An Economic History of South

This book is the first economic history of South Africa in over sixty years. Professor Charles H. Feinstein offers an authoritative survey of five hundred years of South African economic history from the years preceding European settlements in 1652 through to the end of the apartheid era. He charts the early phase of slow growth, and then the transformation of the economy as a result of the discovery of diamonds and gold in the 1870s, followed by the rapid rise of industry in the wartime years. The final chapters cover the introduction of apartheid after 1948, and its consequences for economic performance. Special attention is given to the processes by which the black population were deprived of their land, and to the methods by which they were induced to supply labour for white farms, mines and factories. This book will be essential reading for students in economics, African history, imperial history, and politics.

The late CHARLES H. FEINSTEIN was Emeritus Professor of Economic History at the University of Oxford. His previous publications include *The European Economy between the Wars* (1997) and *Making History Count* (2002).

Ellen Annette McArthur was born in 1862 and educated partly in Germany and partly at St Andrew's School for Girls in Fife. She won a scholarship to Girton College and was placed in Class I of the Historical Tripos at a time when women could sit the examinations but were not awarded degrees by the University of Cambridge. She became the History Tutor at Girton, and in 1893 was the first woman to be appointed a lecturer to the Cambridge Local Lectures Syndicate. From 1902 to 1912 she lectured on economic history to Newnham and Girton students, and was so successful that tutors of mens' colleges asked if their students could be admitted to her courses. In 1925 she was the first woman applicant to be awarded the degree of Litt. D. by the University of Dublin.

Ellen McArthur was invited by W. Cunningham to collaborate with him in writing *Outlines of English Industrial History* (1895). She contributed entries to Palgrave's *Dictionary of Political Economy,* and published a number of articles and notes in the *English Historical Review* on the regulation and assessment of wages in the period 1400–1700.

She died in 1927, following a long illness. Her generous bequest to the University of Cambridge was acknowledged by J. H. Clapham in his preface to the first volume in the series of *Cambridge Studies in Economic History,* published with support from the fund established by: 'that Cambridge economic historian, Ellen Annette McArthur of Girton College, who bequeathed her whole estate to forward the study to which she had first devoted her life'. Since then the Ellen McArthur Fund has been used to support economic history through publications, scholarships, and lectures.

Previous Ellen McArthur Lecturers are:

1968   Alexander Gerschenkron, Professor of Economics, Harvard University
        Europe in the Russian mirror
1970   Edward Miller, Professor of Medieval History, University of Sheffield
        Economic changes in medieval England
1972   Eric Hobsbawm, Professor of History, Birkbeck College *The formation of the industrial working classes*
1975   Carlo M. Cipolla, Professor of Economic History, University of California, Berkeley *Microbes, merchants and health officers in early modern times*
1977   Berrick Saul, Professor of Economic History, University of Edinburgh
        The new deal in action
1979   Emmanuel Le Roy Ladurie, Professor of History, Collège de France
        Peasants, taxes and agriculture in Europe, 1300–1800
1981   Alan Milward, Professor of History, University of Manchester *Recovery and reconstruction in Western Europe after WWII*
1983   François Crouzet, Professor of History, University of Paris-Sorbonne
        Origins and enterprise, the leaders of British industrialisation
1984   Ivan Berend, Professor of History, Karl Marx University, Budapest
        Modernisation in eastern central Europe: economics, ideology, politics, and art in the first half of the twentieth century

1987   Tony Wrigley, Professor of Population Studies, London School of Economics *Continuity, chance and change: the character of the industrial revolution in England*

1989   Herman van der Wee, Professor of History, University of Louvain *Economic and social development before the industrial revolution: the Low Countries, 1000–1750*

1992   Lord Briggs, Worcester College, Oxford *Commerce and culture: the publishing business in Britain*

1996   Robert Fogel, Professor of Economics, University of Chicago *The escape from hunger and premature death, 1700–2100: Europe, America and the Third World*

2000   Jan de Vries, Professor of History and of Economics, University of California, Berkeley *The family and economic growth since the eighteenth century*

An Economic History of South Africa

Conquest, discrimination and development

Charles H. Feinstein

CAMBRIDGE
UNIVERSITY PRESS

CAMBRIDGE UNIVERSITY PRESS
Cambridge, New York, Melbourne, Madrid, Cape Town, Singapore,
São Paulo, Delhi, Dubai, Tokyo

Cambridge University Press
The Edinburgh Building, Cambridge CB2 8RU, UK

Published in the United States of America by Cambridge University Press, New York

www.cambridge.org
Information on this title: www.cambridge.org/9780521616416

First published 2005
Reprinted 2007

A catalogue record for this publication is available from the British Library

ISBN 978-0-521-85091-9 Hardback
ISBN 978-0-521-61641-6 Paperback

Transferred to digital printing 2009

To the memory of my parents

Contents

List of tables	*page*	xii
List of figures		xv
List of maps		xvi
Preface		xvii
A note on terminology, country names, and currency		xix

1 Setting the context: South Africa in international perspective — 1
A unique historical endowment — 1
The economy in an international perspective — 3
The people and economy before 1652 — 13

2 Seizing the land: conquest and dispossession — 22
European expansion into the interior — 22
Abundant land and scarce labour — 32
The roots of conflict — 34
Defeat and dispossession of the Pedi by British and Boers — 37
The final outcome – land allocation in South Africa from 1913 — 43

3 Making the labour force: coercion and discrimination — 47
Black labour for white masters — 47
The use of compulsion to obtain labour — 51
Taxes, restrictions on movement, and other forms of pressure — 55
African labour on white-owned farms — 60
Migrant labour for the mines — 62
The paradox of scarce labour and low wages — 67
The deterioration of the reserves — 70

4 Creating the colour bar: formal barriers, poor whites, and 'civilized' labour — 74
Motivation and methods for creating a colour bar — 74
The conflict with white mine-workers — 77
The 'poor white' problem and the closing of the pastoral frontier — 83
Labour policies of the Pact government, 1924–33 — 85

5 Exporting the gold: the vital role of the mineral revolution — 90
Models of export-led growth — 90
The special features of gold in South Africa — 93

The character and expansion of the mining industry   99
Gold mining as the engine of growth   106
Exploitation of African mine-workers   109

6   Transforming the economy: the rise of manufacturing
      and commercial agriculture   113
      Factories are few and unimportant   113
      The state, tariff policy, and the rise of manufacturing industry   116
      Expansion of industrial output and employment   121
      Faults in the foundation   127
      Inefficiency, low wages, and skill differentials   132
      The destruction of African farming and slow progress of commercial
      agriculture   135

7   Separating the races: the imposition of apartheid   143
      From triumph to disaster – an overview of the post-war period   143
      The political economy of developments after 1948   149
      Apartheid versus urbanization   151
      Trade unions, job reservation, and education   157
      Domination or development?   161

8   Forcing the pace: rapid progress despite constraints   165
      Three more windfalls for the gold mines   165
      Manufacturing: the unprecedented boom   172
      The expansion of the financial sector and the rise of Afrikaner capitalism 176
      State-directed industrialization   180
      Trends in employment, output, and productivity   184
      Weaknesses and constraints – the limits to growth   188
      A revolution finally comes to commercial agriculture   193

9   Hitting the barriers: from triumph to disaster   200
      From growth and stability to stagnation and inflation   200
      The decline of gold mining despite yet another windfall   203
      The expansion of coal and platinum   210
      Manufacturing's failure to achieve export-led growth   211
      The decline in fixed investment   221

10   Confronting the contradictions: the final crisis
      and the retreat from apartheid   224
      Sanctions, capital flows, and the balance-of-payments crises   224
      Changes in the labour market   230
      The retreat from apartheid   240
      The fallacy of 'cheap' labour   244

      Annexe 1: the people of South Africa   252
      The black population before 1900   252
      The white population before 1900   256
      The population in the twentieth century   256

Contents

Annexe 2: the land and the geographical environment   260
The land area and the geological legacy   260
Rainfall, soil, and vegetation   262
Diseases and pests   264
Agricultural regions   266
Annexe 3: the labour force and unemployment   269
The census benchmarks   271
Labour market ratios   273
Interpolation and classification by economic sector   276

Guide to further reading   277
References   287
Index   294

Tables

1.1 Countries comprising a sample of thirty comparable market
economies   4
1.2 Growth of gross domestic product per capita of sample
economies at constant prices, selected periods, 1913–94   7
2.1 Annual average exports from the Cape and Natal, 1807–70   29
2.2 United Kingdom imports by country of origin,
1800s to 1850s   30
3.1 Black labour employed regularly on commercial farms,
1918–54   60
3.2 Source of African labour recruited by mines, 1896–1966   65
3.3 Nominal and real earnings per shift worked of African
workers on the gold mines, 1911–61   67
3.4 Population and income per head in South Africa, 1936   71
4.1 1904 schedule of skilled trades and occupations reserved
for European workers   76
5.1 Annual average exports from the Cape and Natal,
1850–1909   101
5.2 Annual average exports of South African products,
1910–54   102
5.3 South African gold mines: ore milled, output, sales and
price, annual averages, 1885–1948   105
5.4 South African gold mines: working revenue, costs, and
profits, annual averages, 1902–48   106
5.5 Impact on dividends and taxes of a hypothetical
adjustment to wages of black workers,
1911 and 1931   110
6.1 Composition of gross and net value of output in
manufacturing by sector, 1924/5   116
6.2 Output and employment in industry, 1916/17–1948/9   122
6.3 Composition of net value of output in manufacturing by
sector, 1924/5 and 1948/9   126

6.4 Contribution of commodity production to gross domestic product, 1911–48   129

6.5 International comparison of industry, 1938/9   133

6.6 Skill differentials in United Kingdom and South Africa, 1935   134

6.7 Gross value of agricultural production, 1938/9   139

6.8 Indices of output and prices of farm products, 1910/11 to 1945/6   141

7.1 Contribution of commodity production to gross domestic product, 1948–70   144

7.2 Growth of gross domestic product per capita at constant prices, international comparison, selected periods, 1950–94   145

7.3 Growth of real gross domestic product by sector, 1948–94   147

7.4 Level of education of the economically active population, 1970   161

8.1 South African gold mines: ore milled, output, sales, and price, annual averages, 1945–70   169

8.2 South African gold mines: working revenue, costs, profits, and labour productivity, annual averages, 1945–70   170

8.3 Classification of manufacturing establishments by employment size group, 1972   175

8.4 Output and employment in private manufacturing, 1948/9–1971/2   185

8.5 Indices and growth rates of output, employment, fixed capital, and productivity in manufacturing, 1948–74   186

8.6 Composition of net value of output in private manufacturing by sector, 1948/9 and 1975/6   187

8.7 Farm output, prices, labour, and fixed capital, 1948–80   195

9.1 Indicators of a structural break in economic performance *c.*1973   201

9.2 South African gold mines: ore milled, output, price, and sales, 1970–2000   206

9.3 South African gold mines: working revenue, costs, profits, and labour productivity, 1970–2000   209

9.4 Indices and growth rates of output, employment, fixed capital, and productivity in manufacturing, 1974–94   212

9.5 Composition of total and merchandise exports, 1967–96   216

9.6 Composition of exports of manufactures, 1967–93   217

10.1 Current account of balance of payments, 1946–94   226

10.2 Balance of payments, current and capital accounts,
       1946–94   227
10.3 Total and composition of gross foreign liabilities of South
       Africa, 1960–94   229
10.4 Change in labour force participation rates between 1960
       and 1966 by age group, gender, and population group   234
10.5 Employment and unemployment, 1960–96   239
A1.1 European population of South Africa, 1798–1904   257
A1.2 Mid-year de facto total population of South Africa,
       1904–96   258
A1.3 Mid-year de facto population of South Africa by
       population group, 1904–2000   259
A3.1 Population and labour force, benchmark estimates,
       1951–96   274
A3.2 Classification of employed labour force by economic
       sector, 1950–95   275

Figures

1.1 International comparison of gross domestic product per capita in 1913   6

1.2 International comparison of gross domestic product per capita in 1994   10

1.3 Per capita personal income, white and African, selected years, 1917–94   11

1.4 International comparison of Gini coefficients, 1990s   12

5.1 Price of gold in pounds sterling per fine ounce, 1910–70   94

5.2 Comparison of indices of price of gold and of primary products, 1920–70   96

7.1 Growth rates of real gross domestic product (five-year moving average) and population, 1950–95   147

8.1 Farm output, inputs, and total factor productivity, 1947/8–1987/8   198

9.1 Price of gold in US dollars and in rand per fine ounce, 1965–95   204

9.2 Gold produced and ore treated, 1958–98   205

9.3 Fixed capital formation as percentage of gross domestic product, 1954–94   222

10.1 Change in male and female participation rates by age group, 1960–96   235

10.2 Change in male and female participation rates age 20–64 by population group, 1960–96   235

10.3 Employment classified by economic sector, 1950–95   236

10.4 Employment and unemployment, 1950–95   238

10.5 International comparison of labour productivity in manufacturing in 1994   246

Maps

1 Southern Africa, 1910   xxi
2 Cape Colony in the eighteenth century   26
3 European annexation of South Africa, 1652–1900   32
4 The Pedi and the South African Republic   38
5 Agricultural regions of South Africa, c.1960   267

Preface

An earlier version of this material was delivered as the 2004 Ellen McArthur Lectures in the Faculty of History at the University of Cambridge. It was a great honour to be asked to give these lectures and I am grateful to the Trustees of the Fund for this invitation and for their hospitality during my stay in Cambridge. I have made substantial additions and alterations for the present text, but have attempted to maintain some of the informality of approach and greater freedom to express a personal opinion that was appropriate for an oral presentation.

My choice of subject may need some explanation. When I first pondered what theme I should take for the lectures, I realized that I had to choose between two dangers. I did not have any unpublished results waiting to be revealed. I could either select a topic on which I had already written, but at the risk that the response from my audience would be, 'that was all very familiar, it's a pity he couldn't find anything new to say'. Or I could avoid this by lecturing on a subject on which I had done no previous research, at the risk of provoking the reaction, 'that was all very derivative, it's a pity he didn't have anything of his own to contribute'.

In the event I decided that it was likely to be more interesting both for me and for my listeners if I chose something new. I turned to the economic history of South Africa, which I had last studied as an undergraduate at the University of the Witwatersrand in 1950. It was this course, taught with such élan by Helen Suzman around the brilliant book published a few years earlier by Cornelius de Kiewiet, that first attracted me to the idea of a career as an economic historian. The lectures offered an opportune occasion to return to this topic.

As a novice in the field of South African history I am deeply conscious of the extent to which this volume is based on the impressive body of research undertaken by other scholars. It is they who have extracted material from the archives of companies, government departments, and missionary societies, examined unpublished diaries and journals, investigated accounts left by early travellers in southern Africa, conducted oral interviews, studied newspaper and court records, inspected commission reports and minutes of evidence, scrutinized parliamentary papers and government records. My debt to these distinguished historians and economists is enormous and is partially indicated in footnotes and in the 'Guide to further reading' at the end of the volume.

The present text is in no sense a report on further original research. It is an attempt to synthesize the information that now exists. The aim is to provide a broad overview of the character, transformation, initial growth, and final decline of South Africa's economy, and my interpretation of the major factors that explain these developments. The survey begins with the economic conditions of the indigenous people before the arrival of European settlers in the middle of the sixteenth century, and ends with the surrender of power by the white minority at the end of the apartheid period and the election of the first democratic government under Nelson Mandela in 1994. In order to keep the text within a reasonable length, attention is concentrated on the central issues of macroeconomic development in the economy as a whole and in the key sectors of agriculture, mining, and industry, and of the related economic and political policies which influenced the economy. Special consideration is given to policies relating to ownership of land and the supply of labour. Many other aspects, such as public finance, improvements in transport, and the growth of the service sectors, are mentioned only briefly where relevant to the main themes.

The text has benefited immeasurably from the willingness of friends and colleagues to read all or part of preliminary drafts, and I am extremely grateful to Anne Digby, Nicoli Nattrass, Christopher Saunders, Jeremy Seekings, Mark Thomas, Gavin Williams, and Francis Wilson. Without their perceptive comments and constructive criticisms there would be many more errors and oversights, but they do not have any responsibility for those that remain. In addition, I would like to say how much I appreciate the efficient way that Michael Watson expedited publication. I would also like to thank my daughter Jessica for her characteristic helpfulness in compiling the index and for her expert help with proof-reading. My greatest debt is, as always, to my wife Anne, for her unstinting support and encouragement, and for inspiring me by her example.

A note on terminology, country names, and currency

Terminology

All writers on South Africa are confronted by the problem of finding a suitable terminology to describe the different racial groups. All terms are problematic and objectionable to some, and that will no doubt be true of those I use in this volume. I have reserved the term 'African' for the indigenous dark-skinned, Bantu-speaking inhabitants, with no implication that others are not now equally rooted in the continent. Alternative terms, many of which are clearly derogatory, appear only in direct quotations from other speakers or writers. The word 'Bantu', which gained wide currency as the apartheid term for these people, is used here solely as the name for the group of Niger–Congo languages spoken by the indigenous people of central and southern Africa.

'White' is adopted as the generic term for those who came to South Africa from Europe, with 'Afrikaners' used to refer to the Afrikaans-speaking descendants of those who came from Holland, France, and Germany,[1] and 'English' for those from Britain. Other terms – Europeans, Dutch, settlers, colonists, burghers, *boers* (farmers), trekkers, and *trekboers* – are employed as alternatives in appropriate historical contexts.

The other indigenous inhabitants of the southern part of Africa were the hunter-gatherers, previously referred to as Bushmen, but now generally known as San, and the Khoikhoi (previously called Hottentots) who were nomadic herders. Khoisan is the collective term for these two groups. The group referred to as 'Coloured' includes the descendants of the Khoisan, of slaves brought to the Cape by the Dutch, and of black slaves freed at the Cape in the decades after Britain's abolition of the slave

---

[1] The Netherlands East India Company employed large numbers of Germans in its army and administrative service, and some of these were part of the initial settlement established at the Cape. It was these Dutch and German colonists, together with the French Huguenots who were settled among them in the late 1680s, who formed the nucleus of the Afrikaans-speaking Boer population.

trade in 1808, and also many of the children born from the interracial sexual relationships that have occurred throughout South Africa's history. The Asian population was largely created by the decision to bring indentured labourers from India to work in the sugar plantations in Natal. The term 'black' is used as a collective noun for the African, coloured, and Asian peoples.

Country and provincial names

All the countries bordering South Africa have changed their names following independence. In general I have used the name current at the time to which the text refers, but the list given here of the corresponding names by which the countries are now known may be helpful.

Original name	Present-day name
Basutoland	Lesotho
Bechuanaland	Botswana
Nyasaland	Malawi
Northern Rhodesia	Zambia
Portuguese East Africa	Mozambique
Southern Rhodesia	Zimbabwe
South West Africa	Namibia

From 1910 to 1994 South Africa was divided into four provinces made up of the two former British colonies of the Cape and Natal, and the two former Boer republics of the Transvaal (previously the South African Republic) and Orange Free State (see Map 1). From 1994 there was a further subdivision into nine provinces, with the Western Cape, Northern Cape, and Eastern Cape corresponding broadly to the previous Cape Province, and Gauteng, Mpumulanga, Limpopo, and the North West corresponding broadly to the Transvaal.

Currency and exchange rates

From 1825 until the declaration of a republic on 31 May 1961, the South African currency was measured in the same units as Britain's: pounds, shillings, and pence (12 pence = 1 shilling, 20 shillings = £1). When South Africa became a republic in May 1961 a new currency was introduced based on rand and cents (100 cents = 1 rand), with the initial rate of exchange against sterling set at R 2.00 = £1.

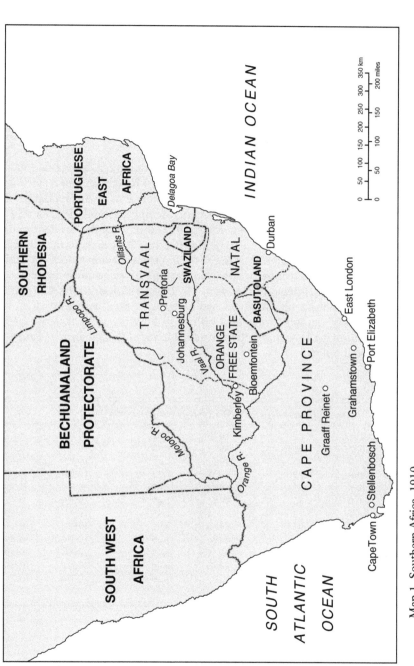

Map 1. Southern Africa, 1910

In Chapters 1 to 6, all monetary sums are given in pounds sterling, and South African readers who want to find the equivalent in rand can simply multiply the published series by 2. However, for the period following the Second World War, covered in Chapters 7 to 10, all monetary sums are given in rand. For current values relating to years before 1967, readers who want to find the equivalent in pounds sterling for comparison with the earlier data can simply divide the published series by 2. For values for years after that date it is necessary to take account of the fluctuations in the rand–sterling exchange rate.

South Africa left the par value of the rand unchanged against the dollar during the 1960s, and did not follow the United Kingdom when sterling was devalued in November 1967. As a result there was an appreciation of the rand against the pound, and a new rate of approximately R 1.72 = £1. The next change occurred in December 1971, following the Smithsonian agreement which marked the end of the Bretton Woods system of fixed exchange rates. From that date the rand fluctuated against sterling and other currencies, occasionally appreciating but more usually depreciating, either by formal devaluation, as in 1971 and 1975, or as the outcome of managed floating in which the exchange rate was determined by a combination of market forces and official policy. By 1994 the rate had fallen to R 5.44 = £1, and in 2003 it was R 12.33 = £1. The annual figures are tabulated below.

SA rand per UK pound, 1961–2003 (annual average, middle rates)

1961[a]	2.00	1978	1.67	1991	4.87
1962–6	2.00	1979	1.79	1992	5.02
1967	1.97	1980	1.81	1993	4.91
1968	1.72	1981	1.77	1994	5.44
1969	1.72	1982	1.89	1995	5.72
1970	1.72	1983	1.69	1996	6.72
1971	1.76	1984	1.95	1997	7.55
1972	1.93	1985	2.91	1998	9.16
1973	1.70	1986	3.35	1999	9.89
1974	1.59	1987	3.33	2000	10.49
1975	1.63	1988	4.40	2001	12.39
1976	1.57	1989	4.29	2002	15.76
1977	1.52	1990	4.61	2003	12.33

[a] From 31 May.

Source: South African Reserve Bank, *Quarterly Bulletin.*

Britain and South Africa use different conventions for presenting numbers, and the present text follows the British practice throughout: the decimal point is indicated by a point rather than a comma (12.33 not 12,33), and thousands are separated by a comma rather than a space (1,450,000 not 1 450 000).

1   Setting the context: South Africa in international perspective

A unique historical endowment

The special character and course of South Africa's economic history was profoundly influenced by its unique endowment of human and natural resources. This created the context within which individuals, ideologies, and institutions shaped the precise outcomes. Other countries possessed one or two of these distinguishing features, but only in South Africa were all of them present together, and it was this combination which proved to be so powerful. The first of these features was that large numbers of Khoisan and Africans already occupied the southern part of the African continent long before the first Europeans arrived from Holland in the second half of the seventeenth century with the intention to settle. There is no basis for an accurate estimate of the size of this population, but a figure of about 1,500,000 may serve as a rough order of magnitude for the beginning of the nineteenth century (see Annexe 1 for an account of the available information on population size). A century later it was close to 4,000,000. The presence of this substantial, and increasing, indigenous population differentiated South Africa from four other regions of European settlement, the United States of America, Canada, Australia, and New Zealand.

The second decisive feature of South Africa's population was the presence from the nineteenth century onwards of large numbers of European settlers. When the Dutch East India Company originally sent Jan van Riebeeck to establish a base at the Cape of Good Hope in 1652, the intention was simply to enable the Company's ships 'to refresh themselves with vegetables, meat, water and other necessities' en route to the East Indies. However, the Company needed greater supplies than a handful of soldiers and sailors could produce from the gardens in Cape Town, and the Directors were soon persuaded to allow a small number of volunteers to settle in the hinterland of the port on a permanent basis. Their task was both to grow wheat and other grains, and to breed cattle and sheep. By the time the period of Dutch rule

over the Cape ended in 1806, the European population numbered
about 27,000.

After control of the colony passed to the British, the process of settlement, and of movement into the interior, gained momentum, encouraged by the temperate climate and absence of tropical diseases. By 1865
the total white population of the two British colonies of the Cape and
Natal and the two Boer republics of the Orange Free State and the
Transvaal had reached 250,000, and by the beginning of the twentieth
century it had climbed above 1,100,000 (see Table A1.1 in Annexe 1).
The settlement of Europeans on this large scale differentiated South
Africa from most of the rest of Africa, and from India and most other
parts of Asia.

From the outset there was a fundamental division between these two
groups of people – the original black majority and the new white minority –
with massive and enduring implications for those who would come to
own the land, water, and other resources, and those who would supply
the manual labour. When conflicts between them were determined by
force, whites possessed superior weapons, mobility, and organization;
when they were determined by legislation, whites alone possessed the
right to vote (except for the relatively few black people who qualified
under the Cape franchise) and to be a member of parliament.[1]

The third special feature was not immediately apparent, but it was
eventually found that the country possessed rich mineral resources, in
particular gold. This mineral wealth differentiated South Africa from
other regions of European settlement with large indigenous populations,
notably those in Latin America. Some of these countries had other
minerals, such as silver, tin, and copper, but what gold there was could
not be compared with the vast quantities found in the Transvaal.[2] Prior to
the discovery of this mineral wealth, South Africa was a relatively backward economy, almost entirely dependent on agriculture. But most parts
of the country lacked the rainfall and other requirements for prosperous

---

[1] The two Boer republics explicitly prohibited black people from participation in their
assemblies, and Natal did so de facto. There was no such barrier in the constitution
introduced in the Cape from 1854, but no black person was ever elected to the old Cape
Parliament. Under the 1910 Act of Union, the Cape franchise was preserved for those
adult black males who met the education and property qualifications, but they could not
become members of the Union Parliament. In 1936, Africans in the Cape were removed
from the common electoral roll for the parliament, and twenty years later Coloureds and
Indians in the province were similarly deprived of the vote.

[2] Substantial alluvial gold deposits were mined by slaves in Brazil from the mid-1600s, but
these were largely exhausted by the late eighteenth century. Mexico took over as the largest
source of gold in Latin America in the twentieth century, but output in 1913 was only
11 per cent of South African production, and by 1938 the proportion had fallen to 8 per cent.

farming. (A more detailed description of environmental conditions is given in Annexe 2.) Markets were small, conditions difficult, and progress slow; this applied equally to the economy of the original inhabitants and to that developed in the eighteenth and early nineteenth centuries by the European settlers. The situation was then totally transformed by the discovery of diamonds and gold in the late nineteenth century. From that point forward the economic history of South Africa becomes, in essence, a story of how this unique combination of the indigenous population, European settlers, and mineral resources was brought together in a process of conquest, dispossession, discrimination, and development to promote rapid economic progress.

The economy in an international perspective

Before we proceed to survey South Africa's history of economic development, it will be helpful to place the country's performance in an international perspective. For the period before 1870 there are no data on overall growth, but such indicators as are available – for example, for trade and immigration – typically showed the country in a relatively unfavourable light when compared with other areas of British settlement. In the 1860s, for example, total exports from South Africa averaged only £2,500,000 per annum, whereas those from Canada amounted to £8,000,000 and Australia's had already reached £19,000,000. By 1870, almost 1,000,000 immigrants had gone voluntarily from the United Kingdom to Australia and roughly 500,000 had settled in Canada. The numbers leaving for South Africa were too small for the United Kingdom authorities to record separately, but there were probably fewer than 100,000 before 1870.

After 1870 growth accelerated, though there is still no overall measure of this. However, we can take the level of total output (gross domestic product – GDP) per capita in 1913 as an indicator both of the progress made since the economic revolution of 1870s and of South Africa's relative international position on the eve of the First World War. All data are taken from the study by Angus Maddison, in which every country's GDP is measured on a comparable basis in 1990 international dollars.[3] For the

---

[3] A. Maddison, *The world economy: a millennial perspective*, Paris: OECD, 2001. Maddison converted estimates of GDP in national currencies in 1990 to international dollars on the basis of purchasing power parities, with individual countries weighted on the basis of their relative GDP. He then extrapolated these estimates back to 1913 (or earlier years) by means of national series for GDP. For South Africa, the population figures underlying Maddison's per capita GDP estimates were adjusted to agree with those given in Table A1.2 in Annexe 1.

Table 1.1. *Countries comprising a sample of thirty comparable market economies*[a]

Africa (six)	**Europe** (seven)	**UK dominions** (three)
Algeria	Austria	Australia
Egypt	Finland	Canada
Ghana	Greece	New Zealand
Morocco	Ireland	
Nigeria	Italy	
South Africa	Portugal	
Asia (eight)	Spain	
Indonesia	**Latin America** (six)	
Japan	Argentina	
Malaysia	Brazil	
Pakistan	Chile	
Philippines	Colombia	
South Korea	Mexico	
Taiwan	Peru	
Thailand		

[a] All estimates refer to the country with frontiers as in 1990; where necessary population and GDP data for earlier years have been adjusted to this basis.

purpose of this and other measures reviewed in this chapter, a sample of thirty broadly comparable market economies was selected. This comprises the three other dominions (Canada, Australia, and New Zealand) with whom, until recently, South Africa was most frequently compared, seven of the smaller, late-developing European economies, six countries in Latin America, eight in Asia and six in Africa (see Table 1.1).[4] Algeria and Nigeria were included in the sample to improve the coverage of Africa, even though data for them are only available from 1950; all the remaining countries are covered from 1913.

The period 1870–1913 was generally one of expansion and prosperity for the world economy.[5] Its most prominent feature might be described as the early development of globalization, characterized by an enormous extension of international communications by rail, sea, and the

---

[4] It is not entirely appropriate to compare a single country with averages of groups of countries, but this procedure was adopted as a reasonable compromise between an unduly complex list of thirty individual countries and a smaller sample. Rates of growth for groups of countries and for the sample as a whole were calculated from weighted totals, not simple arithmetic means.

[5] For a more detailed account of global economic performance in this and other periods see Maddison, *World economy*, pp. 94–167.

international telegraph, and by massive intercontinental flows of both labour and capital. It was also the high point of colonialism, especially in Africa, where European powers imposed their rule on most parts of the continent. World trade was impeded by the introduction of protection by several industrial nations, but despite this it continued to expand at a rapid rate. The rate of increase in output responded favourably to these overall conditions, and in most parts of the world was much more rapid than in earlier decades of the nineteenth century. Following the discovery of gold and diamonds, South Africa was a full participant in this extended phase of growth and trade, with significant inflows of capital and migrants, and increased foreign trade.

Figure 1.1 shows the standing of the country, measured by GDP per capita, at the end of this growth phase. In 1913, at a level in 1990 dollars of some $1,600, South Africa was in twelfth place, a long way behind the three other dominions, each with per capita incomes in excess of $4,000, and also behind most of the European latecomers. However, among the sample countries in Latin America, Asia, and Africa, there were only three – Argentina (at $3,800), Chile (at $2,650), and Mexico (at $1,730) – that had achieved a higher level of per capita income, and the level in South Africa was appreciably higher than the sample average of $1,330. So by 1913 the country could be said to have made a good start on the basis of the mining revolution, and to have moved significantly ahead of many colonial and semi-colonial economies.

For the assessment of comparative economic performance as shown by the subsequent rate of growth of real GDP per capita, the period after 1913 has been subdivided into three phases: from 1913 to 1950, 1950 to 1973, and 1973 to 1994 (see Table 1.2). The most striking feature of this comparison over some eight decades is the remarkable long-run deterioration in South Africa's relative performance, from one of the best economies in the first period to one of the worst in the last.

The first phase covers the two world wars and the Great Depression of 1929–33. Many economies suffered great loss of life and substantial damage to property during either or both of the wars. For many more – including, in particular, the United States and Germany – the years after 1929 were a time of severe recession as output, employment, trade, and prices collapsed. From the mid-1920s, conditions in agriculture deteriorated rapidly in both industrial and developing countries, with massive over-production and tumbling prices of wheat, sugar, coffee, and many other commodities. World trade was severely affected as country after country introduced protective tariffs and other measures in a desperate attempt to maintain their own output, regardless of the consequences for others. There was neither international leadership nor co-operation; the

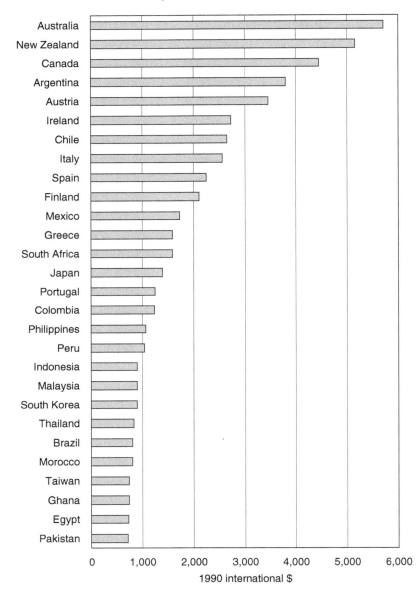

Figure 1.1. International comparison of gross domestic product per capita in 1913

Source: Maddison, *World economy.*

Table 1.2. *Growth of gross domestic product per capita of sample economies at constant prices, selected periods, 1913–94*

	(1) 1913–50	(2) 1950–73	(3) 1973–94
	(annual percentage growth rates)		
South Africa	1.3	2.2	− 0.6
Latin America	1.2	2.7	1.1
Dominions	1.1	2.5	1.5
Japan	0.9	8.0	2.6
Europe	0.6	5.2	2.0
Other African[a]	0.6	2.0	0.8
Other Asian[b]	0.0	3.5	4.3
Total sample	0.5	4.0	2.0

[a] Three in 1913–50.
[b] For South Korea, 1913–40 population and GDP are assumed to have grown at same rate as for Korea as a whole; for Pakistan, 1913 population is based on census data for corresponding areas of India, and per capita GDP is assumed to have grown at same rate for 1913–1950 as in total pre-partition India.

Source: Maddison, *World economy*, pp. 185, 195, 215, 224, 276–9, 288–9, 304–5, and 322–6.

gold standard was finally abandoned by all but a handful of countries, but only after the policies imposed in its name had done considerable damage; and many banks were forced to close as the value of their assets collapsed. The consequences of war and depression were reflected in very slow growth of output, with an average rate for the sample as a whole over the entire period of only 0.5 per cent per annum. However, South Africa was one of a small number of countries that both benefited from the two wars and escaped most of the adverse effects of the depression. Agriculture was not immune from the worldwide collapse of farm prices, but both gold mining and industry prospered in the 1930s and again during the Second World War. GDP per capita was thus able to expand much more rapidly than the sample average, at a rate of 1.3 per cent per annum.

In the next phase, from 1950 to 1973, the world economy enjoyed a long and unique boom; it was a 'golden age' of dynamic growth, unparalleled in the prosperity it created and the range of economies it embraced. Countries which had fallen behind during the world wars and the Great Depression were now able to catch up and to take advantage of advances in technology, economic know-how, and institutions developed by the leading nations. There was scope for unusually rapid growth as under-used resources, especially labour, were drawn into more productive activity. At home, governments were far more willing than before to adopt fiscal and monetary policies designed to promote high levels of demand and full employment. Abroad, capitalist economies worked together harmoniously in the face of the threat posed by the growth of the Soviet Union and other communist countries.

Western policy makers had also learned vital lessons from the disasters of the inter-war years. They co-operated to create an international monetary and financial system under the leadership of the United States which was stable and flexible, and they encouraged the removal of barriers to trade, at least for industrial products. Across the globe, output, productivity, investment, and foreign trade shot forward at an exceptional pace, and employment was high and inflation low. South Africa participated successfully in this golden age, and the increase in its own rate of growth of real GDP per capita from 1.3 to 2.2 per cent per annum was cause for much domestic satisfaction. However, as Table 1.2 reveals, performance in many other countries was markedly superior, and the rate of increase in GDP per capita achieved by South Africa was little more than half the sample average of 4 per cent per annum.

In time, however, the exceptional circumstances that had generated the performance and prosperity of the global golden age came to an end. Some of the factors that emerged were the direct consequence of the preceding era of rapid growth, such as the inflationary consequences of the increased pressure for higher wages that could be exerted in an era of full employment, or the elimination of the exceptional 'benefits of backwardness' that several countries had enjoyed in the early post-war decades. Others were largely independent, such as the activities of the member states of the Organization of Petroleum Exporting Countries (OPEC) which caused the explosive rise in oil prices in 1973, and the increase in oil prices again in 1979. Governments of the leading advanced countries started to give greater priority to curbing inflation – in particular, by raising interest rates – than to promoting growth, investment, and full employment.

Elsewhere, notably in Latin America, there was less acceptance of the need to bring rapidly rising prices under control, and the result was excessive public borrowing which eventually brought financial systems under extreme pressure, with adverse effects on stability and growth. The system of fixed exchange rates established immediately after the Second World War at Bretton Woods proved increasingly unable to withstand the strains of the great change in the relative economic strength of the United States and the other industrial nations, which was itself a product of the golden age. The expansion of world trade dropped sharply, though it was still an impressive 5 per cent per annum.

In this final phase, from 1973 to 1994, there was thus a general deterioration in the performance of the world economy, with the growth in output and trade slowing to a much more sedate pace, inflation accelerating, and unemployment rising. However, it is important to note that for the United States, western Europe, and most of Asia, this deceleration still left per capita GDP increasing at appreciably higher rates than before 1950. For the thirty sample countries, growth in real GDP dropped from 4 to 2 per cent per annum. South Africa shared in the general 'stagflation', but to a much greater extent than elsewhere, and was one of only four sample countries (the others were Peru, Ghana, and Nigeria) to experience an actual decline in real GDP per capita. The net outcome of this long-run relative deterioration was that South Africa was overtaken by many other countries. It was not only that twenty of the thirty sample countries, including several in Asia and Latin America, had attained higher levels of GDP per capita by 1994, but that the gap between them and South Africa had grown progressively larger (see Figure 1.2). Whereas in 1913 South Africa's per capita income had been above the average of the sample countries (see Figure 1.1), by 1994 it had fallen to only 60 per cent of the sample average.

The comparison so far has been concerned with measures of GDP per capita, but in the special circumstances of South Africa it is inappropriate to consider average income without reference to the extreme inequality in the distribution of that income between black and white. Figure 1.3 remedies this deficiency by showing per capita personal income (in constant 1995 rand) for whites and Africans at roughly twenty-year intervals from 1917 to 1994.[6] The boxed figures above the bars show the ratio of white to African average income at each date. At the first three dates, average white incomes were consistently more than eleven times greater than average African incomes. In the period following the Second World War the ratio increased to a peak close to thirteen in the 1960s and then started to diminish, mainly as a result of improvements in African wages and in pensions. By 1994, the gap had narrowed

---

[6] H. Bhorat et al. (eds.), *Fighting poverty: labour markets and inequality in South Africa*, Cape Town: University of Cape Town Press, 2001, p. 2, for 1917 and 1936; H. de J. van Wyk, *Personal disposable income in South Africa by population group, income group and district, 2000*, University of South Africa, Bureau of Market Research, Research Report, No. 279, 2000, p. 27 (adjusted to 1995 prices), for 1960, 1975, and 1994. Personal income is defined as current pre-tax income in cash and in kind earned or received from all sources, including transfers from government and businesses.

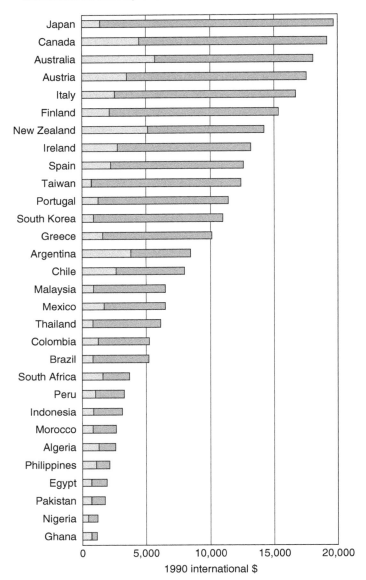

Figure 1.2. International comparison of gross domestic product per capita in 1994

Note: Left-hand part of each bar shows level of per capita GDP in 1913.

Source: Maddison, *World economy.*

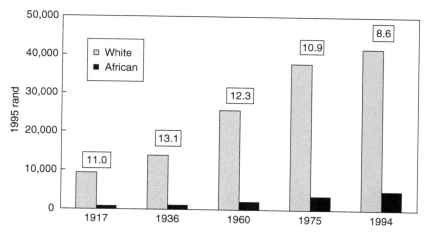

Figure 1.3. Per capita personal income, white and African, selected years, 1917–94

Note: Figure above bars is ratio of white to African per capita personal income.

appreciably, but average white incomes were still more than eight times higher than average African incomes.

We can again put this into international perspective, using one of the standard measures of inequality, the Gini coefficient, as the summary measure. This is done for the sample countries in Figure 1.4, and reveals the striking fact that only one country, Brazil, had a more unequal distribution of pre-tax income than South Africa in the 1990s.[7] This exceptionally inegalitarian income distribution is mainly the result of the large differentials between population groups, but there is also substantial inequality within the groups. In particular, there is a huge disparity in average income of African households between those in large urban centres with one or more members in employment, and those in rural areas.

This review of economic performance in an international perspective thus poses a number of questions that an economic history of South Africa will need to answer. These include the following.

---

[7] Satisfactory data from household surveys for either disposable per capita income or per capita expenditure are available on a consistent basis for all thirty sample countries except New Zealand, Argentina, and Thailand in World Bank, *World development indicators, 2003*, Washington, DC: World Bank, 2003, Table 2.8.

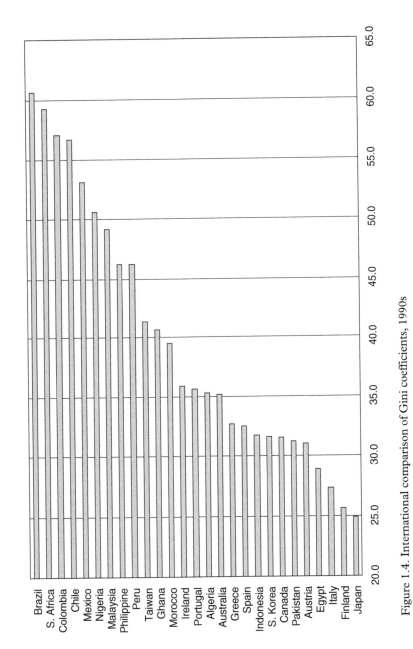

Figure 1.4. International comparison of Gini coefficients, 1990s

Source: World Bank, *World development indicators, 2003*, Table 2.8.

Why was initial growth so slow, both before 1652 and from then to the 1870s?

What was special about gold and what were the sources of growth following the mineral discoveries?

What was the basis for the relatively successful development and structural change during the two world wars and in the years between the wars?

Why did South Africa grow more slowly than other countries in the boom years from 1948 to 1973, even though its own performance improved?

What explains the transition to negative growth in the last quarter of the twentieth century, and how does this relate to the policies of apartheid?

What were the reasons for the exceptionally high degree of inequality between black and white South Africans?

These are some of the issues that will be addressed in this volume, beginning with a brief survey of the economy of the original inhabitants of South Africa before it was disrupted by the arrival of the Europeans.

The people and economy before 1652

Two major groups of people occupied much of southern Africa before the arrival of the first settlers from Holland under Jan van Riebeeck in 1652. It is convenient to consider them separately, but there were many close and complex relationships – from conflict to inter-marriage – both within the two sub-divisions of the Khoisan – the San hunter-gatherers and the Khoikhoi nomadic herders – and between them and the African pastoralists and cultivators.[8] The strength and intimacy of these links is perhaps most vividly revealed by the distinctive clicks that several African peoples adopted from the Khoisan and made an integral feature of their own languages.

It is known from archaeological evidence that the San had occupied South African territory for at least 10,000 years, possibly much longer. They were not acquisitive and did not accumulate property, but they were skilful in their quest for the food nature provided, and adapted exceptionally well to their environment. Their marvellous rock art, with its depictions of elaborate trance visions and symbols of supernatural

---

[8] See the preliminary note for an explanation of the terms used in this volume for the different population groups.

power, survives in caves across the country as a priceless legacy. However, the San were no match for those with whom they shared the continent, and had been marginalized by the Khoikhoi and by African farmers long before the appearance of the Europeans. They survived in remote mountain areas and semi-deserts, but as Europeans expanded their movement into the interior of the western Cape in search of pasture, they took over San hunting grounds, and there was a brutal and one-sided struggle in which large numbers of San people were viciously exterminated:

The tradition early took root among the men of the frontier that the Bushmen [San] were no better than wild animals and that it was justifiable to exterminate them like so much vermin. On their side the Bushmen became fiercer and more predatory as their means of subsistence disappeared before their eyes.[9]

Others were captured in raids, or kidnapped and indentured to farmers for the remainder of their lives. The San also suffered very high mortality during the three major smallpox epidemics that afflicted the region in the eighteenth century. As a result of these cumulative disasters their numbers declined sharply and, by the turn of the century, they had effectively lost their separate identity in South Africa. Those who remained in the country became servants, labourers, and trackers for white farmers, and were absorbed in the wider coloured population (see further Annexe 1). Only those few who took refuge across the border in present-day Botswana or Namibia were able to sustain their traditional way of life.[10]

Khoikhoi herders occupied the winter rainfall region of the south-western Cape at the time the first Dutch settlers arrived, and had been established there since early in the first millennium. They enjoyed a more advanced standard of living than the hunter-gatherers. Evidence from archaeological excavations indicates that in the beginning the only animals they kept were fat-tailed, wool-less sheep, but they later built up big herds of long-horned cattle, possibly obtained initially from contact with Africans in the eastern Cape, from whom they also acquired goats. The cattle needed large amounts of grazing land, and since the western Cape is not rich in grasslands the herders were forced to move seasonally within parts of the region to obtain sufficient grazing. Each of the constituent Khoikhoi communities had land which it used, but their boundaries were not rigidly defined.

Their stock were generally only slaughtered for food on festive and ceremonial occasions, and meat was obtained by hunting wild animals.

---

[9] J. S. Marais, *The Cape Coloured people, 1652–1937*, Johannesburg: Witwatersrand University Press, 1962, p. 15.

[10] In recent years even that has been threatened by a resettlement programme designed to move surviving San from their ancestral lands in central Botswana.

Milk from the cattle provided their staple food; they also took fish and shellfish from the sea, and roots, berries, honey, and insects from the land. Milking was women's work, but everything else relating to the cattle was done by men. There were no individual or family titles to land, but stock was owned by individual households, not communally, and there was considerable differentiation, with wealthy chiefs and headmen owning large herds while many others had no stock. The men of such poor households might, however, be engaged to care for part of the herd of wealthy stock-owners, and be rewarded for their labour by being allowed to take the milk. The Khoikhoi did not develop arable farming, because the hot, dry summer months of this winter rainfall zone were unsuitable for the indigenous grains, millet, and sorghum. Other activities included smelting iron and copper in order to make weapons and implements as well as ornaments for both men and women, carving wood, making pots, weaving baskets and mats, and working skins and hides to provide clothing.

Conflicts over land and water brought the Khoikhoi into dispute with the Dutch immediately following the establishment of European settlement. Despite sporadic resistance the herders soon lost their grazing land, their livestock, and their independence, and were conscripted into menial service as poorly paid and badly treated labourers. The nature of their initial relationship with the Europeans is well illustrated in this extract from the *Journal* kept by van Riebeeck. Following an exchange with the Khoikhoi in 1660, a bare eight years after he landed, about continuing disputes over grazing land in the vicinity of Cape Town, he recorded that their leaders

strongly insisted that we had been appropriating more and more of their land, which had been theirs all these centuries, and on which they had been accustomed to let their cattle graze, etc. They asked if they would be allowed to do such a thing supposing they went to Holland, and then added: 'It would be of little consequence if you people stayed here at the fort, but you come right into the interior and select the best land for yourselves, without even asking whether we mind or whether it will cause us any inconvenience ... As for your claim that the land is not big enough for us both, who should in justice rather give way, the rightful owner or the foreign intruder?' ... They thus remained adamant in their claim of old-established natural ownership. Eventually they had to be told that they had now lost the land as a result of war and had no alternative but to admit that it was no longer theirs, ... their land had thus justly fallen to us in a defensive war, won by the sword, as it were, and we intended to keep it.[11]

[11] H. B. Thom (ed.), *Journal of Jan van Riebeeck*, 3 vols., Cape Town: A. A. Bakema for the Van Riebeeck Society, 1952–58, III, 5 and 6 April 1660, pp. 195–6.

The extract beautifully captures both the arrogance and the aggression that Europeans were to display so frequently over the next three centuries, and also the innocence – and ultimately, despite much spirited resistance, helplessness – of indigenous people, when faced by the superior power and weaponry of newcomers who were always so ready to resort to the sword and the gun.

The second, and numerically far more important group of indigenous inhabitants, were the Africans. We do not know when their ancestors initiated the long overland migration from the Great Lakes region of east Africa, but modern archaeological studies have established that early Iron-Age, Bantu-speaking people were living on the southern side of the Limpopo River by approximately AD 500. Some had travelled south along the coast of the Indian Ocean; others made the journey through the interior of central Africa. In the subsequent centuries, two major linguistic groups, the Nguni and the Sotho–Tswana, continued the slow southward migration. They entered two very different ecological habitats in the eastern and western parts of southern Africa, and adapted their way of life accordingly.[12]

One group, the Nguni-speaking ancestors of today's Zulu, Swazi, and Xhosa people, moved south across the Drakensberg Mountains into the well-watered land between the mountains and the Indian Ocean, an area in which they could practise their skills in both animal husbandry and cultivation. Over time they moved further down the east coast and along the southern coast, and by c. 1000 had penetrated as far as the Great Kei River. The relative abundance of water, good pasture for grazing, and land suitable for arable cultivation in this region promoted a dispersed pattern of settlement, with no large towns. Individual households were largely self-sufficient and could find all their resource requirements close to their homes. The traditional grain crops were millet and sorghum, and these staple grains restricted them to the region of summer rainfall. A divergent rainfall pattern created a natural barrier between the Bantu-speaking cultivators to the north and east of the dividing line, and the Khoikhoi herders who occupied the zone of winter rainfall to the south and west.[13]

The other group were the Sotho (using the term in a broad sense to include also those known as Tswana and Pedi). They migrated into the

---

[12] The three other major groups among the Bantu speakers were the Tsonga, who live chiefly in present-day Mozambique, the Shona peoples of southern Zimbabwe (Mashonaland), and the Herero in Namibia.

[13] The division is not static but runs roughly along a line extending north and west from the vicinity of Port Elizabeth in the south to the coast of the Atlantic Ocean north of the border with Namibia.

huge central plateau north of the Orange River and occupied a broad
swathe of land starting in the west on the edges of the drought and desert
lands of the Kalahari (largely in present-day Botswana), and ending in the
east on the Drakensberg Mountains (in present-day Lesotho). The determining physical feature of the entire region was that there was too little
rain and what there was fell too erratically. Isolated communities could
not survive in these conditions, and settlement was concentrated where
water was available, in large villages and towns, some with more than
5,000 inhabitants.

However, the residents of these settlements were still primarily farmers,
who moved seasonally to their fields. Generally harsh environmental
conditions created the prospect of recurrent crop failures, and the farmers
were also afflicted by cattle diseases, locusts, and other pests. All this
made it an appropriate strategy to spread risk by cultivating several fields
scattered over a wide area, embracing different soils and varied opportunities for rain. As Sansom explains,

Precipitation and soil types are related in complex ways to affect productivity.
This was appreciated and duly comprehended in the individual's calculus of
risk... In other words, there is a choice between investing more or less labour
in soils that will yield bumper crops under optimum conditions or sowing drought
soils that always produce, but do not produce in quantity. The calculation can be
even more complicated. Of the two major traditional grain crops ... millet was a
drought crop while sorghum gave greater yields.[14]

The poor quality of the grassland, and the great distances between
sources of water, also necessitated extensive pastoral farming, with seasonal movements of livestock over a large area.

The Nguni people in the east could largely achieve the necessary
diversification on an individual basis, in a succession of small-scale 'repetitive configurations'.[15] By contrast, a more co-operative relationship per-
mitting a man from one area to use someone else's land in a distant region
was required by the more capricious rainfall and less varied vegetation
and soil types in the vast western territory. This distinction between
concentrated and dispersed settlements became more pronounced the
further west the farmers moved.

Political rivalries and divisions *within* African societies were of considerable importance in the larger history of conflicts and migrations within
southern Africa, and also as a factor in the process of their later conquest
by Europeans. But in the context of an economic history these

[14] B. Sansom, 'Traditional economic systems', in W. D. Hammond-Tooke (ed.), *The
Bantu-speaking peoples of Southern Africa*, 2nd edn, London: Routledge, 1974, p. 144.
[15] Ibid., p. 40.

differences, as well as those between the Nguni and Sotho–Tswana modes of exploitation of their environments, were much less significant than the common features and common destiny of all the African people of southern Africa. They all shared basically the same technology and knowledge of agriculture, and all attached exceptional importance to pastoral farming.

Their cattle, looked after with skilful and lavish care by the men, were not only of great economic value, but also played a vital role in the cultural and social life of their communities. Cattle were the principal means of accumulating, storing, and reproducing wealth, and the primary medium of exchange. Ownership of a large herd conferred power and status; and it permitted the owner to exercise patronage by lending the cattle to those less fortunate, obtaining in return their labour and allegiance. Cattle were not normally slaughtered for food, but only for ritual or ceremonial occasions, such as marriages and funerals, or sacrifices to the ancestors, for example during a drought. Marriage normally required the payment of cattle to the bride's family, and the larger the herd a man possessed, the greater the number of wives he could have. The payment of bridewealth gave a husband the right of access to his wife's labour, both domestic and in the fields, and also to her children, who were greatly valued, both for sociocultural reasons and as potential additions to the household labour supply.

Cattle were owned individually, but land was held communally, and was administered by the chief of the ethnic group and by his sub-chiefs and headmen. Every married man was entitled to receive from the group a site for his house and land to cultivate, but could not claim more than he and his family were themselves likely to use. So long as he maintained his home and cultivated his land it remained in his exclusive possession and could pass on his death to his heirs. He could give away or lend to others land which was temporarily not needed, but no payment could be taken for such transfers; neither sale nor rent of land was recognized in tribal law. Pasture land, forests, and the wild veld were not similarly distributed, but were available, like the English commons, to be freely used by everyone. The chief regulated all use of the resources available to his people. It was he who decided when particular stages of the agricultural cycle such as tilling, planting, harvesting, or cutting grass for thatching should begin, and he who defined which areas were to be used as pasture and which as arable. There were many advantages to this regulation of space and of activity, but it also meant that there was little scope for individual initiative or innovation.

Arable farming, from tilling and sowing to harvesting and threshing, was undertaken mainly by women. In addition to the staple grains, they planted and cared for melons, beans, pumpkins, and root crops. Winter crops such as wheat could not be cultivated because of the practice of turning the cattle on to the fields in the autumn, following the harvest. The techniques employed were generally primitive, notably the widespread use of wooden digging sticks, although there were some iron-bladed hoes. Arable and pastoral activities were never merged into a system of mixed farming, incorporating the systematic use of manure on crops. There was no rotation of crops, and when the fertility of soil was exhausted, the households moved on to freshly cleared land, fertilized by the ash of the burnt cover. Women were also responsible for collecting veld foods, such as wild roots, fruits, and berries, and these could be of vital importance in times of drought and crop failure. The Nguni could have enjoyed a substantial supplement to their diet from the coastal and river resources to which they had access, but generally maintained a taboo against eating fish.

Non-agricultural production was quite limited. In areas where there were iron or copper ores of suitable quality, notably among the Sotho, specialist craftsmen developed considerable skill in mining and smelting, and in the production of metal goods such as hoes, spears, axes, knives, and ornaments. More generally, men used the raw materials from the livestock to make *karosses* (capes or blankets), bags, and shields from the hides and skins, and carvings and receptacles from the bones and horns. They were also skilled workers in wood and ivory, producing utensils, handles for weapons and implements, and ornaments. Women made clay pots, baskets, and mats.

These African subsistence economies were basically self-sufficient and were viable as long as adequate land was available. The people were skilled in a range of crafts and had adapted very intelligently to the hazards of their environment. They enjoyed a decent standard of living, with a healthy diet including milk from cattle and goats, porridge and beer from corn, and meat, which was mostly obtained by hunting the abundant supply of animals in the wild. Their economies were not static; farming and metal-working technologies changed and developed. The introduction of new crops, notably maize – which was probably brought from America by the Portuguese during the seventeenth century, and yielded far more calories per acre – contributed to a slow rise in productivity. However, crop and livestock yields were low. Even the most productive areas, such as some of the land farmed in the east of the country (later part of the Zulu kingdom), were in no way comparable with truly exceptional centres of fertile land in river valleys such as the Nile, or the remarkably well-watered area that produced the outstanding thirteenth-century stone buildings of Great Zimbabwe.

More generally, African societies lacked the conditions essential for sustained economic development. They did not enjoy continuous political and geographical stability, mainly because abundant land made it easy for chiefdoms to fragment. This also meant that societies typically remained small. It is estimated that there may have been as many as a thousand separate ethnic groups, many with fewer than 20,000 members, each largely independent and responsible for managing its own affairs. Within these small units there was no division of labour, other than by gender, and no opportunity for any economies of scale.

Above all, they lacked the potential stimulus of trade. There were no regular markets or trade fairs, of the sort that were common since at least medieval times in England and other countries, and indeed elsewhere in Africa. Specialization in production, and thus inter-tribal trade, was limited by the broad uniformity of economic activity across large areas. Exchange might occur if one group suffered a crop failure and could barter cattle for grain from another that had a surplus, but was otherwise largely restricted to small-scale transactions in metal goods and other locally specific products such as salt or tobacco. External trade was restricted because groups had no access to large, prosperous foreign markets and did not produce suitable export goods. There was a flourishing exchange with the Portuguese at Delagoa Bay in products such as ivory, hides, and metal artefacts in return for beads and cloth, but no systematic production designed specifically for the purpose of trade. Trade in animal products could make chiefs wealthy but did not promote development and innovation in the way that the trade in woollen cloth and other manufactures helped to transform the economies of Europe. Intractable transport problems provided a further obstacle to trade, notably the vast distances to be covered, absence of navigable rivers, frequent mountain barriers, and the need to rely primarily on human carriers (though oxen were used as pack animals in some areas).

The result of all these factors was that the extent of any surplus over minimum levels of subsistence was extremely modest. It was possible only to a very limited extent to support craftsmen and other specialists, encourage learning and formal study, or erect permanent buildings or large religious structures. Any surplus was accumulated primarily in cattle, but cattle were frequently paid to others as dowry or tribute, seized in raids, or lost during droughts. So the typical pattern for any individual society was one of cyclical fluctuation rather than continuous accumulation. Africans were unaware of the spread of literacy and of advances in science and learning in many other parts of the world. There was little technical improvement, and the overall economic and social progress of these societies over many centuries was accordingly slow. Despite this, the indigenous African population might well have been content to continue on their traditional course, but, from the end of the eighteenth century onwards, the possibility was denied to them by the pervasive encroachment of settlers and trekkers on their lands. Through the course of the nineteenth century a powerful new force was superimposed on their way of life.

2 Seizing the land: conquest and dispossession

European expansion into the interior

The process of conquest and dispossession began very early in the history of white settlement at the Cape. As outlined in Chapter 1, the Khoikhoi were forced almost immediately to cede parts of their traditional grazing lands to the Europeans who had landed in Table Bay to develop a refreshment station for the Netherlands East India Company (VOC).[1] Thereafter, the dispossession of the Khoikhoi was swiftly accomplished. In 1672 two of the nomadic tribes were induced to sign treaties under which they surrendered control of a large area of land from Table Bay to Saldanha Bay in the north and to the mountains of Hottentots Holland in the east. The compensation actually paid for this was derisory and only a small fraction of the sums promised in the treaties. The war fought by a third tribe in the mid-1670s was the last occasion on which Khoikhoi in what is now the Western Cape offered organized resistance to white expansion. After that it would take another 100 years before the Europeans expanding eastward from this initial settlement made their first contact with the vanguard of Xhosa farmers moving westward along the coast. From that time forward the economic life of Africans and Europeans would be indissolubly bound together.

One fundamental reason for the slow pace at which the settlers increased both their activity and their numbers, and thus the area over which they operated, was the policy of the VOC. It was never the intention of the Company to promote the development of the colony as an independent territory. On the contrary, their consistent and overriding

---

[1] The full Dutch name of the company was Generale Vereenigde Nederlandsche Ge-Octroyeerde Oost-Indische Compagnie. This powerful institution amalgamated several Dutch trading companies, and from its base in Java it dominated the trade of Europe with the East Indies. The VOC effectively administered the Cape colony as part of the empire of the Netherlands in the east. For further information see M. Wilson and L. Thompson (eds.), *The Oxford history of South Africa*, Oxford: Oxford University Press, 1969, vol. 1, pp. 183–232.

objective, from the first days of their arrival in 1652 until their departure in 1795, was to obtain provisions for the company ships that called at the Cape of Good Hope before embarking on their long voyage out or home across the Indian Ocean. Table Bay was ideally placed roughly halfway between Europe and India, Java, and other territories in the East. In order to provide the necessary supplies, the VOC assisted a small number of 'free burghers' to supplement the fruit and vegetables grown in the company gardens by cultivating wheat and other grains, and keeping cattle and sheep. The farmers soon found that rearing cattle was far more profitable than growing wheat, and that wine could also be produced in the locality.

However, a strict condition was imposed that everything the burghers produced was to be sold to the VOC at low fixed prices. They were not free to sell to the indigenous inhabitants or to passing ships of other nations, still less could they export their wheat, meat, and wine to foreign markets. The rationale for this insistence on a trade monopoly was the Company's fear that if they allowed a free market to emerge, in which burghers could sell their produce to the highest bidder, the effect would be simply to drive up the prices their own ships would have to pay. The VOC also prohibited the cultivation of tobacco, in order to preserve for themselves the profitable barter trade in this commodity with the Khoikhoi. In addition, they were adamant that no form of manufactured goods should be produced at the Cape, since this would both diminish the market for the establishments that produced these goods in Holland, and deprive the VOC of the customs duties that were collected on such goods when they were imported into the colony.

The attitude of the Company was also reflected in their policy with respect to emigration. Once it was realized that there was suitable land available, and that former sailors and soldiers, who became the first colonists, would never make good farmers, small numbers of emigrants were brought from Holland. Some fifty men with experience of farming, and a small number of young women from orphanages in Amsterdam and Rotterdam, arrived in the late 1680s. At the end of that decade some two hundred Huguenots – a small part of the great number of French Protestants who had taken refuge in Holland when Louis XIV revoked the edict which had protected them – were settled by the Company at the Cape. They had the necessary skills and experience for both wheatfields and vineyards, and were dispersed among Dutch- and German-speaking settlers in the areas of Stellenbosch, Paarl, and Franschhoek. After that a handful of individuals came to the settlement of their own volition, but further growth of the white population relied primarily on their natural increase. This took the number of Europeans at the Cape to a mere

1,300 by 1700 and to about 22,000 at the end of the eighteenth century (see further Annexe 1).

Even if the policy of the VOC had been more liberal, and more concerned to promote development at the Cape, however, it could not have overcome the many natural problems that impeded growth prior to the diamond discoveries in the second half of the nineteenth century. The region lacked a suitable staple. It could not produce the fur and timber of Canada, the cotton and tobacco of Virginia and Maryland, or the sugar of the West Indies. Its sheep had no wool, its vines were inferior to those of France and Portugal, its wheat was too expensive. Once outside a small area around Cape Town, and a narrow belt along the coast to the north and east, rainfall was sorely insufficient and unreliable. The rivers were often dry and never navigable, there were no bridges, and the lumbering ox wagons could make only slow progress along roads that were little more than trails and tracks. The Khoisan were the only potential indigenous source of labour, and neither they nor the imported slaves were numerous or industrious. For Europeans, the temperate climate and freedom from tsetse flies and mosquitoes made it a highly attractive country in which to live, but all these other factors made it an extremely difficult one in which to make a living.

The adverse effects of the monopoly of trade maintained by the VOC were not immediately evident, but they emerged early in the eighteenth century when the productive capacity of the colony had finally expanded beyond the needs of the Company. From then onwards, free burghers suffered in good years from a surplus of products and low prices, and in bad years from drought and crop failure. Even with persistent smuggling and illicit trade they did not prosper. Their considerable discontent was further inflamed by the venality, greed, and perquisites of a small number of VOC officials who developed large estates and acquired significant wealth, leaving the great majority of colonists poor and discontented. This enforced lack of opportunity to improve their position encouraged many burghers to escape from the Company's jurisdiction. As they moved further away from the Cape peninsula they found not only greater freedom but also a country rich in game from which they could derive both abundant food and excellent sport. Inevitably, under these conditions, they were largely self-sufficient.

In 1660 van Riebeeck had ordered the building of a hedge of 'bitter almond trees, and all sorts of fast-growing brambles and thornbushes' in order to establish a boundary between the gardens and grain farms of the VOC settlement and the Khoikhoi. He instructed his successor that no extension of the settlement beyond this barrier was ever to be contemplated. More than a century later, in 1778, another of his successors proclaimed that the Great Fish River – just beyond modern Port Elizabeth, almost 500 miles to the east of Cape Town – was to be the boundary between the colony and the Xhosa. Thereafter, the further dispersal of white settlement was checked, for the time being, by the numerous conflicts which followed the meeting of two groups of pastoral farmers as they clashed over land, access to water and good pasture, or allegations of cattle raiding.

From the beginning of the eighteenth century settlers had drifted steadily beyond the mountains that encircled the south-western corner and separated the thin fringe of good land watered by reliable winter rains from the vast, dry, interior plateau known as the Karroo (see Map 2). Once the cattle farmers had forced a way through the first great mountain barrier near Tulbagh, some 75 miles north-east of Cape Town, they followed river valleys towards the coast and then turned eastwards. A village was founded at Swellendam on the Breede River in 1745, roughly on the eastern border of the region in which regular arable farming was possible. Further movement took them into the heart of the eastern Karroo, and in 1786 a magistracy was established at Graaff Reinet. This settlement of some 700 families was about 200 miles from the sea, and about 400 miles from Cape Town, a journey that could take a month travelling by ox wagon, and two or three months driving cattle or sheep. Other settlers spread directly north of Cape Town until they reached the mountains near Calvinia.

In this new frontier economy, land was abundant and cheap, while labour and capital were scarce and expensive. The settlers swiftly adapted to these conditions by abandoning arable farming in favour of an exceedingly extensive and semi-nomadic system of cattle-keeping. Land was effectively given away by the Company under the system of 'loan farms' (leenings-plaatsen). This was a form of leasehold under which anyone could claim a large farm in return for a notional fee; in more distant areas even that fee was not paid. The convention was that the would-be owner of a plot was simply required to walk his horse for half an hour from his chosen central spot to each of the four corners of a rectangle. This normally yielded a diagonal of a little over 4 miles, and a farm of some 6,000 acres, over 9 square miles. These huge farms were about forty times the size of the small, mainly arable, family farms of about 160 acres that were typical in Canada or the United States. They became a fundamental feature of the emerging economy of the roving cattle farmers (trekboers), and persisted even in regions where more intensive farming was possible:

The claim of each man to a farm of not less than 6,000 acres became ultimately an inborn right. In subsequent South African history few factors are of greater

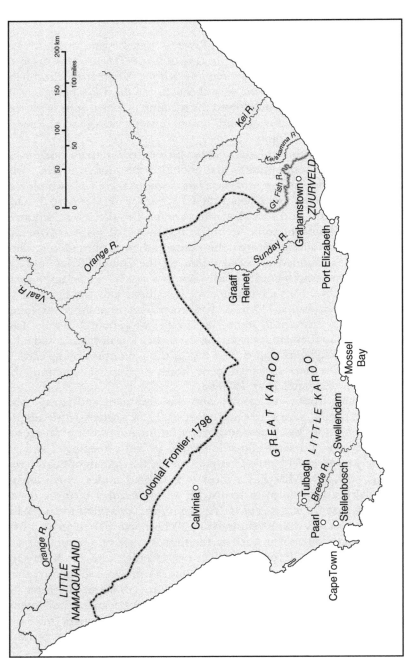

Map 2. Cape Colony in the eighteenth century

importance than the uncontrolled and haphazard method of Boer land settlement and the habits which were bred by the Company's loss of control over Boer expansion.[2]

Farms of this size meant isolation, and isolation was not conducive to the exchange of either ideas or goods.

The pace of economic activity at the Cape quickened slightly after the British recaptured the colony from the Dutch in 1806.[3] The British could not transform adverse natural conditions, but eliminated most of the restraints imposed by the VOC on domestic trade and the supply of passing ships, and allowed the colonists to participate so far as they could in international trade. They were also permitted to 'set up a brewery or any other manufacture not under a general prohibition'. From 1808, a separate branch of the existing government-owned Lombard Bank was formed to undertake a wider range of functions than its parent. The new Discount Bank accepted deposits on which interest was paid, and used the funds to discount bills of exchange and promissory notes, and to make advances against suitable security. In 1825 British silver coinage was declared legal tender and the existing paper currency, the rixdollar, was gradually withdrawn and replaced by sterling notes. The rixdollar had been equal in value to 4 shillings when the British arrived, but had depreciated to 1½ shillings by the time the new coins were introduced. The imperial government's insistence that all holdings of the old currency should be converted at this lower rate was a considerable source of grievance in the colony. The first private banks started operations in the 1830s, typically small 'unit' banks without branches, owned by local merchants. In general they were well managed, but banking made only limited progress until the 1860s.

The authorities slowly recognized the possibilities of systematic colonization of the Cape, and were anxious to consolidate their hold on the frontier district of Albany, a beautiful undulating pastoral area to the west of the Great Fish River – previously called in Dutch the zuurveld (sour grassland) – that was contested by Xhosa and colonists. This concern coincided with severe economic depression and unemployment in Britain following the collapse of farm prices after the conclusion of the Napoleonic wars, and the idea gradually took hold that 'the settlement of a British population fronting the Kaffirs might relieve the poor rates

---

[2] C. de Kiewiet, *A history of South Africa, social and economic*, London: Oxford University Press, 1941, p. 17.

[3] The Cape was occupied by the British in 1795, restored to the Batavian Republic by the treaty of Amiens in 1803, retaken by Britain in 1806, and formally ceded by the Dutch in 1814 at the end of the Napoleonic wars.

and the Army estimates at one and the same time'.[4] The British government was finally persuaded to meet both these home and colonial needs
by assisting some 5,000 settlers to emigrate to the eastern frontier of the
colony in 1820, and to survive an initially difficult time of bad harvests
and floods. There was now a much more substantial English-speaking
element in the colony, and the Europeans had strengthened their position
against the Xhosa.

Further assisted immigration followed after 1837, when some 5,000
artisans and labourers came from the United Kingdom to help rebuild the
population of the Cape following the departure of thousands of trekkers
(see below). The need to ensure a strong base in the newly established
region of British Kaffraria, between the Kei and the Keiskamma rivers,
persuaded the British government to assist further immigration, and in
1857 a large group of Germans who had fought on the side of the British
in the Crimean War were settled on farms in that region. In the two
following years they were reinforced by some 2,300 agricultural
labourers, also from Germany. Other changes affecting the labour supply
for the colony, including the abolition of slavery in 1834, will be discussed
in the following chapter.

Perhaps the main gain to the economic life of the colony from its
absorption into the British Empire was the stimulus given to wine
farms. Under the system of imperial preference operated by the United
Kingdom, Cape wines were allowed to enter on payment of duties appreciably below those charged on wines from France and other foreign
countries. Exports increased rapidly, and wine became by far the largest
item in the Cape's modest external trade until the special benefit given to
the colony was removed in two stages in 1825 and 1831. The product
which emerged to take its place was wool (see Table 2.1). The replacement of the indigenous fat-tailed sheep by wool-bearing Spanish merinos
made slow progress, because many farmers attached greater value to the
meat and fat that they could obtain from the native flocks. However,
production and export of wool eventually started to increase, stimulated
in part by the growing demand from the textile industry in Britain. The
quantity exported was only 20,000 lb in 1822, but climbed to 1,370,000 lb
two decades later, and to almost 26,000,000 lb in 1862. It might not have
compared either in quantity or quality with the wool sheared from the
backs of sheep in Australia and South America, but the Cape had at last
found a major export staple.

[4] E. Walker (ed.), *Cambridge history of the British Empire*, vol. VIII, *South Africa*, 2nd edn,
Cambridge: Cambridge University Press, 1963, p. 224.

Table 2.1. *Annual average exports from the Cape and Natal, 1807–70[a]*

	(1) Food and drink[b]	(2) Raw materials[c]	(3) Other products	(4) Total
		(£ thousand)		
1807–10	–	–	–	36.5
1811–15	–	–	–	93.6
1816–20	–	–	–	194.3
1821–25	142.6	51.5	–2.7	191.4
1826–30	151.2	57.0	13.3	221.5
1831–35	126.8	102.4	5.3	234.5
1836–40	131.5	93.9	28.1	253.5
1841–45	89.6	172.5	36.0	298.1
1846–50	72.5	268.2	32.7	373.4
1851–55	84.0	352.3	248.1	684.4
1856–60	191.2	1,406.9	143.7	1,741.8
1861–65	107.2	1,888.9	119.9	2,116.0
1866–70	112.7	2,251.8	156.1	2,520.6

[a] The series measures the net exports of South African produce; it excludes re-exports and specie and is net of inter-colonial trade.
[b] Including wine, fresh fruit, maize, sugar, and meat.
[c] Including wool, hides and skins, ostrich feathers, and mohair.

Source: C. G. W. Schumann, *Structural changes and business cycles in South Africa, 1806–1936,* London: P. S. King & Son, 1938, p. 44.

Some writers have been keen to assert the importance of commercialization and class formation in the Cape economy from the late eighteenth century, and to emphasize that neither eighteenth-century pastoralists at the Cape, nor later *trekboers* in the interior should be seen as purely self-sufficient, isolated, subsistence farmers. There is no doubt that frontier families did produce for the local market, if only to obtain the various commodities – from sugar and coffee to guns and ammunition – that were important to them. But it is equally clear that the scale of their overall market activity was stunted and puny, especially with respect to exports. As Table 2.2 shows, in the first half of the nineteenth century purchases from the Cape are only barely discernible in total imports into the United Kingdom. In the years immediately following the second British occupation of the Cape, exports from the colony contributed less than 0.1 per cent of that total. By the 1820s the proportion was only 0.4 per cent, and by the 1850s it was still well under 1 per cent. The contrast with the

Table 2.2. *United Kingdom imports by country of origin, 1800s to 1850s*

	(1) 1804–06	(2) 1824–26	(3) 1854–56
	(£ million)		
Total UK imports			
of which from	50.6	57.0	151.6
West Indies	12.4	8.6	8.7
Asia	8.0	11.0	25.7
United States	4.2	6.1	30.3
Latin America	1.3	3.1	9.7
Canada	0.9	3.1	5.7
Africa	0.4	0.7	5.2
Near East	0.2	1.1	6.3
Australia	–	0.2	4.8
Exports from Cape Colony	0.04	0.2	1.2
Cape exports as % of total UK imports	0.1	0.4	0.8

Source: All data on UK imports from R. Davis, *The industrial revolution and British overseas trade*, Leicester: Leicester University Press, 1979, p. 93.

vigorous expansion of production for export to the United Kingdom in other parts of the formal and informal empire is very striking.

While the departure of the VOC brought some improvement in the economic condition of the Cape, many other changes introduced by the British were unacceptable to a large part of the Boer community, and drove them to initiate the next significant phase in the movement of white settlers into the interior. Their trek began late in 1835, continued strongly in the closing years of the decade, and then more sluggishly in the early 1840s. By 1843 some 12,000 Boers had left the Cape. The many social, political, and cultural grievances that lay behind their decision need not concern us here, though antagonism to Britain's interference in what they regarded as 'proper relations between master and servant' figured prominently, and clearly had economic implications. However, the dominant economic factor was the shortage of land. They could not maintain even their extensive system of stock farming in the arid land that remained to the north, and a large body of Africans stood between them and the high-rainfall regions to the east. Their movement accordingly took them in a north-easterly direction between these two barriers. They crossed the Orange River near its southernmost loop, and travelled on to the great central plain known as the highveld.

The main body of trekkers moved into Natal, where they established a republic in 1838, with the extremely enticing prospect that this would give them their own port (then Port Natal, now Durban) free from British control. The initial reaction of Britain to the Great Trek was marked by considerable vacillation, but in 1843 it was decided to annex Natal. This was a significant port on the Indian Ocean that should not be allowed to fall under the control of a group known for their hostility to the United Kingdom, and the decision was also motivated by strategic and humanitarian considerations with respect to the Zulu population of the territory. The annexation caused most of the trekkers to leave the territory and move back onto the highveld, and in 1848–51 some 4,000 British immigrants were assisted to settle in Natal in order to secure the development of British interests in that coastal area.

By contrast, it was argued by many in London that there was little or nothing to be gained by maintaining British claims to jurisdiction over the interior. The existence of an independent Boer state north of the Vaal River was recognized in 1852, and a brief attempt to maintain British rule over the territory between the Orange and the Vaal Rivers was abandoned at the Bloemfontein Convention in 1854. This was a momentous step which effectively divided South Africa into two British colonies and two Boer republics until union in 1910. Three separate groups of trekkers occupied different parts of the territory beyond the Vaal, centred on Potchefstroom to the west, Lydenburg to the east, and Schoemansdal in the Zoutpansberg to the north (see Maps 3 and 4). For a time they were kept apart by bitter personal rivalries, religious disputes, and other controversies, but in 1860 all three combined to establish the South African Republic (or Transvaal). Driven primarily by a belief in the need for economies in government spending, the British government effectively abandoned all responsibility for the African population outside the Cape and Natal. In the northern half of the future South Africa the Boers were now free to do as they wished in their ceaseless quest for land and labour.

The attempt of the British authorities to introduce a more economically rational scheme for the allocation of land than the VOC system of 'loan farms' was alleged to be one of many grievances that had triggered the Great Trek, and the trekkers carried their traditional custom with them into the interior, thus perpetuating the system of extensive pastoral farming for as long as land could be found. In the early years of their advance, the trekkers mainly supplemented their stock farming by hunting and raiding, though it was not long before some among them attempted to develop arable farming in suitable areas such as the fertile Caledon River valley taken from the Basuto. Both types of activity involved conflict with Africans, and the wars to determine who controlled the land that had begun in the late eighteenth century on the eastern frontier of the Cape were continued during the mid-nineteenth century in the interior.

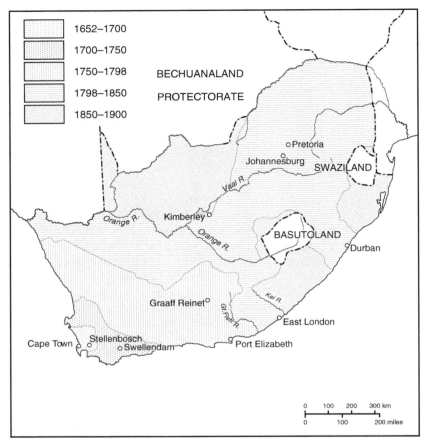

Map 3. European annexation of South Africa, 1652–1900. Adapted from A. J. Christopher, *The atlas of apartheid*, London: Routledge, 1994, p. 15.

Abundant land and scarce labour

Almost immediately after the first contact was made between settlers and Xhosa in the late eighteenth century, the two groups began clashing repeatedly, as white settlers sought to wrest the land from Africans. The first clash with the Xhosa in 1779 was followed by a series of wars, one before the first British occupation and one shortly after, and on four further occasions in the first half of the nineteenth century (in 1812, 1834–35, 1846–47, and 1850). Further battles, though not on the scale of those waged on the eastern frontier, followed as the *trekboers* moved into the land on the other side of the Orange River. The most obvious motive for persistent conflict was that the settlers wanted the land for themselves: for pasture and, where possible, arable farming. From the mid-nineteenth century onwards, there were also many commercial interests anxious to acquire land as a speculation, a trend which later increased strongly after the discovery of diamonds and gold in the interior.

However, there was also another dimension to the process of dispossession, and this has not always received the attention it warrants. This second motive arises in the context of an agrarian economy characterized, as South Africa was, by a relative abundance of land and a scarcity of labour. Under these conditions, according to a well-known thesis introduced in the modern literature by Domar, owners of land will be unable to profit from it.[5] As long as free land exists elsewhere, hired labour would either be unavailable, because those needed to farm the land preferred to work as independent peasants on the free land, or it would be unprofitable, because the minimum wage at which workers were willing to enter the labour market would need to be at least as much as they could earn as independent farmers. However, payment of this 'reservation wage' would leave too little of the income generated from the land at the disposal of the landowners, and was unacceptable to them. Domar used this proposition to explain the introduction of slavery or serfdom, with particular reference to the bonded serfs created in tsarist Russia in the time of Catherine I. The argument in this particular case was that the landowning nobility used their political influence to persuade the empress to impose a system of bondage that would tie labourers to the serf owners. Once legally constrained in this way, they were unable to migrate to areas of Russia with free land, and any possibility of working for themselves as independent peasants was immediately eliminated. In other countries different circumstances led to the imposition of slavery rather than serfdom, but the essential motive and consequences were the same.

In the early period of South African history, settlers did resort to slavery and other systems of coercion in order to ensure a supply of labour and, as we shall see in the following chapter, some forms of coercion continued well into the modern period. But the slaves who were used at the Cape were almost all imported from elsewhere; slavery was never imposed on the indigenous African population, and the settlers effectively sought to solve their critical land–labour problem in another way. Their primary

---

[5] E. Domar, 'The causes of slavery or serfdom: a hypothesis', *Journal of Economic History*, 30, 1970, pp. 18–32, based in part on an earlier formulation of the hypothesis in H. J. Nieboer, *Slavery as an industrial system: ethnological researches*, The Hague: M. Nijhoff, 1900.

answer to the Domar dilemma was not the imposition of slavery or serfdom, *but closure of the escape route to free land*. The more land that settlers could seize and bring under their own control, the more they could deprive Africans of any means of survival other than the sale of their labour to white farmers and other employers. This motivation was recognized by the Rev. J. E. Casalis, of the Paris Evangelical Missionary Society, who was present in Basutoland during the campaigns in the 1860s against the Sotho. He observed perceptively that the Boers took advantage of every opportunity 'to add farm to farm, pasture to pasture', and their aim seemed to be

to force the natives against some impassable range or drive them back into arid deserts; to leave them no space in anticipation of the future and of the increase in population ... to live within such narrow limits that it becomes impossible to subsist on the produce of agriculture and livestock and to be compelled to offer their services to the farmers in the capacity of domestic servants and labourers.[6]

Here and elsewhere, the possibility of Africans continuing to farm independently was to be forcefully eliminated by a sustained process of dispossession. In the South African case, and many others, this strategy was powerfully nourished by racialism and a deep-seated belief in white supremacy, but such dogmas are not a necessary feature of an essentially economic phenomenon, as can be seen in the example of tsarist Russia, where lords and their serfs thought of themselves as part of the same nation, recognized the same emperor, served in the same army, spoke the same language, and practised the same religion.

The roots of conflict

A strategy of conquest and dispossession was pursued energetically by both Dutch and British settlers, and was generally supported in the late eighteenth century by the VOC, and later by Britain, though the imperial government was often critical of settler expansion in the mid-nineteenth century. The process of destruction of the prevailing African polities was also greatly facilitated by serious conflicts and rivalries among the Africans. Nevertheless, white farmers and the British government were the prime movers. All farmers shared broadly the same aims and methods irrespective of whether they were English or Dutch settlers in the Cape Colony or Natal, or *trekboers* in the interior. For all of them, acquisition and control of land, and thus of labour, was imperative if they were to

---

[6] R. C. Germond (ed.), *Chronicles of Basutoland*, Morija: Morija Sesuto Book Depot, 1967, p. 267.

attain a decent standard of living. The territory in which they sought to do this gradually expanded away from their entry point at Cape Town until they claimed possession of almost the entire country south of the Limpopo. The position taken by the imperial government was largely an incidental consequence of other, more powerful, motives, but the movements and policies of the white settlers were a significant factor in the determination of British policies.

Imperial policy evolved over the course of the nineteenth century as the United Kingdom became progressively more involved in military campaigns against the Africans, and as its territorial control expanded with successive annexation of additional parts of the country. It was not a single, unvarying, consistent policy, but one that fluctuated in response to a complex mix of the local interests, attitudes, and ambitions of administrators, merchants, mine-owners, and other influential parties in South Africa; the political and economic objectives of the United Kingdom government and its officials in London, mediated by domestic political rivalry between Tories and Liberals; and by wider international considerations, most notably Britain's concern to maintain control of the vital sea route to India. Whatever the precise combination of factors, it is clear that willingness to intervene gathered pace both in London and South Africa, and by the 1870s was operating powerfully and aggressively. The assertion of British power ultimately required that *all* independent black states should be destroyed, and the imperial government's implementation of this policy thus reinforced the settlers' own programme of conquest and dispossession.

From the 1870s these two groups were supported by a further new and powerful interest group, the rapidly emerging body of mine-owners, operating first in the diamond fields, and later, on a much bigger scale, in the gold mines. A large, regular, supply of labour was an essential requirement for the successful exploitation of South Africa's mineral wealth, and so mine-owners also became enthusiastic proponents of the strategy.

These three groups were deeply divided over many issues, but they were able to make common cause in opposition to independent African polities. All shared the same fundamental belief that their prosperity depended on the overall success of the programme of conquest and dispossession, and did not hesitate to pursue it relentlessly and ruthlessly, regardless of its consequences for the indigenous populations. All three were sustained in their brutal denial of human rights to black people by their conviction that Europeans represented a superior civilization, a doctrine often sustained by an instinctive racialism. The attitudes that prevailed, even at the more enlightened end of a broad range of opinions, are well illustrated by this extract from a report made in 1877 to the governor of the Cape by one of his aides, the Honourable Cecil Ashley, after he had made a prolonged tour of the country. He states that 'better and more settled administration' is one of the essential requirements for rapid development of the country, but that this

can only be obtained by the extension of our authority over such parts of the country, as still are suffered to prolong under the name of independence, a state of barbarism, heathenism, and superstitious abominations which is the cause of endless trouble and constant disturbance within our own territories which now surround them. It is a fresh repetition of the old lesson taught us in India, in Central Asia, in New Zealand, wherever a civilized power is brought in contact with an uncivilized, where law and order find themselves unavoidably neighbour to anarchy, civilization cannot stand still, it must for its own preservation be aggressive lest if law and order be not forcibly imposed anarchy may haply render both impossible.[7]

Ashley's view was more complex than the crude racialism of most settlers, and elsewhere in the report he refers also to Africans as 'sentient, thinking, aspiring men like ourselves'. But it seems clear that in his eyes this was a latent humanity to which savages could lay claim only when they had been civilized, that is to say, had adopted European religion, dress, and customs, lived in square rather than round houses, learned to speak English and acquired literacy, abandoned 'witchcraft' and rejected their traditional healers in favour of 'scientific' medicine. Until then they could be coerced and attacked as superior, civilized authorities saw fit.

At this point in the narrative there is a choice. One alternative would be to provide a broad survey of the working out of this campaign for conquest and dispossession in all parts of South Africa; the other to provide a more detailed case study of one particular region. The latter option was chosen on the grounds that to focus on a single episode allows space for a slightly more detailed and rounded treatment. The case selected is that of the Pedi, one of the Sotho-speaking tribes in the north-eastern Transvaal, and is very largely drawn from the splendid study by Peter Delius.[8]

The events surrounding the conflicts in which the Pedi were involved during the second half of the nineteenth century, first with the Boers and then with the British, obviously have many features specific to the circumstances of this region and to the actors involved in this particular drama. However, the same fundamental features occur in the experience

---

[7] *Further correspondence respecting the affairs of South Africa*, C. 2000, 1878, LV, No. 12, p. 384.
[8] P. Delius, *The land belongs to us: the Pedi polity, the Boers and the British in the nineteenth-century Transvaal*, Johannesburg: Ravan Press, 1983.

of other – perhaps more familiar – groups, in which military defeat was followed by the appropriation of their best land. They appear, for example, in the history of the subjugation of the Khoikhoi in the early eighteenth century, and in the conquest of the main groups of Xhosa in the eastern Cape after nine major wars fought between the late eighteenth and the late nineteenth century. They can be found in the campaigns waged by Boer commandos from the Orange Free State against the Lesotho kingdom of Moshoeshoe, culminating in the defeat of the Basuto in 1867 and the loss of all their best arable land, and in the victory of British regulars over the Tlhaping, one of the Southern Tswana chiefdoms, at the battle of Dithakong in July 1878. One of the last and most crucial acts of conquest was the destruction of the most formidable African military power, the Zulu kingdom of Cetshwayo in Natal in 1879–84 after a combination of external invasions by British and Boers, and ferocious civil wars. These or similar features were also reproduced in many other less well-known episodes across the whole of South Africa.

Defeat and dispossession of the Pedi by British and Boers

A substantial Pedi kingdom first emerged in the late eighteenth century, one of several examples of a process of rapid political change in southern Africa that united previously fragmented chiefdoms under the hegemony of a powerful king. We can pick up the story in the late 1820s, towards the end of the *mfecane*, the period of wars, violent upheavals, and mass migrations of displaced and often dispossessed communities that convulsed most of southern Africa, including the Pedi, in the early nineteenth century, and spread into vast areas of central and eastern Africa.[9] It was during these turbulent conditions that Sekwati, a younger son of the former king, rose to power. He slowly established a paramount position, though with limits to his authority and with potential rivals, and always had to contend with the greatly superior power of the neighbouring Swazi and Zulu kingdoms. The Pedi were attacked by a Swazi army in the 1830s and again in 1869, and by the Zulus in 1851, but on each occasion were able to repel the invading forces.

---

[9] There is still considerable controversy among historians about the reasons for the *mfecane* (or *lifaqane*, the Sotho equivalent of this Xhosa term), and the relative importance of political and military developments in African society – notably among the Zulu – compared with external forces such as the growth of trade in slaves and ivory or changes in climatic conditions. For an account of the debates see C. Hamilton (ed.), *Mfecane aftermath: reconstructive debates in southern African history*, Johannesburg: Witwatersrand University Press, 1995.

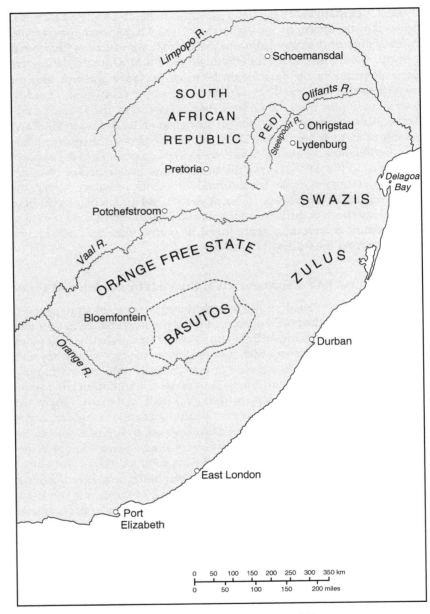

Map 4. The Pedi and the South African Republic

The Pedi heartland lay within the modern province of Limpopo, on the interior plateau known as the highveld, with its northern boundary in mountains around the site described on contemporary British maps as 'Secocoeni's kraal', and extended southwards between two rivers for approximately 100 miles. Their forebears had arrived in this region in about the mid-seventeenth century, and over the next two centuries the population had increased to roughly 70,000. Looser groups under subordinate chiefs owing allegiance to the Pedi king lived outside this core area. Three features of the heartland were of crucial importance to the survival of this kingdom (see Map 4). The area lay between the confluence of the Olifants River to the west and north, and the Steelpoort River to the east, and so was well supplied with water; it was surrounded by three mountain ranges, which provided a superb defensive position; and it was well placed in relation to trade routes between the highveld and the port of Delagoa Bay on the Indian Ocean, where ivory and horns could be traded with the Portuguese for beads, cloth, and copper.

In 1845 two parties of trekkers arrived in the area. They settled at Ohrigstad, a few miles to the east of the Pedi heartland, in a region partially depopulated during the African wars of the 1820s. Some of the new arrivals saw their economic future in raiding African settlements and hunting large herds of elephants and other game that roamed the lowveld (the area that was subsequently to become the vast Kruger National Park), and in trading ivory with the Portuguese, thus escaping from the influence of Britain in the southern ports of Cape Town and Durban. Others envisaged a more stable farming community, grazing cattle and growing wheat, maize, and other crops.

Sekwati was initially apprehensive, but willing to be friendly, and signed a peace treaty with the trekkers' leader, Andries Hendrik Potgieter. The document has not survived, so its exact terms are not known, but there can be little doubt that it was understood in totally different ways by the two parties. The trekkers claimed that this document made over all rights to land, though the precise area to which this was supposed to apply was never specified. Sekwati interpreted it as an allocation to trekkers of land on which they could settle, but without disposing of his people's title to the property; in traditional African style he was granting a right to use the land but not to own it. His position on ownership of land was further demonstrated when the trekkers who wished to establish a permanent farming community offered a payment of cattle in order to obtain full title to the land, and he refused their offer.

The trekkers then tried a second route to acquisition of title, based on a treaty signed in 1846 with the Swazi king, Mswati, under which a large area of land was allegedly ceded to the Boers. This was land well outside the Swazi's own core territory and included a large part of the Pedi heartlands. Sekwati of course repudiated the notion that Swazis had any right to sell land belonging to an independent Pedi kingdom, but the trekkers made effective use of this treaty. After reviewing all the circumstances surrounding the treaty, one historian of the native policy of the *voortrekkers* concluded: 'The circumstances all point to the conclusion that this was some bogus deal designed to supply a title to the land other than that at the disposal of Potgieter. Even if perfectly above-board it is difficult to see what legal right the treaty could have conferred.'[10]

The disagreements reflect the different cultures of the African and Boer communities and a confused situation of frontier societies with no agreed legal system. Matters would ultimately be decided by force, but the immediate reaction of the trekkers was to claim that the land on which Africans actually lived – and had done for centuries – was now their property, and to use this unsubstantiated claim to demand various forms of tribute, including labour, from the Pedi. In 1859 the republic's parliament, the Volksraad, declared that in addition to a freehold farm each burgher could lay claim to one or more *lenings plaatsen* (quit-rent farms), for an annual payment, usually of 30 shillings. This was high for ordinary farmers but enabled some officials, traders, and non-resident landowners from the Cape and Natal to accumulate massive landholdings. The first stage in the dispossession of the Pedi had been accomplished.

The trekkers suffered from what they perceived to be an acute shortage of labour, but as long as the Pedi retained physical control of most of the land, the Boers were unable to extract either labour or tribute on a systematic basis. In 1852 they attempted to rectify this position by organizing a joint attack by commandos from each of the main communities, but a twenty-day siege failed to force Sekwati into submission. Cattle, sheep, and goats were seized, and the power of the Pedi was further weakened, but their kingdom remained intact, and they were not again directly challenged by a Boer army until 1876. Pedi success in battles with the trekkers and with other African societies was in part due to their possession of firearms, which they purchased with earnings from labour in the eastern Cape and, from the 1870s, in the diamond fields. It was a systematic exercise, organized by their chiefs, in which men went as voluntary migrants for as long as was necessary to earn the money needed to buy guns and cattle.

[10] J. A. I. Agar-Hamilton, *The native policy of the voortrekkers, 1836–1858*, Cape Town: M. Miller, 1928, pp. 61–2.

Sekwati died in 1861 and was succeeded by his eldest son, Sekhukhune. The succession was challenged by his other sons, and the resulting conflicts played a significant part in later developments. In 1869 they were attacked by Swazis, assisted by followers of Sekhukhune's brother, Mampuru, but the Pedi again successfully defended their position. For a brief moment the balance of power in the region shifted in favour of the Pedi, and against both Swazis and the South African Republic established by the trekkers in 1860. But by this stage, the position of the Pedi was becoming increasingly anomalous; in most of the rest of the territory of the republic, Africans had been unable to maintain their independence and had lost their land. Some of the vanquished took refuge in Pedi territory, thus strengthening Sekhukhune's position, and he successfully sustained his resistance and continued to rule his kingdom for another fifteen years.

Then in 1876, after some three decades of struggle and uneasy coexistence, the Boers decided that the time had come to launch another full-scale attack on the kingdom. Continuing conflicts over land and labour had been intensified from the 1870s by the consequences of the discovery of diamonds in what is now the Northern Cape, and also of alluvial gold deposits in the eastern Transvaal, on the periphery of the Pedi area. Opportunities to work in these newly opened mines made farm labour even less attractive to the Africans, and the impoverished republic wanted to assert its unchallenged control over these gold fields. There were also fears among the Boers – partly inflated and exaggerated – of the growing strength of the Pedi. The president of the republic, the Rev. Thomas Burgers, assembled an army of over 5,000, of whom about half were Swazi warriors. This was the largest force ever deployed against the Pedi, but it was unable to overcome the Pedi stronghold.

However, even though badly defeated and forced to withdraw, the Boers were able to further weaken the economic base of the African kingdom by seizing cattle, destroying crops, and attacking those who attempted to work the land. The Pedi were also harmed by drought and by internal divisions, and the authority of Sekhukhune was gravely diminished. After the war, the republic started negotiations with the kingdom, including a demand for payment of 2,000 cattle. Further discussion and potential disputes were then overtaken by the decision of the British government to annex the Transvaal Republic in 1877, followed a year later by a British attack on the Pedi stronghold.

The British took this path for a variety of reasons, but there were probably three overriding considerations. The overall perspective was determined by the Confederation Scheme which Lord Carnarvon, Secretary of State for the Colonies, had set out in 1875. This was designed to create a single South African federation joining the Cape Colony and Natal with the two Boer republics, and in order to get the Transvaal to participate it was necessary to defeat the Pedi and also the Zulus. Within this context the British were anxious to ensure the economic viability of their two older South African colonies and of the Transvaal – as always, colonies were expected to pay their way. An essential precondition for this was an adequate labour supply: for the diamond fields in the Cape, for new railway networks that were being built at breakneck speed, and for farmers, especially in Natal and the Transvaal, and this crucial objective was threatened as long as the Pedi retained control of their land and labour. Finally, the British were determined to show their power over the Pedi, and to exact tax revenues from them. There was no room for independent African kingdoms which challenged European property rights and might threaten the whole structure of British political and economic interests, just as there was none for hostile Boer republics.

The campaign against Sekhukhune began in 1878 with a siege lasting two months. This continued the process of disrupting farming and weakening the Pedi's already fragile economic base. In the following year a huge army was assembled under Sir Garnet Wolseley, with combined British and African (mainly Swazi) troops, three times as large as the force deployed by the Boers three years earlier. In a swift campaign, involving heavy casualties on both sides, this massive army conclusively defeated the Pedi. The Swazis continued their onslaught for another ten days, seizing both cattle and captives. Wolseley confided to his diary this revealing comment on the devastation he had unleashed:

Started about 4.45 a.m. for Sikukuni's kraal to see our troops go up the hill. A force of the Swazies also went there, but where the main body of Swazies is, I know not; it has evidently been sent away to raid on cattle: my object is to strike terror into the hearts of the surrounding tribes by the utter destruction of Sikukuni, root and branch, so the more the Swazies raid and destroy, the better my purpose is effected.[11]

In this way, the destruction of the Pedi kingdom was finally accomplished, most of their land was taken from them, and farmers, mine-owners, and land speculators could begin to exercise the control over Pedi labour supplies they so desperately wanted.

Similar campaigns occurred in all parts of South Africa over the course of the nineteenth century. The destruction of African political power was

---

[11] A. Preston (ed.), *The South African journal of Sir Garnet Wolseley, 1879–1880*, Cape Town: A. A. Balkema, 1973, 30 November 1879, p. 179.

followed in each region by appropriation of the most productive land and water rights, together with seizure under some suitable pretext of cattle and other goods. The objective was not only the political defeat of these African kingdoms and chiefdoms, but also the destruction of any possibility of economic independence that would enable black men and women to avoid work on white-owned farms and mines. The only significant exception was the Transkei, which was not appropriated because there was no thought of white settlement in that area.

The final outcome – land allocation in South Africa from 1913

Whites did not immediately take over *all* land, because the British lacked the desire to administer and control the entire African population, while the trekkers lacked the resources to do so. But as the prospects for farming improved, the settlers gradually increased the share of farmland under their control. It was thus not a single act of dispossession but a continuing process, which accelerated after the 1870s and reached its climax in 1913.

Successful attainment of the main objectives of the strategy of conquest and dispossession was embodied in the notorious Natives' Land Act of 1913. This made it illegal for Africans to acquire or rent any land outside the existing reserves. This was qualified by a clause specifying that the prohibition would not apply in the Cape if it would destroy existing and future African franchise rights (which were entrenched in the constitution).[12] In a cynical attempt to show that the measure was even-handed, a matching clause made it illegal for any person who was not an African to acquire or rent land within the reserves. However, the existence of communal tenure and the extent of overcrowding in this very restricted area, made this right to own land in the reserves of little or no value to Africans. A statutory body, the Beaumont Commission, was appointed to recommend the precise composition of the areas in which Africans could acquire or rent land. Until this was done, the status quo would be maintained. Details of the position in 1913 revealed that although Africans constituted two-thirds of the population, the sustained programme of dispossession had reduced the land reserved for them to a paltry 7.3 per cent of the total. Even the Commission recognized that this was too little, but – when it reported in 1916 – its recommendations for a larger area were so strongly opposed by white interests they had to be withdrawn.

---

[12] The qualification was challenged in the courts but upheld by the Appellate Division in 1917. It ceased to apply when the franchise rights of Cape Africans were abolished in 1936.

The ramifications of the Act as seen by African people were exposed in a resolution of the South African Native National Congress passed in 1916, stating that the 'real desire of the white population' was not territorial separation, but

To deprive the natives as a people of their freedom to acquire more land in their own right: To restrict or limit their right to bargain mutually on even terms for the occupation or settlement of land: To reduce by gradual process and by artificial means the Bantu people as a race to a status of permanent labourers or subordinates for all purposes and for all times with little or no freedom to sell their labour by bargaining on even terms with employers in the open markets of labour either in agricultural or industrial centres: To limit all opportunities for their economic improvement and independence: To lessen their chances as a people of competing freely and fairly in all commercial enterprises.[13]

It was not until 1936 that another Act was passed, demarcating further areas for purchase or lease by Africans, and establishing a trust fund to acquire additional land not already owned by the state within designated areas (see Map 5, p. 267). The maximum possible area allocated for African ownership, if it had all been acquired, would still have been only 13 per cent of the total, though in practice purchases of land fell well short of the amount needed to reach this target. This figure exaggerates the disparity in terms of economic potential, in the sense that the African reserves included areas with good rainfall in the Cape and Zululand, whereas large parts of white land were in arid zones in the western half of the country. It also excludes the three areas of African occupation that became British protectorates: Basutoland in 1884 (after first being granted British protection in 1868), Bechuanaland in 1885, and Swaziland in 1907. But even with these qualifications there was no question that the area available for Africans to own or use after 1913 was totally inadequate to sustain an independent and viable peasant economy, and – precisely as intended – left them vulnerable to the growing labour demands of white farmers and the mines.

The close connection between this process of dispossession and the labour requirements of the white economy was further highlighted by the inclusion in the 1913 Land Act of important provisions intended ultimately to prevent black sharecroppers and squatters from farming on white-owned land in any capacity other than as labour tenants.[14] As the Secretary for Native Affairs explained in a Circular Letter,

---

[13] Reproduced in T. Karis and G. M. Carter (eds.), *From protest to challenge: a documentary history of African politics in South Africa*, vol. 1, Stanford, CA: Hoover Institution Press, 1972, p. 87.

[14] See Chapter 3 for further discussion of these various forms of labour service on white-owned farms.

The effect of the Act is to put a stop, for the future, to all transactions involving anything in the nature of partnership between Europeans and natives in respect of land or the fruits of land ... *All new contracts with natives must be contracts of service.* Provided there is a bona fide contract of this nature there is nothing to prevent an employer from paying a native in kind, or by the privilege of cultivating a defined piece of ground or of grazing a certain number of stock on his land, or by any combination of these, but the native cannot pay the master anything for his right to occupy the land; his services or the services of his family ... can be the only consideration.[15]

In the Transvaal and Natal existing tenancy agreements could be continued or renewed, and no Africans were to be evicted until Parliament had increased the area of the reserves. In the Orange Free State, existing contracts for tenancies and sharecropping could run for the period specified but could not be renewed, and there was no moratorium on evictions. Many farmers in this area started immediately to evict Africans from their land, leading Sol Plaatje, an African journalist who travelled extensively in the countryside in the weeks immediately after the Act was passed, to comment that even though he 'knew that this law was as harsh as its instigators were callous', and 'that it would, if passed, render many poor people homeless', he was scarcely prepared for the misery he observed during his time with the fugitives.[16]

The clauses in the Act explicitly prohibiting Africans from paying rent for white-owned land were difficult to enforce in the short term because many of the absentee landowners were influential companies or rich individuals. As Plaatje noted, they 'pocketed the annual rents, and showed no inclination to substitute the less industrious "poor whites" for the industrious natives'.[17] Similarly, many farmers, even in the Orange Free State, were not immediately willing to give up the benefits they derived from sharecropping agreements. However, all Africans farming on white-owned land would in future be dependent on the goodwill and economic self-interest of their landowners, and their prospects were increasingly bleak.

The 1913 and 1936 Acts also facilitated the recruitment of labour by the mines and lowered their labour costs. It enabled them to argue that the subsistence needs of mine-workers' families were met from the income that could be obtained from farming in the reserves, and so did not have to be provided for by the mining companies. When mine wages were investigated in 1943, the representative of the Chamber of Mines

---

[15] *Correspondence relating to the Natives Land Act, 1913*, Cd. 7508, pp 1914, LIX, p. 28, para. 4 (emphasis added).
[16] S. Plaatje, *Native life in South Africa*, London: P. S. King & Son, 1916, p. 81.
[17] Ibid., p. 31.

argued that Africans in the reserves were granted practically free land and pasturage:

In effect he receives in this way a substantial subsidy from the Government which enables him to come out to work in the intermittent fashion which suits him and which accords with his historic background and tribal circumstances. This subsidization of the tribal native by way of free land is a basic factor in the economy of the Union and in any estimate of the economic requirements of that class of native.[18]

The allocation of land under these acts was thus from their point of view a neat solution to their labour problems: Africans were left with enough land to justify – at least in the eyes of mine-owners – the payment of extremely low wages, but not so much that they could avoid periods of work on the mines.

It can thus be said that during the second half of the nineteenth century, the combination of white military and political power finally triumphed over the initial conditions. As far as Africans were concerned, *land was no longer abundant:* no large blocks of fertile, well-watered land remained to which they could move and farm independently for themselves with security of tenure. Domar's requirement of a sufficient labour force to enable owners of land to profit from their possession had been achieved. A more detailed review of the various procedures adopted to ensure the required flow of labour to farms and mines follows in Chapter 3.

[18] Witwatersrand Mine Natives' Wages Commission (Lansdown), *Report*, para. 102.

3 Making the labour force: coercion and discrimination

Black labour for white masters

In the opening decades of the nineteenth century the southern half of Africa was still occupied by three distinct and very disparate groups of people, with only very limited contact between them. In Cape Town and its vicinity there were the commercial interests represented by merchants and traders, and those few farmers who produced for the market. Further afield, and moving steadily away to the east and north, were the majority of white settlers, largely isolated and self-sufficient on their vast farms. In the rest of the territory, African subsistence farmers worked on the land as they had always done.

A century later the urban commercial interests had been powerfully reinforced by mine-owners in Kimberley and Johannesburg, the white community had been augmented by skilled artisans recruited from Europe to work on the mines, and the Africans had lost their independence. But the really crucial change was that all three groups had effectively been integrated in one single, rapidly modernizing economy and would continue to be irrevocably bound together, each making a vital contribution to the economic development of the country. It is this history of the incorporation of the African people to provide the indispensable labour for a modern economy that forms the central theme of this chapter.

As the process of conquest and dispossession was completed over the second half of the nineteenth century, Africans progressively lost the possibility of continuing to farm independently, either in their traditional way on communal land or as individual peasants. In many regions there was a short-lived but very significant development of successful African peasant farming, stimulated by rising demand from the white economy, especially after the mineral discoveries. The new peasants adopted ploughs, experimented with other new techniques, diversified their output, responded eagerly to market incentives, and acquired additional land and stock. But white farmers feared their competition and coveted their land and labour. With government help, laws and practices were imposed to destroy the peasantry and create a rural proletariat. The final outcome of the whole process was that, for the African people of South Africa, land was no longer abundant; in areas they could still own, land was scarce and it was labour that was plentiful.

It thus became possible for South Africa to develop along the lines analysed in models of economic development appropriate for economies with two heterogeneous sectors, in one of which – typically the traditional agricultural sector – there is a surplus of labour and a scarcity of capital.[1] Many individual labourers receive a 'wage' which is greater than the value of the extra output they produce, because other members of the household or village are willing to share the total produced among all members. But the same output could be produced by fewer workers; there is 'disguised unemployment', and the other members would be better off if the surplus labour moved out of the sector. The market mechanism would bring this about if such labour could move progressively into a modern, industrial sector, where it was paid a wage that was higher than, though related to, the shared subsistence level in the traditional sector.

If this industrial wage is below the extra output produced in the modern sector by the additional labour (the marginal product of labour), the process generates additional profits in that sector, leading to capital accumulation and economic growth. Growth in turns draws more labour from the traditional sector, and the process of cumulative expansion of the industrial sector continues as long as there is surplus labour that can be drawn from the agricultural sector. Development is thus achieved by the reallocation of labour from the traditional to the modern sector. Such models are sometimes criticized on the grounds that empirical studies have not found much evidence of the rural unemployment assumed necessary to induce an initial shift to the modern sector. However, this point is not relevant in those cases where the reallocation of labour was not left to market forces; in South Africa extensive state intervention and a substantial measure of coercion and compulsion was applied to bring about the desired transfer.

As soon as Europeans controlled land in any area, they were able to exercise a much greater degree of power over the supply of labour. In the mid-nineteenth century their requirements were still fairly modest. There was some commercial farming – wheat, wine, and fruit in the Cape, wool

---

[1] The model was originally formulated by W. Arthur Lewis in a 1954 article on 'Economic development with unlimited supplies of labour'. For a brief introduction to his model and to later developments see the entry on 'labour surplus economies' in J. Eatwell et al. (eds.), *The new Palgrave: a dictionary of economics*, London: Macmillan, 1987, III, pp. 104–7.

in the Cape and Orange Free State, sugar in Natal – but the extent of cultivation on most European farms in the interior was very limited. The farmers' main need was for herders, shepherds, and domestic servants, supplemented by temporary labour for ploughing, harvesting, and other seasonal tasks in the fields, and this could usually be found without too much difficulty.

From the 1850s, as the economic development of the Cape gathered pace with the expansion of wool exports, the need for additional workers also quickened, and was then dramatically transformed, first by the development of diamond mining from the 1870s, and later – very much more substantially – by the growth of gold mining from the late 1880s. From then on, there was not only a rapid shift from subsistence to commercial farming to feed both the mines and the towns that sprang up to supply them, but also improvements in transport that promoted trade with more distant towns, as well as with overseas markets. The result was that farmers faced mounting competition for labour from the mines, railways, and urban areas, precisely at the time when their own need for workers was rising strongly in response to increased demand. This demand was strongest in the areas that cultivated maize, primarily the 'maize triangle' in the northern Free State and southern Transvaal. Maize was the most important food crop for both blacks and whites, and its cultivation was also far more labour-intensive than the pastoralism which had preceded it on Boer farms.

It was almost entirely men who were required for the mines and farms, and also for the building and transport industries; the only substantial form of paid employment available for black women was as domestic servants, either on farms or in towns. From the first half of the twentieth century, the expansion of industry and commerce created new employment opportunities, but the increase in demand for female workers was very slow, and for black females even slower. Even after the Second World War, the census data for 1951 show only 680,000 economically active black women, of whom 530,000 were employed either in domestic service or in community and social services, and about 100,000 worked on farms. The total number of black women in other non-farm employment was little more than 50,000, about 2.5 per cent of the total.[2] Within industry, the largest concentration was in the Cape, where coloured women were the mainstay of the food and garment industries.

However, these figures substantially understate the contribution made by women. In the formal economy it was the custom in farming for

---

[2] The increased demand for female labour during the second half of the twentieth century is discussed in Chapter 10.

employers to call on the labour of the wives and children of their male workers when extra hands were needed; and there were significant numbers of women who supported themselves in an informal urban economy of shebeens (illegal drinking places), gambling, dressmaking, and street trading that went largely unrecorded. Furthermore, the whole system of farm and migrant labour was underpinned by the reproductive and unpaid domestic and child-rearing contribution made by women in rural and urban households. Maintaining a household was particularly arduous in the countryside, where wives and daughters were compelled to spend long hours each day walking to fetch water and to find wood for fuel.

Before elaborating on the methods used to obtain the necessary labour for farms, mines, and other sectors, reference should be made to the ubiquitous conviction of white settlers that manual work was not something they should perform. When Baron van Imhoff, Governor-General of the Netherlands East Indies, visited the Cape in 1743 he observed:

I believe it would have been far better had we, when this colony was founded, commenced with Europeans ... But having imported slaves every common or ordinary European becomes a gentleman and prefers to be served than to serve. We have in addition the fact that the majority of farmers in this Colony are not farmers in the real sense of the word, but owners of plantations, and that many of them consider it a shame to work with their own hands.[3]

Some one hundred years later, a local magistrate reported this same attitude in Natal:

It would be very difficult to contemplate any kind of product of labour, except skilled labour, which does not involve that of the Kafir in this district. On a farm he does almost everything. He herds the cattle, milks the cows, churns the butter, loads it on the wagon, the oxen of which he inspans and leads. He cuts wood, and thatch, he digs sluits [ditches], and makes bricks, and reaps the harvest; and in the house invariably cooks. There is little that I ever see a farmer do, but ride about the country.[4]

In 1877 Anthony Trollope similarly found 'that in the Free State, as in all the other provinces and districts of the country so much of the work as is done for wages is invariably done by coloured people'.[5] With this deeply

---

[3] Van Riebeeck Society, *The reports of Chavonnes and his council and of van Imhoff on the Cape*, van Riebeeck Society, vol.1, 1918, p. 137.

[4] Natal Native Affairs Commission, 1852–4, *Proceedings*, IV, evidence of Mr Peppercorne, p. 6, quoted in S. van der Horst, *Native labour in South Africa*, London: Oxford University Press, 1942, p. 47.

[5] A. Trollope, *South Africa*, ed. J. H. Davidson, reprint of 1878 edition, Cape Town: A. A. Balkema, 1973, pp. 397–8.

entrenched outlook, whites relied on African or coloured labourers to work for them. But how was this black labour to be obtained? Military conquest could deprive Khoikhoi and Africans of ownership of their land, but that did not automatically detach them from the soil. As long as black people were able to continue farming for themselves in some form, their labour was not available to white farmers, with the consequence that various methods had to be devised to overcome this critical deficiency.

The use of compulsion to obtain labour

One set of methods soon adopted involved overt compulsion. The first and most extreme instance of this was the introduction of slavery into the Cape by the VOC. The first slaves were brought to the colony in 1658, and rapidly became an essential part of its labour supply. Most households had at least one slave, mainly for house work, and there were larger numbers on arable farms in the vicinity of Cape Town, although they were less important on cattle and sheep farms.

However, when slavery was abolished in 1834 the total slave population was only 36,000 (see Annexe 1). By contrast, in the late eighteenth century there were over 1 million slaves in the British and French islands in the Caribbean, the slave population of Brazil reached a peak of around 2 million in the first half of the nineteenth century, and on the eve of the Civil War in the United States the slave population was close to 4 million. A variety of factors, discussed in the previous chapter, had restricted the growth of farm output, so that the Cape slave economy never reached a scale remotely comparable with cotton and tobacco plantations in the southern United States or sugar plantations in the West Indies. Every act of enslavement is a denial of human rights, and Cape slavery had enduring social and cultural consequences for descendants of both slaves and slave owners, but it was not of prime significance in the formation of the labour force required for the development of the modern economy.

The same is broadly true of the labour of the Khoikhoi, many of whom were driven to take work on white farms when they lost access to the land on which their nomadic existence had depended. From 1808, when the supply of imported slaves was cut off by the abolition of the slave trade to British possessions, they became an important additional source of labour for Cape farmers. For the majority, who could not take refuge in missionary institutions such as Genadendal or Bethelsdorp, the choice was either the precarious and unlawful life of a vagrant in remote border regions, or the dependent status of a labourer working on terms dictated by white farmers that were only marginally better than slavery. One study of labour contracts in the districts of Tulbagh and Graaff Reinet during the first two decades of the nineteenth century concluded that nearly half the Khoikhoi were paid only in food and clothing.[6]

The British authorities recognized the many unsatisfactory features in the condition of the Khoikhoi, and in 1809 the Governor, Lord Caledon, attempted to regulate matters. His proclamation included some provisions that were meant, in principle, to improve their situation, but the overall effect in practice was to bind them more tightly to the farmers. This remained the position until 1828, when the British authorities at the Cape responded to pressure both from Dr Philip, the chief representative of the London Missionary Society in South Africa, and from the Society and philanthropic members of parliament in London, by passing the highly controversial Ordinance 50. This repealed all former laws affecting 'Hottentots and other free persons of colour', making them equal to Europeans in the eyes of the law. The ordinance was bitterly resented by the colonists, and precipitated some disturbance in the labour market, but did not change the fundamental position of the Khoi.

Although slavery was officially abolished in 1834, all slaves were obliged to serve another four years as 'apprentices', and so were not finally emancipated until 1838. It was the wheat and wine farmers in the south-western Cape who had relied most heavily on slaves and were forced to adjust to the end of this form of labour. During the transitional period they attempted to have other coercive policies introduced, such as a vagrancy law, but the British government wanted to see the emergence of free labour and to uphold Ordinance 50, and so did not support such measures. After a brief period of dislocation and difficulty, farmers developed a new pattern of employment consisting of a small regular labour force supplemented by a much larger number of seasonal and casual workers, and found that this gave them a workable and flexible system. Except for domestic servants, those employed were overwhelmingly male, but when farmers hired a freed male worker they assumed that this also allowed them to call on the labour of his wife and children when necessary.

Initially many freed slaves sought to leave their masters, but quickly found that there were few alternatives open to them, and they had no land, livestock, or other resources to enable them to farm independently. The Colonial Secretary explicitly rejected proposals to provide former slaves and Khoisan with small plots of land, because this would frustrate his objective of creating a force of free labourers working for wages. However, a crucial aspect of the new conditions was that most workers

---

[6] The study by Reyburn is quoted in Marais, *Cape Coloured people*, p. 129.

received only part of their remuneration in money wages. Many became labour tenants, working in return for the right to use small plots of land, or were paid in food, housing, and clothing, and in wine or brandy under the notorious *dop* system. These arrangements served to tie the labourers to their former owners and to perpetuate a cycle of dependency, debt, and drunkenness, which persisted through the twentieth century with devastating effects.

Compulsion was also clearly involved in the system of indentured child labour. This had originally been introduced at the Cape in 1775 for children of slave men and Khoikhoi women, and was extended to Khoikhoi children by a law of 1812. In the mid-nineteenth century the trekkers applied this system, in conditions amounting in many instances to virtual slavery, to Africans in the Transvaal and Orange Free State. The children (known as *inboekelinge*) were captured in wars or in special raids, often undertaken for that specific purpose. They might also be handed over by their parents in return for land, food, or other goods, as in the following extract from the journal of the *landrost* (magistrate) of Lydenburg:[7]

22 June 1864
To-day appeared Mr G. T. Becking giving notice that he wished to register 4 kaffir orphans named Joseph, Oortman, Windvogel, and Roos, estimated age 6 years, 2nd 4 years, 3rd 3 years, [4th] 2 years. G. T. Becking aforesaid declares that he obtained or bartered these from the kaffirs of Mswazi and gave for them 8 blankets.
    'This done on date as above.
    'G. T. Becking.'

Inboekelinge were given food and lodging, but no pay. Girls were normally used for domestic work, which could cover everything from cooking and childcare to making butter, soap, and tallow. Boys were usually employed in herding sheep and cattle, or as hunters; some might also learn trade skills, for example as carpenters or blacksmiths. In the Transvaal females were supposed to be released at the age of twenty-one, males at twenty-five, but they were not necessarily freed at the prescribed age in less regulated frontier districts. Even if they were, they had by that time been effectively socialized in a Boer community, isolated for many years from both their families and their culture. The result was that many remained on the white farms as supervisors, as hunters, or even as part of white militias.

---

[7] Agar-Hamilton, *Native policy*, p. 221. *Inboekeling* is sometimes translated as 'apprentice' but the normally positive connotation of apprenticeship in a European context makes it an inappropriate term in this setting.

Another form of overt compulsion was a system under which indentured labourers were brought to South Africa from abroad. This was first
introduced in 1860, after Natal sugar planters had persuaded Sir George
Grey, Governor of the Cape Colony and high commissioner of South
Africa, that they were unable to recruit sufficient Africans, and that
workers should be imported from India. The attraction for London was
that indentured labour might help to make the newly established sugar
industry, and thus the settlement in Natal, economically self-supporting.
The initial scheme operated until 1866, was suspended for eight years
following a serious depression in the Colony, and then continued until
1911. Over that period, the Indian labourers provided about 70 per cent
of the labour force in the cane fields. They were indentured for five years,
with the advantage for the employers that wage costs were fixed for this
period, and that their labour could be tightly controlled. The majority
were allocated to the plantations as field workers, but they were also
employed as domestic servants and in government departments. On
completion of their contracts the labourers could either opt for repatriat-
ion to India, or – as the great majority did – remain in South Africa as
'free' Indians.

The scheme was emulated on the Witwatersrand in 1904, when mine
owners reacted to a serious shortage of labour by persuading the authorities to agree to the importation of indentured labour from China, with
the understanding that they would not compete with white workers but
would be employed only on unskilled work. It was intended to be a
substantial operation, and within two years some 50,000 labourers were
working in the mines. However this 'Chinese slavery' aroused such hostility in Britain that it contributed to the Liberal Party victory in the
general election of 1906, and the new government prohibited the issue
of further licences to bring in indentured labourers. Those already on the
Rand were sent home as their contracts expired.

Two more direct forms of compulsory labour were the system of labour
tax or tribute, and the use of prison labour. Under the former, the
obligation to supply labour for public works and farms was imposed on
tribes defeated in battle, or on those who asked permission to settle in
territory controlled by the trekkers. It was typically used to obtain up to
fourteen days' labour for road-making, and for seasonal activities such as
ploughing and harvesting. Effectively, it was a tax in kind, and was
probably the only form in which a tax could be levied in the Boer republics
at a time when a money economy had not yet developed.

Convicts were used to build many of the early Cape roads, including
the spectacular Sir Lowry's Pass over the Hottentots Holland Mountains
in 1830, Michell's Pass, cut for some 5½ miles of solid rock through the

Breede River valley to Ceres in 1846–8, and a further series of highways, bridges, and mountain passes in the Cape and Natal during the following decades. The use of convicts for public works is found in many countries, but from the late 1880s the Cape government extended the scheme to the private sector and made convicts available to wine farmers. This arrangement continued for many years and was increased massively after the Second World War, with the construction of special farm jails, paid for by the local farmers, in many parts of South Africa.

Taxes, restrictions on movement, and other forms of pressure

None of the forms of compulsion outlined above were able to meet steadily increasing demands for labour, especially after the increasing pace of commercial activity from the 1870s, so government and employers also resorted to three formal, institutionalized mechanisms to exert pressure on black men to work for white masters. The first was the use of taxation, mainly in the form of hut or poll taxes which could be levied on all residents of a district irrespective of their income. As the Holloway Commission subsequently acknowledged,

In the past difficulty was experienced in obtaining a sufficient supply of labour for the industries of the country. The native in a tribal reserve … felt no urge to go out to labour. Not accustomed to anything more than his simple wants of tribal life he had really no incentive to work for more. The European Governments, wanting labour for their industries, decided to bring pressure to bear on the Native to force him to come out to work, and did this by imposing taxation.[8]

In some instances, a further motive for such taxes was to raise revenue, but these had the same effect as taxes explicitly adopted to increase the supply of labour. When this was clearly the objective, the tax was deliberately set at a level that would force young men to leave their rural areas in order to earn enough to pay the amounts due for themselves and other members of their family. Taxes were levied on occupants of segregated locations and reserves set aside for Africans (and in the Cape also for Khoikhoi), on those referred to as 'squatters' who were living on land over which Europeans claimed ownership, and on those occupying crown land.

The first hut tax was levied in Natal in 1849 at a rate of 7 shillings per hut, but was doubled to 14 shillings in 1875 as the need for labour increased following the mineral discoveries. In the Cape, a tax of

[8] Native Economic Commission (Holloway), *Report*, para. 532.

10 shillings per hut was normally introduced as each reserve was established. In 1869 a tax at the same rate was imposed on huts on crown land occupied by Africans or Khoikhoi, and in 1876 this was extended to those on private property. In order to discourage the owners of such property from maintaining a potential source of future labour for themselves by allowing Africans to live on their land without immediately requiring labour from them, the second act limited the application of the tax to 'any of the native races ... in the *bona fide* employment of the owner of the land'. In 1884 this restriction was further tightened by stipulating '*bona fide* and continuous employment'. A further amendment in 1892 took a slightly different form by imposing a charge of £1 on the owner of private land 'for every male adult Native resident on his land who was not required for the due working of any private property'. The effect in this case was to induce the owners to evict such Africans, thus forcing them onto farms where they could only obtain land in return for labour.

In the Transvaal, during its short period under British jurisdiction, the administrator, Sir Owen Lanyon, imposed a uniform tax of 10 shillings per hut, replacing a number of differential taxes levied previously by the republic, and this remained in force until 1895. It was then revised to put more pressure on able-bodied rural Africans to work for Europeans. The rate of 10 shillings was retained for males above twenty-one years of age who were unmarried or had only one wife, but each further wife was assessed as an additional hut. On top of that, a poll tax of £2 was levied on males aged twenty-one and over, with exemption for 'Natives who resided among white people as servants'. In the Orange Free State, the great majority of the African population were dispersed on white-owned farms, but a tax of 10 shillings per hut was levied on the occupants of Witzieshoek, the largest of three small reserves.

The second major and continuing legal intervention in the labour market was the enforcement of pass laws. These were used in two ways and – until the 1950s – were generally applied only to men, reflecting the need for male workers. They were adopted in the Cape to restrict movement into the colony from African territories to the east while they were still independent, so that only those who were coming to work were permitted to enter. In this form they were the precursor of policies formulated in the inter-war years – and, more stringently, in the apartheid era – to limit the number of African residents in urban areas. They were also deployed in all parts of the country as a means of binding labourers to a particular employer, generally reinforced by Masters and Servants Acts which made breach of contract a criminal offence. Farmers were especially keen to take advantage of these laws to prevent workers leaving their employ, whether to move to another farm offering better wages and conditions, or to abandon agriculture entirely and move to urban areas. Passes were everywhere a symbol of the personal control exercised by whites over blacks. They were often abused by whites and always bitterly resented by blacks. Naboth Mokgatle burned his pass in a protest in 1930, and recorded his feeling that if more Africans had made the gesture 'they would have demonstrated their hatred for the badge of slavery, the pass, which restricted their movements since its inception. The pass denies the African privacy, choice, dignity, movement and everything which makes a man.'[9]

The desire of whites to regulate the freedom of movement of black people by the use of passes has a long history. From 1760 onwards every slave moving between town and country had to carry a pass signed by his or her master, and in 1797 the Swellendam authorities required that 'all Hottentots moving about the country for any purpose should carry passes'. This was extended as a central feature of the system created by Lord Caledon in 1809, under which no Khoikhoi could move anywhere without an official pass. Failure to produce such a document on request made him liable to 'arrest as a vagabond and treatment accordingly'. What this meant in practice was that he would be placed under contract with any farmer known by the local officials to be short of labour. The system thus effectively enabled farmers to control their labourers' freedom of movement and prolong their contracts beyond the period of one year specified by the law, until it was swept away by Ordinance 50 in 1828.

In 1841 the government agreed to support the labour system that had evolved in response to the abolition of slavery by passing a Masters and Servants Ordinance which imposed penalties on workers who broke their contracts. It thus helped farmers to secure a stable labour force, though not to the extent they thought necessary. A new Masters and Servants Act was passed by the recently formed Cape Parliament in 1856, replacing earlier laws, and became the model for laws subsequently introduced in Natal and the Boer republics. It made it a crime for a servant to break a contract, made either orally or in writing, by such acts as desertion, disobedience, wilful breach of duty, or absence without leave. Servants were also given protection against masters who could be proved guilty of assault or who failed to pay wages or provide food as specified in the contract. This became the prototype for similar legislation in other parts

---

[9] N. Mokgatle, *The autobiography of an unknown South African*, London: Hurst & Co, 1971, p. 180.

of the country. In the Orange Free State an act of 1873 criminalized not only the breaking of contracts but also

carelessness or irresponsibility in the carrying out of duties, incapacity for work as a result of drunkenness, use for the servant's own purposes of his/her master's property, disobedience, the use of insubordinate language toward anyone in authority, and losing, damaging or enrisking the master's property as a result of dereliction.[10]

Both parties found it difficult to enforce these acts, and there were numerous amendments, but the scales of justice were heavily weighted on the side of the employer, and the principal effect of the corporal punishment, imprisonment with hard labour, and other penal sanctions provided by these acts was to put servants yet more tightly under the control of their masters.

In 1857 restrictions on movement were introduced in the Cape for 'foreign' Africans attempting to enter the colony. Effectively they could only do so if a settler had first obtained a pass for them. Once they had entered the first contract of service a new pass had to be obtained, valid for the period of contract, which was to be not less than one year or more than five. This system undoubtedly impeded the movement of labour into the Colony, and was greatly disliked both by employers and workers. However, it gradually became less significant as the borders were extended during the last quarter of the nineteenth century through the progressive annexation of Griqualand East, Pondoland, and other Transkeian territories. A vagrancy law of 1879, which made it an offence for any person to be without 'legal and sufficient means', should also be noted, and may have served as an additional pressure on Africans within the Colony to find work. Pass laws were also introduced in Natal and the Boer republics, but did not yet have much impact in this period.

From the late nineteenth century, the need for greater control over the freedom of movement of African males was sharply increased by the new demand for labour for the gold mines, and the adverse effects that this had on the numbers of workers available to white farmers. Further legislation in the period before the election of the National Party in 1948, notably the Natives (Urban Areas) Act of 1923 and later amendments, was essentially concerned to use the pass system to limit the number of Africans in urban areas. In doing so, the pass laws simultaneously helped the commercial farms to meet their growing labour requirements. Throughout this period the farming sector continued to rely heavily on these restrictions on free

---

[10] T. J. Keegan, *Rural transformations in industrializing South Africa: the southern highveld to 1914*, Braamfontein: Ravan Press, 1986, pp. 131–2.

movement, and frequently demanded that they be strengthened and extended, rather than trying to meet competition from the mines and factories by raising wages.

The third mechanism to increase the supply of labour was the progressive whittling away of opportunities to farm on land designated as part of the area reserved for white ownership and occupation. As white farmers' access to capital and government aid increased, and they were able to improve their own economic position by extending the share of their land that they farmed themselves, there was a steady erosion of the land available to Africans on white farms in these areas. This trend was especially strong in the inter-war period.

These three specific and calculated methods were supplemented by two more general sources of pressure on African men to work for whites. The most powerful was the increasing poverty of the land that remained for Africans as a growing population struggled to maintain itself in a shrinking area. The nineteenth-century process of continuous reduction in the amount of land available to an independent African population was described in Chapter 2. It was followed in the twentieth century by a serious deterioration in the condition of land in these areas, a ruinous and unremitting phenomenon examined more fully below. When the Africans in these areas could no longer grow sufficient food to keep themselves and their families alive, their only option was to leave and seek work on commercial farms or mines.

Trade was also an effective form of pressure, often in association with generous offers of credit, and was promoted for many reasons. When bi-annual fairs (which later developed into regular weekly markets) were instituted at Fort Willshire on the Keiskamma River in 1821, the acting governor aimed 'to transform the Kaffers from a thieving nation into a commercial one', and believed that trade would have educative and civilizing effects. The missionaries were pursuing their evangelizing aims when they introduced Africans to a variety of goods, and placed particular emphasis on the wearing of European clothing. Farmers wanted a larger market for their produce; traders wanted to expand their activity. The authorities encouraged Africans in the Cape to develop new wants by including goods such as coffee, sugar, and tobacco as part of the payment made to those employed on public works projects. Whatever the motive, Africans were induced and assisted to acquire a taste for European goods – everything from food, liquor, and clothing to blankets, guns, and ploughs. They were steadily drawn into a cash nexus, their self-contained subsistence economy was broken down, and their traditional crafts of iron smelting and pottery making were destroyed. When they wanted cash to satisfy these newly inculcated needs they had little alternative but to enter the market to sell their labour.

African labour on white-owned farms

When Africans had been driven into service for the whites by one or more of these methods, there were several different ways in which their labour was used on white farms. Four main forms can be identified, and they will be discussed in order of increasing proletarianization, but there was no simple or orderly progression towards capitalist farming, as is sometimes suggested. It was a complex and varied system, with different forms of labour utilization applied according to the different conditions and circumstances in individual regions. The total number of black workers employed on commercial farms from 1918 to 1954 is shown in Table 3.1.

Rent tenancy (also known as 'kaffir farming') was a system under which whites with too much land – essentially speculators and absentee landowners – allowed Africans to work their land in return for a payment of rent. It was very common in the late nineteenth and early twentieth centuries, but was extremely unpopular with working farmers, both because it deprived them of labour and because they perceived it to be unduly favourable to Africans. Without resident landowners Africans allegedly were not kept under proper European control and could do as

Table 3.1. *Black labour employed regularly on commercial farms, 1918–54[a]*

	(1) African	(2) Coloured and Asian	(3) Total
	(000s)		
1918	359	74	433
1925	435	93	528
1930	476	88	564
1937	658	106	764
1947	–	–	831
1952	801	117	918
1954	840	124	964

[a] Includes domestic servants on farms, excludes casual and seasonal labour; in 1954 there were 130,000 African domestic servants and 23,000 Coloured and Asian.

Source: Bureau of Census and Statistics, *Union statistics for fifty years* (hereafter *Union statistics*), G-3.

they liked. The 1913 Natives Land Act attempted to eliminate this system, but could not easily or quickly overcome the interest of large landowners in deriving incomes from their property in this way.

The second arrangement was sharecropping or 'farming-on-the-half', under which Africans obtained the use of land for cultivation or grazing stock, and also somewhere to live. In return for this they provided their own ploughs, oxen, and seed, and had to give half (or more) of their crop to the white landowner. It meant that African farmers had to produce at least twice their own subsistence, but it was popular with the more enterprising Africans, and gave them a much better reward for their labour than other systems. Because the sharecroppers had a direct interest in the size of the crop they were likely to produce a larger output than other workers, and so the arrangement was attractive to absentee landowners. It was also advantageous to white farmers as long as they were short of capital and so could not afford to purchase additional cattle for ploughing. However, once the shortage of capital was overcome, they usually wanted to farm the land themselves, believing that they could obtain higher outputs at lower cost, and Africans found it increasingly difficult to obtain land as sharecroppers.

Sharecropping was greatly weakened, though not completely destroyed, by the 1913 Natives Land Act. In response to requests from farmers, the Act included further clauses under which many relatively prosperous African farmers were forced to leave the land, to dispose of their stock at notional prices in a buyers' market, and to become labour tenants. This occurred particularly in the Orange Free State and Transvaal; it was one of many instances of a cruel process in which white South Africans deliberately destroyed successful African enterprise, then condemned and scorned black people for their poverty and incompetence, and used their impoverished condition as justification for their continued subjugation.

The third system, labour tenancy, was essentially a relationship under which Africans provided a specified amount of labour, and the farmer allowed the labourer and his family land on which to reside, plus grazing rights and a small plot to cultivate. It was most common in the Transvaal and Orange Free State, and least used in the Cape, where relatively few Africans lived on European farms. The terms of the relationship varied enormously both by region and over time. In its most primitive form, it was very close to the feudal *corvée* in France or *barshchina* in Russia. Labour was provided by the whole family throughout the year for the equivalent of two days a week; no wage was paid for that labour, and tenants supplied the ploughs and oxen needed for cultivation. In its most advanced form, labour was required for a fixed period, usually 90 days but raised to 180 in some areas, they were paid wages in cash and kind for their period of service, and the landowner provided the capital equipment – increasingly tractors rather than oxen. For the remainder of the year, labourers were free to go elsewhere if they wished, for example to take work in the towns or as transport riders, subject always to getting their employer to sign a pass.

As attempts to suppress the two previous systems, rent tenancy and sharecropping, were pursued more vigorously, labour tenancy became the most common form of exploitation of African labour. For farmers who were land rich but income poor, it was the ideal way to secure the necessary supply of labour. It became the dominant system from about 1913 until the end of the Second World War, and survived even longer in some areas. It was associated with a variety of 'squatters' laws' designed to limit the number of families on any one farm or part of a farm (typically not more than five), and thus ensure that labour was shared among all white farmers.

The final arrangement, wage labour, was becoming increasingly common throughout the inter-war period, and by the early 1930s it was estimated that some 70 per cent of tenant income in Natal and the Orange Free State was received in the form of wages in cash and kind. It replaced labour tenancy once land was no longer a free resource that could be used by farmers as a cheap form of remuneration, and became the predominant system after the Second World War. Land taken over from African tenants could be farmed more intensively and efficiently. In addition, as farming developed and modernized, it was preferable to employ permanent workers who could acquire skills, especially those essential for mechanization, and who were more efficient than intermittent, poorly motivated tenants. Wages were paid in cash and kind. The cash wage was not only very low, but also showed little or no improvement in monetary terms from the 1870s to the 1940s, and almost certainly declined in real terms, while the real value of the accommodation and rations provided probably changed little.

Migrant labour for the mines

The early development of the diamond fields and the swift transformation from cheap open quarrying to capital-intensive underground mining is described in Chapter 5. From the late 1870s a small group of skilled technicians and mechanics – roughly two out of three of whom were recruited from Europe – operated and maintained the capital equipment, and supervised the manual labour of approximately 10,000 Africans. Africans quickly appreciated that a short period of work at the diggings would earn enough to buy guns or cattle, and the mines never experienced any difficulty in recruiting labour. The normal arrangement was for very short-term contracts, typically of three months, though workers might immediately re-engage for a total of nine months or longer. By the end of the 1880s the system of closed compounds had become standard. It was introduced primarily to make it more difficult for Africans to steal diamonds for sale to illicit dealers, but it also gave the mines greater control over their workforce, and eliminated drunkenness and absenteeism.

From the 1890s demand for labour accelerated with the expansion of gold mining. Agriculture was still the dominant employer, but from now on it faced serious competition for labour from the mines. By 1911 some 260,000 Africans were employed on gold and other mines compared to 360,000 on commercial, white-owned farms; by 1960 the numbers had increased in roughly the same proportions to 520,000 on the mines and 770,000 on commercial farms.[11] The labour force in the gold fields incorporated three key features first developed on the diamond diggings: a rigid demarcation in which occupations designated as skilled were reserved exclusively for highly-paid white workers while manual work was performed solely by low-paid black workers; an African workforce that was recruited as short-term migrants; and the housing of Africans in closed compounds.

The gold mines quickly understood that the fundamental requirement for profitable operation was the recruitment of large numbers of Africans at low wages. In 1897 George Albu, chairman of the Association of Mines, explained to a Commission of Enquiry how he proposed to cheapen labour 'by simply telling the boys that their wages are reduced'. What he had in mind was a reduction of a third, from 2s 3d per shift to 1s 6d for skilled labour. In the following exchange his views were expressed with revealing clarity:

Commission: Suppose the kaffirs retire back to their kraals? Would you be in favour of asking the Government to enforce labour?

Albu: Certainly ... I would make it compulsory ... Why should a nigger be allowed to do nothing? ... I think a kaffir should be compelled to work in order to earn his living.

Commission: If a man can live without work, how can you force him to work?

Albu: Tax him, then...

Commission: Then you would not allow the kaffir to hold land in the country, but he must work for the white man, to enrich him?

Albu: He must do his part of the work of helping his neighbours.[12]

[11] The figures for commercial agriculture are based on the agricultural censuses; they exclude casual labour but include domestic servants on farms. Those for mining are from Bureau of Census and Statistics, *Union statistics*, G-4 to G-5.

[12] Witwatersrand Chamber of Mines, Industrial Commission of Enquiry, 1897, *Evidence*, p. 22.

So it was that mechanisms such as taxation, pass laws, Masters and Servants Acts, the extension of credit by traders, and rural poverty, discussed above in relation to farm labour, also played an absolutely essential role in securing men for the mines. In 1895 the Chamber of Mines drafted a law designed to give it greater control over the labour that had been recruited. They persuaded the Transvaal Volksraad (people's assembly) to pass the law, which required an African in a proclaimed labour district to obtain a pass that would be held by his employer until he was discharged. Anyone found without a pass was liable to be arrested. This law was difficult to administer, and was soon replaced by a system under which the pass laws made breach of contract by Africans a criminal offence, with inspectors appointed to detect and punish deserters.

Immediately following the attainment of political union in 1910, the Native Labour Regulation Act of 1911 perpetuated the system that had operated in the Transvaal, making the breach of contract provisions of the Masters and Servants Acts specifically applicable to any African labourers employed on the mines. As a result of these penal sanctions for breach of contract, any strike action by African mineworkers was made illegal. A similar breach of contract by a white worker was not a crime; it was only subject to civil penalties. The act also made all Africans working on the mines subject to the pass laws. This was both a further means of preventing desertion and a system of identification that restricted their ability to move freely about the country.

By preventing Africans from entering urban areas, so leaving mining and farming as the only alternative employment, subsequent pass laws and influx controls favoured these sectors at the expense of manufacturing. While this was the general context for the creation of a mine labour force, its recruitment was distinguished by a number of more specific, interrelated features, all established early in the history of the industry and maintained broadly unchanged until the beginning of the 1970s. Unlike the multiplicity of arrangements in agriculture, there was essentially only one system for mines.

All African miners were recruited on a temporary basis as migrant labour. The usual contract was for twelve to eighteen months, and for the period of the contract they were prohibited from seeking or taking up any other job. While on the mines they were housed and fed in large single-sex compounds, and at the end of their contracted period they were required to go back to the area from which they had come. The combination of fixed-term contracts, penal sanctions, and controlled compounds gave the companies great power over their workers, and minimized the possibility of trade union or political organization.

Table 3.2. *Source of African labour recruited by mines, 1896–1966[a]*

	(1) South Africa	(2) British protectorates[b]	(3) Mozam-bique	(4) Other (mainly Malawi)	(5) Total employed
	(per cent)				(000s)
1896–8	35.5[c]	3.9	60.2	0.5	54
1906	22.8	3.7	65.4	8.0	81
1911	40.4	6.4	51.6	1.7	174
1921	38.7	14.0	47.1	0.3	188
1926	41.3	14.0	44.5	0.2	203
1931	49.8	17.4	32.7	0.1	226
1936	52.2	19.0	27.8	1.1	318
1946	41.3	16.6	31.5	10.6	305
1951	35.3	16.5	34.8	13.5	306
1956	34.7	16.6	30.8	17.9	334
1961	36.5	17.8	24.2	21.5	414
1966	34.1	22.9	28.4	14.7	383

[a] Africans employed in the Transvaal gold- and coal-mining industries.
[b] Lesotho, Botswana, and Swaziland.
[c] Lesotho and Swaziland are included with South Africa.

Source: Van der Horst, *Native labour*, pp. 216–17, F. Wilson, *Labour in the South African gold mines, 1911–1969*, Cambridge: Cambridge University Press, 1972, p. 70, D. Innes, *Anglo American and the rise of modern South Africa*, Johannesburg: Ravan Press, 1984, pp. 248–9.

The oscillating migrant workers were recruited from the reserves within South Africa, as well as from the three British protectorates, Mozambique, and Malawi, and typically returned to the mines several times for further periods of service. As shown in Table 3.2, the proportion drawn from the different regions varied considerably over time, with the share recruited within South Africa almost always well under half the total. In the early years of the industry, Mozambique was by far the largest source and provided 60 per cent or more of the labour employed in South Africa's mines, but from about 1907 there was a long-run downward trend in recruitment from the east coast, though it remained important. The proportion recruited in South Africa fluctuated between 40 and 50 per cent from before the First World War until the end of the Second World War, and then declined to about 35 per cent. In the two decades after 1945 the territories to the north of South Africa, especially Malawi, became the source for a substantial proportion of the mine labour force.

The enormous labour turnover and constant reinduction of the work-force required by reliance on oscillating migration imposed heavy costs on the mining companies. However, from their perspective, these losses were handsomely compensated for by the benefits of not having to pay sufficient in wages to house and feed African mine-workers' families, and by the control they exercised in the compounds. In addition, there were economies of scale in mass housing and feeding, and the scale on which they recruited gave them access to labour outside the borders of South Africa. Use of migrant labour also enabled them to evade responsibility for the incidence of silicosis (also referred to as miner's phthisis) among African mine-workers. This was an incurable, often fatal, occupational disease caused by prolonged exposure to fine particles of dust, which also made miners' lungs more vulnerable to tuberculosis. Mine medical officers claimed that migrant workers were less at risk because of their short spells of work, and that they could 'shake off' these diseases once they had returned home to the 'open-air life' of the rural areas. Naturally, this calculation of the private costs and benefits for the companies took no account of the wider costs to the economy and society of the enormous damage done by migrant labour to the economy of the reserves and to family life: the long separation of husband and wife, the absent father, the increased death rates.

In the very early years of the industry, the different mines competed for labour, but it did not take them long to recognize that this tended to drive up wages and that it would be in their common interest to eliminate such competition. From the 1890s attempts were made to centralize recruiting for the mines with the formation of the Rand Native Labour Association in 1896. After some initial disagreements among the mining houses, and opposition from independent recruiting agents, the mines established a system under which recruitment of all African labour was undertaken on their behalf by special organizations. In its final form the system involved one such body (the Native Recruiting Corporation) operating inside South Africa and the British protectorates, and another (the Witwatersrand Native Labour Association) responsible for recruiting in foreign countries. Thus in any one area there was only a single powerful agency to which potential workers could sell their labour and, once operative, this effective monopsony had a very strong impact. Between 1889 and 1911 the companies were able to recruit large numbers of mine labourers at the same time as they were cutting the annual average cash wage by over a quarter.

Individual mining companies not only allowed the recruiting body to prevent them from competing for labour by specifying rates for different classes of time-work, they also colluded in accepting the imposition of a

Table 3.3. *Nominal and real earnings per shift worked of African workers on the gold mines, 1911–61*

	(1) Earnings (including food)	(2) Retail price index	(3) Index of real earnings
	(cents)	(1911=100)	
1911	24	100	100
1916	24	116	86
1921	28	168	69
1926	26	136	80
1931	25	128	82
1936	26	120	90
1941	28	138	85
1946	37	171	90
1951	45	218	86
1956	56	263	89
1961	62	293	88

Source: (1) Wilson, *Labour,* p. 66; (2) *Union statistics,* H-23; (3) = (1) ÷ (2) converted to index with 1911=100.

'maximum permissible average' on daily earnings from piecework. As a result of these practices, mining houses were able to hold down African wages very effectively. The wages paid in cash and kind were not only very low, both absolutely and as a fraction of those paid to white workers, but actually declined over time. As Table 3.3 shows, wages for African miners were 14 per cent lower in real terms in 1961 than they had been fifty years earlier.

The fixed price of gold (a subject that will be discussed in Chapter 5) was a powerful constraint on the mine companies, but it could not justify the ruthless manner in which they relied on a combination of military conquest, discriminatory legislation, and collusion to destroy the bargaining position of African mine-workers, and allow them no share in the growing prosperity of the mines and the country over the long period from the 1880s to the 1960s.

The paradox of scarce labour and low wages

A striking feature of the situation just outlined is the paradox of persistent complaints from both farms and mines of their difficulty in obtaining labour, coexisting for roughly a hundred years with their equally persistent refusal to pay higher wages. Why was this? An explanation frequently offered by employers for this phenomenon, for example when interrogated by commissions and enquiries, was that the labour supply would not respond to higher wages. In other words, unlike any normal market, in which a higher price evokes a larger supply, the supply curve for African labour was actually 'backward sloping' so that a higher wage would call forth a smaller amount of labour. This doctrine was enunciated endlessly by farmers, mine-owners, politicians, and even economists. For example, according to Sir Arnold Plant, Professor of Commerce at the University of London, writing in 1936:

The paradoxical situation in which a scarcity of African labour is accompanied by average wages of about one-quarter (including rations) of those paid to Europeans is explained in part by the peculiarities of the labour supply. So long as the African peoples remain out of contact with European modes of life, the wage incentive exerts only a limited influence upon their willingness to work for European employers. In so far as Africans work for only a more or less a fixed sum, whether to pay taxes or to purchase commodities, higher rates of wages may for a period actually reduce the amount of work which they are willing to do.[13]

An obvious weakness in this explanation is the treatment of all Africans as though they were a single homogeneous group, which manifestly they were not. It was probably true that an African leaving an isolated rural area for the first time, with no previous contact with urban conditions and goods, would have in mind a target income to meet a specified need for cash, and would work only as long as required to meet that target. However, the proportion of Africans in this position must have diminished rapidly during the course of the nineteenth century. By the time Plant was writing it is unlikely that any significant number of Africans entering employment were not already well acquainted with European goods and the benefits of a larger money income, and so ready to supply more labour when given an incentive to do so. On a more analytical level, there was also frequent confusion between individual responses and the aggregate supply of labour. Even if it were true that one man might work for a shorter period when offered higher wages, it is likely that more men would be attracted into the labour market at the better rate, so that the total number of man-hours available to employers would have increased.

There is copious evidence, at many dates and many places, that Africans were sensitive to different levels of wages. As early as the 1850s it was reported that a public works project in the eastern Cape had found no difficulty in recruiting 'any number of Kaffir workmen' when it offered

---

[13] Walker (ed.), *Cambridge history*, p. 836.

better pay for higher grades of work. Workers in the top grades 'have never left, and others remain on the works in the hope of making themselves eligible for promotion'. In Natal a commission set up to investigate the problem was told that 'any amount of native labour may be procured at five shillings a month, by rational treatment of the natives'.[14] In the early years of the mining industry, individual employers were fully aware that workers were attracted to those mines which paid higher wages, and the introduction of monopsonistic recruiting was a direct response to this. Conversely, when they attempted to reduce wages in 1890 they immediately experienced difficulty in obtaining sufficient workers. Farmers complained that their supply diminished when the mines offered higher wages; the mines complained when they in turn found their labour drawn away by higher wages paid by manufacturing or the railways.

Exponents of the backward sloping supply curve could claim that such examples only serve to establish that Africans prefer higher to lower wages, or that they would work harder or better in response to higher wages, not that they would work longer. But since the mines continued to deploy the argument even when they were in a strong position to control the minimum period for which workers were recruited, it seems likely that there were other factors behind their refusal to pay higher wages, and that the idea of a backward sloping labour supply curve was simply a convenient rationalization. One such factor was the legacy of the pre-mineral era, in which defeated Africans lived on land taken from them by whites, and worked for farmers who either conscripted their labour, or paid them only the barest minimum as labour tenants. As Trollope commented on those he met in the Orange Free State on an extensive tour of South Africa in 1878:

The Dutch Boer does not love to pay wages ... He prefers to keep what he has and to do what can be done by family labour. He will, however, generally have a couple of black men about his place, whose services he secures at the lowest possible rate. Every shilling so paid is grudged. He has in his heart an idea that a nigger ought to be made to work without wages.[15]

This view persisted among farmers and was shared by the mine-owners. However, it is likely that a more important explanation was simply that higher wages meant lower profits. As a result, both farmers and mine-owners naturally preferred to rely on other methods of obtaining labour, such as land restrictions, taxation, and pass laws, as long as the political instruments necessary to achieve these were available to them.

---

[14] For the views reported in this paragraph see van der Horst, *Native labour*, pp. 19 and 46.
[15] Trollope, *South Africa*, p. 398.

The recruitment and employment policies of agriculture and mining that have been summarized above interacted with – and were reinforced by – conditions in the reserves, and this very important influence on the labour supply must now be examined.

The deterioration of the reserves

The areas left for exclusive African occupation were originally called locations, but were later referred to as reserves, and still later, under apartheid, as 'homelands'. The three largest were the Transkei and Ciskei in the eastern Cape and Zululand in Natal, and these were reasonably compact areas. Elsewhere reserves were mainly small, dispersed pockets of land. Even the largest, potentially fertile areas were under extreme pressure, with the population increasing and the condition of the land deteriorating. This problem was already acute in some areas by the late nineteenth century, and was evident almost everywhere by the 1920s. For the reserves as a whole, farm output per head at constant prices was appreciably lower in the 1930s than in the previous decade, although it was not until the post-war period that there was a really sharp decline.[16]

In the inter-war period, the reserves were already unable to maintain even a very low level of self-sufficiency. Data on population and income per head in 1936, derived from a very thorough study of the available evidence, are set out in Table 3.4. In the upper panel, the population is divided into three groups, showing that while overall income per head in South Africa averaged £36, the figure for 2,000,000 whites was £130 and for 6,600,000 Africans it was only £10. In the lower panel that average for Africans is then sub-divided into three components, comprising 1,400,000 in towns and mines with an average income of £31, 2,200,00 on white farms with an average of £7, and 3,000,000 in reserves with an average of only £3 per year, including in this miserable sum the value of food produced and consumed.

A survey of conditions in the Ciskei at the end of the 1940s concluded grimly that without the earnings of the emigrants, the population of the district would starve. In fact, even with migrant remittances, the toll of death and disease was exceedingly high. South African statistics do not include data on mortality among Africans, and the following information relates to the 1960s. However, it is particularly germane, since it refers to

---

[16] This statement is based on estimates by C. Simkins, 'Agricultural production in the African reserves of South Africa, 1918–1969', *Journal of Southern African Studies*, 7, 1981, p. 263.

Table 3.4. *Population and income per head in South Africa, 1936*

	(1) Population (millions)	(2) Income per head (£)
Whites	2.0	130
Asians and Coloureds	1.0	21
Africans	6.6	10
Total population	9.6	36
Africans		
Towns and mines	1.4	31
Farms	2.2	7
Reserves	3.0	3
Total Africans	6.6	10

Source: Department of Economics, University of Natal, 'National income', in E. Hellmann (ed.) *Handbook on race relations in South Africa*, London: Oxford University Press, 1949, Tables I, VII, and XII.

conditions in the Sekhukhuniland reserve, effectively the area that remained to the Pedi after the defeat and dispossession that was reviewed in the previous chapter, and is an astounding indicator of the malnutrition prevailing in that area. It is a quotation from a paper by two doctors, based on an investigation conducted at the Jane Furse Memorial Hospital: 'Figures do not exist for infant and child mortality rates, but from retrospective questioning of mothers of children admitted to the hospital it would seem that at least 50 per cent of all children born alive fail to reach their fifth birthday, and the majority of those who die do not reach their third birthday.'[17]

An initially appalling situation in this and other reserves from the late nineteenth century onwards was made cumulatively worse by the total lack of financial support from the government. This was in stark contrast to their generosity to white farmers in numerous and varied forms including subsidies, grants, loans, and railway rebates, together with large outlays on irrigation, fencing, and other improvements. Expenditure from 1910 to 1936 on European farms and farming was £112m; on African farms and farming it was £660,000.[18]

[17] P. M. Leary and J. E. S. Lewis, 'Some observations on the state of nutrition of infants and toddlers in Sekhukhuniland', *South African Medical Journal*, 39, 1965, p. 1157.
[18] S. H. Frankel, *Capital investment in Africa, its course and effects*, London: Oxford University Press, 1938, p. 120 and fn. p. 127.

These last three indicators – average income, infant mortality, and government expenditure on agriculture – graphically reveal the true meaning and unbridled extent of the discrimination prevalent in South Africa. The tragedy of the reserves created by this discrimination was an integral part of the measures adopted to ensure the necessary supply of labour for the modern sector of the South African economy. Its fundamental cause was undoubtedly the grossly inadequate share of land left for Africans by the process of dispossession already described. Taken together with the policies pursued by the government to ensure the required supply of labour for the mines and white commercial agriculture, the endemic poverty and lack of capital of African farmers, and the competition they faced in the market from white farmers, there is more than sufficient to explain the desperate conditions and continuous deterioration of the reserves. But to complete the picture, certain features of African farming methods that aggravated the process of deterioration should also be mentioned.

The traditional custom of migration to new land was no longer possible, but Africans were unable to adapt to the new circumstances that had been imposed on them. The depth of their attachment to cattle was one of the major obstacles. Where white agronomists saw too many cattle, African farmers saw too little land. Tragically both were correct and neither could persuade the other. When a commission examined conditions in the Ciskei in 1932 they described the disappearance of good grazing and the worsening conditions in vivid terms:

The worst effects of overstocking may be seen in some parts of the Ciskeian area ... In Middledrift there are large areas where the surface soil has been entirely eroded and no grass whatever grows. In adjoining parts the grass is being speedily supplanted by *helichrysum* and similar weeds ...

Unless precautionary measures are taken against overstocking the condition in the Transkei and the Native Areas in the rest of the Union will be tomorrow what the Ciskei is today. The same causes are at work there, and they will inevitably produce the same effect in the near future – denudation, donga-erosion, deleterious plant succession, destruction of woods, drying up of springs, robbing the soil of its reproductive properties, *in short the creation of desert conditions*.[19]

On the arable side, monoculture exhausted soil that could no longer be left to recuperate properly. Lack of capital and absence of many men did not help, but those who remained on the land failed to introduce even such minimal improvements as crop rotation and fertilization. Yet another

---

[19] Native Economic Commission (Holloway), *Report*, paras. 72 and 73 (emphasis in original).

legacy of the African past was communal tenure and the duty to share access to land and output. While admirable in some respects, it was a potential barrier in the reserves to those few who might have wished to be more innovative and entrepreneurial.

In other economies a collapse of agriculture like that described above would almost certainly have been followed by a steep rise in food prices as the shrinking farm sector struggled to feed a growing urban population. The difficulties faced by the Bolsheviks in interwar Russia are a classic example of this phenomenon. However, this problem did not emerge in South Africa because of the successful expansion of commercial agriculture by white farmers (see further Chapters 6 and 8). Their experience was totally different from that suffered by African subsistence farmers in the reserves, and the commercial sector was generally able to meet the country's food requirements.

4 Creating the colour bar: formal barriers, poor whites, and 'civilized' labour

Motivation and methods for creating a colour bar

In the previous chapter the supply of black labour was considered solely in terms of the numbers available, and the manner in which it was induced to serve on white-owned farms and mines. There was, however, another extremely important dimension to the making of the labour force: the creation of a 'colour bar' that rigorously excluded all Africans from any skilled or semi-skilled work. Similar but not quite so stringent restrictions were applied to coloured and Asian workers. This colour bar is one of the most distinctive aspects of South Africa's economic history. Other countries have similar histories of conquest and dispossession, even if not on the same scale, but no other country has used its political and legal system to create and maintain such a comprehensive and formal colour bar.

Discrimination by race in South Africa is as old and pervasive as European settlement, and can be seen at numerous points from the treatment of slaves and the extermination of the San in the seventeenth and eighteenth centuries to the *Grondwet* (constitution) adopted in the 1850s by the Transvaal republics stipulating that 'the people desire to permit no equality between coloured people and the white inhabitants, either in church or state'. However, it was not until the expansion of economic activity and non-farm employment, stimulated by the mineral revolution in the last quarter of the nineteenth century, that it was considered necessary to make explicit provision for discrimination in the work that could be undertaken by whites and blacks. It did not take long for a clear dividing line to be drawn in the diamond fields, with skilled jobs reserved for Europeans and manual work undertaken only by black workers, but this demarcation was at least partly justified by the fact that it was initially only Europeans who possessed the necessary skills. Legal provisions were not yet required.

The first enactment of a formal colour bar in mining occurred in the Transvaal, where the Volksraad adopted a regulation in 1893, ostensibly for reasons of safety, stipulating that blasting underground could be performed only by a qualified white person. A further act of 1898 stated explicitly that no coloured person was permitted to hold an engine-driver's certificate of competency. This discrimination was gradually extended to other classes of skilled and semi-skilled work, especially in the first decade of the new century. When agreement was given to the importation of indentured labourers from China in 1904, the Chamber of Mines accepted that the Chinese would be employed only on unskilled work, and would thus take the place of black, but not of white, miners. A schedule to the ordinance passed by the Transvaal Legislative Council listed over fifty separate skilled trades and occupations from which the Chinese were specifically excluded.

Even though the importation of Chinese labourers was rapidly sus-pended, the schedule became a de facto basis for the range of occupations claimed exclusively for Europeans. The full list, set out in Table 4.1, contains a few occupations specific to mining, such as machine rockdriller, drill-sharpener, and cyanide shiftsman, but the great majority are standard industrial trades required for the maintenance and repair of buildings and equipment above ground: blacksmiths and bricklayers, mechanics and millwrights, painters and plumbers. Underground, the actual work was done by black miners; the white miner was effectively only a supervisor, and the real need for him to perform that function was questionable.

The fundamental reason for these restrictions was not the inability of Africans to undertake such work, but the desire of white miners to protect their jobs and their very large income differentials. These differentials were introduced originally in the diamond fields in the 1870s, and then reproduced in the gold mines in the 1890s, because a genuine scarcity of skilled artisans made it necessary for mining companies to offer high wages to attract workers from Europe. White workers naturally sought to retain this premium, even when the initial scarcity was no longer operative and increasing numbers of the recipients were born in South Africa. Economic motives preserving skilled work for whites were power-fully reinforced by social prejudice in favour of this particular manifesta-tion of innate white supremacy, and by its long-standing obverse, that whites should not have to perform unskilled work.

The issue was addressed by the new South African Parliament in the first year after the formation of the Union. The Mines and Works Act of 1911 was designed to regulate the working and inspection of mines, works, and machinery, and gave the Minister of Mines power to frame regulations, particularly for the safety of mining operations. The govern-ment took advantage of these powers to incorporate provisions continu-ing the colour bar restrictions previously practised only in the Transvaal, and to extend these for the first time to the three other provinces. It was

Table 4.1. *1904 schedule of skilled trades and occupations reserved for European workers*

amalgamator	engineer	painter
assayer	engine-driver	patternmaker
banksman	fireman-overseer	pipeman
blacksmith	fitter	plasterer
boiler-maker	ganger	plate-layer
brass-finisher	ironmoulder	plumber
brassmoulder	joiner	pumpman
bricklayer	machine rockdriller	quarryman-overseer
brickmaker	machine sawyer	rigger
carpenter	machinist	sampler
clerk	mason	signaller
coppersmith	mechanic	skipman
cyanide shiftsman	miller	stonecutter
drill sharpener	millwright	timberman
driver of air	mine carpenter	timekeeper
or steam winch	mine overseer	tinsmith
driver of mechanical	mine storeman	turner
or electrical machinery	onsetter	wiresplicer
electrician	overseer[a]	woodworking machinist

[a] In any capacity other than the management and control of labourers.

Source: Van der Horst, *Native labour,* p. 171.

doubtful in law whether the Mines and Works Act authorized the issue of such a discriminatory regulation, but it was not challenged initially because it was well understood that the practice was sanctioned by custom as well as by the influence of white trade unions.

It was possible for the Union government to introduce such discriminatory legislation because, in the discussions preceding the formation of the Union in 1910, the British authorities had accepted the view of the Boer republics they had just defeated on the battlefield that only whites should have the vote. In the search for unity, the historical concern for equality before the law that had shaped earlier British policy in the Cape and Natal in the nineteenth century was discarded. Some residual elements of the franchise remained in the Cape for Africans and coloureds, but they were too limited by educational and property qualifications to be of much consequence. The consequences of this momentous decision were spelled out by Selope Thema:

While we do not wish to encroach upon the society of the whites, nevertheless we claim our rights of citizenship first as the aboriginals of this country, and second as British subjects ... Under democratic institutions it is only the interests of those who have the power of the ballot that are considered and safeguarded. And in my opinion no justice can be done to the African until he has been equipped with this power. Today he is being rendered LANDLESS and HOMELESS, taxed heavily and cruelly exploited, because he has no voice in the making of the laws. Daily he is coming more and more to look upon the laws of the country not as protecting safeguards, but as sources of humiliation and oppression.[1]

Efforts to promote and extend the colour bar created by the 1911 Mines and Works Act continued after the First World War. In 1918 a further nineteen defined occupations on the mines were added by agreement to the original list of thirty-two job categories formally reserved for whites under the 1911 Act. In other industries a similar policy was implemented by measures that effectively prevented Africans from acquiring the formal qualifications necessary for performance of skilled work. For example, minimum educational qualifications were specified which in practice most Africans would be unable to attain, or it was made a requirement to attend industrial classes which were not available to them. The 1922 Apprenticeship Act, which set Standard VI (the top grade in primary schools) as the minimum requirement for apprenticeship, provided a good illustration of this procedure, since very few African children had the opportunity to reach this level. In 1938 only 2 per cent of African children at state and state-aided schools were receiving post-primary education.

The conflict with white mine-workers

The desire of white mine-workers to maintain the colour bar, and protect their skill differentials, inevitably brought them into direct conflict with the mining companies. The companies were in a difficult position because of certain intrinsic features of the mining industry. Under the gold standard, the mines received a fixed price for their product and could do nothing to change this. This made it imperative for them to maintain strict control over their expenses if operations were to be profitable, and wages accounted for a very high proportion of their total costs. If mine owners had been allowed to choose their labour on a purely profit-maximizing basis, they would undoubtedly have opted to employ a much larger proportion of Africans at rates substantially below those paid to white workers.

[1] R. V. Selope Thema was one of the early leaders of the African National Congress and a distinguished editor and politician. The quotation is from an article in 1922, 'The race problem', reproduced in Karis and Carter, *From protest to challenge*, vol. 1, p. 214.

Africans were not only much cheaper but also – because of the 1911 Native Labour Regulation Act described in Chapter 3 – much easier to control. They had also shown that they were perfectly able to do many of the skilled jobs from which they were excluded by the colour bar. This had been amply demonstrated before the full range of restrictions was imposed, as indicated in the following testimony by the general manager of one of the companies in 1907:

We have some of the Kaffirs who are better machine-men than some of the white men. I have boys who have been working on the mine from twelve to fifteen years, and they are better than many on the Rand nowadays.

Can they place holes [for blasting]? – Yes they can place the holes, fix up the machine and do everything that a white man can do, but, of course, we are not allowed to let them blast.

If the law was not what it is, do you think they could blast with safety? – I do not think, I feel sure about it. I have had experience with natives since 1879, and I know what a native can do.[2]

The competence and experience of African miners was shown again during the First World War, when many skilled white workers left the mines to serve in the armed forces. Their absence forced some relaxation of the colour bar, especially for semi-skilled work such as drill sharpening or pipe and track laying; it also caused the companies to hire unemployed Afrikaners from the rural areas, with no previous experience of the mining industry. These new recruits had to learn the skills they needed from the African workers, as reported in this interchange between the Low Grade Mines Commission of 1919–20 and a consulting engineer at one of the larger mines:

You say that in many cases the native teaches the white man his work underground? – Yes, in very many cases I might say.

But how does that come about? – Well a man comes from the back veldt and goes down the mine for six months. Sometimes he learns and he finally gets a machine to work himself. He is not able to do it but his natives do it, and if he were not there the natives could do it. They are skilled machine men some of these natives.

And you maintain that the men from the back veldt know so little that the boys are teaching them? – It is quite clear that it is so. I can take you down and show you, any mine any time.[3]

At every stage white miners fought strongly to prevent any dilution of their monopoly of skilled work. Because of the artificial and uneconomic

---

[2] Transvaal Mining Industry Commission, 1907–08, *Evidence*, Qs 13,372–3.
[3] Low Grade Mines Commission (Kotze), Evidence of Mr C. D. Leslie, consulting engineer to the Simmer Deep mine, paras. 445–50, quoted in F. A. Johnstone, *Class, race and gold*, London: Routledge & Kegan Paul, 1976, p. 106.

nature of this monopoly, their position was actually quite weak, so requiring both strike action and the support of wider public opinion in the white community. In 1907 white miners went on strike to prevent the companies allowing Africans to do skilled work, and the government was compelled to intervene and insist that the mines maintain a definite ratio of white to black labour. In 1913 a strike was called over the refusal of a particular mine to recognize a white trade union, a tactic which white miners correctly saw as a preliminary to an attack on their exclusive right to undertake certain semi-skilled jobs. The strike dragged on for a considerable time, and when management eventually decided to restart operations with new workers, other miners struck in sympathy. The position in Johannesburg deteriorated to the point where the government of Louis Botha thought it necessary to call in British forces, which opened fire on the demonstrators. There was a brief lull, and then renewed hostility at the beginning of 1914, with a strike that started in the coal mines, and spread rapidly to both the railways and the gold mines. On this occasion the government was better prepared and promptly called in the recently formed Union Defence Force. The strike collapsed and nine of the leaders were deported without trial.

There was a temporary truce between owners and workers during the war years, though the issues discussed at a conference between the Chamber of Mines and the Mine Workers' Union in 1917 included a demand from the Union for the exclusion of black workers from semi-skilled work. The Chamber refused to agree to this, claiming that it would be unjust, but also indicated that it was not opposed to a white monopoly of skilled work. Conflict with the companies then resumed as soon as the Armistice was signed in 1918. There was a new militancy among the white miners, particularly the recently recruited Afrikaners, who were increasingly inclined to take unofficial action to achieve the removal of black workers from semi-skilled jobs that had been assigned to them during the war years. In 1918, under pressure from white trade unions, the companies agreed to maintain the status quo with regard to the relative scope of employment of black and white miners, but it was soon evident to them that this was not a financially sustainable position.

In 1919 Britain had suspended the gold standard, allowing sterling to float against the dollar, until it could reduce prices and wages sufficiently to restore the conditions necessary for its successful operation. In the same year the Bank of England reached agreement with South African gold producers that all their output would be sold in London on the free market. As long as sterling remained below its pre-war parity of $4.86 to the pound, this effectively meant that the fixed dollar price of gold translated into a higher sterling price, and the mines received a premium for their gold. In 1920, when the exchange rate had depreciated substantially, the price received by the mines, including the premium, was some 112 shillings, 32 per cent above the price fixed by the gold standard. However, this premium would be eroded as the United Kingdom moved closer to a return to gold at the pre-war parity, at which point the price received by the mines would revert to the fixed level of 85 shillings per fine ounce.

There had been an inflationary rise in all costs of production during the war, with the biggest increase in the bill for wages and salaries of white employees. It was thus essential for the companies to find some means of reducing their costs; they knew that many of them could not survive if gold returned to its pre-war price while their cost structure remained at its inflated post-war level. Since the average pay of a white miner in 1921 was more than twelve times the average cost in cash and food of an African worker, the most obvious way to achieve the necessary economies was to replace some of the white labour force by Africans. At the end of 1921 the Chamber of Mines announced that it proposed to revoke the status quo agreement 'so as to permit the elimination of a number of redundant unskilled and semi-skilled Europeans'. The proportion of black to white miners would be increased from the prevailing ratio of about 8:1 to a new level of 10.5:1. To make its intentions perfectly clear, the Chamber also informed a conference with white workers convened by the Prime Minister that the companies thought it necessary to 'be at liberty to allocate and distribute and use their labour in whatever direction it thought fit, without the operation of any trade unions restrictions'.[4]

This was a direct challenge to the position of the white miners, and was made in the context of a post-war depression which began in the middle of 1920 and reached its lowest point two years later. The general fall in activity and rise in unemployment over this period intensified the insecurity and militancy of the white mine-workers, and there were also disputes in the engineering and power industries. The announcement by the Chamber of Mines led rapidly to a major strike in both gold and coal mines, and early in 1922 this was backed on a limited scale when a general strike was called in the Transvaal. The strike in turn became an armed rebellion, as Afrikaner workers mobilized in commandos, and invoked in industrial warfare the spirit and tactics they had developed in their fight against the British. General Smuts (who had by then succeeded Botha as

[4] Minutes of the conferences between the Prime Minister and representatives of the Transvaal Chamber of Mines and the white workers, quoted in Johnstone, *Class, race and gold*, p. 129.

Prime Minister and leader of the governing South African Party) responded by calling in the army, supported by artillery and aircraft. The rebellion was suppressed after fierce fighting, in which over 200 people were killed and many more wounded. The strike and rebellion were a remarkable demonstration of the triumph of racial over class solidarity, with white miners and their supporters marching under the banner: 'WORKERS OF THE WORLD, UNITE and FIGHT for a WHITE SOUTH AFRICA'. Four leaders of the rebellion were sentenced to death and walked to the gallows singing the Red Flag!

The strikers returned to work on terms dictated by the Chamber of Mines. The companies took advantage of their victory to improve their position in a number of different ways. Wages of white miners were immediately reduced by about 25 per cent, though the cost of living was also falling quite sharply at this time, so that the reduction in real earnings was much less substantial. The ratio of black to white workers was raised to about 10:1, allowing for the displacement of white by African workers in certain semi-skilled tasks such as drill sharpening, timbering, and pipe fitting. However, this higher level was not sustained; from 1925 onwards, following the election of the Pact government there was tacit recognition of the need for compromise to achieve better industrial relations, and the ratio was held steady at between 9:1 and 8:1 until the 1960s.

The third benefit that the mines extracted from their defeat of the white mine-workers was a very substantial improvement in the productivity of African miners. The technical basis for this was the general introduction of small jackhammer drills in place of large hand drills for stoping – breaking the rock in which the gold-bearing ore was imbedded. This was a major part of mining operations underground, and the revolution in drilling resulted in a huge reduction in costs. The jackhammers could be operated by only one worker, and he could drill very much further in a given shift, so that the efficiency of rock drilling more than doubled between 1921 and 1925. The new drills had been available on the Rand since 1916, but it was only after 1922 and the end of the status quo agreement with white miners that it was feasible to use them on a large scale, and to do so with maximum advantage. The key factor here was a reduction in the time that African miners were underground but unable to work because they were required to wait for a white miner to perform various tasks designed to ensure the safety of the day's operations. Once Africans were allowed to undertake the necessary preparatory and safety work without waiting for a white man to watch over them, a significant increase in the time they actually worked during an eight-hour shift became possible.

The interdependence of the technical advance with a change in labour relations was underlined in 1925 by Ernest Oppenheimer, chairman of Anglo American Corporation:

It must not be overlooked that without the reorganization of underground work dating from the 1922 strike and without the introduction of overlapping shifts the industry could not have attained the results of which they are now justly proud. The improved fathomage broken is not only due to the better type of machines and drills now used, but also largely to the fact that the effective drilling time has been practically doubled.[5]

The companies had won the immediate struggle, but they were able to derive only a limited benefit from their success, and were subsequently constrained by fear that any renewal of their attack on the still privileged position of white miners might provoke further unrest. They also paid a heavy price at the subsequent general election, when the ruling South African Party under Smuts was defeated, and replaced by an administration far less sympathetic to their interests.

Two years after the rebellion, the general election of 1924 was won by an alliance between the National and Labour parties. The National Party represented the interests of rural Afrikaners, small property owners, and the mostly unskilled Afrikaans-speaking workers who had migrated to the towns. The Labour Party was mainly supported by urban, English-speaking workers, including many immigrants from Britain, and drew much of its backing from the poorer sections of this community. These two rather disparate parties gained a majority of seats in the election, and combined to form the Pact government. Their electoral success reflected the bitter opposition of white artisans to the policy of the Chamber of Mines, and to the party of Botha and Smuts that had supported them. It was also a consequence of resentment in the Afrikaner community at the growing poverty among whites, a resentment felt as keenly by their compatriots as by those who were actually suffering. All agreed that whites should not be forced into a position where they had to compete with Africans for unskilled jobs. This problem of the 'poor whites' was not only a significant factor in the election of 1924, but also played a pivotal role in the subsequent formulation of policy by the Pact government, and we need to examine its nature and origins.

---

[5] Speech to shareholders, May 1925, quoted in T. Gregory, *Ernest Oppenheimer and the economic development of southern Africa*, Cape Town: Oxford University Press, 1962, p. 499.

The 'poor white' problem and the closing of the pastoral frontier

The life of Boer farmers in the interior of the country in the second half of the nineteenth century was captured superbly by the Transvaal Indigency Commission of 1908:

Two features of the early conditions in the Transvaal must be noted: the isolation of the lives of its white inhabitants and the large size of the farms. The daily life of the early Transvaal farmer consisted mainly in supervising the work of natives in the mealie lands or among the stock, in tending his animals, in shooting game for the pot and in an annual trek to the Low Veld for winter grazing. The land owner could not cultivate the soil because there was no market for agricultural produce. He did not even farm to supply his own wants. Except for the small supply of mealies which he grew he lived almost entirely on the game which fell to his rifle. . . . He did not use [his stock] for food, but grew rich or poor as their numbers increased or diminished. His homestead was usually some miles from that of his nearest neighbour, and there were few strangers with whom he ever came into contact. It was, therefore, but natural that his outlook was both circumscribed and essentially uncommercial.[6]

As Frankel had shrewdly observed, this was essentially 'that type of farming from which the Bantu had failed to extricate themselves for centuries'.[7] The Boers also lacked education, skills, and capital. They suffered from the same lack of access to prosperous markets and inability to produce appropriate export goods, the same inadequate transport, and the same isolation from modern ideas and scientific developments. They too experienced the ravages of drought and disease, of storms and locusts.

By the early 1880s the possibility of the continuation of this static, simple, and largely subsistence mode of life was drawing to a close. The time-honoured custom of entitlement to at least one farm of about 6,000 acres had led to rapid exhaustion of the vast territories the trekkers had first entered in the late 1830s, so that by the end of the century most of the desirable land had been appropriated. Further expansion was blocked by the desert, by the African population in the limited areas that remained to them, and by international boundaries, notably the acquisition of South West Africa by Germany in 1884, the annexation by the British government of Basutoland in 1868, and the granting of protection to Bechuanaland in 1885. The closing of the pastoral frontier to a growing population occurred at roughly the same time as the virtual extinction of

[6] Transvaal Indigency Commission, 1906–8, *Report*, para. 15.
[7] Frankel, *Capital investment*, p. 45.

the vast game herds that had previously provided such an ample supply of free sustenance.

It is in these developments, combined with the relatively unfavourable conditions for farming outlined in Annexe 2, that the origins of the poverty of the farming community are to be found. From the 1880s, as the frontier closed, and speculators attracted by the mineral discoveries drove up land prices, it became increasingly difficult for new generations to acquire their own farms, and they were forced to share the land with parents and siblings. This situation was exacerbated by a high birth-rate in Boer families, combined with an inheritance system prescribed by Roman-Dutch law that entitled every child to a 'legitimate' share of the estate and, in the common case of intestacy, to an equal share. Initially large farms were split and split again, and the process of subdivision of estates continued even after the legal requirement was formally abolished. Eventually many of the farms were too small to support either the owners or the large numbers of *bywoners* (people, often relations, who squatted on someone else's land without any clearly defined rights or duties). They had been easily accommodated when land was more abundant, and thought nothing of being occupiers rather than owners. As long as they could graze their land and hunt their game, what more was needed? But by the early twentieth century their existence was seriously threatened: 'In course of time as families multiplied and game grew scarce, some of the farms began to prove incapable of supporting the increasing numbers who had to get a living from them.'[8]

Farms were further impoverished by rinderpest, a cattle disease which swept through South Africa in 1896–97 with devastating effect, and many farmers were unable to raise the loans required to restore their herds. In addition, they could not afford the expensive fences that were necessary for improvements in their livestock, their strips of arable were too small and too scattered to be farmed efficiently, and their grasslands had been reduced in size and quality to the point where they could no longer sustain grazing. Rural poverty was then greatly exacerbated by the South African War of 1899–1902, when Britain decided that extensive destruction of Boer farms was necessary in order to prevent the Afrikaner commandos living off the land while waging their guerrilla campaigns against the British army.

The end result of all these varied forces was that thousands of Afrikaner farmers were reduced to a position of extreme destitution. There was no precise definition of 'poor white' and thus no means of counting them

---

[8] Transvaal Indigency Commission, 1906–8, *Report*, para. 18.

accurately, but it was estimated that by 1920 the number was at least 100,000. A decade later, during a worldwide depression in which agriculture was particularly badly affected, an estimate made for a special report by the Carnegie Commission put the number as high as 300,000, or about one in three of the Afrikaans-speaking white population. The great majority were unwilling or unable to become wage-earning farm workers and drifted to the towns; but there, too, all they had to offer was unskilled manual labour. This involved competing for jobs with African workers, for which they were ill-equipped and which they regarded as socially and politically unacceptable. As the Transvaal Indigency Commission reported in 1908, explicitly endorsing the observations from much earlier reports quoted in Chapter 3,

We have been impressed with the frequency with which it has been stated in evidence that unskilled work was 'Kaffir's work' and as such not the kind of work which a white man should perform ... This attitude of the white man has greatly affected his efficiency as a labourer. He has never regarded unskilled labour as an ordinary field of employment. When he has had to do unskilled work he has done it grudgingly as being Kaffir's work, and therefore inefficiently ... The white man's prejudice against 'Kaffir' work, his inefficiency as an unskilled labourer and the higher wage he requires, have had the natural result that coloured labour, inefficient though it is, is cheaper to the employer for unskilled work than white labour.[9]

This unwillingness to perform unskilled work which Africans could do more cheaply and more efficiently – an attitude attributed by one distinguished witness before the Commission to the legacy of slavery[10] – was the crux of the 'poor white' problem: it was both an economic and a social crisis, and it fell to the new government to attempt to find a solution.

Labour policies of the Pact government, 1924–33

The Pact government, with General Hertzog as Prime Minister, represented the sectional interests of its rural and urban supporters outlined above (p. 82), and of burgeoning Afrikaner nationalism. One strand of its policy making was designed primarily to appeal to its Labour Party constituency, the skilled, mostly English-speaking, workers. These policies included creation of a new Department of Labour, extension of the scope of the Workmen's Compensation Acts, improvements in the

---

[9] Transvaal Indigency Commission, 1906–8, *Report*, para. 46; For the earlier observations, by van Imhoff in 1743, Mr Peppercorne in the early 1850s and Trollope in the late 1870s, see p. 50 above.

[10] Transvaal Indigency Commission, 1906–8, *Report*, para. 40; the witness was J. H. Hofmeyer, a subsequent Deputy Prime Minister.

standards specified under the Factories Act, and the introduction of old age pensions to cover whites and – at a lower rate – coloureds.

The second, and far more important strand, was the rapid introduction of a series of major policy changes designed to promote the interests of the Afrikaans-speaking poor whites who were moving to the towns in large numbers. This involved measures to create employment for unskilled and semi-skilled white workers, to improve wages, and to protect both them and the skilled artisans from competition from Africans. In the previous chapter it was observed that farmers and mine-owners preferred to rely on political powers of coercion and discrimination rather than allow normal market forces to generate higher wages for African workers when there was a shortage of labour. What the Pact government was now attempting to do was once again to suppress the operation of normal market forces, but this time to raise wages for whites rather than depress them for blacks. By the 1920s there was no longer a scarcity of skilled and semi-skilled labour which could justify the exceptionally high premium paid to white workers, but white political power was to be deployed to maintain this differential.

The government immediately introduced a discriminatory employment policy for what was officially described as 'civilized' labour. Those who produced this tortuous definition presumably failed to appreciate the irony of issuing it as a *Circular*:

Civilized labour is the labour rendered by persons whose standard of living conforms to the standard of living generally recognised as tolerable from the usual European standpoint. Uncivilized labour is to be regarded as the labour rendered by persons whose aim is restricted to the bare necessities of life as understood among barbarous and undeveloped peoples.[11]

Under the cover of these definitions, whites were to be employed on unskilled and semi-skilled work at wages in excess of those normally paid for such work. In government departments and other parts of the public sector, notably the railways and harbours, this policy was vigorously pursued. Many thousands of black workers were dismissed and replaced by whites.

Application of this policy was more difficult in the private sector, since business was less willing than government to meet the additional costs imposed by the employment of 'civilized' labour, and had to be prevented from adopting a low-wage policy using cheap black labour. In its first two years in power, the new government passed two major Acts, both

---

[11] FN 10 *Circular* No. 5 (Pretoria, Oct. 1924), and Union Office of Census and Statistics, *Official Year Book* (hereafter *Year Book*), 9, 1926–7, p. 203.

designed, in part, to protect white workers from African competition. The Industrial Conciliation Act of 1924 was concerned primarily with skilled labour and organized groups of white workers, and incorporated a legal definition of 'employee' which effectively excluded almost all Africans. However, the industrial councils established under the Act were subsequently authorized to recommend minimum wages for Africans employed in industries covered by the Act, and were thus able to set their wages at levels at which it ceased to be profitable for firms to employ Africans. The Wages Act of 1925 established a three-man Wage Board to regulate wages and conditions of work in industries (other than agriculture and domestic service) in which employers and workers were not organized. The provisions of the Act effectively precluded the Board from recommending wages for unskilled workers below the rate at which employees could support themselves 'in accordance with civilized habits of life'. The Board was thus either unable to make a recommendation for unskilled workers because it judged that employers would be unable to pay the statutory rate or, where it did recommend a minimum wage, it promoted the employment of white workers at the expense of black. It was inevitably a complex and difficult task to improve wages for white workers while preventing employers from hiring black workers, and both acts had to be amended on several occasions, but the legislation finally succeeded in its primary aim. The acts were backed up by pressure on private employers exercised by the government through the tariff system (see Chapter 6), and by wider cultural pressures to conform exerted by white society as a whole.

The Pact government also took steps to re-establish the legality of the colour bar after it brought a test case in 1923, and the Supreme Court held that reliance on the 1911 Mines and Works Act for this purpose was *ultra vires*: the act itself did not authorize racial discrimination, and it could not be imposed by regulation. The mining industry ignored this temporary 'freedom' to employ Africans on skilled work, and continued to operate as if the regulation was still in force. Despite this, white workers saw in the judgement a serious threat to their already weakened position. Since the failure of the 1922 strike, the mining companies had been primarily concerned to replace semi-skilled white miners, but there were fears that they had now been given the opportunity to start displacing skilled workers. Accordingly, white workers and their supporters used their political influence with the new government to secure their position.

A Mining Regulations Commission was appointed to examine the issues, and reported in 1925. It found that the process of displacement of white workers was already far advanced in semi-skilled work, and endorsed the fears of the Mine Workers' Union that this would in due course apply also to skilled work:

Taking general mining as a skilled work, as surely it is, there is an abundance of examples of what are virtually encroachments of the native into it. The undue enlargement of the European miner's area of responsibility ... has led to the employment of a large number of native boss-boys in what is essentially a skilled position, where they are called upon to exercise over their subordinates wide powers of control and supervision. Into drill-sharpening, too, which when in the most competent hands we agree is a skilled occupation, the native has undoubtedly made his entry, with the result that has attended his advent into other skilled occupations, of degrading it to the rank of the semi-skilled.[12]

The same factors which made it more profitable for the mining companies to employ African rather than white workers in semi-skilled jobs, would operate with equal force in skilled jobs. It quoted the view of the Government Mining Engineer:

I have no reason to doubt that, as natives become more skilled in various occupations, economic law will in years to come operate as it always has, and that the more expensive white man will be replaced to an increasing extent by native labour. The refusal of the white man to do what is called Kaffir work accelerates his own displacement. By letting the native do the work he also lets the native get the training, and when he is sufficiently trained, the temptation to the employer to put him in the place of the more expensive white man becomes irresistible.[13]

It was thus clear to the commission that Africans must be prevented from performing such work, not because they lacked the competence to do it but, on the contrary, precisely because they were, or soon would be, competent. A new colour bar act was urgently required.

In 1926, after a fierce political struggle and an initial rejection by the Senate, a Mines and Works Amendment Act was passed, legalizing the old regulation and enabling the government to extend the new prohibition to all classes of skilled work throughout South Africa. From now on an overt, legal, colour bar could be established by regulation in industry as well as in mining. It was immediately implemented on the mines to exclude African and Asian (though not coloured) workers from specified occupations, but was not at that stage applied to the industrial sector. Though the Chamber of Mines made plain its displeasure, it had little option but to accept that the monopoly position of the white mineworkers with respect to these job categories had been secured.

---

[12] Mining Regulations Commission (Pittman), *Report*, para. 114.
[13] Ibid., para. 113.

The economic interests of skilled white workers who could vote had triumphed over those of skilled black workers who could not. South Africa may have been, as some have argued, part of the system of international monopoly capitalism in the era of imperialism, with the giant mining and finance houses as the dominant fraction of the ruling class and owners of the means of production; the white mineworkers may have been part of the proletariat, owning no property and with nothing to sell except their labour; but the state had not acted as the instrument of the ruling class. The pursuit of profit by the mining houses was now firmly constrained by the need to accommodate the interests of the white working class.

5   Exporting the gold: the vital role of the mineral revolution

This chapter begins with what may seem to be a digression, but is actually central to the explanation of how South Africa – and more especially the northern republics of the Transvaal and Orange Free State – escaped from the parlous situation in which the country languished until the 1860s, and was at last enabled to embark on a transition to a dynamic, modern economy.

Models of export-led growth

The really hard part of economic growth is getting the process started, and this is particularly difficult to achieve on the basis of internal demand alone. Undeveloped economies are usually trapped in vicious circles of poverty. Because income is low there is little demand, and consequently very little output other than subsistence production of food. Low levels of output in turn close the circle by perpetuating low incomes. To make matters worse, low incomes mean that there is little possibility of saving and so of making capital investments, with the result that productivity cannot be improved, and there is thus no escape from the low level of income.

The expansion of exports to overseas markets provides one of the best means for a country to break out of this trap and enjoy export-led growth. It is a commonplace of the historiography that gold was the export staple that played this role for South Africa, and provided the basis for rapid economic development. However, the comparative historical record shows very clearly that exports do not always have this beneficial effect, so it cannot simply be taken for granted that all that is needed is an export staple, any staple. If the experience of a range of countries is examined, it is possible to identify two broad types of export economy, distinguished by the technology used in the staple industry.[1] Both involve production

---

[1] This is not a comprehensive classification. The export economies based on peasant producers, for example, of rice in Burma and Thailand or palm oil and cocoa in west Africa, are the most obvious omission. Their output was normally sold to foreign firms

for export, but their features are quite dissimilar and the consequences for overall economic growth very different.[2]

The first type covers small-scale, intensive, homestead farming of products such as wheat, wool, meat, and milk, and is exemplified by regions of the United States, Canada, Australia, and New Zealand. Historically, this model has provided an extremely effective basis for economic growth. The gains originating in the export sector were largely retained in the country, and spread out from the staple producers until the economy as a whole attained high levels of physical and human capital, productivity, and living standards.

This type of export economy has a bundle of interdependent core features. The first, and most fundamental, relates to the scale of production. The optimum technology for these products allows highly efficient results to be achieved on the basis of small-scale family farms. There are no economic advantages from growing bigger (or as the economists would say, no economies of scale), and consequently there is no tendency to expand into larger units. Pastoral farming may require large areas of land – as with the vast sheep stations in eastern Australia – but is not labour-intensive, and so the unit of production remains small. In many instances family members provide all the labour required; in other cases, for example cattle ranching, only a small number of hired workers are employed to assist the family. The resulting distribution of income in the community of small farmers is thus relatively egalitarian. Second, because output is produced by small family units, there is little or no place for direct investment of foreign capital in the export sector itself, though there may be a significant flow of capital from abroad for investment in the construction of the regional infrastructure, especially railways, which play a vital role in transporting products from farms to points of export at the coast.

The third set of features is associated with the fact that this form of production encourages a search for ways to substitute capital for labour. Notable examples include the introduction of mechanical reaping and binding and the use of steam threshing machines in the United States

who had a monopoly of the trade and captured most of the gains from any expansion of exports, so that there was typically very little impact on the growth of the overall economy. The very successful experience of Taiwan, Malaysia, and other small Asian economies after the Second World War might be presented as a fourth type, based on exports of manufactures, but that was only possible under the different economic and technological conditions of that period, and is less relevant to the analysis of economic growth in the nineteenth and early twentieth centuries.

[2] Many of the ideas in the following paragraphs are drawn from the illuminating paper by R. E. Baldwin, 'Patterns of development in newly settled regions', *Manchester School of Economic and Social Studies*, 24, 1956.

from the mid-nineteenth century, later developed into effective combine-harvesters, and the invention of the stump-jump plough in Australia. In the twentieth century the major labour-saving advances in mechanization came from the use of the internal combustion engine and electricity, for example the introduction of mechanical sheep shearing. There is also more general promotion of technical advance and progressive introduction of improved farming methods, including the adoption of new seeds or fertilizers, scientific breeding to obtain the livestock best suited to the prevailing conditions in these new countries, and erection of fencing. In New Zealand, for example, agricultural research and extension work raised farm productivity by raising the output of milk per cow and the butterfat content of the milk. The revolution in transport and the advent of refrigeration encouraged the promotion of an export trade in dairy products based on significant improvements in the production of butter and cheese.

These conditions in turn foster a high standard of education and advances in human capital and, together with the egalitarian distribution of income, create a social and political environment in which democratic political systems can flourish. Finally, this system of small-scale family units supports the development of local suppliers; as family incomes rise, demand diversifies away from food, clothing, and other basic needs, and local production of a more extended range of goods and services is encouraged. These include equipment, seeds, technical services, and other goods and services for the farms, as well as manufactured consumer goods, and services such as schools, hospitals, and newspapers for farm families.

The second type of export economy consists either of large-scale plantations for growing tropical crops such as sugar, bananas, cotton, rubber, palm oil, sisal, coffee, tea, and cocoa, or of large-scale mines or oil wells. The former can be immediately identified with countries in many parts of central and southern America, Asia, east and west Africa, and the West Indies. Examples of the latter include the production of copper in Zambia and Chile, of tin in Malaysia, and of oil in Venezuela, Mexico, and Nigeria. The core features of this second type are essentially the antithesis of those outlined above. Economies of scale in the relevant technologies lead to large units, employing substantial numbers of hired labourers. The prevailing under-development and its corresponding social and political structures make it possible for the firms to recruit all the labour they require at very low wages, and working conditions are usually appalling. The giant enterprises are usually owned by foreign multinational companies and dependent on foreign capital and senior management. The distribution of income is highly skewed, with a majority of the local population living in poverty while a few businessmen and politicians enjoy high rewards for their co-operation with the foreign owners.

These conditions are associated with low standards of education, very limited advances in human capital, and authoritarian political systems. The plantations, mines, and oil wells are generally enclaves in the larger economy. They generate only modest local demand, and a large proportion of the gains from production are taken out of the region in profits for the owners and payments to their expatriate managers and specialists, whose children are sent back to the home country for their education. Historically, such enclaves have failed to lead to development of other sectors. This type of export economy is profitable for the foreign owners and for selected local interests, but not for the host economy and society as a whole.

For South Africa, the export staple was gold. What makes South Africa both anomalous and interesting as a case study in successful economic development is that in terms of its technological conditions, gold has far more in common with the failed large-scale plantation/enclave model than with the conditions conducive to export-led growth associated with small-scale family farming. In terms of the bundle of core features, the mines were operated by very large-scale enterprises, and over 90 per cent of the labour force consisted of unskilled African migrant workers paid abysmally low wages. The companies were mainly owned abroad and heavily dependent on foreign capital. Little or no training or general education was provided for African miners, and they were denied any right to participate in electoral processes. Most of the cash income received by African miners was remitted to the rural reserves, and spent on food for their families, or on taxes; there was almost no expenditure to provide a stimulus for local industry. On the face of it, therefore, all these features made gold an unlikely source of export-led growth. How then was it able to perform this vital function?

The special features of gold in South Africa

Part of the answer is that gold was not just another commodity. It played a unique role in international finance as the metal on which the world's money supply was based. One consequence of this special status is that the world price of the metal was fixed in dollars, first under the gold standard, and then under the Bretton Woods arrangements that were introduced after the Second World War, and it remained in place until the system broke down in 1971. During that entire period there was only one change in the dollar price: in January 1934, when President Franklin

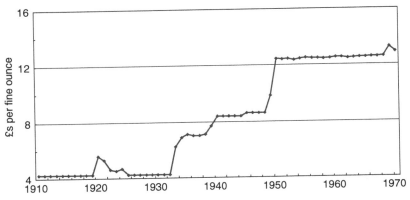

Figure 5.1. Price of gold in £s per fine ounce, 1910–70

Source: Chamber of Mines, *96th Annual Report*, p. 58.

Roosevelt wanted to see a devaluation of the US currency and fixed the relationship between the dollar and the monetary metal at $35 per fine ounce, compared with the previous value of $20.67. The underlying reason for this unique change in US financial policy was the belief that devaluation of the dollar would help to bring about a general rise in commodity prices in the United States, especially for farm products, and thus relieve an exceptionally severe depression.

However, the exchange rate at which the fixed dollar price was converted into South African currency could and did change, and the gold mines received a boost each time this occurred. The first occasion (described in the previous chapter) followed the end of the First World War, when Britain allowed sterling to float, but was reversed when it returned to the gold standard in 1925. The three following changes were cumulative, and their combined effect, together with the devaluation of the dollar in 1934, raised the sterling price obtained by the gold mines from £4.25 per fine ounce before 1932 to £12.50 in 1950. The successive changes from 1910 to 1970 are shown in Figure 5.1 (and also in column (5) of Table 5.3).

The most controversial of all the changes was made some fifteen months after the Great Depression had already forced the United Kingdom and thirty-one other countries to abandon the gold standard, and with it their fixed exchange rates, in September 1931. Throughout 1932 South Africa stood resolutely alone, offering various objections to any suggestion that it too should leave gold. The main economic argument was that gold was the essential bulwark against rising prices, and its removal would simply lead to inflation. This was hardly a telling point at a time when the world was suffering from an unprecedented fall in prices and incomes, and South African farmers, in particular, were in great distress. As Keynes observed when the same argument was raised in the context of a controversy in the United Kingdom in 1929, 'To bring up the bogy of inflation ... at the present time is like warning a patient who is wasting away from emaciation of the dangers of excessive corpulence.'[3] Other objections did not have sufficient strength to withstand mounting economic pressures from ruined farms and businesses, and from unemployed workers.[4] After a year of further economic decline and heated political controversy, the gold standard was eventually abandoned at the end of December 1932. The result was a return to parity with sterling, and thus a substantial devaluation of the South African currency against the dollar, with a corresponding increase of almost 50 per cent in the sterling price of gold between 1932 and 1933.

Roosevelt's increase in the dollar price of gold followed in 1934, though much of the potential gain from this was lost because sterling had by that time appreciated against the dollar, leaving only a relatively small rise in the sterling price of gold to add to the previous increase.[5] In the remainder of the decade the price received in South Africa fluctuated within narrow limits according to the exchange rate set for sterling during the period of its 'managed float' against the dollar. There was a further small increase in the price of gold on the outbreak of the Second World War, when sterling was allowed to float downwards against the dollar, and Pretoria immediately followed London. Finally, in September 1949 the United Kingdom announced a substantial devaluation of sterling in an acknowledgement of the extent to which its financial position had deteriorated during the war while that of the United States had strengthened. On this occasion there was no hesitation; it was accepted that the United Kingdom was South Africa's major trading partner, and that failure to

---

[3] J. M. Keynes, *Collected works*, Vol. 9, *Essays in persuasion*, London: Macmillan, 1972, p. 118.

[4] It was also claimed that it was wrong for a gold-producing country to do anything which might weaken support for the role of gold as the basis of the world monetary system; it would be the equivalent, said the governor of the Reserve Bank, of 'the village bootmaker declaring boots expensive and unhealthy and parading himself and his family barefoot'. A further argument was that a government determined to establish its complete independence from the United Kingdom did not need to keep its currency tied to sterling.

[5] In 1932 and 1933, when the official price of gold was still $20.67, the annual average exchange rate depreciated from $4.86 for £1 while South Africa remained on the gold standard, to $3.30 after parity with sterling was restored. The sterling price of gold thus increased from £4 5s to £6 5s per fine ounce. In 1934, when the dollar price of gold was $35 per fine ounce, the exchange rate had appreciated to $5.07, and the sterling price was thus £6 18s per fine ounce.

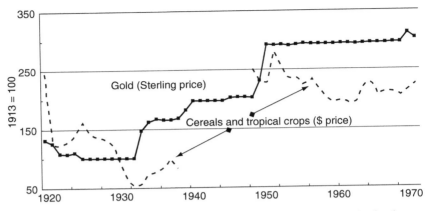

Figure 5.2. Comparison of indices of price of gold and of primary products, 1920–70

Source: Lewis, *Growth and fluctuations,* pp. 280–4.

keep the sterling parity unchanged would make it difficult to maintain non-gold exports. Accordingly, the South African currency was devalued against the dollar to the same extent as sterling, with a corresponding increase of over 40 per cent in the sterling price of gold.

The overall result of these changes in the sterling price of gold was that the experience of gold provided a much more favourable platform for economic development than that of other primary products. In Figure 5.2 the movement in the price of gold from 1913 to 1970 is compared with an index of primary product prices covering the main cereals and tropical products.[6] From the late 1920s, South Africa benefited from a stable or rising price for gold, whereas the prices of primary products were reduced catastrophically during the years of overproduction and farm crises at the beginning of the Great Depression. The general decline in raw material prices meant that the Rand mines also enjoyed lower working costs. Both gold and commodity prices increased between 1938 and 1948, and the latter also rose sharply during the Korean War, but gold was again immune from the general fall in commodity prices that began after 1951 and continued strongly until the mid-1960s. The stability or rising price of gold thus made it a much better basis for development than the

---

[6] No general index of primary product prices is available for the relevant period, but a broadly reliable comparison can be made by taking an unweighted average of series for cereals and tropical crops (in terms of current US dollars) given in W. A. Lewis, *Growth and fluctuations 1870–1913,* London: George Allen & Unwin, 1978, pp. 280–4. Both this series and the price of gold are shown as indices with 1913=100 in Figure 5.2.

volatile prices of other commodities, which tended to climb rapidly during inflationary periods such as the two world wars, and then fall sharply, with severely disruptive effects on their economies.

However, this one favourable aspect was almost certainly not in itself sufficient to outweigh the adverse impact on export-led growth of the other technological and related features of gold mining noted in the first part of this chapter. It seems reasonable to conclude, therefore, that if goldfields identical to those in South Africa had been discovered elsewhere in Africa or Asia, they would not have been the source of general growth in the wider economy. They would have remained enclaves with limited effects similar to those in other economies of this type. What, then, was the critical feature of South African conditions which made it possible for gold to act as the growth engine for a more general process of economic expansion? The answer is that it was the wider consequences which flowed from a geographical environment and climate which attracted people with modern economic skills to settle in South Africa in large numbers, becoming permanent residents rather than temporary expatriates.

This applied not only to the thousands of immigrants recruited from Europe as skilled workers on the diamond fields and gold mines, but also to many of those who were involved in the finance and management of these industries, men such as Cecil Rhodes and Barney Barnato from the United Kingdom, or George Albu and Ernest Oppenheimer from Germany. The first consequence of their presence was that they and many others brought with them valuable entrepreneurial, managerial, and technical skills, both for mining and for other sectors. The Jewish immigrants from Lithuania and other parts of eastern Europe attracted to South Africa after the mineral discoveries were also a valuable addition to the economic and entrepreneurial resources crucial for successful development. These new arrivals in South Africa were typically well paid, some prospered in business and the professions, and a few became exceptionally rich. Their spending created a good market for the domestic production of goods and services, supplementing expenditures by the mines on stores and equipment and on professional and financial services. The overall result of this settlement by immigrants from Europe and elsewhere was that the Rand was not an enclave; the gold mines were not isolated from, and independent of, the rest of the economy.

A further and even more fundamental consequence was the European impact on South Africa's institutional framework. The transplanting of European institutions in the southern part of the African continent began with the arrival of the first Dutch settlers in the seventeenth century, and was renewed and revivified after control of the Cape passed to the British.

A notable early illustration of the changes was an 1811 proclamation requiring two justices of the High Court to go on periodic circuit to the outlying districts, thus bringing the rule of law to the borders of the Colony for the first time. This was followed by reform of the judiciary and introduction of the English jury system in 1834, the granting of municipal government to Cape Town in 1840, and the establishment of representative government in the colony, with an elected lower house, in 1854. In 1861 the Legislative Council passed the Joint Stock Companies Limited Liabilities Act. Institutions such as these matter – they are an essential requirement for dynamic economic growth.

There is good evidence from a large set of countries that appropriate institutions are very closely associated with the presence of settlers from Europe who introduced the traditions of their home countries in areas to which they migrated.[7] These traditions included institutions such as property rights and respect for contracts, the rule of law and an efficient, independent judiciary, and competent, democratic government, subject to checks on its power and not dominated or corrupted by vested interests. Such institutions are in turn the necessary foundation for transactions to buy and sell goods and property, for lending and borrowing, for the formation of industrial and financial joint stock corporations, for saving and investment, and for the allocation of resources for the expansion of physical and human capital. All of these are prerequisites for modern economic growth and rising incomes.

Of course, like almost everything else in South Africa, these institutions were warped by racism. Property rights, lack of arbitrary rule, a democratic vote, and compulsory education were assured for whites, and withheld from blacks. In the Transvaal goldfields, for example, this discrimination was made quite explicit: under various laws black people were precluded from acquiring mineral licences, trading in minerals, and establishing

---

[7] The importance of appropriate institutions for economic growth has been the subject of a number of distinguished theoretical and empirical studies. One of the most persuasive is an elaborate econometric study recently published by D. Acemoglu, S. Johnson, and J. A. Robinson, 'Colonial origins of comparative development', *American Economic Review*, 91, 2001. They took per capita GDP in 1995 as the dependent variable, and differences in settler mortality at various dates in the early colonial period as a proxy explanatory variable for the influence of current institutions, which are in turn assumed to derive from earlier institutions dating from the time of the first settlers. Their estimates imply that differences in institutions explain approximately three-quarters of the differences in per capita incomes across a sample of sixty-four former colonies. Furthermore, the results are quite robust: the omission from the sample of either very high-income countries such as the United States, or of very low-income African countries does not change the results. Their estimates also changed remarkably little when they controlled for a large range of other factors that might be correlated with settler mortality (and thus with institutions) and income levels, for example, geography, religion, or the current disease environment.

shops or residing in mining areas. It was specifically laid down that 'No coloured person may be a licence holder, or in any way be connected with the working of the gold mines, except as a working man in the service of the whites.'[8] Nevertheless, what ultimately mattered, when the issue is viewed solely from the perspective of South Africa's initial economic development, was not this relentless denial of rights to the majority of the population, but their establishment and development for some. Even in the presence of massive racial discrimination, it was ultimately the existence of advantageous institutions derived from European settlement that enabled gold to drive forward South Africa's economic transformation.

The character and expansion of the mining industry

Within a few years of the discovery of the first diamond in 1867 in the north-eastern Cape, there were thousands of diggers in the area, white and black, but the day of the small independent digger and open quarrying of alluvial deposits did not last long. It was soon found that the diamond-bearing 'blue ground' was concentrated on four adjoining farms in deep, cylindrical 'pipes', and the economic logic of the underground mining this required led rapidly to two radical changes. The first was the amalgamation and consolidation of more than 3,000 individual claims until they were all owned by a few large joint-stock companies. This process had effectively been accomplished by the late 1880s, with De Beers Consolidated Mines, under the control of Cecil Rhodes, in complete command of the industry. The second was the investment of significant sums of capital for the sinking of proper shafts and the replacement of spades, buckets, and ladders by machinery for pumping, hoisting, and washing.

Output climbed rapidly, passing 1,000,000 carats by 1872, 2,000,000 carats by 1879, and 3,500,000 carats in 1888. By the end of the 1880s, Rhodes had attained a position by which he could control the total output of diamonds, and thus prevent the fall in prices that would have been the inevitable result of an excess supply on world markets. Operations were concentrated at two of the four mines, and output was generally held steady at a level of between 2,500,000 and 3,000,000 carats a year until demand for this luxury item collapsed during the depression of the 1930s.

These revolutionary developments in the diamond fields were rapidly surpassed by the exceptional pattern of growth in the Transvaal goldfields.

---

[8] Transvaal Laws 15 of 1898 and 32 of 1908, quoted in Johnstone, *Class, race and gold*, p. 23.

The unique gold-bearing conglomerate reef of the Witwatersrand was discovered by two brothers near its north-west extremity in 1884, and the first mining operations on the Rand followed rapidly. Within two years the brothers had traced the gold eastward to the main reef, and preliminary results of tests on ore from these reefs were so satisfactory that the Transvaal government proclaimed the area a public goldfield in September 1886. Johannesburg, the town that was to become the industrial and financial centre of the new industry and of South Africa, was founded in the same year. The exciting news spread rapidly to London and Paris, and hundreds of companies were eagerly floated to purchase farms in the new district and to participate in the boom in land and gold that was confidently predicted. The fortunes made, and experience gained, in the diamond industry were a powerful influence on the early development of the gold mines, and the international financial connections established in Kimberley were a significant factor in raising capital for Johannesburg.

Production and exports of gold expanded at what was – by South African standards – a phenomenal pace, and within a few years the nature and scale of the whole economy had been dramatically transformed. In the 1860s, after more than two centuries of hard toil and slow progress on South Africa's farms, total exports of all agricultural and pastoral products had only just reached £2,500,000 a year. In the first half of the 1890s, after fewer than ten years of mining, exports of gold had raced to £4,500,00 a year. By 1906–10 the annual average was over £27,000,000, and by the late 1930s it had soared to £80,000,000 (the figures are shown in column (5) of Table 5.1 for 1875 to 1909, and in column (4) of Table 5.2 for 1910 to 1954). A similar picture of progress to new heights that would have been unimaginable before the mineral discoveries can be seen in many other indicators of economic activity, including immigration and urbanization, banking and the growth of a money economy, government revenue, and transport.

The Witwatersrand goldfield was marked by an exceptional continuity and uniformity in the length and breadth of its reefs, but the gold was not located in easily accessible alluvial deposits such as those discovered earlier in the eastern and northern Transvaal, or in the mid-nineteenth century in California and Australia, which could be mined with pick, shovel, and pan. Nor did it occur in veins of metal ore such as those in almost all other countries where gold is mined. The Rand's gold existed in minute particles embedded in huge quantities of hard quartz rock, and the reefs extended at an angle from the surface to depths of many thousands of feet. The visible 'outcrops' where the reefs appeared on the surface were quickly exhausted, and from early in the 1890s the industry was reconstructed on the basis of deep-level mining. By 1913 more than

Table 5.1. *Annual average exports from the Cape and Natal, 1850–1909*[a]

	(1) Wool	(2) Hides, skins, ostrich feathers[b]	(3) Other products[c]	(4) Diamonds	(5) Gold	(6) Total Cape and Natal	(7) Gold as % of total
			(£ million)				
1860–4	1.51	0.18	0.63	–	–	2.32	–
1865–9	1.80	0.51	0.31	0.01	–	2.63	–
1870–4	2.79	0.49	0.94	1.03	–	5.24	–
1875–9	2.68	0.72	0.96	1.90	0.04	6.30	0.6
1880–4	2.58	1.34	1.21	3.42	0.02	8.57	0.2
1885–9	2.45	0.86	1.38	3.72	0.30	8.71	3.5
1890–4	2.55	0.97	1.46	3.82	4.15	12.94	32.1
1895–9	2.36	1.12	2.72	4.52	11.29	22.01	51.3
1900–04	1.80	1.37	3.85	5.14	7.00	19.16	36.5
1905–9	2.93	2.33	5.03	7.23	27.30	44.82	60.9

[a] Including re-exports of imported goods and a small amount of inter-colonial trade.
[b] Excluding any exports of these products from Natal.
[c] Mainly mohair, wine, fresh fruit, maize, sugar, and meat.

Source: Year Book, 5, 1922, pp. 692–3.

half the mines were working at depths of between 2,000 and 4,000 feet below the surface; by the 1930s depths of 4,000 to 5,000 feet were common and some mines had already reached 8,000 feet. Several years of costly trial and error were required by engineers and geologists to develop the appropriate techniques for the exploitation of the gold-bearing conglomerate reefs on the Witwatersrand at these great depths.

The miners working deep underground drilled holes in the rock, inserted dynamite, and blasted the quartz loose from the face. From there it was hauled to the shafts and hoisted to the surface. Expensive physical and chemical processes were then applied to extract the gold. The millions of tons of rock brought to the top each year were first reduced in size in gyratory stonebreakers, then crushed into progressively finer pieces in powerful stamp and tube mills. After that, the finely crushed ore was carried in a stream of water over plates covered by strips of corduroy cloth, where particles of gold were caught in the pile. This use of corduroy cloth was a significant innovation, first introduced in

Table 5.2. *Annual average exports of South African products, 1910–54*

	(1) Agricultural and pastoral products	(2) Diamonds	(3) Other products [a]	(4) Gold and specie [b]	(5) Total	(6) Gold and specie as % of total
	(£ million)					
1910–14	10.3	8.7	4.0	32.9	55.9	58.9
1915–19	18.0	6.3	5.8	38.1	68.2	55.9
1920–4	21.9	6.3	7.0	41.6	76.8	54.2
1925–9	28.2	10.5	6.2	44.1	89.1	49.5
1930–4	16.5	3.2	4.1	53.7	77.5	69.3
1935–9	22.1	2.8	5.7	80.4	111.0	72.4
1940–4	19.9	4.6	22.7	86.5	133.7	64.7
1945–9	52.1	11.2	32.7	135.4	231.4	58.5
1950–4	127.8	18.5	82.2	146.1	374.6	39.0

[a] Includes other mining products, manufactured goods, and coal bunkers and other ships' stores.
[b] The value of gold exports includes the premium received as a result of currency fluctuations, for example in 1933–38; exports of semi-processed gold and of gold and silver plate and plated ware in 1949–53 are included with gold.

Source: Union statistics, N-4 and N-5. There are a number of omissions and inconsistencies in the series given in this source for gold, and I have attempted to correct these and to include exports of specie (coin) on the basis of data in *Year Book,* 20, 1939, p. 956; 25, 1949, p. 1046, and in other issues.

1923, at a time when the mines were searching anxiously for ways to reduce costs.[9]

The finer gold which escaped the corduroy cloth or the mercury plates which it superseded, was dealt with by the Macarthur–Forrest cyanide process. This was a revolutionary innovation, by which gold that was either too small to be caught by the earlier processes, or was combined with impurities, was dissolved in solutions of potassium cyanide. Costs were initially prohibitive, but after improvements were made the process was adopted in the 1890s, and had such a powerful effect on the performance of the industry that one historian referred to its role

---

[9] The less efficient system replaced by the corduroy cloth had carried the coarser free gold over mercury-coated copper plates, where the gold was caught as an amalgam by the mercury and then had to be separated from the mercury by heating the amalgam in special retorts.

as 'salvation by cyanide'.[10] It enabled the proportion of gold recovered from the ore to be increased from 60 to almost 100 per cent, and permitted the treatment of a large quantity of ore that would not otherwise have been profitable to mine. In subsequent years the costs of the separation process were appreciably reduced by additional technical advances. The introduction of the small jack-hammer drills after 1922 (discussed in Chapter 4) was also of considerable importance in reducing costs by raising labour productivity. Successful operation of the Transvaal mines was greatly assisted by large seams of good-quality coal which were discovered in close proximity to the reefs. The first coalmines were opened on the East Rand in the late 1880s, and cheap fuel from this area was a crucial element in the rapid exploitation of the goldfields.

In most mines on the Witwatersrand there was considerable variation in the grade of ore, that is, in the ratio of gold to rock. The average grade mined each year was typically about 6.5 dwts until the decline in the 1930s explained below, but most mines would have a large quantity of low-grade ore and a relatively small quantity of high-grade ore.[11] A crucial variable for the mines was the average grade of ore which it was profitable to mine after allowing for all costs and overhead charges (but not for interest or amortization of capital). If working costs were reduced or the price of gold increased, the quantity of payable ore increased and more gold could be extracted, though the average grade would fall. The law required each mine to work to the average grade of its declared ore reserves – it could not look for a quick profit by mining only the high-grade ore and ignoring the rest.

Mining of the form and on the scale determined by the nature of the Witwatersrand reefs obviously required large corporations to raise the substantial sums of capital that were needed, both to carry the considerable risks of a speculative enterprise and to sustain the activity through the long gestation period necessary to bring a deep-level mine into operation. They also had to provide the essential expertise for sinking and operating deep shafts, and undertaking the complicated ore reduction processes. Within a short time the industry was highly concentrated under the control of six giant mining and finance houses. Given their inordinate power and their influence on the economic history of South Africa it

---

[10] Owen Letcher, quoted in H. Rockoff, 'Some evidence on the real price of gold, its costs of production, and commodity prices', in M.D. Bordo and A.J. Schwartz (eds.), *A retrospective on the classical gold standard 1821–1931*, Chicago: Chicago University Press, 1984, p. 629.

[11] 20 dwts (pennyweights)=1 fine ounce, and the average grade of ore was measured in dwts of gold per ton of rock milled.

seems appropriate to list them by name, with their share of gold production in 1936 shown in parentheses. They were Rand Mines (34 per cent) Johannesburg Consolidated Investment Company (24 per cent), Anglo American (14 per cent), Consolidated Gold Fields (11 per cent), Union Corporation (8 per cent) and General Mining and Finance Corporation (5 per cent).

The distinctive feature of gold was that all mines produced an identical product for which there was an unlimited market: the industry could sell as much as it could produce. The critical determinant of production was thus not on the demand but on the supply side – as long as it was profitable to mine the gold, it would be produced and sold. Profitability, in turn, was a function of the costs of mining and of the price of gold. Because they did not compete over sales, mining houses were willing to pool their expertise and experience, and to co-operate to reduce costs. And because the price of gold was fixed by forces over which they could exercise no control whatsoever, these measures to reduce costs were vitally important for them. A demonstration of this co-operation in relation to one of the major elements in their costs, the wages of African miners, was referred to in Chapter 3. They also worked together to reduce other costs such as those for shaft sinking and rock drilling, or for mine administration. In this way, technical advances and best practice in any one mine were swiftly diffused, and the whole industry became highly efficient.

By their success in increasing efficiency, the companies were able to expand output even when the price of gold remained constant. They did even better when the price increased as a result of changes in the exchange rate of sterling against the dollar. Each rise in price (shown above in Figure 5.1) transformed conditions; in particular, higher sterling prices enabled mines to extract gold from rock with a lower gold content and still cover their costs. It was especially profitable when the extra output could be obtained from existing mines and shafts with no additional capital outlays. By 1931 profits had dipped below 8 shillings per ton milled; by 1934 the figure had climbed to over 15 shillings. Activity, employment, and profit per ton of ore milled all surged when prices rose in the 1930s and surged again in the 1950s (see Chapter 8), and the life of the mines was greatly extended. The relevant figures for output milled, gold produced, and average grade are given in columns (1) to (3) of Table 5.3, with the value of gold sales and the price received (in £s per fine ounce) in columns (4) and (5). The consequent variations in working revenue, costs, and profit per ton of ore milled are set out in Table 5.4.

During the 1930s the main effect of the rise in the sterling price of gold following the currency devaluation was on tonnage milled, and – for the

Table 5.3. *South African gold mines: ore milled, output, sales and price,*
annual averages, 1885–1948

	(1) Ore milled (million tons[a])	(2) Output of gold (million fine ounces)	(3) Average grade (dwts per ton[b])	(4) Value of gold sales (£ million)	(5) Price received (£ per fine ounce)
1885–9	–	0.13	–	0.53	4.24
1890–4	–	1.06	–	4.50	4.25
1895–9	4.86	2.85	11.8	12.10	4.25
1901	0.37	0.26	13.8	1.10	4.25
1902–4	5.32	2.82	10.7	11.98	4.25
1905–9	14.33	6.30	8.9	26.77	4.25
1910–14	22.98	8.42	7.3	35.75	4.25
1915–19	24.88	8.83	7.1	37.52	4.25
1920–1	22.06	8.14	7.4	44.34	5.45
1922	18.26	7.01	7.7	32.34	4.61
1923–4	25.71	9.36	7.3	43.16	4.61
1925–9	27.72	10.09	7.3	42.85	4.25
1930–2	31.51	11.04	7.0	52.38	4.74
1933–4	35.71	10.75	6.0	70.50	6.57
1935–9	48.40	11.77	4.9	84.84	7.20
1940–4	60.24	13.53	4.5	113.68	8.40
1945–8	53.24	11.73	4.4	101.17	8.62

[a] Metric tons of 2,004.6 lbs.
[b] 20 dwts (pennyweights)=1 fine ounce.

Source: Chamber of Mines, *96th Annual Report*, 1985, p. 58.

reasons explained earlier – there was a sharp fall in the average grade
of the ore mined. The net result was that there was initially a fall in the
output of gold, and it was not until 1937 that output regained the 1932
level. This trend towards extraction of rock with a lower gold content was
also encouraged by the special excess profits duty levied from 1933,
which operated so as to benefit mines which milled a larger tonnage of a
lower grade of ore. The companies, supported by the government, thus
took advantage of the increased price to extract gold which would otherwise have been left underground. Mining lower grades of ore did not
maximize the immediate profits of the companies, but it extended the life
of the mines and ensured greater profits over the long term. However, the
primary concern of the mines was not the quantity of gold they mined, but
its value and thus their profits on the operation. The fluctuations in
working costs and working profits per ton milled are shown for selected

Table 5.4. *South African gold mines: working revenue, costs, and profits, annual averages, 1902–48*

	(1) Working revenue	(2) Working costs	(3) Working profit
	(£ per ton of ore milled[a])		
1902–4	2.21	1.37	0.84
1905–9	1.81	1.12	0.70
1910–14[b]	1.54	0.98	0.55
1915–19[c]	1.54	1.09	0.45
1920–1	1.95	1.42	0.53
1922	1.74	1.30	0.44
1923–4	1.64	1.10	0.55
1925–9	1.56	1.08	0.48
1930–2	1.65	1.07	0.58
1933–4	1.96	1.07	0.89
1935–9	1.76	1.05	0.71
1940–4	1.91	1.19	0.72
1945–8	1.91	1.41	0.51

[a] Metric tons of 2,004.6 lb.

[b] Data corrected for apparent error in source for these years.

Source: Chamber of Mines, *96th Annual Report*, 1985, p. 87.

years in Table 5.4. The former varied in response to the efforts of the companies to reduce wages and other costs, and were also affected by wider trends in prices at home and abroad. The profits per ton milled reflected both these fluctuations in costs and those in revenue per ton milled, with the latter determined mainly by the average grade of the ore and the price received for gold.

Gold mining as the engine of growth

Numerous metaphors have been adopted to describe the unique and indispensable role of gold (and to a lesser extent, diamonds) in promoting the economic development of South Africa: for Frankel the industry was the 'power-house of modern enterprise'; for de Kiewiet it was the 'life-blood of the Union'; for a 1941 government commission it was the 'mainspring of the Union's economic system'; for Hobart Houghton, mining had been the 'leading sector of the whole economy of southern Africa' ever since the discovery of diamonds.

Gold mining certainly made a substantial direct contribution to output, income, and employment. In 1911, the first year for which an estimate of the national income is available, its share of GDP was almost 20 per cent, and in the period from 1920 to 1939 it was normally between 12 and 18 per cent. In 1910, gold gave employment to 224,000 miners, of whom 199,000 were black; in 1940 the corresponding figures were 428,000 and 380,000. But agriculture was even larger in terms of its contribution to GDP until the depression of the 1930s, and was always a far larger source of employment. Clearly the metaphors were intended to convey something more significant than this.

One way in which gold was said to play a special role was through its backward linkages, the demand from the mines which fostered the growth of a range of industries and services to supply its needs. This claim was rebutted by Lehfeldt on the grounds that all industries are interdependent:

It is often said that the importance of the mines is not to be estimated merely by their direct revenue, but by the support they give to other industries, to the supply of foodstuffs, to the production of mining machinery, to the railways and so on. The argument is fallacious: everyone is everyone else's customer, but that is no more true of mining than of any other occupation – for instance, a farmer spends his income and so gives employment to manufacturers of implements, of clothes, to the railway; there is nothing peculiar to mining in the matter.[12]

Lehfeldt's point is valid in relation to an analysis of a static situation, of the sort that would be reflected in a standard input–output table, but it is not well taken in the context of a dynamic process. The mines were able to increase production rapidly because there was an unlimited export market for their gold, and their expansion was in turn the prime mover for the growth of other sectors. Mining could have increased its output at roughly the same pace even if no local industries had existed to supply its inputs. The scale of the protective tariff barriers needed to enable South Africa to compete with imported goods is sufficient indication that supplies of manufactures (though not coal) could have been acquired from overseas at lower cost. By contrast, the development of manufacturing would have been far slower without the tremendous stimulus given by the gold mines, directly and indirectly, to the growth of a domestic market.

Their direct purchases encouraged the growth of industries producing machinery, electrical equipment, explosives, wire cables, cement, and

---

[12] R. A. Lehfeldt, *The national resources of South Africa*, Johannesburg: University of the Witwatersrand Press, 1922, p. 29.

miners' footwear. The mines stimulated coal mining and electricity generation to provide their enormous power supplies. They were a major force behind the development of internal transport, with an increase in the railway network from less than 100 miles in 1870 to over 7,000 by 1910 and 10,000 by 1924, as trunk lines raced from the coast, first to Kimberley and then to Johannesburg. They needed doctors and lawyers, geologists and accountants; they supported the expansion of banking and financial services; and they also looked to the future by assisting the expansion of higher education in subjects such as engineering and science.

The mining industry played an even more vital role in sustaining the country's balance of payments and earning the foreign exchange needed by other sectors. At the end of the 1890s, gold accounted for over 50 per cent of South Africa's total exports; by the eve of the First World War the proportion had risen to almost 60 per cent, and at the end of the 1930s it was over 70 per cent (see the final columns of Tables 5.1 and 5.2). As a primary industry the input requirements of the mines were very low, and much of that was obtained from local sources, so gold mining's high exports and low imports made a substantial positive contribution to the current account. This was especially important for overall economic development, since the position in manufacturing was the exact opposite, with high import content and low exports. The growth of manufacturing was only possible, therefore, because the balance of payments was supported on this massive scale by the exports of gold.[13]

A further sense in which mining was a critical force for development that could not otherwise have occurred was through its contribution in taxes and royalties to government revenue. These taxes on the gold mines were discriminatory, in the sense that they were levied at special rates not applicable to other industries, and were massively increased in 1933 when the state moved to appropriate part of the windfall gains from devaluation by introducing an excess profits duty. Two years later a further gold profits surtax was imposed on the profits of the gold mines. By 1936, total government receipts from mining were approximately twelve times larger than in 1913, whereas the value of the gold produced and the dividends declared had only doubled. It was revenue raised from the gold mines that enabled the state to give huge sums to other sectors, especially the white commercial farmers, with an array of subsidies, relief grants, capital works, and loans.

---

[13] See Chapters 6 and 8 for further discussion of this issue.

Mining gave further vital assistance to industry when from 1925 a system of protective tariffs was brought in with the explicit aim of promoting the expansion of manufacturing, a policy discussed more fully in Chapter 6. The tariff raised costs to the mines, to a very slight extent by directly raising the price of stores purchased, though most materials used by the mines were deliberately exempt from duty, but more substantially indirectly, by making it necessary to increase salaries and wages for white workers to offset the effect on the cost of living. Similarly, they effectively subsidized agriculture because the state-owned railways charged higher rates on goods carried for the mines in order to offset lower freight charges for products brought to, or taken from, farms. Their charge on mining machinery, for example, was almost double that on agricultural machinery. The ability of mining to shoulder these extra burdens was thus essential to the success of the government's policies to promote industry and commercial agriculture.

Finally, mining was a powerful magnet attracting foreign capital to South Africa from Europe and the United States. In addition to the large sums invested directly in the gold mines, their prosperity and fame helped to attract capital, entrepreneurs, and skilled labour to other industries. As the economy developed, the relationship between mining and other sectors deepened. The giant mining houses had always had some industrial interests, largely related to their needs for items such as chemicals and explosives, but after the Second World War the nature of their involvement increased dramatically. A massive programme of diversification of their investments was a major force behind the modernization and mechanization of industry, and the mining groups were a substantial source of funds, technical expertise, and managerial skills for manufacturing and other sectors.

Exploitation of African mine-workers

Gold was thus the export staple that enabled South Africa to break free from the constraints which had for so long held back its economic development, and gold was the source of the riches on which other sectors were able to draw. But all these benefits were only possible because of the structure of legislation and conventional discrimination built on the past conquest and dispossession of black people. This enabled the mining companies to force African wages down, and to hold them for many decades at minimum subsistence levels. The ways in which this was achieved were described in Chapter 3, and the consequences for black wages were demonstrated in Table 3.3. The indispensable part played by this extreme exploitation of the African workers was widely acknowledged, both within the

Table 5.5. *Impact on dividends and taxes of a hypothetical adjustment to wages of black workers, 1911 and 1931*

	(1) 1911	(2) 1931
	(£ million)	
Actual allocation of total revenue		
Stores, other costs, etc.	11.5	18.8
Cash earnings of white workers	8.6	8.7
Cash wages of black workers	5.8	7.3
Dividends	8.1	8.1
Taxation	1.2	3.4
Total revenue	35.1	46.2
Hypothetical adjustment to dividends and taxes		
As above	9.3	11.5
After doubling cash wages of black workers	3.5	4.2
Per cent fall	62	64

Source: Data on allocation of total revenue from Wilson, *Labour*, pp. 159–60.

industry and by outside commentators. A calculation made in 1912 concluded that if the native labourers had been replaced by Europeans, 'the annual bill for unskilled workers would have been twice the value of the production and six times the net profit'.[14]

However, it can easily be claimed that this *reductio ad absurdum* was too extreme: it is not normal in any country to pay skilled and unskilled workers at the same rate. Instead a more reasonable calculation can be made, for which it is assumed that average cash wages for unskilled African mine-workers were merely doubled. This would still have left them below one-fifth of those paid to white workers, a markedly greater differential than is normal elsewhere.[15] The data used for this hypothetical calculation are set out in the upper part of Table 5.5, which shows the allocation of the aggregate revenue of the gold mines for 1911 and 1931, two representative years before the increase in price that followed devaluation in 1932. It is then shown in the lower panel that doubling the cash wages of black workers would have cut total profits (dividends and taxation) by well over 60 per cent. In principle, it would also have been

[14] D. W. Gilbert, 'The economic effects of the gold discoveries upon South Africa', *Quarterly Journal of Economics*, 47, 1933, p. 579.
[15] The issue of comparative skill differentials is discussed more fully in Chapter 6.

possible for the mining houses to increase black wages by cutting those of white workers, but this option was effectively ruled out by the political power of the white miners described in Chapter 4.

The impact on profitability of this hypothetical increase in African wages can be assessed in the light of Frankel's calculation that the net rate of return to the gold mines over the period 1887–1932 averaged 4.1 per cent (including capital gains), and was thus broadly in line with the rate earned elsewhere in a competitive international capital market.[16] It can be concluded, therefore, that foreign and domestic investors would certainly not have made capital available to South Africa on the scale required if the return on the investment had been reduced to anything like this extent. Furthermore, this aggregate calculation combines mines with varying proportions of high- and low-grade ore, and many individual mines with a larger proportion of low-grade ore would have been even worse off.

It thus seems clear that for a period of some five decades from the beginning of mining to devaluation in 1933, the industry as a whole would not have survived if obliged to pay its black workers even the modest improvement assumed in this exercise. Higher wages for black miners were simply not consistent with minimum levels of profitability, and production could not have been sustained except on a small minority of mines with the richest seams. The need to hold down black wages became even more essential after the 1926 Mines and Works Amendment Act (discussed in Chapter 4) restricted the ability of the mines to displace semi-skilled or skilled white labour by black labour. If this had been permitted, the companies could simultaneously have reduced their total labour costs and increased African earnings, but the opposition of the white working class and the changed political situation after the 1924 general election made this impossible. Some limited increase in earnings for unskilled black workers might have been granted after the windfalls in 1933 and 1934, but this was not done, partly because the industry was by that stage firmly in command of its labour supplies and could recruit all the workers it needed, partly because it would have been seen as a hostile act by other sectors, as well as by the government that wished to promote the development of those sectors.

Economic historians are familiar with an impoverished standard of living for the mass of the labour force as a feature of initial periods of industrialization; for example in the United Kingdom in the late eighteenth and early nineteenth centuries, in the United States in the

---

[16] S. H. Frankel, *Investment and the return to equity capital in the South African gold mining industry*, Oxford: Blackwell, 1967, p. 27.

late nineteenth century, or in Soviet Russia under Stalin in the 1930s. But in South Africa the incidence of this burden was grotesquely distorted and magnified by racialism, so that a disproportionate share of the burden was borne by the black workers. This fundamental inequity must be seen, therefore, as an indispensable element in the process by which gold made possible the growth and transformation of the South African economy.

6 Transforming the economy: the rise of manufacturing and commercial agriculture

The growth of diamond and gold mining, described in the preceding chapter, proceeded at a remarkably swift pace. No encouragement was needed from the government and little assistance, apart from certain regulations designed to facilitate recruitment and employment of the necessary supplies of black labour at extremely low wages. The history of the expansion of manufacturing and commercial agriculture was utterly different, and the attempt to make these two sectors economically viable was a central concern of government economic programmes from the formation of the Union. Manufacturing was given protection from foreign competition; farming received extensive support and financial assistance over a sustained period. The first part of this chapter is devoted to the methods adopted to promote the development of the manufacturing sector; the second to the policies required to assist white farmers to sustain themselves on the land and to feed a steadily increasing urban population.

Factories are few and unimportant

Manufacturing was slow to start in South Africa and slow to develop. It was initially stifled by deliberate action of the VOC, which did not wish to see any production in the Cape that might compete with their factories in Holland.[1] Even after such restrictions were removed by the British there was little progress during the first three quarters of the nineteenth century. The urban commercial centres of the Cape and Natal were essentially trading entrepôts, where wool, hides, feathers, and other agricultural products brought in from the interior were exchanged for imported manufactured goods such as machinery, clothing, and household articles. By the mid-nineteenth century the industrial occupations in Cape Town, Grahamstown, Durban, and other towns were still almost

---

[1] See Chapter 2.

exclusively those of individual artisans: predominantly carpenters, masons, coopers, and smiths, together with the tailors, seamstresses, and cobblers who made and repaired clothing and shoes. There were a handful of small-scale craft workshops, such as those producing rough furniture, coaches, and wagons, but there were no factories. The railway workshop established at Salt River in Cape Town in 1859 can claim to be the colony's first industrial establishment, and more general factory production followed at a leisurely pace from the 1880s.

Progress everywhere was stimulated by the mineral discoveries in Kimberley and the Witwatersrand, but for several decades production of manufactures was still almost entirely restricted to processing local food and raw materials, and making simple clothing. Activities such as fruit canning, cigarette making, and garment manufacture were largely undertaken by women, while iron foundries, breweries, flour mills, brick-fields, soap and candle works, and tanneries provided jobs for men. Some of these industries enjoyed a limited measure of protection, as the accidental result of increased customs duties intended to provide more revenue for the two colonies, but there was no concerted policy to promote industrialization, either there or in the Boer republics.

Both skill and capital for more advanced development were lacking, and domestic markets were too restricted to support an efficient scale of production. The cash incomes of the great majority of people were too meagre to provide much purchasing power, and much of the population was rural and isolated. Most of the food and clothing consumed by white farm families, as well as articles such as soap and candles, were made at home by farmers' wives and daughters, while each farmer built and repaired his own wagon, and made his rough harness and boots; there was almost no market for factory goods. Despite the natural protection provided by costs of transport from Europe, local factories were unable to compete with imported articles, even those made with wool that might first have been shipped from South Africa. As noted in a report on the country in 1875, 'Formerly Graham's Town, too, had its cloth factory and hat factory, but it was found cheaper to import than to work up wool.'[2] Foreign industries thus continued to provide the bulk of the manufactured consumer goods and equipment required by the colonies. A few steam engines were at work in flour, sugar, snuff, and saw-mills, but water and animal power still played a larger role. When the first industrial census was taken in the Cape in 1891, only 327 establishments (out of some 2,000) employed steam or gas engines. Other activities listed

[2] J. Noble, *Descriptive handbook of the Cape Colony*, Cape Town: Juta, 1875, pp. 195–6.

in almanacs and blue books – such as wool-washing, fish-curing, blubber-boiling, and coffee pulping – can hardly claim to be part of the growth of manufacturing.

Developments in Natal and the two Boer republics moved even more sluggishly than in the Cape. At the beginning of the twentieth century it was observed that

A beginning has been made with manufacturing industry in the Transvaal, but as yet factories are few and unimportant. The great engineering works on the Rand have been called into existence by the requirements of the mines, and might more properly be considered as part of the mining industry. They are extensive and well-equipped; some of the workshops can turn out heavy machinery well made and well fitted, and all can execute repairs, make castings, and fit parts with efficiency and dispatch. But so far the great cost of skilled labour, and other items of expenditure, have made it impossible to compete with home and American industry in machinery manufacture.[3]

On the eve of the First World War manufacturing was still largely confined to the production of fairly basic consumer goods, produced by small-scale, labour-intensive processes, and of certain products – such as explosives and mining boots – required by the gold mines. It contributed only £15,000,000 to the country's GDP in 1913, less than 5 per cent of the total, compared with £60,000,000 from agriculture and £87,000,000 from mining. When external supplies were cut off during the First World War, a welcome stimulus was given to expansion of industries producing goods such as textiles, leatherware, and furniture, and local industries also benefited in these years from the exceptional rise in foreign prices associated with wartime inflation. Nevertheless, when the fighting was over and shipping resumed, manufacturing in South Africa remained a small and vulnerable sector, with strictly limited prospects for development.

The continued predominance of basic consumer industries, and of industries such as chemicals and metal-working with close links to the mines, is evident in the detailed structure of the manufacturing sector in 1924/5. Gross value in column (1) of Table 6.1 measures the value of the goods made and work done by each industry; net value in column (2) measures value added and is equal to gross value less the cost of materials, fuel, and power. The former is a broad indication of the size of an industry in terms of its sales (at factory prices), the latter is a better measure of its contribution to national income and of the sum available for wages, salaries, rent, and profits. In 1924/5, processing food, drink, and tobacco

[3] W. E. Bleloch, *The new South Africa, its value and development*, London: Heinemann, 1901, p. 236.

Table 6.1. *Composition of gross and net value of output in manufacturing by sector, 1924/5*

	(1) Gross value of output	(2) Net value of output
	(per cent)	
Light industry		
Food, beverages, and tobacco	46.1	32.4
Textiles, clothing, leather, and footwear	10.8	10.0
Wood and furniture	5.9	6.9
Paper, printing, and publishing	6.7	11.2
Other manufacturing	2.3	2.7
	71.8	63.2
Heavy industry		
Chemicals and chemical products	11.6	12.1
Pottery, glass, and other non-metallic mineral products	4.6	7.0
Basic metal industries	6.0	8.9
Metal products and machinery (incl. electrical)	2.5	3.3
Transport equipment	3.2	5.3
Rubber products	0.2	0.2
	28.1	36.8
Total manufacturing	100.0	100.0

Source: Union statistics, L-6 to L-33.

accounted for almost half of gross output, and light industries as a whole for almost three-quarters. The contribution of food, drink, and tobacco to net output was significantly lower, indicating the large share of raw materials in the value of the articles produced. Among heavy industries, the production of metals, metal products, machinery, and transport equipment (mainly work done in railway workshops) was responsible for only 12 per cent of gross output, though for almost 18 per cent of net output.

The state, tariff policy, and the rise of manufacturing industry

As soon as the Union government and its advisers started to ponder what might be done to promote the more rapid development of manufacturing, their thoughts turned to protective tariffs. This was not a new idea: factories for the manufacture of matches and soap had been established with tariff protection in the Transvaal by the late 1890s. When the Cullinan Commission was appointed in 1910 to investigate whether it was feasible to develop local manufacturing, it recommended that industry should be given protection subject to certain conditions:

> The Commission has, in many instances, been asked to recommend prohibitive rates of duty, but its aim is not to coddle but to assist, by determining on the measures that should be taken to enable an industry to compete, provided it shows sufficient evidence of industrial efficiency ... The Commission has generally taken into account three factors, which it considers essential before any industry can be recommended for favourable consideration: (1) that a fair proportion of the raw material used is or can be obtained in the country; (2) that a fair percentage of white labour is employed; and (3) that there is a reasonable chance of the industry becoming established.[4]

The *Report* is interesting for its early recognition of what was to be a recurrent theme of government commissions on industrial policy for the next sixty years: the inescapable tension between providing protection and coddling inefficiency. The proposal to use the tariff to create employment for white workers is also noteworthy.

The outcome of the *Report*, the Customs Tariff Act of 1914, gave a moderate measure of protection to certain products, but was essentially a victory for supporters of free trade, led by the Chamber of Mines. The revenue bias of the Act is shown by the fact that at least 120 out of some 193 items of that tariff were either admitted free of duty or at only 3 per cent if not from the United Kingdom.[5] The mining companies had consistently opposed the establishment of local industries if that could only be done behind tariff walls which would increase costs of production on the Rand, and they were strongly supported in their anti-tariff campaign by merchants and traders who stood to lose from any curtailment of imports. In 1923, when the Board of Trade and Industries again suggested increased tariffs, it drew only a half-hearted response from the Smuts government, which was reluctant to introduce a full-scale policy of protection in the face of continued opposition from mining and commercial interests.

From 1924, however, the situation was radically altered by the election of the Pact government of the National and Labour parties. They immediately introduced a policy designed to promote industrial development,

---

[4] Commission on Trade and Industries (Cullinan), *Report*, p. 13.
[5] Board of Trade and Industries, Report No. 282, *Investigation into manufacturing* (Pretoria, 1946), para. 325.

and this was continued by the coalition and fusion ministries which held office from 1933 to 1939.[6] The growing scale of poverty among *bywoners* and other white families who had no prospects in the rural areas, and were drifting into the towns in large numbers, was one powerful motive for such a policy.[7] The Pact government drew much of its political support from this group of people, and from fellow Afrikaners who sympathized with their plight, and there was strong pressure to create jobs for them. The reservation of existing jobs in the public and private sectors for white workers – by means of the colour bars and 'civilized' labour policies described in Chapter 4 – could help to alleviate the poor white problem, but was not by itself sufficient. It was also necessary to create *new* jobs, and the government recognized that this could best be done by encouraging expansion of secondary industry. Manufacturing could employ a much higher proportion of white workers than mining because of its greater need for semi-skilled or skilled labour which could be reserved for white men and women; perhaps 40 per cent of its labour force would be white, compared with only 10 per cent on the gold mines. It was, for example, white Afrikaner females from rural backgrounds who provided most of the labour for the developing food, textile, and clothing industries.

There were also two other strong motives driving the new policy. General Hertzog, the leader of the National Party – and from 1924 Prime Minister – was an ardent Afrikaner nationalist, and a sovereign and independent South Africa was among his highest priorities. He believed that a robust, self-sufficient, industrial base would promote this and help to weaken the position of the mining companies, whose directors and shareholders he suspected of being more sympathetic to foreign interests. The government also recognized that mines were a 'wasting asset' which would ultimately become exhausted, so that it was necessary in the long run to replace them as a major primary source of production, employment, and government revenue. Given the unsatisfactory state of agriculture, only manufacturing had the potential to do this. 1924 thus marks a critical turning point in the history of manufacturing in South Africa.

---

[6] The National Party under Hertzog and the South African Party under Smuts entered into a coalition agreement for the general election in 1933. They then merged to form the United Party in December 1934, with Smuts agreeing that his former rival, Hertzog, should be leader of the new party and Prime Minister. Unity continued until September 1939, when the party split over the issue of South Africa's participation in the Second World War. Smuts obtained a majority for his view, became Prime Minister, and took the country into the war on the side of the United Kingdom.

[7] See Chapter 4, pp. 83–5 for a discussion of the factors responsible for the emergence of the 'poor white' problem.

The central element in the policy of industrial development adopted by the new government was tariff protection to promote import substitution. The main concern of previous tariffs had been to provide additional revenue for the state; this one was deliberately aimed at protection for industry. The tariff would be set at a level that would raise internal prices until it became profitable for industries to manufacture certain products in South Africa which had previously been imported. In its general features, the policy followed many other developing economies in invoking 'infant industry' arguments for protective tariffs. These included both early industrializers, for example the United States and Germany, and also latecomers such as Russia, Canada, Australia, and Argentina. What was unique to South Africa was the attempt to link this to policies designed to create employment specifically for one group in the labour force, those of European descent.

A revised Customs Tariff Act was passed in 1925 to give effect to the new programme. Industries already protected from foreign competition by earlier tariffs were granted additional protection, and new industries were added to the list. The broad policy was designed to avoid increases in customs duty on capital goods or on the materials required for farming and mining, but mining could not avoid the indirect costs of the general rise in wages and prices caused by the tariff. An attempt was also made to exempt from duty those imported raw materials and semi-manufactures that were needed for a range of manufacturing products, such as leather for footwear, timber for furniture, and steel for machinery. The policy initiated by the Pact government was maintained throughout the inter-war period, and at the end of the Second World War it was stated that 'The policy of protection inaugurated in 1925 has been continued ever since and, except in the case of industries supplying mining and agricultural requirements, the vast majority of existing industries in the Union enjoy protection to a greater or lesser degree.'[8]

The 1925 Act also gave a reconstituted Board of Trade and Industries wide powers and advisory duties for the protection of secondary industry, and the board played a major part in the implementation of the 'civilized' labour policy. Special clauses were introduced to penalize industries that 'maintained unsatisfactory labour conditions', a euphemism for failure to give preference to white employees, or that failed to meet other conditions laid down, including job creation. They could lose the customs duty rebates on certain of their raw materials, and could also be excluded

---

[8] Board of Trade and Industries, Report No. 282, *Investigation into manufacturing*, para. 329.

from the list of firms approved to tender for orders from the government and railways.

Protection was the most wide-ranging of the policies inaugurated by the Pact government and continued by its successors, but it was only one aspect of the growing role played by the state in relation to the functioning of the economy:

Though the economic system has remained dependent on private enterprise, the conditions under which the individual has been allowed to operate have been closely controlled by the fiscal and monetary powers of the State, by public regulation of wages and labour conditions, by the control of agricultural marketing, and by means of State ownership and control of the principal means of transport.[9]

State ownership of the railways was followed in 1923 by the establishment of the Electricity Supply Commission (ESCOM) to operate and expand electricity supply undertakings. The government then took the significant decision to intervene more directly in industry by the creation in 1928 of an Iron and Steel Industrial Corporation (ISCOR), designed to exploit South Africa's rich resources of coal and iron ore. These two major public corporations, producing electricity and steel, would thus provide two of the essential requirements for a more mature pattern of industrialization.

There had been a number of early attempts, both before 1910 and in the early 1920s, to develop a South African iron and steel industry using local materials, but they were effectively defeated by the scale of the investment required. Hertzog's government attached considerable importance to reducing the country's dependence on imports for 'every bit of iron and steel used', and also believed that this could be done at a lower cost, so that the new works 'would immediately stimulate the creation and establishment of other industries in this country which use steel for their raw materials'. It recognized that this would only happen if there were a major long-term investment by the state:

Further, it is clear that if the establishment of such a works was not going to be postponed into the indefinite future, if we were not going to be content with simply making steel out of scrap or with tentative experiments in making pig iron, that you must have ample capital resources, and the history of the matter showed that it would only be by the Government themselves stepping in and cutting this Gordian knot and providing the security of Government interest and a substantial amount of the financial responsibility.[10]

---

[9] Industrial and Agricultural Requirements Commission (Van Eck), *Third Interim Report*, para. 130.

[10] House of Assembly, *Debates*, 1927, col. 521, speech of the Minister of Defence moving the second reading of the Iron and Steel Industry Bill. The corporation was established

The original expectation was that the public would subscribe for a substantial part of the capital, but when they failed to do so the shares were taken by the government, so that the corporation was effectively owned by the state. This establishment of a state corporation to produce steel was a bold and far-sighted move for a conservative government. They had to face accusations of advancing 'in a socialistic, even a Bolshevistic, direction', as well as savage criticisms from academic economists who assailed the 'hopelessly uneconomic' performance of ISCOR in its early years, when there was worldwide excess capacity in steel plants, and steel could be imported very cheaply.

The massive project was based near Pretoria, in close proximity to large deposits of high-grade iron ore and coal, and also to the principal market for ISCOR's output on the Witwatersrand. It included coke ovens, blast furnaces, by-product plants, and rolling and sheet mills, and produced the first steel in 1934. After an initially difficult period, in which its labour costs were unnecessarily increased by the decision to 'man the works with white labour', it was eventually successful and made a major contribution to the development of secondary industry. By the early 1940s additional capacity was needed, and a new site with scope for substantial expansion was selected in Vereeniging, close to the Vaal River. In 1940 ISCOR produced 320,000 tons of steel and met about one-third of the country's requirements; by 1950 this had increased to over 600,000 tons, almost half of the steel used in South Africa.

Expansion of industrial output and employment

The progress of the industrial sector – broadly defined to cover all private and government undertakings (including railway workshops) in manufacturing, construction, and electricity, gas, and steam supply – can be traced in Table 6.2 for selected years from 1916/17 (the earliest year for which consistent data are available) to 1948/9. The level of gross output is shown in column (1), and a rough measure of the movements in the volume of output (after elimination of the effect of changes in price) is given in column (2). Columns (3) to (5) show the number of wage and salary workers.

Output growth continued strongly until 1929, but then fell sharply as secondary industry was hit by the international depression. The impact on South Africa of the worldwide decline in output, employment, and prices was aggravated during fifteen months when the Union remained

in 1928 and commenced production in 1934. For the economists' critique, see C. S. Richards, *The iron and steel industry in South Africa with special reference to ISCOR*, Johannesburg: Witwatersrand University Press, 1940.

Table 6.2. *Output and employment in industry, 1916/17–1948/9[a]*

Census year[b]	Gross value of output		Number of employees			(6) White as % of total
	(1) At current prices	(2) At 1938/9 prices[c]	(3) Total	(4) White	(5) Black	
	(£m)		(000s)			
1916/17	49.5	39.4	124	46	78	37.2
1924/5	84.2	66.7	192	71	121	37.1
1929/30	111.8	98.1	218	91	127	41.6
1932/3	91.0	91.4	192	87	105	45.3
1938/9	199.6	199.6	352	145	207	41.1
1948/9	674.6	402.2	668	228	440	34.1

[a] Private, municipal, and government undertakings (including railway workshops)
employing three or more workers in manufacturing and construction, and electricity, gas,
and steam.
[b] A census year, for example 1924/5, covers data reported by firms on the basis of their
financial years ending on any date between 1 July 1924 and 30 June 1925. On average the
results reported for 1924/5 are likely to refer mainly to the calendar year 1924, and so on.
[c] This measure of the volume of production was obtained by dividing column (1) by the
Bureau's index of the price of manufactured articles, constructed on the basis of a sample of
manufactures (covering about 60 per cent of total output) for which separate information
was available on both quantities and values.

Source: Year Book, 22, 1941, pp. 853 and 862, and 27, 1952–3, p. 980.

on the gold standard after the depreciation of sterling and other currencies. The direct impact on manufacturing of the relative appreciation of
the currency was limited by the small proportion of output that was sold
outside the Union, but the sector could not avoid the substantial indirect
effects of the severe decline in farm incomes and of the collapse in world
demand for diamonds.[11] Between 1929/30 and 1932/3 the value of output plunged by 19 per cent in nominal terms, and the volume by 7 per cent.
The highly discriminatory impact of the 'civilized' labour policy is
also very evident. In the period of growth to 1929/30, employment of
white workers increased by 20,000 but that of black workers by only
6,000, while in the recession only 4,000 white employees lost their jobs
compared with 22,000 black employees. The share of white employees

[11] The collapse of exports of agricultural and pastoral products from an annual average of
£28m in 1925–9 to only £16m in 1930–4 can be seen in column (1) of Table 5.2. The
corresponding figures for diamond exports in column (2) are £10m and £3m per annum.

reached its high point during the depression, at 45 per cent of the industrial labour force.

From the beginning of 1933 circumstances changed dramatically. Manufacturing was swept forward by the remarkable surge on the Witwatersrand that followed the increase in the price of gold discussed in Chapter 5. This boom in gold mining reinforced the continuing assistance from the tariff, and South African industry made a rapid escape from the Great Depression. The currency devaluation helped industry's competitive position by raising the relative price of imported manufactures, although complementary imports of manufactured materials became more expensive. The development of industry also enjoyed the benefits of a cumulative process of expansion. As output expanded, unemployed or low-paid workers were absorbed by industry, incomes increased, and a larger proportion of the population moved to the towns. The more incomes rose and the urban share of the population increased, the more industry gained from higher demand for its products. By 1938/9 the volume of output was more than double its previous peak level in 1929/30, and employment had increased over the same period by 60 per cent. A small white population could no longer supply a disproportionate share of the increased demand for industrial labour, and 102,000 additional black employees were recruited between 1932/3 and 1938/9, against a rise of only 58,000 in the number of white employees.

The Second World War then provided a further powerful stimulus to local industry, and this time, after its vigorous growth in the 1930s, South Africa was in a much better position to capitalize on the forced withdrawal of foreign competition than it had been in 1914–18. Manufacturers responded vigorously to the opportunities created by wartime shortages of imported products, and to the new demands made by South Africa's war effort, so that the volume of output (at constant 1938/9 prices) doubled from nearly £200,000,000 in 1938/9 to just over £400,000,000 in 1948/9 (see column (2) of Table 6.2). Light industry stepped up production in the drive to maintain supplies of food and clothing in the absence of goods from abroad, but the most significant development was the rapid expansion and changed character of the engineering industry. Before the war the industry was largely confined to jobbing and maintenance work, rather than large-scale standardized production, and had been described as a 'vast repair shop for the mines'. From 1939, however, the industry was transformed, and mass production techniques – which until then had been successfully kept out by white trade unions – were introduced, notably for munitions and electrical goods. Armoured vehicles, weapons, shells, and trucks were produced, using high-grade steel made by ISCOR; and a domestic machine tools industry was fostered by the rapid mechanization of the engineering industry.

The new administration under General Smuts continued its predecessor's policy of giving strong support to industrial expansion. The Industrial Development Corporation was established by the government in 1940. Its prime function was to 'facilitate, promote, guide and assist' the development of industry by private enterprise, and it was empowered both to make loans and to acquire shares. Resources were made available for the further expansion of ISCOR, and direct assistance was provided for private industry by building and financing additional premises for factories. The application of the protective tariff policy became 'more dynamic and positive', and there was a far-reaching shift in the way in which it was applied.[12] Instead of requiring an industry to demonstrate its potential by attaining a certain size before protection could be granted, the government announced that it was prepared to give an undertaking that tariff protection would be granted to a prospective essential industry if it complied with certain conditions stipulated in advance. Such assurances were given during and after the war to a number of industries, including agricultural implements, electric motors, the manufacture of yarn and cloth, pulp and paper, certain chemicals, and sheet glass. Furthermore, there was now a willingness to extend tariff protection to earlier stages of production, including materials processing and semi-manufactures. The authorities were also anxious to ensure that the progress made during the war years was not disrupted by the revival of foreign competition when trade resumed (as had happened after 1918), and from 1946 various amendments to the Customs Act were introduced specifically to prevent such imports.

Over the whole period covered by Table 6.2, from 1916/17 to 1948/9, the volume of output increased tenfold, an impressive rate of growth of 7.5 per cent per annum. If the period is divided in 1924/5, performance was only marginally more rapid after the election of the Pact government (at 7.8 per cent per annum) than it had been before (at 6.8 per cent per annum). The corresponding rate of increase in employment over the full period of thirty-two years was 5.4 per cent per annum. Employment of additional labour thus accounted for almost three-quarters of the increase in output, and an improvement in output per employee (labour productivity) for about one-quarter. The rate of growth of productivity was respectable but not exceptional at 2.0 per cent per annum, but that was to be expected given the initial emphasis on the 'poor white' problem

[12] A. J. Norval, *A quarter of a century of industrial progress in South Africa*, Cape Town: Juta, 1962, pp. 116–17.

and the need to create as many jobs as possible. However, there appears to have been a marked slow-down in the rate of growth of productivity during the war, with a decline in the rate of increase from just over 2.5 per cent per annum until 1938/39 to a bare 0.5 per cent per annum across the war years. This probably reflects the need to adopt labour-intensive techniques because of the inability to acquire machinery and equipment from abroad, as well as the change in the composition of the labour force noted below.

The overall change in the composition of net output by industry is set out in Table 6.3, with the data for 1924/5 reproduced from Table 6.1 for ease of comparison with those for 1948/9. By the latter date, heavy industry had expanded to roughly equal parity with light industry. The share in net output of the largest consumer goods sector – processing food, drink, and tobacco – fell by 13 percentage points, from 32 to 19 per cent, and there was also a sharp decline in the contribution of paper, printing, and publishing. The only light industry that raised its relative share was textiles, clothing, leather, and footwear, with an increase from 10 to 15 per cent. The heavy industries that expanded most rapidly relatively to the rest of the manufacturing sector were production of basic metals (especially iron and steel), which doubled its share of net output from 9 to 18 per cent, and transport equipment, which increased from 5 to 8 per cent.

This growth in the output of secondary industry before and during the Second World War was accompanied by substantial changes in the character and structure of production. A substantial increase in the size of firms between 1916/17 and 1948/9 was reflected in a twofold increase in the average number of employees per establishment (from 23 to 46), and a fourfold increase in average gross output per establishment (from £7,400 to £28,000 at constant 1938/9 prices).[13] There were advances in the technical level of industry, but additional investment in buildings, plant, and machinery only marginally outpaced the rise in employment, so that total capital per worker was 15 per cent higher in 1948 than in 1924.[14]

Within the still severe confines of the limited size of its domestic market, South African industry had embarked on the momentous

---

[13] Based on data in columns (2) and (3) of Table 6.2 and figures for the number of establishments from *Year Book*, 21, 1940, p. 875, and 27, 1952–3, p. 973.

[14] Based on data for numbers employed from column (3) of Table 6.2 and the net stock of fixed capital in manufacturing at constant 1938 prices, from D. G. Franzen and J. J. D. Williers, 'Capital accumulation and economic growth in South Africa', in R. Goldsmith and C. Saunders (eds.), *The measurement of wealth*, Income and Wealth series VIII, London: Bowes & Bowes, 1959, p. 313.

Table 6.3. *Composition of net value of output in manufacturing by sector, 1924/5 and 1948/9*

	(1) 1924/5	(2) 1948/9
	(per cent)	
Light industry		
Food, beverages, and tobacco	32.4	19.0
Textiles, clothing, leather, and footwear	10.0	15.2
Wood and furniture	6.9	6.4
Paper, printing, and publishing	11.2	7.7
Other manufacturing	2.7	3.4
	63.2	51.7
Heavy industry		
Chemicals and chemical products	12.1	9.5
Pottery, glass, and other non-metallic mineral products	7.0	6.0
Basic metal industries	8.9	17.6
Metal products and machinery (incl. electrical)	3.3	5.0
Transport equipment	5.3	7.8
Rubber products	0.2	2.4
	36.8	48.3
Total manufacturing	100.0	100.0

Source: Union statistics, L-6 to L-33.

transition from small-scale craft workshops to large-scale factory production. The former system was characterized by skilled artisans working alone or with one or two assistants – exemplified by craftsmen such as those in clothing and shoemaking or in the furniture trades – producing non-standard individual items, with little or no division of labour. They decided what was to be produced, created any necessary designs, selected the appropriate materials, undertook every part of the actual work of making the product, and – if it was not a bespoke item – found a buyer. If they used machinery, for example the sewing machines that were available to tailors and dressmakers, it was entirely under their control, as were the pace of production and the length of the working day.

In total contrast, the characteristic feature of the factory system of mass production that progressively replaced this was that the workers acted on orders from managers or supervisors; they did not make decisions. In its extreme form this system culminated in the system of continuous flow production and the assembly line associated with Henry Ford and the automobile industry. South Africa had not yet reached this level by 1948, but large-scale, factory production of completely standardized items, and more extensive division of labour, had been gradually introduced into a wider range of industries, with each stage of the production process broken down into limited, repetitive, specialized activities. The transformation began in the 1920s in consumer goods industries such as clothing, leather, and furniture making, and was extended during the war years to the engineering and metal working industries. A start had been made, but there was still a long way to go.

It was a development of potentially huge importance in the context of South Africa's racially segmented labour force. It would progressively erode the need for highly skilled workers that had originally underpinned the special position of white artisans, and enhance the opportunities for black workers to move from unskilled to semi-skilled occupations. The process accelerated during the war years, when large numbers of skilled white workers left industry for the armed forces, causing acute shortages of labour. Employment of black workers outstripped the increase in white labour, with a steady shift of the former into semi-skilled and skilled jobs, and by 1948/9 the share of white employees in the total industrial labour force had fallen sharply to 34 per cent. This was below its level in 1924/5.

A sample of some 300,000 workers covered by wage determinations made by the Wage Board from 1937 to 1956 showed that 16 per cent of the skilled and 72 per cent of the semi-skilled workers were black. The latter were subdivided into 42 per cent African, 20 per cent coloured, and 10 per cent Indian.[15] Among the occupations in which Africans were increasingly employed, especially in the Transvaal and Natal, were machine minders, spinners, weavers, and carders in the textile industries, and operators of motor vehicles, bulldozers, mechanical shovels, and tractors. Coloured people in the Cape and Indians in Natal were employed in semi-skilled and skilled occupations in the textile and clothing, food, tobacco, building, leather, printing, and furniture industries.

Faults in the foundation

Superficially the expansion of secondary industry thus appeared to have made excellent progress, and much quiet satisfaction was derived from contemplation of statistics such as those in Tables 6.2 and 6.3. Beneath

---

[15] Department of Labour, *Report for the year ended 31 December 1955*, pp. 29–30. The data relate to the time at which each investigation was made by the board, and exclude determinations in respect of general unskilled labour.

the surface, however, there were significant faults in the foundation, and if not controlled these would in time undermine the prospects for future development. The two critical structural weaknesses were the small size of the domestic market for manufactured goods and the low level of efficiency of local industry.

The fundamental source of both problems was the context in which manufacturing was expected to operate. As previous chapters have demonstrated, during the late nineteenth and early twentieth centuries, an economic system rooted in discrimination and inequality was created by and for white farmers, and was carried over into mining. Its core elements included an array of pressures – notably alienation of land, rural poverty, pass laws, taxes, denial of basic human rights, and, on the mines, the compound system – that compelled black workers to sell their labour for exceptionally low wages. The critical issue that emerged for South Africa was whether such a low-wage, low-productivity system could also be an appropriate basis for the expansion of secondary industry.

As long as the economy was dominated by farming and mining, this vital question could be ignored, particularly as the economic interests of these two sectors were strongly reinforced by the perceived sociopolitical interests of a majority of white voters. However, economic conditions were changing, and the importance of the two primary sectors was steadily shrinking, while that of secondary industry (including construction, gas, and electricity supply) was rising. Columns (1) to (3) of Table 6.4 show the share of these three sectors in GDP at current factor cost at selected dates; column (4) gives the ratio of industry to agriculture and mining. In 1911 the contribution of industry to GDP was only 12 per cent of the combined contribution of the two primary sectors; by 1938 it was over 54 per cent, and by 1948 it was almost 90 per cent. But the interests of gold mining, on which the past had been built, and of manufacturing, on which the future would depend, diverged in two crucial respects.

First, their markets were completely different. There was a market abroad for every ounce of gold produced by the mines, so that they had no direct interest in the size and prosperity of the local market. For manufacturing, however, the domestic market was of critical importance, since the efficiency of most firms was too low for them to be able to compete successfully overseas. Furthermore, a larger home market would permit essential economies of scale. The low wages paid by the mines had a beneficial effect on their costs of production and profits, and there was no adverse impact on their market to be set against these gains. For manufacturing, however, one firm's gain from low wages was another firm's loss from a smaller market. Even if each individual capitalist thought the system worked to his or her advantage, the market for

Table 6.4. *Contribution of commodity production to gross domestic product,* [a] *1911–48*

	(1) Agriculture	(2) Mining	(3) Industry [b]	(4) Ratio of share of industry to share of agriculture and mining
		(per cent of GDP)		
1911	21.5	27.3	5.9	0.12
1918	24.2	18.0	9.7	0.23
1928	18.9	15.7	12.4	0.36
1938	12.7	18.3	17.0	0.55
1948	16.4	10.0	23.3	0.88

[a] GDP at factor cost at current prices.
[b] Manufacturing, construction, electricity, gas, and water.

Source: South African Statistics, 1992, p. 21.8.

manufactured products as a whole was restricted by the low incomes of the mass of the population.

The second difference was in the nature of their labour requirements. Profitable mining operations were based on large numbers of oscillating migrant black workers. Before the Second World War new recruits were sent underground without training; they were expected to acquire what skills they needed on the job. The companies could see no benefit from expenditure on training workers who were employed on short-term contracts and who would leave the mine after working for only twelve months or a little longer. There was some slight improvement in the approach to training during and after the war, but it was not until the 1960s that the mines started to take any serious interest in raising the skill levels of their black workers.

The labour requirements of manufacturing were very different. There was an increasing need in almost all branches for trained, adaptable, motivated workers who were able to exploit technical progress and achieve higher productivity. The greater the progress of industrial output and of global technology (from which South Africa acquired its techniques), the larger the need for skilled and semi-skilled labour, and the more difficult it would become to meet this from the restricted pool of white workers. What South Africa required was better general education for black workers, as well as specific training to enable them to improve their skills and undertake more specialized and complex tasks. Migrant workers, rapid labour turnover, and formal and informal colour bars preventing black labour from doing semi-skilled or skilled work were all totally inconsistent with this. The nature of industry's labour requirements thus went to the very heart of a social system rooted in migrant labour, pass laws, and rural poverty. If the country wanted a truly viable, self-supporting, industry it would eventually have to accept that fundamental changes in education, urbanization, and occupational mobility were required for the black labour force. This in turn would have far-reaching implications for their wages and purchasing power, and for their demands for social and political rights.

The two sectors also had different views about industrial relations, though this issue was not as crippling for industry as the first two. Mining companies were generally content to operate under a coercive system in which trade unions were illegal, and little attention needed to be paid to industrial relations. Many industrialists, on the other hand, appreciated the benefits of good industrial relations in terms of higher productivity and uninterrupted production, and could see the advantages that would accrue from trade union recognition and the creation of suitable procedures for negotiation with representative leaders.

Analysed in the light of these fundamentals problems of market size and productive efficiency, tariffs could offer only short-term gains for which they exacted a heavy long-term penalty. First, industries protected by the tariff were deprived of the vital spur to search for greater efficiency that only competition gives. Sheltered infant industries showed little sign of growing into economically viable adults, able to survive without protection. Second, the protection from foreign competition that tariffs afforded to certain industries directly raised costs for all those that purchased from the sheltered industries. An official commission which attempted to calculate the scale of this levy in the mid-1930s estimated that the minimum excess cost over free imports was equivalent to almost one-fifth of the value of the goods made behind tariff walls.

[I]t is clear that in various directions protected industries have, by increasing the level of costs in South Africa, impinged on economic industries, and reduced both the income derived from them and their capacity for employment. The balance between protected industries and industries which bear the cost of protection has been upset. It is our considered conclusion that ... protection of secondary industries by ordinary customs duties has reached the limit that the country can reasonably bear.[16]

---

[16] Customs Tariff Commission (Holloway), *Report*, 1936, paras. 28, 43–60; the value of the output of protected industries was estimated at £19.3m in 1933, and the costs of protection at £3.5m. The quotation is from para. 201 and was subject to a reservation regarding the need to avoid harming protected industries by withdrawal of protection.

However, the commission recognized the need to avoid harming industries already subject to protection, so that it might be necessary to 'grant more protection to a promising industry to safeguard what has already been built up'; and they were also very conscious that the exceptionally high wages paid to European workers were entirely dependent on the tariff. In the end they compromised by recommending the continuation of 'moderate' protection, equal to an *ad valorem* rate of 25 per cent.

In 1941 a substantive review of the *Fundamentals of Economic Policy in the Union* was published by the Van Eck Commission. They recognized the steady development achieved since the First World War, but again found that the bulk of the country's manufacturing structure was not self-supporting and depended on protection which they estimated was costing in the vicinity of £10,000,000 a year by 1939/40.[17] The commission considered that the high industrial cost structure was indicative of a low level of efficiency and an extensive need for rationalization, and urged that the state should not in the future make 'an indiscriminate use ... of customs duties, import restrictions, or other forms of assistance' as a means of promoting and accelerating the Union's industrial development. They also made the absolutely fundamental point that when gold mining declined (which they expected to happen by the early 1950s), industrial development could 'provide a substitute ... only if it is ultimately established on a self-supporting basis'.[18]

This was a long way from being achieved, however. Confined by its small scale and low efficiency to its protected home market, the manufacturing sector remained heavily dependent on foreign supplies for a large proportion of its manufactured and semi-processed materials such as iron and steel, cotton and woollen cloth, or electrical materials. The result was an enormous deficit in the balance of payments of the industrial sector. In 1938/9, for example, manufacturing spent almost £12 on imported materials for every £1 earned in exports.[19] The disproportion would be even more glaring if imported machinery and capital goods were included in the calculation. This huge imbalance could be sustained only as long as mining was able to earn the necessary foreign exchange. The country was thus in the deeply unsatisfactory position that South Africa's manufacturing industries could survive only as long as they were supported by the gold mines they were supposed eventually to replace.

---

[17] Industrial and Agricultural Requirements Commission (Van Eck), *Third Interim Report*, paras. 104 and 251–2.
[18] Ibid., para. 163. The forecast of the future of gold mining is in paras. 150–51.
[19] The value of imported materials for industry was £38.6m (out of a total £87.7m), and the value of exports of manufactures was approximately £3.2m; *Year Book*, 22, 1941, pp. 860–1, and *Union statistics*, N-4 and N-5.

Inefficiency, low wages, and skill differentials

How, then, should South Africa's industrial performance in the period from Union to the end of the Second World War be assessed? The countries which presented themselves as natural benchmarks against which South Africa could be measured were Australia, Canada, and New Zealand. All four had achieved their initial growth in the nineteenth century by exporting primary products from their farms, forests, and mines, and were seeking in the twentieth century to develop their secondary industries with the aid of protective duties. All four were relatively small, and struggling to compete with larger, well-established industrial nations such as Britain and the United States. Together they had resisted demands from Britain at the 1932 Imperial Economic Conference in Ottawa for a reduction in their tariff barriers that would enable the United Kingdom to increase its exports of manufactures at the expense of their fledgling industries. Each year the official South African *Year Book* provided the latest data on industrial performance in the four dominions and the results were not encouraging.

Those reproduced in Table 6.5 for 1938/9 reveal the chronic problems of inefficiency and low average incomes which were characteristic of South African industry. In that year net output per employee in manufacturing (in column (1) of the table) was only 70 per cent of the level attained in Australia and New Zealand, and less than 60 per cent of the Canadian figure. The much lower level of fixed capital per employee in column (2) was indicative of the extent to which South Africa lagged behind its competitors in the mechanization of industry, and helped to account for the poor standard of productivity. The large gap in average salaries and wages shown in column (3) – £131 in South Africa compared with a range from £189 to £226 in the other dominions – was a direct consequence of this low productivity; the share of profits in net output was broadly the same as in the other economies.

Moreover, for South Africa the average remuneration tells only a small part of the story. As can be seen in the last two lines of Table 6.5, where pay is distinguished by race, the average for white workers was £240 while that for Africans was only £47.[20] As with mining, the expansion of manufacturing in the inter-war and wartime periods was based on egregious discrimination against black workers. Table 6.6 shows a comparison of the average wage of skilled and unskilled male workers in the

---

[20] This comparison is not entirely accurate because the figure for Europeans includes salaried workers (which overstates the difference) and females (which understates it). A more reliable comparison covering male wage-earners only is given in Table 6.6.

Table 6.5. *International comparison of industry, 1938/9*

	(1) Net output per employee	(2) Fixed capital per employee[a]	(3) Salaries and wages per employee	(4) Wages as % of net output
		(£)		
Canada	457	1,120	226	49
New Zealand	366	750	217	59
Australia	360	490	189	53
South Africa	261	320	131	50
White			240	
African			47	

[a] Separate figures for plant and equipment only are not available for Canada, but the value per employee for New Zealand was £480, for Australia, £250, and for South Africa, £190.

Source: Year Book, 22, 1941, p. 863, and Board of Trade and Industries, Report No. 282, *Investigation into manufacturing*, Annexure G, p. 147. The average remuneration for all black employees was £55.

United Kingdom in 1935 with corresponding data for South Africa for manufacturing and mining. In the United Kingdom wages for all male unskilled workers were 69 per cent of those for skilled workers, and this is broadly in line with many other countries, where the ratio typically falls in a range from 50 to 75 per cent.[21] The ratio in South Africa was a completely different order of magnitude: about 18 per cent in manufacturing and 10 per cent in mining.

What had begun as a valid reflection of a scarcity of skilled labour, and an abundance of unskilled labour, was reinforced and rigidified by artificial barriers to mobility created by discriminatory legislation, the power of white trade unions, and social custom in the white polity. The result of these policies and practices was that levels of pay for skilled workers in South Africa were raised markedly above those elsewhere. The true disparity was not as large as the gap in nominal pay, because the cost of

---

[21] The Board of Trade and Industries, Report No. 282, *Investigation into manufacturing*, Annexure F, p. 156, gave an international comparison of hourly wage rates for male workers in industry in 1938, based on a different set of sources and procedures. According to these figures, the unskilled wage was 17 per cent of the skilled wage in South Africa, while in nine other countries the proportion was between 53 and 82 per cent. See also H. Phelps Brown, *The inequality of pay*, Oxford: Oxford University Press, 1977, pp. 70–4.

Table 6.6. *Skill differentials in United Kingdom and South Africa, 1935*

	(1)	(2)	(3)
	Average wage per male wage-earner		Ratio of unskilled
	Skilled/white	Unskilled/African	to skilled
	(£)		
United Kingdom (1935)			
Bricklayers and building labourers	176	131	0.74
Turners and engineering labourers	212	144	0.68
All male wage-earners	197	136	0.69
South Africa (1935/6)			
Industry[a]	240	42	0.18
Gold mines[b]	393	40	0.10

[a] Includes manufacturing, construction, electricity, and gas supply. The average for European male wage-earners was derived from the average for all European wage-earners, and data on the relative number of males and females in 1935/6, on the assumption that the ratio of female to male average wages was the same as in 1947/8 and 1948/9 (0.47), the first year for which this split was published.
[b] Includes cost of food for black workers.

Source: For the United Kingdom, G. Routh, *Occupation and pay in Great Britain, 1906–70*, 2nd edn, London: Macmillan, 1980, pp. 101, 115. For industry in South Africa, Board of Trade and Industries, Report No 282, *Investigation into manufacturing industries in the union of South Africa*, Annexure G, p. 147 (for average European wage, excluding salaries); *Union statistics*, G-8 (for relative numbers of male and female production employees); and *Census of industrial establishments, 1948/48 to 1949/50*, Table 15, pp. 116–7, 123–5 (for average male and female wages). For mining, Wilson, *Labour*, pp. 166, 169.

living was appreciably higher in South Africa, especially for manufactured goods. It is difficult to get a precise comparison of the difference in purchasing power, although the subject was investigated by several government commissions. One of the best of the available estimates – based on data for matched adult male artisans in building and engineering in Johannesburg and London – indicates that skilled workers in South Africa enjoyed a *real* advantage of the order of 10–25 per cent.[22]

There can be little doubt that the exceptionally high real wage paid to white employees exceeded their marginal product (the value of the output which each additional worker produced), or that this premium to which 'civilized' labour claimed entitlement was not paid from the profits of

[22] Economic and Wage Commission (Clay), *Minority Report*, para. 23.

employers, but from the already miserable wages of the mass of low-productivity black workers. The depressed wage of unskilled black workers was thus the principal source of the huge differential in remuneration for skill that was ubiquitous in South Africa.

Black workers in manufacturing were not only grossly underpaid; they were also – like their fellow workers in agriculture and mining – denied any share in the growing income of the new economy they were creating. In the report published in 1941, the Van Eck Commission cited the candid recognition by the Secretary of Labour (in his department's 1938 *Annual Report*) that 'the unskilled … did not secure that share of the increased prosperity of industry to which they were in equity entitled', and offered a succinct explanation:

Such a development is not in the least surprising if regard is had to the strong racial prejudice which pervades the Union, to the exclusion of Natives from the collective wage regulating system, and to the resulting practice by which in many industries Native wages are fixed by negotiation between representatives of the European trade unions and employers.[23]

It is thus not possible to present any simple assessment of the position of the South African economy at the end of the Second World War. It was clearly in a far stronger position than it had been in 1910. The new industrial policy introduced by the Pact government had initiated a significant move away from farming and mining, and laid the foundations for the development of a modern economy. Secondary industry had responded energetically to the opportunities for import substitution and expanded rapidly, attaining a higher technological level and producing a wider range of products. But the fundamental underlying weaknesses of the industrial sector had not been remedied. It was locked into the constraints of low wages and low productivity, it was preventing most of its population from obtaining training and exercising their skills, it was restricted by the limited size of its home market, and it remained totally dependent on gold mining to pay for its imported materials and capital goods.

The destruction of African farming and slow progress of commercial agriculture

While industry was bounding forward for some three decades at an impressive rate of 7.5 per cent per annum, commercial agriculture was

---

[23] Industrial and Agricultural Requirements Commission (Van Eck), *Third Interim Report*, paras. 111–2.

unable to increase its volume of output by more than a dismal 2.2 per cent per annum over the period from Union in 1910 to the end of the Second World War. Before examining the factors responsible for this poor performance it is necessary to consider why commercial agriculture was essentially confined to white farmers. One leading authority on the South African economy identified a fundamental cleavage in agriculture:

> [T]here may be said to be two different types of rural economies existing side by side in the same country. One is the essentially market-oriented farming, as practised by white farmers, and the other is the largely subsistence-oriented farming of African peasants in the reserves. The difference between the two is deep-seated and manifests itself in a variety of ways reflecting cultural differences and fundamental attitudes to the exploitation of the natural environment ... The white farmers are scientific and experimental in their approach, while the African is traditional, and even the few progressive individuals are hampered by the communal system of land tenure and other social restraints.[24]

This characterization is, however, significantly flawed by its complete omission of any reference to African farming outside the reserves, and by its failure to recognize the powerful role played by state policy, racial prejudice, and the economic self-interest of white farmers in deliberately stunting and stifling the commercial activity of African farmers.[25]

Even after Europeans gradually claimed title to most of the land of South Africa by the processes described in Chapter 2, substantial numbers of African farmers remained in occupation of European-owned land. Outside the Cape, the largest category were labour tenants, but they were subject to increasing pressure to reduce their own activity and increase the labour they provided for white farmers. Their cultivation and grazing rights were progressively reduced as farms rose in value, and the more the state assisted white farmers to acquire resources and techniques to cultivate their land more efficiently, the more farmers sought to restrict what they saw as its primitive and unprofitable use by Africans. The former labour tenants were gradually compelled to become wage labourers, and allowed at most token plots which could not provide a genuine basis for subsistence. They, or more commonly their children, increasingly moved away from the farms to find better paid and more attractive employment in mines and factories.

In the early 1920s appreciable numbers of sharecroppers also survived, and they typically farmed with great effort, enterprise, and skill. When the author of an oral history project interviewed Nkgono Mma-Pooe, the

---

[24] D. Hobart Houghton, *The South African economy*, 4th edn, Cape Town: Oxford University Press, 1976, p. 45.

[25] For conditions inside the reserves see Chapter 3, pp. 70–3.

widow of Naphtali, who had been a sharecropper in the northern Free State during and after the First World War, she referred to the white landowner, Theuns, saying of her husband:

Theuns would remark that he had at last got the real '*Vrystaatse mense*' (Free State people) – people who are used to work and did do proper farming wherever they came from. He would say that before anyone could wake up Naphtali's span [of oxen] was already in the fields with most part of a day's work behind him.

She also recalled the success Naphtali achieved in the early 1920s:

People in the neighbourhood of Lindequesdrif, other croppers, tenant-labourers, farm-owners and *bywoners*, black and white alike, talked about Naphtali's harvest. Many whites in fact remarked that Tol [the farmer] should be very pleased that he had engaged a cropper of Naphtali's ability. I remember Piet Smit, a white farmer from another section [of the farm] ... brought his own maize for threshing. His maize stack was far smaller than ours. We beat him by far.[26]

Sharecroppers were, however, always vulnerable to the demands of their landowners and to implementation of the provisions of the 1913 Natives Land Act. Naphtali and Nkgono were forced to move farms many times, and in 1939 he divided his crop with the farmer for the last time. After that he was unable to continue, but became a foreman, and was allocated only three acres of land for his own use. White farmers who thought that they could benefit from the labour and capital provided by Africans working on their land under contracts for 'farming on the half' would enter into such arrangements and continue them from year to year. But as soon as they decided that their interests were better served by farming all the land themselves, the contracts were terminated and the sharecroppers evicted. As this process of attrition continued through the post-1913 decades, it became progressively more difficult for Africans to survive as independent farmers, and the only terms on which they could do so became increasingly more onerous. Many families were unable to find a farmer who would permit them to occupy any land on which they could plant their seed or graze their animals.

Those few Africans who had the fortitude and fortune to survive on European-owned land as independent producers were subjected to extreme direct and indirect discrimination. They were explicitly denied all the many forms of financial and technical assistance – to be described below – that the state made available to European farmers. When they needed to acquire equipment they lacked access to capital and had great difficulty in obtaining credit. When they entered the market to sell their

---

[26] T. Matsetela, 'The life story of Nkgono-Pooe', in S. Marks and R. Rathbone (eds.), *Industrialisation and social change in South Africa*, Harlow: Longman, 1982, pp. 226–8.

produce they did so in an inferior position and subject to the hostility of European farmers who resented their competition. There were exceptions to this, as to any generalization, and a few white people were sympathetic and helpful. But overall it was a matter of deliberate and sustained policy by European farmers, and the government which they elected, that made commercial farming synonymous with white farming, not some aberrant cultural attitude on the part of Africans.

Even though white farmers enjoyed such a privileged position relative to Africans, conditions were not easy for them. The great difficulties which they faced with the closing of the pastoral frontier in the late nineteenth century were outlined in Chapter 4. Growing poverty forced many off the land, and those who remained battled against unfavourable natural conditions with inefficient techniques and inadequate facilities. Details of the problems of erratic and often inadequate rainfall, soil deficiencies, and insect pests are given in Annexe 2. The director of the Transvaal Department of Agriculture reflected in a paper written in 1908:

For various reasons the Europeans who settled in South Africa did not apply themselves to the development of the soil with the same zest and dogged determination that they had displayed in acquiring it ... Consequently, while agriculture was making such great strides elsewhere, here it moved so slowly as to appear almost stationary ... It may safely be asserted that there are few parts of the world occupied by Europeans which are so little understood from an agricultural point of view or in which farmers are exposed to so many risks and difficulties as South Africa, or where judged by the standards attained elsewhere ... agriculture is in such a backward condition.[27]

Conditions and practices were slow to change. In 1936, 33 per cent of the total working population of the Union (excluding casual farm labour and Africans in reserves) was dependent on farming but produced less than 12 per cent of the national income. As the Van Eck Commission observed, this disparity was 'striking evidence of the unremunerative position of the farming industry'.[28]

Deficient rainfall determined that only about 8 per cent of the total land area owned by Europeans could be used for arable farming (before the irrigated area was increased after the Second World War), and the remainder was suitable only for pastoral farming, mainly sheep. However, as can be seen from Table 6.7, the value of output produced by the sector in 1938/9 was more evenly divided between the two

---

[27] F. B. Smith, *Some observations upon the probable effect of the closer union of South Africa upon agriculture*, Pretoria: Government Printer, 1908, p. 4.
[28] Industrial and Agricultural Requirements Commission (Van Eck), *Third interim report*, para. 90.

Table 6.7. *Gross value of agricultural production, 1938/9*

	(1) £ million	(2) per cent
Field crops		
Maize	12.9	19.0
Wheat and other cereals	7.0	10.3
Fresh fruit	5.2	7.6
Sugar cane	3.5	5.1
Vegetables and potatoes	3.0	4.4
Vineyards	1.2	1.8
Other crops[a]	4.6	6.8
Total	37.4	55.0
Livestock products		
Animals slaughtered	12.1	17.8
Wool	8.0	11.7
Milk and dairy products	6.5	9.5
Poultry and poultry products	3.5	5.1
Other livestock products	0.6	0.9
Total	30.6	45.0
Total agricultural production	68.0	100.0

[a] Including hay, wattle bark, and tobacco.

Source: Union statistics, I-23 to I-25.

divisions. Over time the share of field crops increased slowly, largely as a result of the dramatic losses of stock in the 1930s. Maize was the principal cereal crop and was the staple diet for a large proportion of the population. In 1938/9 about 82 per cent of the total crop was produced by the commercial farming sector, about 8 per cent by Africans on white-owned land, and about 10 per cent by Africans in the reserves. The European producers were mainly concentrated in the 'maize triangle' in the northern Orange Free State and southern Transvaal (see further Annexe 2). Yields were persistently low by international standards, less than 40 per cent of those in the United States, 35 per cent of those in Australia, and 30 per cent of the level obtained in the Argentine.

The first agricultural schools and experimental farms were established in the Cape Colony in 1898, and together with agricultural extension services embarked on the long task of assisting farmers to raise their efficiency and to adapt their farming techniques so as to make the most of the unfavourable conditions. From the late nineteenth century farmers started on an extended process of installing windmill pumps, digging boreholes, erecting barbed-wire fencing, and introducing mechanization. The first two increased water supplies and enlarged the areas in which stock could be grazed; the fences had a beneficial effect on livestock farming, making it easier for individual farmers to introduce improvements and control grazing practices. Progress was made, but only very slowly; for example, by 1946 there were still only 20,000 tractors for 112,000 farms. Irrigation projects brought water to only a limited additional area of white-owned land. In the northern Cape, for instance, the Vaal-Haarts scheme irrigated 90,000 acres, and in the Transvaal a major government scheme, the Hartebeespoort Dam, provided 38,000 acres of irrigated plots. Despite these improvements, overall management of the land remained a cause for great concern. By 1944 an official enquiry was compelled to observe:

The march of veld deterioration, fertility depletion, erosion and desiccation over all parts of the country points unmistakably to the wide prevalence of unsound or exploitative farming in the Union today, farming which is ill-adapted to the natural controls and characterised by inefficient or abusive methods of using the land.[29]

Table 6.8 traces the pattern of growth and fluctuations in output and prices between 1910/11 and 1944/5. The livestock farmers suffered from a series of severe droughts in the 1920s, as grass disappeared from grazing lands and water resources dried up. From the mid-1920s farmers had to cope with the disastrous worldwide collapse in prices and markets during the Great Depression. The farm prices received by South African producers (columns (4) to (6) of the table) plunged by a staggering 56 per cent between 1924/5 and 1932/3, and were still 38 per cent below their earlier peak in 1938/9. The war years brought some relief by removing much of the competition from imported products, and there was also an increase in demand for certain foods, especially meat and dairy products, as a result of higher employment and incomes. Farm incomes and prices also benefited from lucrative bulk purchase contracts for food placed by the UK government. However, this was partly offset by the reduction in general exports caused by lack of shipping (see column (1) of Table 5.2), and by shortages of imported fertilizers and machinery. The cereal harvest also suffered from poor weather. The net effect of these various factors was that the volume of farm production increased at a rate of only 1.5 per cent per annum over the whole period from 1924/5 to 1945/6.

[29] Department of Agriculture and Forestry, *Report of the reconstruction committee*, 1944–5, para. 85.

Table 6.8. *Indices of output and prices of farm products, 1910/11 to 1945/6 (1936/7–1938/9=100)*

	Physical volume of production			Producers' prices		
	(1) Total	(2) Livestock products	(3) Field crops	(4) Total	(5) Livestock products	(6) Field crops
1910/11	47	53	43	101[a]	66[a]	119[a]
1924/5	74	74	80	150	182	133
1929/30	90	97	88	99	85	106
1932/3	80	100	57	66	52	74
1938/9	106	100	110	93	79	100
1945/6	103	112	94	170	118	197

[a] 1912/13.

Source: Union statistics, H-29 and I-27.

The persistent poverty and slow progress created strong economic and political pressures on the government to intervene in support of white farmers, and they responded vigorously. Academic economists, who were harshly critical of their policies, measured the scale and counted the mounting cost to the rest of the community. Richards listed eighty-seven bills passed by parliament between 1910 and 1935; almost all were designed to assist farming by such means as land acquisition, improvements such as irrigation, fencing, and dipping tanks, land grants, long-term loans from the Land and Agricultural Bank, short-term credit, scientific research, dissemination of information, and technical assistance.[30] Frankel calculated that over the same period the government raised over £71,000,000 in loans funds for agriculture and spent a further £41,000,000 from revenue. Farmers received export subsidies, interest subsidies, and rebates on railway rates; they were assisted to purchase seed and fertilizer; they were given grants for drought relief and rural unemployment.[31]

The collapse of world farm prices evoked a succession of schemes designed to maintain domestic prices for farm products above the levels set by world market conditions. Starting with sugar, and extending successively to include dairy products, wheat, maize, meat, and wool, these

---

[30] C. S. Richards, 'Subsidies, quotas, tariffs and the excess cost of agriculture in South Africa', *SAJE*, 3, 1935, pp. 371–3, gives the full list of titles of these acts.
[31] Frankel, *Capital investment*, pp. 119–20.

schemes typically imposed tariffs or restrictions on imports, paid subsidies or bounties on exports, withheld produce from the market, and fixed prices. This process of state intervention in support of the farmers culminated in the Marketing Act of 1937, which provided machinery for co-ordinating existing schemes and bringing new products under control. Boards were established to administer marketing control schemes for particular products. They could prohibit the sale of a product at a price other than the one they fixed, and were given monopoly powers over disposal of those products.

These boards were dominated by producers and had little regard for the interests of consumers; they attempted to raise prices by restricting output rather than by increasing efficiency. According to one estimate, in 1939–40 a sum of at least £7,500,000 was transferred to farmers from other sections of the community, and more than two-thirds of this amount was paid by consumers in the form of higher prices.[32] To an even greater extent than manufacturing, farming was so effectively protected from foreign competition that there was nothing to prevent such increases in prices. A large part of this burden was carried by black consumers of staple foodstuffs such as maize, milk, and sugar, even though their standard of living was so much lower than that of the white farmers who were the principal beneficiaries of this policy.

In terms of farm output and incomes there was not much to show for the effort and expenditure undertaken in the years from Union to 1945, and the inefficiency of commercial farming was severely criticized by individual economists and official commissions. However, despite the many problems and weaknesses that prevented rapid progress in the inter-war and wartime period, the foundations were greatly improved, and there was finally a basis for more rapid advance and modernization in the post-war years.

---

[32] Industrial and Agricultural Requirements Commission (Van Eck), *Third interim report*, para. 89.

7 Separating the races: the imposition of apartheid

This chapter and the following three chapters are devoted to the economic history of South Africa from the end of the Second World War until the transfer of power to the first democratically elected government in 1994. Both government and business embarked on post-war economic development with considerable optimism, and for a time the economy appeared to make excellent progress, aided by a booming world economy and exceptionally favourable conditions for the gold mines. However, even in these good years there were significant underlying problems, and from the early 1970s there was a drastic deterioration in performance. The primary aim of these final chapters is to analyse the background to, and reasons for, this transition from relatively successful growth to the abysmal economic record of the final phase, and to explore the latter's relationship to South Africa's distinctive economic and social system.

In order to set the record before and after the critical turning point in a clear perspective, the present chapter begins with an overview of the whole period from the end of the war to 1994, including a comparison of growth of real GDP per capita in South Africa and a sample of other countries. The following sections outline the apartheid policies of the new National Party government, focusing particularly on those with a direct bearing on the economy, especially the attempts to control urbanization and promote separate development. The final section examines some general propositions that were advanced in debates about the relationship between apartheid and the development of the economy.

From triumph to disaster – an overview of the post-war period

In the period following the Second World War, South Africa faced a fundamentally new challenge. The economic and political system that had evolved since the mid-nineteenth century had been designed to further the sectional interests of white agriculture and mining. It had

143

Table 7.1. *Contribution of commodity production to gross domestic product,*[a] *1948–70*

	(1) Agriculture	(2) Mining	(3) Industry[b]	(4) Ratio of share of industry to share of agriculture and mining
	(per cent of GDP)			
1948	16.4	10.0	23.3	0.88
1954	16.1	10.4	26.4	1.00
1960	12.4	12.7	26.6	1.06
1965	10.1	11.0	30.4	1.44
1970	7.9	9.0	30.8	1.81

[a] GDP at factor cost at current prices.
[b] Manufacturing, construction, electricity, gas, and water.

Source: South African statistics, 1992, p. 21.8.

successfully developed the gold mines, sustained commercial white farmers in an unpropitious environment, and assisted industry to make vigorous progress. Now the crucial question was: could this system continue to promote the expansion of an economy in which the contribution of mining was expected to diminish, and growth would have to depend predominantly on the ability to generate further and *more self-supporting* advances in manufacturing? By 1954 the industrial sector was responsible for over a quarter of GDP, and its contribution was as large as that of agriculture and mining combined (Table 7.1). Its relative importance continued to increase, while the share of agriculture declined sharply and that of mining remained broadly stable, so that by 1970 the industrial sector produced almost 31 per cent of GDP, 1.8 times the contribution of the other two commodity-producing sectors.

In the initial post-war period this transition did not seem to present any problem, in large part because an anticipated downturn in production of gold did not occur. In column (1) of Table 7.2, South Africa's performance from 1950 to 1973 is shown in international perspective, as one of a sample of thirty countries. Over this period, growth of real GDP per capita increased at a reasonable pace, accelerating to 2.2 per cent per annum (compared with 1.3 per cent per annum between 1913 and 1950) as South Africa participated in the remarkable worldwide upsurge in

Table 7.2. *Growth of gross domestic product per capita at constant prices, international comparison, selected periods, 1950–94 (annual percentage growth rates)*

	(1) 1950–73	(2) 1973–94	(3) 1973–83	(4) 1983–94
Japan	8.0	2.6	2.3	2.9
European (seven)	5.2	2.0	1.8	2.1
Other Asian (seven)	3.5	4.3	3.6	4.7
Latin American (six)	2.7	1.1	1.1	1.2
Dominions (three)	2.5	1.5	1.3	1.8
South Africa	2.2	−0.6	0.0	−1.2
Other African (five)	2.0	0.8	1.6	0.0
Total sample	4.0	2.0	1.6	2.2

Source: Maddison, *World economy*, pp. 185, 195, 215, 224, 276–9, 288–9, 304–5, and 322–6.

output and trade.[1] The rate was broadly in line with that of many other countries in the sample, though not nearly as good as that of Japan and other Asian and European latecomers, and well below the average of 4 per cent per annum for the sample as a whole.

In these decades there was thus no obvious indication of any incompatibility between satisfactory growth and the traditional character of the South African socioeconomic system. Within South Africa, the performance of the economy was hailed as a triumph. It was possible for sober economists to contemplate grand projections:

[I]f these rates could be maintained until the end of the century, South Africa would by then have the same per capita income as the United Kingdom has today, and this in spite of the fact that population numbers would have nearly doubled. The country would have become a major economic power. What is even more important is that poverty as a mass phenomenon among the Blacks would have largely disappeared as it did among the Whites in the 'thirties and 'forties.[2]

---

[1] For details of the composition of the sample of thirty countries, and some additional comments on international economic conditions in the two contrasting post-war phases, see Chapter 1, p. 3.

[2] S. P. Viljoen, 'The industrial achievement of South Africa', *SAJE*, 51, 1983, pp. 31–2. The only qualification noted was that 'present world conditions' might make it difficult to maintain a high rate of growth for the next two decades.

It was claimed by both right-wing supporters and left-wing critics of apartheid that the government's policies were helping to *boost* the rate of growth. As the table indicates, this was not the case. Apartheid did not enable South Africa to grow more rapidly than countries that did not have similar low-wage, labour-repressive economies, but neither did it prevent a successful performance.

But in the early 1970s triumph turned to disaster. Growth rates for real GDP per capita declined in almost all countries as the prosperity of the 'golden age' gave way to the years of 'stagflation', but – as column (2) of Table 7.2 demonstrates – South Africa's record was singularly inferior. For the sample as a whole, the average rate of growth from 1973 to 1994 was a slow 2.0 per cent per annum; for South Africa it was a disastrous –0.6 per cent per annum. It shared with Peru, Ghana, and Nigeria the distinction of being the only countries in the sample in which real GDP per head actually declined over the post-1973 period as a whole. Furthermore, while growth in most developed economies started to recover after the worst years of the slowdown at the beginning of this phase, South Africa's performance continued to deteriorate, and was markedly worse from 1983 to 1994 than from 1973 to 1983 (see columns (3) and (4) of the table). It was initially suggested by some commentators that the problem was simply a reflection of the wider downturn in the world economy, but before long it was realized that the crisis went far deeper, and was more directly related to distinctive features of South Africa's socioeconomic system.

Underlying this fall in per capita real GDP after 1973, was the decline in the rate of growth of real GDP, that is to say, of total output, not output per capita. The growth rates for the successive sub-phases are shown in Table 7.3 and the annual growth rates for both real GDP and population in Figure 7.1. It is evident that the fundamental problem was slower growth of the economy, not acceleration in the growth of population. The contrast between the earlier phase of rapid expansion of real output, from 1948 to 1973, and the dismal record after 1973 is very striking, with a deteriorating performance in all sectors of the economy. The average annual rate of growth of real GDP in column (6) crashed from almost 5 per cent between 1948 and 1973 to a miserable 1 per cent in the long final phase from 1981 to 1994.

The vital industrial sector (see column (4) of the table) was stagnant during those years, compared with a growth rate of 7 per cent in the earlier good years. In the mining sector, the poor growth rate reflected an abrupt fall (not just slower growth) in the physical quantity of gold produced (columns (2) and (3)). Many of the services – notably whole-sale and retail trade, transport and communications, and financial and

Table 7.3. *Growth of real gross domestic product by sector, 1948–94 (annual percentage growth rates)*

	(1) Agriculture, forestry, and fishing[a]	(2) Mining and quarrying	(3) of which gold	(4) Industry[b]	(5) Services	(6) GDP at factor cost
1948–64	2.8	5.8	5.9	6.5	4.0	4.9
1964–73	3.2	0.5	−0.6	7.6	5.5	4.6
1973–81	3.1	−0.5	−3.3	4.6	3.8	3.5
1981–94	0.7	−0.1	−0.9	0.0	1.8	0.8

[a] Centred three-year averages were used in place of annual data for this sector.
[b] Including construction and utilities.

Source: Calculated from data on gross value added by industry at constant 1995 prices, *South African statistics*, 2002, pp. 19.3–19.4.

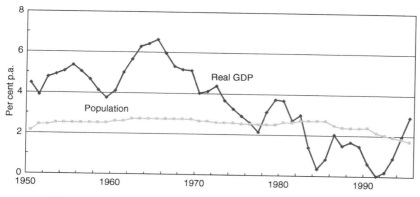

Figure 7.1. Growth rates of real GDP (five-year moving average) and population, 1950–95

Source: GDP: *South African Statistics*, 2002, p. 19.4.

business services – depend to a large extent on the growth of the primary and secondary sectors, and thus show broadly the same general pattern. The average annual rate of growth of the service sector as a whole first accelerated to 5.5 per cent from 1964 to 1973, but then fell away to less than 4 per cent in 1973–81 and dropped further, to below 2 per cent, in 1981–94. The growth of output in services in the final phase was thus markedly better than in mining and manufacturing, but the main contribution to this growth came from the expansion of government service and of social, communal, and personal services. Over 1,700,000 additional service jobs were created between 1975 and 1995 (see Annexe 3), but the bulk of these were in activities in which there were only limited possibilities for improvements in the rate of growth of output per head, and the services were unable to compensate for the poor performance of the rest of the economy.

Other symptoms of the worsening economic position included more rapid inflation, soaring unemployment, and a growing problem with the balance of payments. From 1948 to 1973 the average annual rate of increase of consumer prices had been reasonably stable at 3.5 per cent, but over the next two decades the rate accelerated to more than 13 per cent per annum. As the growth of output declined the number of unemployed increased. Previous complaints of labour shortages faded away and were replaced by the anguished cries of millions of South Africans who wanted work but were unable to get it. By the end of the apartheid era there were over 6,000,000 people of working age who were either unemployed or so discouraged that they had withdrawn from the formal labour market because they saw no hope of finding a job.

There was also a significant deterioration in the balance of payments. In the initial post-war decades South Africa was normally considered to be an attractive destination for foreign investors, and a substantial inflow of capital from abroad made it possible for the country to run a persistent deficit on its current account. This was the case from 1946 to 1959 and again from 1964 to 1973. The pattern was disrupted in the intervening years during the political crisis that followed the events at Sharpeville in 1960, when the police opened fire on a large crowd of predominantly unarmed Africans demonstrating against the pass laws, killing 69 and wounding 178, the great majority shot in the back as they were running away. There was a large flight of capital and a short economic downturn, but the economy recovered, confidence was restored, and overseas capital once again poured in to cover the country's current-account deficits.

In the two following decades, however, from 1974 to 1994, the appeal of South Africa for foreign investors diminished sharply as a consequence of worsening economic performance, mounting political unrest, and the increasing impact of external financial sanctions. There was a substantial net outflow of direct investment and other forms of private capital (including heavy overt and concealed flows by residents anxious to move their funds out of the country), and the net inflow of portfolio investment included substantial borrowing by the government and public corporations. This drain on the capital account compelled the authorities to take action to eliminate the deficit on the current account, with further adverse consequences for growth and employment. These adverse developments in the labour market and in the balance of payments will be discussed more fully in Chapter 10.

This dramatic transition in these different dimensions of macroeconomic performance in the early 1970s was not the only momentous change in South Africa at that time. There was also a remarkable renewal of the political struggle against apartheid, with a tremendous upsurge in the range and intensity of protest. This movement gathered strength at home and support abroad, and finally culminated in the release of Nelson Mandela in 1990, followed by negotiations between the government and the African National Congress, leading in 1994 to the country's first free and democratic elections. The government's inability to prevent, or bring to an end, the economic downturn was only one of the causes of this extraordinary political revolution, but the distressed state of the economy increased the militancy of the oppressed and undermined the confidence of the oppressors. It was thus a major factor in the collapse of white rule and the transition to a government representative of all the people of South Africa.

The political economy of developments after 1948

The significant and largely unexpected new feature of the post-war political economy of South Africa was the victory of the National Party in the general election of 1948. This was the party of the Afrikaner *volk* (people and nation), elected on a platform of apartheid. It was not immediately clear exactly what this meant, and the party had not formulated a master plan. There were undoubtedly important elements of continuity with previous policies of segregation under the earlier governments of Botha, Hertzog, and Smuts. However, as apartheid evolved and gathered momentum in response to economic and political developments, the National Party government became more confident in its political and administrative powers, and more fervent in its ideological beliefs. It was made clear that it was aiming to go markedly further than its predecessors, and this determination was especially evident after Hendrik Verwoerd became the dominant force, first as Minister of Native Affairs in 1952 and then as Prime Minister from 1958 until his murder in 1966.[3] Here too, however, in the political sphere as in the economic, there was a significant turning point in the early 1970s. The legal and administrative

---

[3] The successive prime ministers in this period were D. F. Malan (June 1948 to Dec. 1954), J. G. Strijdom (to Sept. 1958), H. F. Verwoerd (to Sept. 1966), B. J. Vorster (to

structures erected during the strong, confident, doctrinaire advance in the 1950s and 1960s were progressively dismantled in the course of a slow, irresolute, pragmatic retreat in the late 1970s and 1980s.

Almost immediately after coming to power, the National Party government began to strengthen and intensify many of the most discriminatory features of the South African economic, social, and political system. The measures introduced included more thorough suppression of African political organizations, elimination of the last vestiges of voting rights for the coloured population in the Cape, and the enforcement of numerous forms of social apartheid. The Population Registration Act of 1950 provided for the classification of every South African by race, and of Africans and coloureds by ethnic group. Two further acts prohibited mixed marriages between whites and members of other population groups, and extended a 1927 prohibition on sexual intercourse between whites and Africans to cover coloureds and Indians as well.

In 1953 the Reservation of Separate Amenities Act was passed in order to amend the situation created when the Appellate Court upheld a ruling that if different racial groups were segregated in public buildings, the facilities provided must be substantially equal. The Act gave the appropriate authorities power to introduce segregation in any public premises or public vehicles, and stipulated that separate facilities need not be equal, leaving no room for further judicial intervention. What had previously been done informally and with a degree of flexibility was now made legally binding and rigid. Whites would in future be separated from blacks in post offices, railway stations, town halls, libraries, and swimming pools. They could not travel on the same trains and buses, or be carried in the same taxis and ambulances; they were unable to sit on the same benches, ride in the same lifts, play in the same parks, or swim from the same beaches.

Subsequent legislation sought to prevent any interracial contact in churches, schools, hospitals, and similar institutions, in cinemas and concert halls, in restaurants and cafes, and on the sports fields. The 1956 Industrial Conciliation Act aimed to create separate unions (or separate branches) in existing trade unions with both white and coloured members, and to prevent the formation of any new mixed unions. The Group Areas Act of 1950 and later amendments were used to compel many thousands of coloured and Indian people to leave District Six in Cape Town, Cato Manor in Durban, and similar areas in many other large and small towns across the country where their communities had

Sept. 1978), and P. W. Botha (to Sept. 1984). Botha then became the first executive state president under a new constitution, and held this office until September 1989, when he was succeeded by F. W. de Klerk (to May 1994).

lived and traded for many decades. They were moved to remote, segregated, and often barren, ghettos, while the areas they were forced to abandon were taken over for exclusive occupation by whites. Other laws were used to forcibly resettle millions of African people in already overcrowded reserves or homelands. The Surplus People Project estimated that the total number of removals between 1960 and 1983 was about 3,500,000, including 1,130,000 evictions from white-owned farms, 860,000 under the Group Areas Act, 840,000 from urban areas, and 610,000 made in pursuit of homeland consolidation and clearing of so-called 'black spots'.[4]

All these measures were cruel and discriminatory, they caused great harm and pain to millions of people, but yet they were only secondary aspects of the government's programme.

Apartheid versus urbanization

Apartheid was designed, above all, to sustain and strengthen racial separation in order to ensure white domination. When Strijdom was Prime Minister, he expressed his policy with brutal clarity:

I say that the White man today has *baasskap*, paramountcy and domination because the franchise laws of the country put the vote into his hands ... The franchise laws of the country do not give the natives the slightest chance of ever gaining power, not on merit or on any other grounds ... That power is vested in the White man and for that reason the White man is master.[5]

His successors learned to be more diplomatic but the fundamental aim did not change. The central thrust of the programme designed to perpetuate this domination was to be an attempt to reverse the powerful long-run trend towards integration of black and white in urban areas that had developed over the first half of the century.

The logic of domination dictated that the majority of the black population should remain isolated and dispersed in rural areas and mine compounds; the logic of industrialization dictated that they should concentrate in urban areas to provide the labour necessary for economic expansion. This was a contradiction with which all white politicians had grappled since the formation of the Union. In 1922, the Stallard Commission attempted to defy the logic of industrialization by laying

---

[4] L. Platzky and C. Walker, *The surplus people – forced removals in South Africa*, Johannesburg: Ravan Press, 1985, p. 10. 'Black spots' was the term used to refer to African freehold land and land owned by churches and missions in areas defined by the government as for white ownership and occupation only.
[5] *House of Assembly Debates*, 19–21 April 1955, cols. 4141 and 4198.

down the principle that 'The Native should only be allowed to enter urban areas, which are essentially the White man's creation, when he is willing to enter and to minister to the needs of the white man, and should depart therefrom when he ceases so to minister.'[6] Migrant labour would thus have to be the means by which the white economy obtained its workforce while white society maintained its dominance of the urban areas. This policy was incorporated in the 1923 Urban Areas Act, and with each of the subsequent amendments to the Act more barriers were erected to prevent Africans moving to the towns and settling there with their families. Despite all this, previous governments were unable to control the trend towards urbanization, and the proportion of the growing African population living in towns increased steadily, from 350,000 (10 per cent) in 1904 to 1,690,000 (22 per cent) in 1946.

During the Second World War, rapid economic growth and the departure of many white workers for the armed forces encouraged a degree of relaxation in the application of the pass laws and of informal colour bars. Better training facilities were provided for black workers, and there was a clearer recognition that industry required a stable urban labour force rather than oscillating migrants. A report by the Social and Economic Planning Council in 1946 was highly critical of the harm that had been caused by the migrant labour system, and the threat which it posed to the entire society:

The past half-century has witnessed a decline in the stability of Native family life which constitutes a danger to the whole nation – black and white alike – in the spheres of health, of morality and of general social structure, peace, order, reasonable contentment, goodwill, and a sense of national solidarity. The situation is too grave to be dismissed lightly. The nation as a whole must fight for its family life and for sound and sane tradition.[7]

The wartime Smuts government appointed a commission under Justice Fagan (a former Minister of Native Affairs in Hertzog's cabinet) to investigate these issues, and it reported in 1948:

From what we have already said it should be clear, firstly, that the idea of total segregation is utterly impracticable; secondly that the movement from country to town has a background of economic necessity – that it may, so one hopes, be guided and regulated, and may perhaps also be limited, but it cannot be stopped or turned in the opposite direction; and thirdly, that in our urban areas there are not only Native migrant labourers, but there is also a settled, permanent Native population. These are simply facts, which we have to face as such. The old cry, 'Send them back!' ... no longer offers a solution.

[6] Transvaal Local Government Commission (Stallard), *Report*, 1922, para. 42.
[7] Social and Economic Planning Council, *Report No. 9*, 1946, para. 11.

A policy based on the proposition that the Natives in the towns are all temporary migrants – or can be kept in the stage of temporary migrants – ... would be a false policy, if for no other reason, than because the proposition itself has in the course of time proved to be false. It is, however, precisely this proposition of the Stallard Commission which ... lies near the root of many provisions of the legislation relating to Natives in urban areas and has had far-reaching effects in the administration of that legislation throughout the Union. An admission, therefore, that it is an untenable proposition – and that is an admission which is simply forced upon us by hard facts – makes it necessary for us to find a new formula.[8]

But by the time the Fagan Commission submitted this clear case for realism the National Party was in office and had already firmly repudiated such ideas. It had fought the election on the basis of an unpublished document, the Sauer Report, which presented total apartheid as the 'eventual ideal and goal', while recognizing that this would have to be achieved gradually and with due regard to the economic interests of the country. This ambivalence reflected the wide span of opinion held by party supporters: at one extreme, Afrikaner intellectuals who wanted complete segregation, and who could envisage a situation in which whites would 'satisfy the demand for labour from within their own ranks'; at the other, businessmen in industry and trade with a stronger sense of what was feasible. Thus the Sauer Report was not a straightforward blueprint for a new government to follow: the details of apartheid remained to be specified.

Once in power the National Party made explicit its intention that the trend towards African urbanization should first be controlled and then reversed, and it effectively endorsed the Stallard Commission's recommendation that African workers 'should only be permitted within municipal areas in so far and for so long as their presence is demanded by the wants of [the] white population'.[9] African labour might be indispensable for industrial growth, but it should be primarily migrant labour, entering on a temporary basis and for a limited purpose, with no entitlement to political, social, or other rights in the urban areas. Only a small minority of Africans – those already urbanized and 'detribalized' – were to be allowed to remain in the towns. Section 10 of the 1952 Urban Areas Act specified that in order to qualify for this special status African men and women had to prove that they were either born in a town and had lived there continuously, or had worked continuously for one employer for at least ten years, or had lawfully lived in the town without interruption for at least fifteen years; spouses, unmarried daughters, and sons

---

[8] Native Laws Commission (Fagan), *Report*, 1948, para. 28.
[9] Transvaal Local Government Commission (Stallard), *Report*, 1922, para. 267.

under eighteen could also qualify. All others were required to register as work seekers within seventy-two hours of coming to town, and, if unable to find a job, were forced to leave.

The government relied primarily on enforcement of an elaborate set of laws and procedures in its attempt to bring the flow into the towns under control. It was in this context that passes were introduced for women, despite the intense hostility this aroused. Unlike men, it was not their labour that the government wanted to control, but their freedom of movement and their presence in urban areas. Until the National Party came to power African women had enjoyed virtual exemption from the obligation to carry a pass. In 1952, however, the Natives (Abolition of Passes and Co-ordination of Documents) Act was passed, introducing a single reference book in place of all previous passes, and making it mandatory for both men and women to carry this at all times. The law was not immediately implemented for women, but the authorities started to issue reference books to them in 1956, and from 1963 it became compulsory for women to carry a book and to produce it on demand.

At the core of the apartheid system was a colossal bureaucratic apparatus of influx controls and labour bureaux, backed up by the oppressive powers of the police. Under regulations introduced in Johannesburg, for example, Africans who became unemployed were required to report to a bureau within three days, and were placed on a waiting list. Employers were required to register a vacancy within three days of its occurrence, and would then be sent an applicant for the type of work concerned. Both employers and work seekers were entitled to refuse to enter into a contract of service, but Africans were not encouraged to return to the bureau to ask for a different job. Africans on an urban waiting list for whom there were no jobs were referred to district labour bureaux, where the employment offered to them was on farms and in rural industries. As noted by an official commission in 1958, the whole system was clearly detrimental to the improvement of efficiency and productivity. The regulations 'had the tendency to separate the various European areas into separate water-tight compartments'. Each local authority 'tended to limit its recruitment activities to the labour resources within its own area and to resist the drafting of surpluses to areas where shortages existed'.[10]

What seems to be of more importance is that the system reduces the scope of the employers to select suitable employees. The recruits sent by the local bureaux frequently do not possess the physical or mental aptitudes necessary for the work that they have to perform. There is still too great a tendency on the part of the

---

[10] Commission of Enquiry into Policy Relating to the Protection of Industries (Viljoen), *Report*, 1958, para. 256.

authorities, in the words of the Secretary for Native Affairs, to regard 'the native as an interchangeable unit of a large undifferentiated mass of individuals', an attitude that may pass muster in the selection of labourers for purely manual work, but which is not suitable for industry where aptitude and dexterity are becoming increasingly important in the selection of employees.

The result … is to aggravate the already high labour turnover, with a consequent increase in labour cost and ill effects on the efficiency of industry.[11]

The scale of the extraordinarily grievous intrusion into the lives of the African population which this policy necessitated, and the criminalization of millions of people, can be glimpsed in the number of convictions under the pass laws. They increased steadily from 232,000 in 1951 to 414,000 in 1959, and then dipped slightly, following an attempt to reduce tensions after Sharpeville. The upward trend was quickly resumed, and by 1967 the figure had soared to 694,000. The two most common charges under which Africans were convicted were failure to possess the documents which establish their right to be in the prescribed area, and being in a prescribed area for more than 72 hours without permission.

The government recognized, however, that their ambitious aims could not be achieved simply by restricting residence in, or access to, the urban areas. The centrepiece of their alternative policy was to be separate development in the former reserves, now renamed 'homelands'. A commission under Professor Tomlinson was appointed in 1950 to investigate the socioeconomic development of the reserves; its brief, in effect, was to ascertain what was required to increase the capacity of these areas to support a larger number of Africans, thus reducing the pressures pushing them towards the urban centres. Four years later the commission published a summary of its mammoth report recommending a large-scale, ten-year programme of land reclamation and development. It involved the expenditure of over R 200,000,000, major reforms in agriculture, and the establishment of white-owned industries – both inside the reserves and on their borders – to provide alternative sources of income and employment. They noted that only industries *within* the reserves would enable Africans to develop fully as skilled workers and entrepreneurs, 'since there alone all restrictions on such development will be removed'.

The commission estimated that by 1981, after some twenty-five years of intensive development and industrialization undertaken in accordance with their proposals, the reserves might be able to support about 7 million persons on the basis of earnings within those areas, with a further 2 million (including absent migrant labourers) housed there on the basis of incomes earned in the border areas or other parts of the Union. In total

[11] Ibid., paras. 257–8.

this would cover about 60 per cent of a projected African population of some 15 million. Peering even further into the future, it was suggested that by 2000 the proportion accommodated within the reserves would have risen to about 70 per cent of the African population, which was projected to reach about 21 million by that date.[12] This was the fantasy with which the Commission confronted Fagan's facts. Its goals became even more fanciful when the government – with Verwoerd's influence now much stronger than when the Commission was appointed – rejected many of its key recommendations, including proposals to introduce individual in place of communal tenure, or to allow the purchase of more than one lot by a single farmer, the ten-year programme of expenditure, and the suggestion that white-owned enterprises should be established inside the reserves. It was decreed that private white capital and entrepreneurship could only operate inside the white areas of South Africa, though they would be encouraged to move to border areas, where employees could work while still leading a family life inside the reserves.

In practice very little was achieved. The government's policy envisaged that European entrepreneurs would establish new labour-intensive plants outside the borders of the homelands, while more modern, capital-intensive industries would operate in well-established industrial regions such as the southern Transvaal or Durban. The attraction of the border areas was meant to be the availability of cheap labour, supplemented by subsidized power, water, and transport, but distance from their main markets, absence of the external economies enjoyed in the principal centres, and other excess costs of the proposed decentralization made businesspeople very reluctant to move to these areas. Neither generous incentives in such forms as tax concessions, cheap finance, subsidies, and exemption from minimum wage stipulations, nor controls on new industrial development in the traditional centres proved sufficiently persuasive.

As a consequence, there was minimal development in or near the reserves, and the new jobs created were only a small fraction of the numbers Tomlinson had envisaged, although some propaganda claims for greater success were made after parts of existing metropolitan regions were redesignated as 'border areas'. When the census was taken in 1970, over 5 million Africans were counted in urban areas. This was almost certainly an underestimate, but even so it amounted to one in three of the total African population and was three times the number in 1946. It was also more than 50 per cent greater than the number of whites, whereas in

[12] Commission for the Socio-Economic Development of the Bantu Areas (Tomlinson), *Report*, 1955, p. 184.

1946 the two groups had been of roughly equal size. Not all those so enumerated were permanently urbanized and 'town-rooted', with a wife in the town and no intention of returning to the reserves, but a large and steadily increasing proportion were settled town-dwellers. The figures would no doubt have been even larger without the government's draconian restrictions on residence in the towns, but the results could scarcely be hailed as a success for the policy of separate development. Economic reality was stronger than political fantasy.

Trade unions, job reservation, and education

Three further aspects of government policy were also of great importance from an economic perspective; none would have been contemplated by a government that gave greater priority to economic progress than to white supremacy. The Native Labour (Settlement of Disputes) Act of 1953 redefined the term 'employee' to exclude Africans. It also renewed a wartime measure prohibiting strikes by African employees and, although African trade unions were not prohibited, they were denied official recognition. The law did not prevent strikes by African workers, and a small number occurred each year, but it meant that the strikers could be prosecuted for striking illegally. Following from the provisions of the Act, registered unions were prevented from having mixed white and African membership, there was no possibility of direct collective bargaining between African workers and their employers, and unofficial African unions were precluded from participating in the activities of Industrial Councils or the proceedings of the Wage Board which fixed wages in specified industries.

A second set of policies included legislation to provide further reservation of jobs on a racial basis. This was usually applied in order to designate occupations exclusively for white workers, but could also be used to protect coloureds and Indians from African workers. The colour bar legislation that was introduced in 1911 and confirmed in 1926 (see Chapter 4) had excluded Africans from many occupations on the mines, and the 1922 Apprenticeship Act had effectively prevented them from entering a wide range of skilled jobs in other industries. But now the scope of the formal and informal restrictions was to be greatly extended. In 1951 the Native Building Workers Act prohibited Africans from undertaking skilled building work outside their own areas, and from 1956 the Industrial Conciliation Act and later amendments provided for the extension of job reservation to 'any undertaking, industry, trade or occupation or class of work'. It was no longer only skilled workers who were to be protected; statutory exclusion could be applied to semi-skilled occupations, the number of which was increasing rapidly with mechanization of industry. Other mechanisms could also be used to prevent Africans from entering certain occupations; for example, since Africans were not allowed to be members of a trade union, they were automatically excluded from any occupation covered by a closed-shop agreement, of which there were many.

When the Minister of Labour explained why certain occupations should be reserved for whites, he acknowledged a possible conflict between economic and political principles:

> The European worker in this country must be protected or else European civilization will go under. Even though it might intrude upon certain economic laws, I would still rather see European civilization in South Africa being maintained and not being swallowed up than to comply scrupulously and to the letter with the economic laws.[13]

The new provisions were first applied in the clothing industry, reserving exclusively for white workers the jobs of machinists, supervisors, cutters or choppers-out, and table-hands. In subsequent years, job reservation was extended to a number of other occupations, including several relating to the assembly of motor vehicles, a major growth industry. The significance of these determinations was enhanced by informal and social pressures on employers even where there was no legal barrier to the employment of black workers. The effect was to prevent more black workers from moving into the more skilled and better-paid occupations that employers were finding it increasingly difficult to fill, and thus to retard the progress of the economy. In the 1960s there was increasing concern over the shortage of skilled labour, but official policy remained firmly committed to the preservation and extension of job reservation.

The final aspect of the apartheid programme that must be reviewed is the approach to African education, initiated in 1953. The Bantu Education Act brought school education and teacher training under the control of the Department of Native Affairs. The church and mission schools that had previously been responsible for 85 per cent of African education were effectively informed that if they wished to continue they would have to do so without the benefit of any financial support from the state. 'If there is a church which is prepared to maintain schools entirely at its expense that is their affair. They have to be registered. For that purpose such a church can train its own teachers but also entirely at its own expense.'[14] The Act also pegged the financial contribution that would

[13] *Senate Debates*, 21 March 1957, col. 2425.
[14] Minister of Native Affairs, *House of Assembly, Debates*, 3 June 1954, col. 6222.

be made by the 'general taxpayer' at the existing level. Any expenditure in excess of that would have to come from direct taxation of Africans; the much larger amounts they paid in indirect taxes were not to be counted.

Having ousted the churches and obtained control of the schools, Verwoerd set out the policy he intended to follow.

It is the policy of my department that education should have its roots entirely in the Native areas and in the Native environment and Native community ... The Bantu must be guided to serve his own community in all respects. There is no place for him in the European community above the level of certain forms of labour ... For that reason it is of no avail to him to receive a training which has as its aim absorption in the European community while he cannot and will not be absorbed there. Up till now he has been subjected to a school system which drew him away from his own community and practically misled him by showing him the green pasture of the European but still did not allow him to graze there.[15]

Central aspects of this new doctrine were the progressive introduction of the pupil's mother tongue as the medium of instruction, and the requirement that equal treatment be given to the teaching of English and Afrikaans. Many educationalists would approve of the use of a mother tongue as a means of improving literacy in the first few years of schooling. However, in the context of 'Bantu Education' its imposition lowered standards in the early school years, because of the lack of text-books for pupils and of suitable training and handbooks for teachers. The inadequate terminology in indigenous languages for describing modern scientific concepts was also a weakness. The associated deterioration in the standard of English had a detrimental effect on the education of the minority who advanced to the higher primary and post-primary years, where English remained the usual medium of instruction.

What this combination of aims and methods meant in practice was illustrated by a commission appointed in 1962 in the Transkei. It reported that it

found much evidence of dissatisfaction with the syllabuses in the primary schools on the grounds that too much time was devoted to the practical subjects and religious instruction. It was asserted that an over-emphasis had been made on fitting the child at too early an age for his post-school life, to such an extent that insufficient time was being allocated to the basic skills in the languages and arithmetic.[16]

---

[15] Senate, 7 June 1954, from H. F. Verwoerd, *Verwoerd speaks, speeches 1948–1966*, ed., A. N. Pelzer, Johannesburg: APB Publishers, 1966, p. 83.

[16] Commission of Inquiry into Teaching in Transkeian Primary Schools, *Report*, pp. 12–13, quoted in South African Institute of Race Relations, *A survey of race relations in South Africa, 1963*, p. 223.

It was also announced by the Minister of Bantu Education that it was the intention to make education up to the level of Standard 2 (the fourth primary year) available wherever possible, but that for higher primary and secondary levels, schools in the reserves would be given preference over those in urban areas, because 'this is the first place where the Bantu development must be promoted generally'. As he further explained, 'To train the Bantu to be of service in the European area simply means that you then train him to come into competition with the European.'[17]

There was a substantial increase in the proportion of African children who received some schooling, but the overwhelming majority left before finishing even the primary years. Data on the distribution of African pupils in 1964 showed that 72 per cent were in lower primary classes (the first four years), 25 per cent in higher primary classes (the next four years), and only 3 per cent in secondary classes. In relation to the total economically active population (all those between fifteen and sixty-four who were either at work or unemployed), data collected in the 1970 census are summarized in Table 7.4. Some 79 per cent of urban Africans and 93 per cent of those in the rural areas had not attained Standard 6 or higher, compared to a mere 4 per cent of the white labour force. Some 51 per cent of the urban Africans and 79 per cent of those in the rural areas – accounting together for 46 per cent of the total economically active population – had not even passed Standard 3.

The educational level of the white population can be taken as a broad indication of what is required to underpin a functional working population, that is, one that is literate, numerate, and competent, and includes a proportionate number of more highly qualified managers, professionals, and technicians. Against this benchmark, the total inadequacy of black education is quite obvious. The teaching content and financial restrictions imposed by 'Bantu education', together with gross deficiencies in the training and remuneration of teachers and in school facilities, were all part of the context for these abysmal standards. But so too was a society which sent children to school suffering from hunger, disease, and chronic malnourishment, which systematically undermined their self-confidence and extinguished their motivation for learning. These deeper roots of educational failure could not easily be eradicated, and explain why glib assurances from the Riekert Commission and other would-be reformers that the problem was 'receiving serious attention' were so ineffectual.

---

[17] *Senate, Debates*, 2 June 1959, col. 3466.

Table 7.4. *Level of education of the economically active population, 1970*

	(1) White	(2) Asian	(3) Coloured	African	
				(4) Urban	(5) Rural
			(per cent)		
None	1.1	8.5	22.4	34.8	63.4
Up to Standard 2	–	–	–	16.1	15.3
Standards 3–5	–	–	–	27.8	14.7
Less than Standard 6	2.8	35.9	45.3	–	–
None or below Standard 6	3.9	44.4	67.7	78.6	93.4
Standards 6–7	23.1	33.5	22.3	15.3	4.6
Standards 8–9	31.9	13.4	6.7	4.8	1.2
Standard 10	25.6	5.1	1.4	0.6	0.2
Degree and/or diploma	15.5	3.7	1.9	0.7	0.6
Total	100.0	100.0	100.0	100.0	100.0
Number (000)	1,509	716	182	2,706	2,996

Source: Data from 1970 Population Census, reproduced in Commission of Inquiry into the Utilisation of Manpower (Riekert), *Report*, 1979, p. 21.

Domination or development?

Although the primary purpose of the apartheid policies was racial separation and *wit baasskap* (white domination), the crucial point in relation to the economic development of the country is that, in these early decades of apartheid, the National Party was confident that its political imperatives were fully consistent with its economic objectives. When his policies were challenged on the grounds that they were damaging to the economy, Verwoerd's rejoinder was: 'I say again therefore that far from bringing about economic stagnation, apartheid is the fountain-head of the economic prosperity of South Africa.'[18] Underlying this assertion was his conviction that the system of migrant labour that had worked so well on the gold fields would be equally successful in industry and, as was characteristic of him, he was sure that his policy was what the Africans themselves really wanted:

[18] House of Assembly, 9 March 1960, from Verwoerd, *Verwoerd speaks*, p. 342.

The migratory labour system in which the Bantu sell their capacity for work, their capacity for labour far away from their homes, has been in force for many generations. Everyone knows that as far as mine labour is concerned, it is the best and probably even the only practicable and workable system. My contention is that the strengthening of this system and the expansion of the system to most of the other spheres of labour would be in the interests of the Bantu because the established business interests in the European towns still ensure that the urban locations will never be able to expand to fully-fledged Bantu townships, and because such a development would also not run in accordance with the Government policy. There is further good reason to believe that the Bantu prefers, because of the social consideration, the migratory labour system to removal to the European areas.[19]

The government was thus convinced that under their rule South Africans could enjoy economic growth and prosperity as well as white supremacy and racial separation. Was this really possible?

The question provoked a sustained and vigorous controversy. In academic circles it was one of many elements in a wide-ranging debate between traditional or 'liberal' scholars and a new school variously labelled 'revisionist', 'radical', or 'Marxist'. In relation to this specific issue, proponents of the 'liberal' view contended that because apartheid was driven primarily by ideological considerations, it was economically irrational and incompatible with a dynamic economy, and would ultimately prove damaging to the country's growth and prosperity. In particular, they argued, migrant workers, high labour turnover, inferior education, job reservation, and other apartheid policies all had powerful adverse affects on the productive efficiency of black workers and thus severely retarded economic growth.

In diametric opposition to this, radicals and Marxists maintained that there was no conflict between the state's political and economic objectives. On the contrary, they argued, apartheid was designed to serve the interests of the dominant class and was the means by which capitalism could thrive under the conditions prevailing in post-war South Africa. Their analysis – though not of course their political objective – was thus similar to that of the government and its supporters in industry and mining who saw the battery of apartheid policies as supportive of economic growth. Thus, for Johnstone,

[I]t is a mistake to believe that the continued and increasing use of African labour in 'white' industry is a contradiction of apartheid ... The actual goal of apartheid policies is the pragmatic development of an economically powerful white

---

[19] Senate, June 1955, ibid., p. 91.

supremacy. The whites want continued prosperity and continued supremacy, and the government is seeking to secure both of these goals together.[20]

He further argued that 'Capitalist business, far from being incompatible with the system, secures high profits through very cheap, unorganised and rightless labour.'[21] This focus on supposedly 'cheap' labour for the factories was also prominent in the analysis of apartheid by two of the most influential members of the Marxist school, Martin Legassick and Harold Wolpe:

Apartheid ... was the application of the cheap forced labour system established under segregationism, now applied to secondary industry rather than to mining and farming alone.[22]

Apartheid, including separate development, can best be understood as the *mechanism specific to South Africa* in the period of secondary industrialization, of maintaining a high rate of capitalist exploitation through a system which guarantees a cheap and controlled labour force under circumstances in which the conditions of reproduction (the redistributive African economy in the reserves) of that labour force is rapidly disintegrating.[23]

As these statements indicate, Marxists saw the maintenance of 'cheap' labour for industry as the principal purpose of post-1948 apartheid. The entire edifice of influx controls, labour bureaux, and political suppression was, in their view, designed to maintain a supply of low-paid, pliable, docile black workers. They saw no fundamental distinction between the earlier phase of development dominated by farming and mining, and the new phase dominated by manufacturing, and drew many of their conclusions from an analysis of the earlier period.

Cheap labour was not, however, the only potential economic benefit that might be claimed for apartheid. From a macroeconomic perspective, a racially discriminatory, low-wage economy should have a number of other consequences that might be favourable to the promotion of growth. Higher profits should lead to higher savings and thus more rapid improvements in the stock of capital, one of the principal sources of growth. In addition, for any given level of capital expenditure, systemic under-investment in social infrastructure for blacks (for housing, piped

---

[20] F. A. Johnstone, 'White prosperity and white supremacy in South Africa today', *African Affairs*, 69, 1970, p. 126.

[21] Ibid., p. 136.

[22] M. Legassick, 'Legislation, ideology and economy in post-1948 South Africa', *JSAS*, 1, 1974, p. 9.

[23] H. Wolpe, 'Capitalism and cheap labour power in South Africa: from segregation to apartheid', in H. Wolpe (ed.), *The articulation of modes of production*, London: Routledge, 1980, p. 296.

water, schools, hospitals, and urban transport) should allow a disproportionate share of savings to be concentrated on productive investment.
Higher profits based on cheap labour should also raise government
revenue from taxes, and so make possible higher public expenditure
which could be used either to sustain weaker sectors of the economy
such as commercial agriculture, or to increase current outlays on education, health, and other services for whites. There would, of course, be
costs to set against these gains, but apartheid theorists tended to ignore
the adverse effects of inferior education, slum housing, malnutrition,
disease, and political discontent on the productive efficiency of the
black workers who bore the burdens of this discriminatory system.

In the three following chapters these varied abstract considerations will
be tested against the actual historical record. There is no place for simple
dichotomies, and it must be recognized that the application of apartheid
policies in a capitalist economy was likely to have both functional and
dysfunctional elements. Furthermore, it should not be assumed that all
industries or firms would respond to given policies in the same way. For
example, opportunities for mechanization and greater use of semi-skilled
labour, or dependence on the domestic market, would differ across
industries; and within industries there were significant differences
between the minority of large, mechanized, capital-intensive companies
and the majority of smaller, more labour-intensive firms. But on balance,
over the economy as a whole, which outcome would prevail? Was cheap
labour really the essential requirement for successful industrialization?
Would racist ideology, migrant labour, and low wages promote or prevent
economic growth?

8 Forcing the pace: rapid progress despite constraints

This chapter is devoted to a detailed examination of the developments in mining, manufacturing, and agriculture in the years prior to the turning point in the early 1970s identified in Chapter 7. The domestic and external reasons for the deterioration in economic performance after this point are discussed in Chapters 9 and 10.

The period from the end of the Second World War to the crisis of the early 1970s was one of exceptionally rapid growth. It was a time of great optimism and confidence in the development of the South African economy, and there was indeed much to celebrate. But the attempt to achieve rapid industrial growth within a system of apartheid designed to secure racial discrimination and separation was being tested to destruction. The economy was rushing forward at great speed, especially in the 1960s, but it was out of control; it was racing towards barriers that were inherent in the framework of laws and institutions erected in pursuit of white supremacy. When it reached those barriers a crash was inevitable; no recovery was possible without fundamental change; growth could not be resumed.

Three more windfalls for the gold mines

Contrary to initial expectations, gold mining flourished remarkably during the initial postwar decades. The very pessimistic estimates prepared by the Government Mining Engineer in 1941 for the Van Eck Commission (referred to in Chapter 6) had predicted that the annual tonnage of gold would decline steeply by 1965. This was based on two rather cautious assumptions: that it would not be economically viable to mine ore of a lower grade (gold content), and that no areas not yet developed and prospected would come into production. By the end of the 1940s both assumptions had already been proved false. Vast new reefs were discovered in the Transvaal and the Orange Free State, and the simultaneous devaluation by the United Kingdom and South Africa in September 1949 raised the sterling price of gold by over 40 per cent, a level that was maintained until 1970.

The discoveries were the result of prolonged and expensive activity, initiated after the departure from the gold standard at the end of 1932 (see Chapter 5). The resulting increase in the price of gold transformed the finances of the mining houses and revived their zest for new ventures. Exploration was first undertaken to the west of the original Rand, and it was established that there were new payable reefs in the Transvaal, both in the Far West Rand and also further west, near Klerksdorp. Stimulated by this success, in 1936 the large mining houses started to make a careful investigation of large areas south of the Vaal River, in the Orange Free State. The existence of gold in this region had been suspected since the nineteenth century, but previous explorations had failed to discover payable quantities, and the reef which was to form the basis for the country's richest goldfield was not discovered until 1939. In total contrast to the discoveries by individual prospectors on the Witwatersrand in the 1880s, the new finds were the result of systematic, scientific exploration by large mining corporations, using geophysical and magnetometric surveying, and drilling boreholes on an unprecedented scale. Even so, a vast amount of exploratory work was required and many options on potential sites were abandoned as worthless before the new reef was finally 'proved'.

The exploitation of the Orange Free State discovery, and of most of the potential mines in the Far West Rand and Klerksdorp, was delayed by the war. When development started it was a long, costly process, and the prospects were very uncertain. The gold reefs in the Orange Free State were lying at depths of over 8,500 feet, and were covered by thick layers of lava. The rise in temperature as the mine descended (the geothermic gradient) was much steeper than on the Rand, so that large additional outlays on ventilation and refrigeration were required, as well as the substitution of 'dry' for 'wet mining' below a certain depth. Shaft sinking in this region commenced in 1946, but it was not until 1951 that the first gold was produced at the St Helena and Welkom mines.

In addition to the cost of developing the mines, huge outlays were required to provide the necessary transport, electricity, and water, and to build housing, shops, schools, and hospitals in Welkom and other new towns that sprang up on what ten years earlier had been remote and isolated mealie farms. By 1955 over R 400,000,000 had been spent on the development of the Orange Free State goldfield. By the end of the decade, twenty-two new mines had begun production in the three new fields, and these produced 60 per cent of South Africa's total output of gold and 79 per cent of the working profit. Further mines were started in these areas during the early 1960s, and a small number of new mines were also opened to the east of the original field on the Rand.

Anglo American became the dominant mining house in the new Orange Free State goldfields and thus in the country as a whole. This was the result of the remarkable entrepreneurial vision and judgement of Ernest Oppenheimer, his son Harry, and their associates, together with their ability to raise large sums of capital abroad, especially in the United States, and the enormous resources that their corporation effectively controlled, not only from diamond and gold mining in South Africa, but also from copper mines in Northern Rhodesia. The power of this giant corporation in the economic life of South Africa was still further enhanced by its steady diversification into industry (described below). The creation of such an overwhelming position of strength was all the more remarkable because Anglo American's initial explorations in the Orange Free State were all unsuccessful, and by 1939 it looked as though it would have no mines in this potentially rich field. However, it successfully built up its stake in the new area by a massive programme of acquisition, deploying its immense resources to buy shares in companies that had been more successful in the initial exploration. In this way the share of the country's total gold output produced by its mines climbed from 14 per cent in 1936 to 41 per cent in 1969, but this later figure actually understates its full power and influence because it also held (or later acquired) significant shareholdings in other houses.

These shifts in the location of the goldfields, and revolutionary advances in the methods of exploration, shaft sinking, and mining, were introduced with only minimal adjustments to the traditional system of labour relations and labour utilization. The agreed ratio of black to white miners of about 8:1, and restrictions on the work that could be done by the black labour force, were all carried forward from the 1920s (see Chapter 4). Despite the higher gold price and the profitability of the new mines, the wages (including food) of black labour were held down as they always had been, and in real terms were only 6 per cent higher in 1969 than in 1946. The excuse for sustaining monopsonistic collusion was invariably that there were some marginal mines with low-grade ore which could not afford to pay higher wages, and the survival of these mines was always given a higher priority than increases in the living standards of African miners.

There were minor improvements in the standard of housing provided in new compounds, but migrant labour remained the basis of the system. In the early 1950s Anglo American did contemplate the establishment of villages for some of its married African employees on the Orange Free State mines. However, when the Minister of Native Affairs (Verwoerd) was asked to define his attitude to this experiment, his reply was: 'I want to state quite unequivocally that I am opposed to that development.' The general principle subsequently enunciated by the government was that married quarters could only be provided up to 'an absolute limit of 3 per cent of the total Native labour complement of any mine', and only for 'Native personnel who are employed on a permanent basis because of specialized training and experience and who are required to be continuously on the mine property'.[1] In the event, even the 3 per cent limit was not reached.

Within the traditional structure, the new mines did make significant advances in the mechanization of their operations, both underground and on the surface, aided by the widespread use of electricity in place of steam power. The use of mechanical scrapers to clear broken rock from the rock face represented a considerable saving of unskilled manual labour, as did other equipment developed for lifting and loading the ore. Locomotives were used in place of labourers to move underground wagons along tracks from the face to the shaft, and hand tools were replaced by pneumatically operated machinery. Mechanization called for greater numbers of semi-skilled workers, and the mines started to pay slightly more attention to the selection and training of their African workers.

Despite this, labour productivity measured by the amount of ore treated for person employed (see column (4) of Table 8.2 below) remained absolutely flat, at a little over 160 tons per worker, from the end of the Second World War to the early 1960s. It thus appears as if all the investment in mechanization over these two decades was required simply to offset the more difficult geological conditions in the new fields. The process of bringing new mines into production may also have retarded improvements in productivity until the mines were operating at their full capacity. The mining companies found it increasingly difficult to obtain the number of skilled white workers they required, but occasional attempts to erode restrictions on the employment of African miners in skilled or semi-skilled jobs were always thwarted by the white trade unions, with support from the government.

However, in the early 1960s there was a sudden and significant break in the previously static performance. By the middle of the decade the quantity of ore treated for each worker had risen to 179 tons, and it continued upwards to reach 190 tons by the end of the decade. At about a 1 per cent increase per annum this was not a spectacular rate of progress, but it had at least shown improved efficiency in the use of labour. It was achieved partly by the delayed effect of mechanization, enabling the quantity of ore treated to increase far more rapidly than the expansion of the labour

---

[1] Gregory, *Ernest Oppenheimer*, pp. 579–80.

Table 8.1. *South African gold mines: ore milled, output, sales, and price, annual averages, 1945–70*

	(1) Ore milled (million tons[a])	(2) Output of gold (million fine ounces)	(3) Average grade of ore (dwts per ton[b])	(4) Value of gold sales (R million)	(5) Price received (R per fine ounce)
1945–8	53.2	11.7	4.4	202.3	17.24
1949	53.9	11.7	4.3	229.7	19.42
1950–4	56.8	12.0	4.2	298.8	24.83
1955–9	63.4	17.0	5.4	425.6	24.97
1960–4	71.4	25.3	7.1	632.9	25.04
1965–9	74.9	30.9	8.2	787.2	25.50
1970	80.0	32.2	8.0	831.2	25.84

[a] Metric tons of 2,004.6 lbs.

[b] 20 dwts (pennyweights)=1 fine ounce.

Source: Chamber of Mines, *96th Annual Report*, Johannesburg: Chamber of Mines, 1985, p. 58.

force, and partly by more efficient use of African mine-workers. From 1967 the white unions finally agreed to allow certain changes, but only on condition that the greater part of the gains from elimination of restrictive practices would accrue to them and not to the black miners who would do the actual work. The most important of the concessions permitted an African 'boss-boy' to inspect the workplace at the beginning of a shift and decide whether or not it was safe for his gang to start work. This saved as much as an hour of working time that was previously wasted while African miners waited for a white man to arrive and authorize them to start. Africans were also allowed to handle explosives and to drive underground locomotives hauling white miners. The formal colour bar was retained but its application was becoming more flexible.

The net outcome of these various changes can be seen in Tables 8.1 and 8.2. The average grade of ore was appreciably higher in both the Orange Free State reefs and those on the Far West Rand than in the older Witwatersrand mines, and this difference was more than sufficient to offset the fact that the increase in the sterling price of gold had made it possible to reduce the average grade of ore that could be profitably mined. As a result the companies increased the output of gold by 175 per cent – from just under 12,000,000 fine ounces in 1949 to over 32,000,000 in 1970 – while the tonnage of ore milled increased by only 48 per cent (compare columns (1) and (2) of Table 8.1). This contrast is reflected in

Table 8.2. *South African gold mines: working revenue, costs, profits, and labour productivity, annual averages, 1945–70*

	(1) Working revenue	(2) Working costs	(3) Working profit	(4) Ore milled per worker (tons[a])
	(rand per ton of ore milled[a])			
1945–8	3.83	2.82	1.01	159
1949	4.29	2.97	1.32	162
1950–4	5.30	3.77	1.53	164
1955–9	6.82	4.87	1.95	162
1960–4	9.41	5.67	3.74	164
1965–9	11.09	6.75	4.33	183
1970	11.24	7.34	3.90	193

[a] Metric tons of 2,004.6 lb.

column (3) in a marked rise in the average grade of ore over the same period, from 4.3 to 8.0 dwts per ton milled.

These favourable developments in ore grade and labour productivity, combined with sustained resistance to any significant improvement in real wages for African mine-workers, meant that working revenues per ton milled rose markedly more rapidly than working costs (see columns (1) and (2) of Table 8.2). As a result, working profits per ton milled, shown in column (3) increased almost threefold, from R 1.32 in 1949 to R 3.90 in 1970. These two decades were, therefore, a very profitable period for the companies, and this was not the end of their good fortune.

In addition to the higher price of gold and the discovery of new fields, yet another large windfall fell into the laps of the mining corporations early in the post-war period. It had long been known that uranium could be obtained from the residues of some of the ores mined for gold, but there was little demand for this metal and thus no profit to be made from it. However, during the Second World War and in the subsequent period of the cold war, the need for uranium for nuclear weapons suddenly became extremely urgent, and the United States and Britain were prepared to provide the capital for the rapid development in South Africa of the necessary supplies, and to pay very high prices for the vital metal. In later years additional demand was created by the development of peaceful uses for atomic energy.

The first pilot plant to produce uranium concentrate came into operation in 1947, and a full plant was completed in 1952. By 1958, seventeen mines were already functioning, with an output of 5,670 tons of uranium, and others were to follow. The operation generated enormous profits; in 1958, for example, the working profit from gold was R 123 million and an additional R 75 million was made from uranium. The material also represented a substantial addition to South Africa's exports, amounting in the same year to R 107 million or 9 per cent of the total (including gold), and thus made a valuable contribution to the balance of payments. The construction of these large plants for the recovery of uranium had further beneficial effects through backward linkages to the chemical industry, especially for sulphuric acid, and the engineering industry. Production reached a peak in 1959 and then declined slightly, but still averaged 3,170 tons at the end of the 1960s.

South Africa's diamond industry was also in an extremely strong and profitable position in the early post-war period, when there was an unprecedented demand for gemstones. As Oppenheimer explained in 1953 to the shareholders of De Beers Consolidated Mines, large quantities of unsaleable diamonds had been acquired at very low prices during the depression of the 1930s, and the corporation had carried these stones for many years. 'When we could at last dispose of our stocks, we were in the midst of the greatest boom the diamond trade has seen, prices of diamonds had recovered and benefited from the two devaluations of the pound sterling. We reaped a golden harvest'.[2] This was an exceptional, one-off profit. A large part was used to fund Anglo's investments in the new goldfields described above, and a stabilization fund of R 40 million was set aside for the future protection of the industry.

In subsequent years diamond mining continued to prosper, with demand for industrial stones supplementing the gem market. The volume of diamonds produced by South Africa increased roughly fourfold between 1950 and 1970, but there was also a rapid expansion of other sources of supply, notably in the Congo and other parts of central and west Africa, and in the USSR. The De Beers group lost its position as the largest producer by weight, though it remained a major source of world sales by value because of the higher ratio of gemstones to industrials in the output of the South African mines. In the 1960s, large quantities of rough diamonds were imported from other producers and then re-exported after sorting and grading in Kimberley and Johannesburg. However, rising political hostility to South Africa made it difficult for De Beers to maintain this aspect of the group's operations, and much of this activity was subsequently switched to London, while still preserving the group's

[2] Ibid., p. 105.

crucial role in the centralized marketing of diamonds. Some of the new producers were reluctant to exercise the restraint in relation to sales that was required by De Beers and the Central Selling Organisation, the cartel through which the world market for diamonds was controlled. However, the influence of De Beers in the trade, the length of their purse, and a very successful advertising campaign (based on the slogan 'Diamonds are forever'), enabled them to prevent a more serious over-supply.

The other significant feature of the early post-war decades was the rise in the contribution of minerals other than gold, coal, and diamonds from 14 per cent of the value of total sales in 1950 to 35 per cent in 1970. This increased share was not only a consequence of the fixed gold price, it also reflected the extensive diversification of a wide range of new mines in this period (see also Annexe 2). A large-scale open-cast copper mine was developed at Phalaborwa in the north-eastern Transvaal, and by 1970 the value of copper sold had reached R139 million, temporarily over-taking coal as the most important mineral after gold. Other metallic and non-metallic minerals produced included asbestos, iron ore, manganese ore, vanadium, antimony, chrome ore, phosphates, tin, and fluorspar. For a number of these and other minerals the value of the output was relatively small in relation to total sales by the mining industry, but they ranked among the major sources of supply available to the Western world during the cold war era.

Manufacturing: the unprecedented boom

By the beginning of this post-war period, following the boom of the 1930s and further strong expansion during the war years, the foundations had been laid for the development of a mature, well-capitalized, industrial sector.[3] The years that followed, from the end of the Second World War to the early 1970s, were a time of spectacular growth, structural change, and modernization. Industry was well placed to take advantage of the significant internal boost provided by the expansion of gold mining described earlier in this chapter. It was also able to benefit from the unusually favourable external conditions during the post-war 'golden age' outlined in Chapter 1. It was well endowed with capital and entre-preneurship, and there was initially an elastic supply of labour, so that the industrial workforce could be increased substantially without driving up its cost.

---

[3] For these earlier developments see Chapter 6.

Like Germany, France, Japan, and other countries that had either fallen behind during the two world wars and the Great Depression, or were late starters, South Africa had the capacity to take advantage of the 'opportunities of backwardness'. Countries in this position could advance to the 'best-practice' technological frontier at an exceptionally rapid pace in the early post-war decades because they could borrow from leading industrial nations already on the frontier. They could acquire the most advanced physical equipment and machinery and the most up-to-date scientific knowledge and technical expertise. They could also build on the experience of the industrial leaders to improve the performance of crucial economic and social policies and institutions, such as company laws, corporate structures, management hierarchies, banking systems, financial intermediaries, and industrial relations.

As in earlier phases, South Africa's dominant strategy in a process of cumulative expansion was import substitution, so that a large part of the market for the rapidly increasing output came from replacement of imports. It was thus a period of sustained innovation and modernization on the supply side and of expanding markets on the demand side. There seemed to be no limits to what might be achieved. Businesspeople, policy makers, and academics were enthusiastic; confidence was high. In 1962 the chairman of the Board of Trade and Industries boasted that 'in no other country has there, within the brief compass of twenty-five years, been a more complete metamorphosis of its economy and a more spectacular development of its industries ... than in South Africa'.[4] A decade later, Hobart Houghton, a leading economist, reflected on 'a long period of almost uninterrupted prosperity' that had started in 1933, and on the expansion of the industrial, market-oriented sectors of the economy:

These processes are not yet ... complete, for there are still pockets of low productivity particularly in the African peasant areas. Modernization of the whole economy appears, however, to be merely a matter of time, for a stage has been reached when economic progress is self-generating, and South Africa has the capacity to maintain a rate of capital formation adequate to provide rising *per capita* income for its whole population.[5]

The contribution of industry (including construction, electricity, and gas supply) to GDP at current factor cost climbed from 23 per cent in 1948 to almost 31 per cent in 1970. At the earlier date it was still less than that of agriculture and mining combined; at the later date it was 84 per cent greater (see Table 7.1). It was widely considered that manufacturing

[4] Norval, *Industrial progress*, p. vii.
[5] Wilson and Thompson, *Oxford history*, p. 32.

was not only surging forward, it was taking over the role of driving the economy that had formerly been played by gold: 'The importance of manufacturing in the future economic development of South Africa cannot be too greatly stressed because all the indications are that it must be the cornerstone of future expansion.'[6]

The large orders placed by the new gold mines and uranium plants for capital equipment and industrial stores were only one aspect of the crucial contribution that the giant mining houses made to industrial transformation during the 1950s and 1960s. Even more significant were the resources that they made available in the course of a continuing process of diversification, with Anglo American in the forefront of a massive programme of investment and expansion in industry. They had vast capital, managerial, and technical resources at their disposal; they could operate on a huge scale; they could afford to initiate projects which would take many years to come to fruition. In all these respects their capacities far exceeded those of other private industrial concerns, and it was above all their increasing involvement in secondary industry that was responsible for consolidating the transformation of South African manufacturing during these two post-war decades.

Further vital support for this progress to superior forms of production came from foreign companies that were induced to establish local production facilities in order to circumvent the tariff and other barriers raised against imports. Investment by overseas multinationals was valuable as an additional source both of savings and of foreign exchange, and because it was typically associated with the introduction of new technology. There were still many small firms operating in the Union, using high-cost, labour-intensive techniques, but they had been relegated to a subordinate position; an increasingly large share of output was being produced in modernized, mechanized, mass-production plants. The distribution of establishments by size group in 1972 is set out in Table 8.3. The smallest units – employing fewer than twenty workers – accounted for 47 per cent of all establishments but produced only 4 per cent of total net output. By contrast, the largest units – employing 500 or more workers – accounted for only 3 per cent of all establishments, but produced 45 per cent of total net output.

Before the 1950s, the industrial interests of mining groups were primarily confined to the manufacture of products required for their own operations; for example, African Explosives and Chemical Industries Ltd (AE & CI) produced both the chemical raw materials and the finished explosives for blasting, as well as calcium cyanide for the extraction of

---

[6] Hobart Houghton, *South African economy*, p. 137.

Table 8.3. *Classification of manufacturing establishments by employment size group, 1972*

(1) Employment size group	(2) Percentage of establishments	(3) Percentage of total employment	(4) Percentage of net output
1–9	30.7	1.7	1.7
10–19	16.4	2.6	2.5
20–49	21.4	7.7	7.1
50–99	12.7	10.0	8.9
100–199	9.0	14.2	12.8
200–499	6.6	22.3	21.7
500–999	2.1	16.2	17.0
1,000+	1.1	25.3	28.2
	100.0	100.0	100.0
Total number / value	12,671	1,131,061	R3,749m

Source: South African statistics, 1976, p. 12.39.

gold from the crushed rock. However, from the late 1950s the mining houses began to expand the scope of their industrial activity, and this process of diversification accelerated in the 1960s. The key to this increased involvement in other sectors was the success of developments in the Orange Free State: their new gold mines were no longer absorbing all their vast resources, and instead were starting to create surplus capital which could be invested outside mining.

The principal advances in scale, technology, and capital intensity that were the consequences of this decision to diversify were made in heavy industry, but light industry also participated. The giant concerns had access to the most advanced scientific and technical information and the most modern capital equipment, typically through links with foreign concerns, such as the relationship between AE & CI and Imperial Chemical Industries (ICI) in the United Kingdom. Across a range of manufacturing industries – including metals, heavy engineering, chemicals, fibres and textiles, brewing, grain milling, and paper making – companies in the Anglo American group built large, capital-intensive plants. They also had substantial interests in civil engineering and construction, property, cement, timber, and printing and publishing. Other mining groups owned broadly similar portfolios of industrial companies, though not on the same scale as Anglo American.

The general process can be illustrated by the pattern of development followed by three of the leading Anglo American companies. In the 1950s AE & CI began to extend its output from explosives for mining to a wide

range of products required by other sectors, including nitrogenous fertilizers, plastic materials such as polyethylene and PVC, synthetic fibres
(nylon), and many industrial chemicals. By the end of the 1960s it was
one of the largest industrial concerns in the country (measured by the
value of its assets), and had a total labour force of about 15,000. The
second company, Boart and Hard Metals, had been established in 1936
to explore possible markets for industrial diamonds, and turned first to
improved drilling techniques for the mines. In the post-war period it
expanded from this to produce a range of specialized high-quality drilling
tools tipped with diamonds or tungsten carbide for mining concerns, as
well as tools and abrasives for general industrial drilling, grinding, and
cutting. A large share of its output was sold abroad, and it was an
acknowledged world leader in its field.

Scaw Metals was acquired by Anglo American in 1964. It had started in
the 1920s as a manufacturer of steel castings and parts for the mines, but
branched out in the 1930s to produce cast steel grinding balls. In the post-
war period it first expanded its capacity to produce rolled steel, primarily
for the new gold mines, and then broadened into a more general engineering company. It developed technical links with leading steel corporations in the United States and Britain, and began to manufacture cast
steel bogies and goods wagon wheels for the railways, as well as steel
castings for equipment used for moving metals at high temperatures. It
was this which fostered the closer relationship with Anglo American,
since one of their companies was the source for the special high-quality
steel required by Scaw Metals. The specialized producer, Highveld Steel
and Vanadium, was Anglo American's largest industrial undertaking in
the 1960s. It had been established to exploit South Africa's vast reserves
of vanadium (an element used for strengthening some steels), together
with the iron ore in which it was found, and this was achieved after an
intensive programme of research and investment in co-operation with US
and British companies. The costly and innovative plant was designed to
operate on an extremely large scale, and Anglo American considered that
it was essential to secure control of the market for Highveld Steel's output. This led to a process of forward integration in which Scaw and other
major consumers of specialized steel were acquired.

The expansion of the financial sector and the rise of Afrikaner capitalism

The growth of industry was also assisted by the expansion of the financial
sector. From the 1860s the small, local 'unit' banks in the Cape Colony
were reinforced by larger 'imperial' banks linked to the City of London, and

they swiftly developed stable networks of branches across the country. This was followed by a lengthy process of amalgamation and concentration, leading ultimately to a position in which banking was totally dominated by two concerns: the Standard Bank of South Africa and Barclays Bank (Dominion, Colonial and Overseas). These two powerful banks, both owned by British interests, provided essential short-term credit and other banking functions for business and personal customers. The Johannesburg stock exchange, founded in 1887 immediately following the gold discoveries on the Witwatersrand, evolved into an active and efficient market for long-term capital. However, other institutions were lacking.

In the late 1940s the South African Reserve Bank was keen to promote the growth of a money market in order to broaden the market for government securities; this would in turn strengthen its position as lender of last resort and controller of credit. A government-sponsored National Finance Corporation was established in 1949 and accepted short-term funds (call money) that had previously been placed in London by the mining houses and other large institutions. In the next few years Anglo American, working in partnership with firms in London, played a significant part in the development of a more comprehensive financial system, and its lead was followed by others. A number of private discount houses and merchant banks were cautiously established, but soon expanded and diversified vigorously to create a variety of sophisticated markets and perform a range of functions. Short-term liquidity was greatly increased, temporarily idle funds were mobilized, financial expertise and capital were more readily available to industry, large sums were raised for both the public and private sectors, and credit was extended to help exporters. Also in this period, insurance companies and pension funds started to broaden their portfolios to include industrial equities. These financial innovations made a significant contribution to the development of a more flexible interest rate structure and to the exercise of monetary policy; they also greatly improved the financial infrastructure to which industry could turn for advice and for credit or capital.

The development of financial institutions was a primary factor in the rise of Afrikaner capital in the non-farm economy. At the beginning of the post-war period Afrikaners produced well over 80 per cent of all marketed farm output, but their involvement in all other sectors of the economy was still quite insignificant. It was estimated that the proportion of turnover sold by Afrikaner firms in 1948/9 was only 1 per cent in mining, and only 6 per cent in both manufacturing and finance.[7] It was slightly larger, at

---

[7] D. O'Meara, *Volkskapitalisme: class, capital and ideology in the development of Afrikaner nationalism, 1934–1948*, Johannesburg: Ravan Press, 1983, p. 182.

25 per cent, in commerce, but the great majority of these businesses were either small one-man and family operations, or co-operatives formed to purchase agricultural supplies and market farm produce. The only exceptions were Die Nasionale Pers (National Press), formed in 1914 to publish a pro-Hertzog newspaper in the Cape, and two financial institutions. The most important was Sanlam, which was established in 1918 to sell life insurance, and over time developed into a massive concern, forming subsidiary finance and investment companies that were not as restricted by legislation in their investment policy as insurance companies. The other was Volkskas (People's Treasury), which began as a co-operative loan bank in 1934, but was registered as a commercial bank in 1941, and built up a network of branches across the country.

The driving force motivating sponsors and supporters of both institutions was that of mobilizing and centralizing the savings of the *volk* (people or nation) and deploying these in order to build a stake in industry and commerce controlled by Afrikaners. A proposal for Sanlam to take the initiative in forming a large finance company was advocated in the following terms:

> I cannot propose a more effective method than this, to employ the mobilised capital of the Afrikaner in the furtherance of his national interests in the spheres of commerce and industry, and to capture key positions. Such a finance company appears to be the appropriate means through which the Afrikaner can realise his legitimate struggle to assert himself in the economic domain.[8]

The proposal was accepted at an economic congress convened by the Federation of Afrikaans Cultural Associations in 1939, and was indicative of the extremely close ties between this economic movement and the activities and ambitions of the leaders of Afrikaner political and cultural organizations. However, progress was initially very slow. The main source of potential funds was the farming community, but their resources were limited, especially during the depressions in the inter-war years. In addition, there were divisions among the *volk*, with many strongly opposed to the idea of supporting such urban, capitalist organizations which seemed no different from those of the 'imperialists' they disliked so intensely; and Sanlam and Volkskas also faced fierce competition from larger and better-established institutions such as Standard Bank and Barclays.

From 1948, however, their drive for greater economic power for Afrikaner business was transformed by the election victory of the

---

[8] Memorandum in 1938 to the Sanlam board from M. S. Louw, their actuary and financial strategist, quoted (and translated) in O'Meara, *Volkskapitalisme*, p. 109.

National Party. Government bodies and local authorities transferred their accounts and deposits to Volkskas and other Afrikaner institutions, while public corporations and government agencies awarded contracts to Afrikaner companies for the supply of material and equipment. The state-owned Industrial Development Corporation was also used to strengthen the economic position of Afrikaner firms. A further substantial boost followed during the early 1960s in the aftermath of the Sharpeville crisis (see p. 189 below), when there was an exodus of foreign capital, and Sanlam was well placed to acquire large quantities of shares at bargain-basement prices in companies operating in vehicles, computers, and electronics.

A third major group that emerged after the remarkable growth in the early post-war decades was the Rembrandt Corporation, led by Anton Rupert. His firm initially prospered during the war years in the Cape wine and brandy trade, but then evolved into a huge cigarette manufacturer, building up its domestic market by making extensive use of Afrikaner nationalism and its cultural symbols. It also expanded abroad by establishing a series of international partnerships. By the 1970s it had become a massive tobacco multinational as well as a financial and industrial company, with investments inside South Africa in a wide variety of sectors including banking and finance, mining, and engineering.

The main Afrikaner expansion into mining came in 1963, when Anglo American – who could no doubt see the advantages of having Afrikaans financial interests inside the capitalist tent – sold a substantial part of its interest in a leading mining house, General Mining and Finance Corporation, to Federale Mynbou (Federal Mining – Fedmyn), a subsidiary of Sanlam. A few years later Fedmyn purchased a majority of the shares and took control of the corporation. This was followed in 1976 by the takeover of a second mining house, Union Corporation.

By the mid-1970s the Afrikaner economic movement had effectively accomplished its primary aims. It was true that the share of turnover in Afrikaans ownership had declined in the commercial sector to 16 per cent. This was because many small stores had been put out of business by the rapid expansion in the 1960s of more efficient and cheaper chain stores such as O. K. Bazaars and Woolworths, and from the 1970s by the growth of Pick 'n Pay and other food supermarkets. But the share of turnover in Afrikaner hands in manufacturing and construction had risen to 15 per cent, in finance to 25 per cent, and in mining to 30 per cent.[9] This success was not only a crucial aspect of the decisive (though

[9] M. Lipton, *Capitalism and apartheid: South Africa, 1910–1986*, London: Gower/Temple Smith, 1985, p. 411.

ultimately temporary) rise to dominance of the Afrikaners; it was also of considerable significance for the subsequent formation of economic and social policies. By the 1970s, the position of farmers and small business-people and traders within the National Party was markedly weaker than it had been in the early years of the apartheid government; the power of Afrikaner capitalists and of large industrial and commercial firms was very much greater. These firms had very different views on issues such as the colour bar, black wages, education, and urbanization, and their concerns – articulated by organizations such as the Afrikaanse Handelsinstituut (Afrikaans Commercial Institute) – became increasingly influential. The rise of Afrikaner capitalism was thus a highly important element leading to bitter divisions within the National Party and also to the erosion of the original apartheid policies that will be discussed in Chapter 10.

State-directed industrialization

Although many of the major industrial concerns were backed by the massive resources of the mining groups, the sector continued to rely heavily on the state for various forms of protection and assistance. The National Party government elected in 1948 maintained the policy of wholehearted support for industrialization and tariff protection that its predecessors had initiated, and protective measures were considerably strengthened and widened in scope as compared with the inter-war period, so that industries were 'much less exposed and vulnerable to disruptive influences emanating from outside the Union's own economy'.[10] The system of protection also encouraged a high level of foreign direct investment to establish or expand production facilities in South Africa, as this was often the only way in which overseas companies could maintain their position in the local market.

However, the government was compelled to make a significant change in the way in which protection was applied. As a signatory in 1947 to the General Agreement on Tariffs and Trade (GATT) – the body established by the international community to promote free trade, particularly in manufactures – South Africa was unable to maintain its previous system of customs tariffs. In its place it instituted a system of import licensing, covering almost all imports. Quantitative controls on imports were first introduced in 1948 in response to a serious balance-of-payments deficit, but were subsequently retained and developed through the 1950s and

---

[10] Commission of Inquiry into Policy relating to the Protection of Industries (Viljoen), *Report*, 1958, para. 189.

1960s as one of the principal instruments that could be used by the government to promote domestic industry. Only a small range of goods (raw materials such as petrol, oil, and yarn) could be imported without a permit; all other imports required either a specific permit, or a general permit issued in accordance with quotas specified from time to time. Only holders of valid licences were allowed to acquire the necessary foreign exchange to pay for imports, and the number of licences issued could be increased or reduced according to the state of the balance of payments. Imports of raw materials and capital goods were given priority over consumer goods, and the import of certain consumer goods regarded as inessential was prohibited.

Importers of goods subject to licensing were informed by the authorities that no permits would be issued until it had been established that it was not possible to obtain similar materials (or satisfactory substitutes) from South African suppliers. The policy of advance guarantees of market share, initiated during the war (see Chapter 6), was also continued to good effect. The history of SAPPI (South African Pulp and Paper Industries Ltd) illustrates this procedure very clearly. This major company was set up by Union Corporation, one of the mining houses, to produce paper and newsprint from domestic supplies of timber. The large, capital-intensive plant required for this would involve massive capital outlays. Before SAPPI was established all newsprint had been imported, and the import control authorities effectively removed any market risk from Union Corporation's investment by agreeing that they would refuse to make any new import permits available for either newsprint or any other type of paper until the local market had taken up the entire output of SAPPI mills. The company was also assured that any future increases in capacity would be given the same protection from foreign competition. This was clearly very helpful for the shareholders of SAPPI; whether it and similar uses of the system of import restrictions were the best way to promote efficiency and reduce the cost structure of South African industry is more questionable.[11]

Government control of imports was also a fundamental element in the development of a motor vehicle industry, in this instance in co-operation with the major international automobile companies from Europe, the United States, and Japan. The first vehicles sold to South African motorists were imported fully assembled, but as early as the 1920s Ford and General Motors established local assembly plants. They were later followed by others, but all these plants continued to rely predominantly on

---

[11] This topic is discussed in Chapter 9, p. 219.

imported components, and at the end of the 1950s the proportion (by weight) of components produced within the country was still only 17 per cent. The main local manufactures were not functional parts but tyres, window glass, and batteries, all of which could easily be excluded from imported packs of 'completely knocked-down' components. The growth in local demand for vehicles was adding to the country's already high propensity to import, and in 1960 the government decided to initiate an import-replacement programme for motor cars.

The expectation was that this key industry would both act as a 'catalytic agent' in the expansion of South African manufacturing and also improve the balance of payments. The policy was designed to ensure that assembly plants progressively increased the local content of their vehicles. Assistance was given to the industry in various ways, including tariff protection on a list of items to be manufactured locally and excise duty rebates for those manufacturers who exceeded the specified minimum level of local supplies. Phase II of the programme was initiated in 1964 with the aim of moving rapidly to a position where at least 55 per cent by weight of components were obtained from local sources, and the local market was effectively reserved for cars approved as 'made in South Africa' in accordance with this formula. Phase III, announced in 1969, required the proportion of local content to be raised to 66 per cent by 1976, and commercial vehicles were also gradually included in the programme.

The major multinational producers were thus induced to extend their investment in assembly plants, and also to provide capital and expertise for the production in South Africa of engines and other parts. The programme was successful in promoting the expansion of output and employment in the motor vehicle industry and its local suppliers, but at a high cost in foreign exchange. The use of weight as the criterion for local content encouraged the companies to purchase domestic components with a relatively high mass but low value, so that 66 per cent by weight was equivalent to only 40 per cent by value. The import bill for vehicle components, taken together with the costs of the foreign capital equipment required by both assembly plants and component manufacturers, remained a major burden on the balance of payments.

Furthermore, the government accepted from the outset of the local content programme that further intervention in the vehicle industry would be inconsistent with its general commitment to free enterprise. It declined, therefore, to place any restrictions on the number of manufacturers that could be given a share of the market in return for meeting the specified requirements. The result was that a relatively small demand was divided among a large number of producers: by 1965 five companies were producing fifteen models with the 'made in South Africa' label, and over the course of the next two years the number more than doubled, to thirty-one. Each plant was thus operating well below the output regarded as the minimum efficient scale of production, and this applied also to independent suppliers of parts, since they too were working on short production runs in order to meet demands for this multiplicity of models. Despite paying what by US standards were derisory wages, the cost of production of a motor car in South Africa was calculated to be 45 per cent higher than in the United States in 1965, and the gap increased to 62 per cent by the time the third phase of the local content programme was implemented in 1976.[12] This is a vivid illustration of how much South Africans had still to learn about the distinction between 'cheap labour' and low labour costs per unit of output.

More direct state intervention in the economy was also maintained, mainly through the state-owned Industrial Development Corporation (IDC), created during the Second World War (see Chapter 6). The IDC operated like an industrial bank, providing capital for new firms, establishing new ventures in partnership with domestic or foreign companies, and launching new projects of strategic importance. It gave special attention to the promotion of industries in which there was scope for technical progress and rationalization. By 1973 it had a portfolio of assets worth R 484 million and had made funds available for further expansion of the iron and steel corporation, ISCOR, and for the creation in the 1950s of the Phosphate Development Corporation (FOSKOR) to produce superphosphates for agricultural fertilizers.

One of its most important projects was its support for the South African Coal, Oil and Gas Corporation (SASOL), a major new public corporation formed in 1950 to convert coal into gas, and then gas into petrol, diesel, and other liquid products. This was again a project too large and uncertain for the private sector to undertake, and was initiated largely for strategic reasons when foreign sanctions posed a threat to the country's external supplies of oil. It absorbed vast sums of capital, mainly provided by the IDC, but eventually succeeded in its primary aim, and also played a major role in the development of a wider petro-chemical industry. Many chemical by-products were obtained in the course of the main process and these supplied the raw materials for a variety of different plants in the chemicals industry. External pressure also led to the formation of another

---

[12] A. B. Julius and A. B. Lumby, 'Phases I, II and III of the local content programme in the South African motor car manufacturing industry, 1961–1976', *SAJEH*, 13, 1998, p. 33, based on data supplied by a South African-based subsidiary of a US motor vehicle manufacturer.

large state corporation, ARMSCOR, to manufacture armaments. The stimulus in this instance came from the embargo on sales of arms to South Africa imposed by the United Nations in 1963. In response, the government attempted to ensure that there was sufficient local capacity to supply all the military equipment it required, from ammunition to military aircraft. This was achieved mainly through appropriate support for private-sector companies but, where this was not possible, the work was done by ARMSCOR.

Trends in employment, output, and productivity

Employment in the private manufacturing sector increased almost three-fold, from about 440,000 in 1948 to 1,160,000 in 1971 (rounded from data given in column (4) of Table 8.4). At that date there were also some 520,000 occupied in construction and electricity, gas, and water supply, making the total number in secondary industry almost 1,700,000. Of these, approximately three out of four were black, predominantly African. Further information on the growth of private manufacturing is shown in Table 8.4. As shown in columns (1) and (5), the number of establishments increased from 8,500 to over 14,000, and the average size of establishment in terms of employment grew from 52 in 1948 to 82 in 1971. There were still large numbers of small establishments, but they accounted for only a small fraction of total output.

Value added at constant prices increased sixfold over the period from 1948 to 1974, an impressive long-run rate of growth of over 7 per cent per annum. As shown in the first column of Table 8.5, there was considerable variation around this high average rate. The pace reached almost 8 per cent per annum from 1948 to 1954, slowed to 5 per cent per annum in the late 1950s, and then accelerated to a peak rate of almost 10 per cent per annum in the first half of the 1960s. It then dropped slightly in each of the last two sub-periods, ending at 6.5 per cent per annum from 1969 to 1974.

This rapid growth can be attributed to the combination of an increase in the use of labour at a rate of over 4 per cent per annum, with an improvement in labour productivity (value added for each worker), for which the rate of increase was almost 3 per cent per annum (see the second and third columns). However, this improvement in labour productivity was in turn based largely on the extremely rapid expansion of the stock of fixed capital (measured at constant prices) that was associated with the process of modernization and mechanization outlined above. As shown in columns (4) and (5) of Table 8.5, this massive expenditure on buildings, plant, and machinery resulted in fixed capital per worker more

Table 8.4. *Output and employment in private manufacturing,*
1948/9–1971/2[a]

Census year [b]	(1) Number of establishments	(2) Gross output at current prices	(3) Net output at current prices	(4) Total number employed [c]	(5) Average number employed per establishment
		(R million)		(000)	
1948/9 [d]	8,510	1,016	397	439	52
1954/5	9,685	2,123	837	605	62
1960/1	10,661	2,974	1,198	662	62
1965/6	12,894	5,104	2,038	957	74
1971/2 [e]	14,169	9,276	3,820	1,166	82

[a] Public-sector undertakings, construction, and electricity and gas supply are not included.
[b] For the period covered by census years see note *a* in Table 6.2.
[c] Includes working proprietors and unpaid family assistants.
[d] The definition of manufacturing was changed after 1954/5 to exclude repair and service work and certain other activities. Data were given on both definitions for 1954/5 and the same proportional adjustment was made to 1948/9 to obtain figures for this year consistent with those for later years in the table. For this reason the figures for 1948/9 differ from those in Table 6.2.
[e] The Standard Industrial Classification was revised from 1970, resulting in a small reduction in the scope of the manufacturing sector. Data were given on both definitions for 1969/70 and the same proportional adjustment was made to 1971/2 to obtain figures for this year consistent with those for earlier years in the table.

Source: Union statistics, L-3 and *South African statistics, 2002,* Table 12.1.

than doubling between 1948 and 1974. This increase was due partly to the substitution of capital for labour that occurred in many industries, and partly to the increasing share of manufacturing output produced by highly capital-intensive industries such as metals, engineering, and chemicals. The stock of fixed capital increased even more rapidly than real output, so that there was a small rise in the capital/output ratio (see column (6) of Table 8.5). When this higher capital stock is taken into account, it emerges that roughly 90 per cent of the impressive growth of output was accounted for by increased inputs of labour and capital, so that only about 10 per cent was the result of greater efficiency in the use of these inputs.[13]

[13] This calculation is based on standard growth accounting procedures. An index of total factor inputs was derived by combining indices for labour and capital with weights based on their respective shares in total factor income. These were 0.46 for labour and 0.54 for capital; see J. Nattrass, *The South African economy, its growth and change,* 2nd edn, Cape

Table 8.5. *Indices and growth rates of output, employment, fixed capital, and productivity in manufacturing, 1948–74*

	(1) Value added at constant prices	(2) Employment	(3) Labour productivity	(4) Fixed capital at constant prices	(5) Capital/ labour ratio	(6) Capital/ output ratio
Indices, 1948=100						
1948	100	100	100	100	100	100
1954	157	142	111	170	120	108
1960	210	154	136	225	146	107
1965	336	216	156	356	165	106
1974	616	297	207	699	235	113
Annual percentage growth rate						
1948–54	7.8	6.0	1.7	9.2	3.0	1.3
1954–60	5.0	1.4	3.5	4.8	3.4	−0.1
1960–5	9.8	6.9	2.7	9.6	2.5	−0.2
1965–9	7.6	3.4	4.1	6.6	3.1	−0.9
1969–74	6.5	3.9	2.5	8.8	4.7	2.1
1948–74	7.3	4.3	2.9	7.8	3.4	0.5

Source: (1) and (2) *South African statistics, 2002*, Tables 19.1.2 and 7.1.1; (3) = (1) ÷ (2); (4) South African Reserve Bank, *Quarterly Bulletin*, June 1999; (5) = (4) ÷ (2); (6) = (4) ÷ (1).

The inverse of the rise in the capital/output ratio is a decline in output per unit of capital, and the fall in this measure of the productivity of capital was even more marked if both series are converted to current prices, because there was a persistent tendency for the price of capital goods to rise more rapidly than the price of goods produced.[14] In addition, there was a downward trend in the share of profit in value added in manufacturing. This was a consequence of the dual effect of sustained pressure for higher wages, and a continual rise in the price of material inputs relative to the price of the final output. The result of this combination of a fall in both the ratio of output to capital at current prices and the share of profit in value added, was a steep fall in the rate of profit on

Town: Oxford University Press, 1988, p. 184. The resulting average annual growth rates for 1948–74 were 6.5 per cent for total factor inputs and 0.7 per cent for total factor productivity, compared with 7.3 per cent for output.

[14] This can written as $\frac{P}{K} = \frac{P}{Y} \times \frac{Y}{K}$ where Y = net output (value added) at current prices and K = net stock of fixed capital at current replacement cost, Y_c and K_c are the corresponding estimates of output and capital stock at constant prices, and Π_y and Π_k are the respective deflators (price indices) for output and the capital stock. When the relationship is converted to rates of change over time, the left-hand side is approximately equal to the *sum* of the changes in the two terms on the right-hand side.

Table 8.6. *Composition of net value of output in private manufacturing by sector, 1948/9 and 1975/6*

	(1) 1948/9	(2) 1975/6
	(per cent)	
Light industry		
Food, beverages, tobacco	19.0	14.1
Textiles, clothing, leather, and footwear	15.2	10.4
Wood and furniture	6.4	3.2
Paper, printing, and publishing	7.7	7.7
Other manufacturing	3.4	3.3
	51.7	38.7
Heavy industry		
Chemicals	9.5	11.4
Pottery, glass, and other non-metallic mineral products	6.0	5.3
Basic metal industries (ferrous and non-ferrous)	17.6	13.0
Fabricated metal products	1.9	9.5
Machinery (including electrical)	3.2	13.2
Transport equipment	7.8	7.2
Rubber products	2.4	1.7
	48.3	61.3
Total manufacturing	100.0	100.0

Source: Union Statistics, L-6 to L-31.

capital.[15] It is particularly significant that the rate of profit was falling even during the period of rapid growth before the 1970s, indicating that 'There was never any honeymoon period for the marriage of apartheid and capitalism in terms of a *stable and reproducible growth path.*'[16]

In the early post-war decades there was a continuation of the trend towards a more mature structure of production observed in the years before 1948 in Chapter 6. The focus shifted further from consumer goods such as food and textiles towards intermediate and capital goods. The composition of net output in 1948/9 and 1975/6 is set out in Table 8.6,

---

[15] The relationship can be written as $\frac{Y}{K} = \frac{Y_c}{K_c} \times \frac{\Pi_y}{\Pi_k}$ where P = profits, and K and Y are as defined in the previous footnote.

[16] N. Nattrass, 'Economic power and profits in postwar manufacturing', in N. Nattrass and E. Ardington (eds.), *The political economy of South Africa*, Cape Town: Oxford University Press, 1990, p. 121 (emphasis in original).

showing a rise in the contribution of heavy industry from 48 to 61 per cent of the total. This was almost entirely the result of the above-average rate of expansion of two metal-working industries: fabricated metal products and mechanical and electrical machinery. The contribution to total net output of the former increased from 2 to 9.5 per cent, and that of the latter from 3 to 13 per cent. On the eve of the Second World War the economy was still almost wholly dependent on foreign producers even for many basic consumer goods; by the early 1970s it was not only largely self-sufficient in consumer goods but was also producing a considerable part of its intermediate semi-manufactures and capital goods.

Weaknesses and constraints – the limits to growth

Nevertheless, even in this period of dynamic growth, significant weaknesses and constraints were evident in the industrial sector, some arising from critical socioeconomic problems already identified with respect to the pre-war period in Chapter 6, others emerging for the first time in the post-war period. The former included the small size of the domestic market for manufactured goods (which made it difficult to achieve optimum economies of scale), the low level of efficiency of a large part of the workforce, and the enormous sectoral deficit on the balance of payments. The major new problem was a growing shortage of skilled labour, though this too had its roots in the discriminatory racial system consolidated in the 1920s, and in the even older deficiencies in basic education for black workers. Manufacturing remained uncompetitive, and relied heavily on a varying combination of tariff duties, foreign exchange controls, quantitative import quotas, and licences to keep foreign competitors out of domestic markets. It was necessary to raise these barriers over the course of the post-war period and to extend protection to the great majority of industries. By 1971 the commission appointed to investigate the export trade concluded that South African protective tariffs could no longer be regarded as 'low', and that 'there were not many existing branches of manufacture to which relatively effective protection had not been extended'.[17]

The balance-of-payments problems arose from a combination of short-term cyclical crises and long-term structural disequilibrium. The short-term crises could occur on either current or capital account, and could have either domestic or foreign origins. In 1948–9, for example, there was a surge in imports as a result of the abnormal pent-up demand for both

---

[17] Viljoen, 'Industrial achievement', p. 46.

consumer and capital goods that had accumulated during the war. This was exacerbated by a steep rise in domestic liquidity in 1947 as British investors transferred their funds from the United Kingdom to South Africa in fear of nationalization and a sterling devaluation by the post-war Labour government. The Union authorities responded by imposing import controls on a long list of commodities, and subsequently added to this an elaborate system of import licensing as described above. This was then further supplemented by exchange controls, which gave them power to regulate movements on the capital account of the balance of payments. Both these forms of direct control were retained long after the initial crisis had been dealt with.

A more serious crisis erupted in 1960, and continued until 1963, when capital streamed out of the country as overseas investors lost confidence in South Africa following the mass shooting of largely unarmed black protestors at Sharpeville. The government's reaction was decisive and wide-ranging. It obtained loans from the International Monetary Fund (IMF), intensified and extended import controls, raised interest rates and restricted credit, and tightened exchange controls on residents. In June 1961, after the formation of the Republic, it added a critical new weapon to its armoury by introducing a system of 'blocked rand'. This effectively stopped South African residents from remitting funds abroad and non-residents from repatriating the proceeds of sales of local securities. These stringent measures successfully adjusted the current account, by holding imports down, and the capital account, by first stemming and then reversing the flow of capital. A further significant factor in the swift recovery of international confidence was the willingness of Anglo American, Sanlam, and other South African finance houses to acquire any holdings of industrial and financial securities that overseas investors wanted to sell. This was a very visible demonstration that local belief in the South African economy remained high, and foreign investors were quick to read these signals.

The more fundamental issue of long-term disequilibrium was created by difficulties in relation to both imports and exports. On the import side, demand for overseas manufactures remained stubbornly high, despite the long-standing policy of import substitution that was intended to reduce the country's dependence on foreign goods. By the 1950s this had been successfully achieved for a wide array of consumer goods, but the outcome was not a significant decline in the propensity to import, it was a shift to imports of intermediate industrial products (such as synthetic and plastic materials, fabricated metal products, and motor vehicle components), to capital equipment and, to a lesser extent, to raw materials. In 1935–9 the ratio of merchandise imports to GDP was 0.23, in 1965–69, after three decades of energetic import replacement, it was 0.20 and on a rising trend. The underlying causes of this inability to make substantial inroads into the country's dependence on imports can be found in the small size and high cost of the intermediate and capital goods industries, an issue to which we return below.

On the export side, although mechanization and the shift to modern, capital-intensive methods of production sucked in semi-manufactures and capital goods from abroad, it did not – except in a very few instances – generate compensating sales of South African manufactures in foreign markets. Export performance was generally poor; low productivity meant that South Africa was unable to compete effectively in world markets, and its share in exports of manufactured products by developing countries dropped sharply from 12.6 per cent in 1955 to 4.3 per cent in 1975.[18] Other reasons for the inability to achieve a faster rate of growth of exports included the poverty of many of the country's natural markets in Africa; the high transport costs necessary to reach other continents; and the fact that subsidiaries of large multinationals were usually established in order to get behind South Africa's tariff barriers, but were precluded from competing in third markets that were reserved for the holding company itself or for its other subsidiaries. As in the 1930s, manufacturing was running a massive foreign-exchange deficit, and was able to survive only because mining earned a handsome surplus. In 1975, for example, manufacturing imports amounted to R 5,700 million while exports were only R 1,800 million, leaving the sector with a deficit of R 3,900 million.[19] This was tolerable only because gold and other mining industries had an excess of exports over imports of R 2,200 million, and this was supplemented by a smaller current-account surplus in agriculture, and by net receipts of capital from abroad.

The general quality of labour at any given skill level remained far too low for a country seeking to compete in the international economy. The process of mechanization and modernization that had taken place had fundamentally changed the nature of industry's labour requirements. Demand for highly skilled craftsmen and for unskilled labour had declined; demand for skilled and semi-skilled operatives, mechanics, and technicians had increased. In the post-war period the dominant employee was a semi-skilled worker or machine operator, and increasingly he or she was black. The two largest job categories in a sample of over 1,100,000 industrial workers analysed by the Federated Chamber of

---

[18] T. Moll, 'Did the apartheid economy fail?', *JSAS*, 17, 1991, p. 282.
[19] Nattrass, *South African economy*, p. 146. See also J. C. du Plessis, 'Investment and the balance of payments of South Africa', *SAJE*, 35, 1965, p. 329, for data for 1956–64.

Industries in 1969 classified 485,000 as operators and 323,000 as semi-skilled workers. Some 52 per cent of the operators and 89 per cent of the semi-skilled workers were African; the corresponding proportions for coloured or Asian workers were 35 per cent and 11 per cent.[20] The industrial sector depended overwhelmingly on black labour, but was unwilling or unable to pay appropriate wages (though there was a short period in the early 1960s when wages for black workers were raised quite sharply), provide proper training, or create commitment and motivation – all of which were essential prerequisites for the improvement in productivity that was desperately needed.

Skilled work remained almost exclusively a white preserve until the late 1960s, and there were persistent shortages of skilled artisans, revealed, for example, in surveys conducted by employers between 1969 and 1971, in the furniture, motor, metal, clothing, and construction industries. As the economy continued to expand there were no longer enough white workers to provide all the artisans required. In the mid-twentieth century one in five of South Africa's population was white, but the proportion was declining steadily, and by the end of the century the ratio would be close to one in ten. The unemployment that had existed among whites in earlier periods had effectively been eliminated, and the shortage faced by industry was aggravated by the tendency for increasing numbers of white employees to choose higher status, white-collar occupations in preference to manual work. In 1971 data from Manpower Surveys showed 380,000 white workers (27 per cent of those covered) in manual occupations; by 1990 this had fallen to 312,000 (18 per cent).[21] Any one employer who was willing to pay higher wages could bid labour away from other firms, but for the economy as a whole the supply of skilled labour was becoming an increasingly serious bottleneck.

Industry would have to find an increasing number of skilled black workers to meet its requirements. Nevertheless, as outlined in the previous chapter, the government – with the general support of white society – erected and maintained many formal and informal obstacles designed to bar the progress of African and other black workers into skilled occupations. Among the barriers to better utilization of black labour were industrial colour bars reserving specified jobs for white workers; resistance to the registration of black apprentices; insistence by white trade unions on 'the rate for the job' to discourage the employment of cheaper

---

[20] S. Biesheuvel, 'Black industrial labour in South Africa', *SAJE*, 42, 1974, p. 311.
[21] Based on the classification of Manpower Survey data by O. Crankshaw, *Race, class and the changing division of labour under apartheid*, London: Routledge, 1997, pp. 148–51; the Survey does not include agriculture or domestic service.

blacks; fears on the part of employers that the employment of black workers would antagonize their white employees and/or customers; and gross deficiencies in the education and training available for black workers.

Even before the post-war boom had run its course there was concern about this array of issues and widespread recognition by the government and its advisers that the economy was close to the limits of what could be achieved on the basis of the original strategy of import substitution. For manufacturing as a whole, the proportion of total supply (gross output plus imports) produced in South Africa had increased from 44 per cent in 1926/7 to 71 per cent in 1956/7, and then more slowly to 77 per cent in 1967/8.[22] Little further scope remained for light industries to displace imports, while comparable displacement of more complex intermediate and capital goods was severely constrained by several factors, including the small scale of South Africa's domestic market, the lack of the necessary skills and technological capabilities, and the inability to raise protection of these industries sufficiently to displace imports without doing great damage to other domestic industries.

The desperate poverty of the black urban population also effectively closed off another possibility touted by some: so-called 'inward industrialization'.[23] The underlying proposition was that the removal of influx controls would initiate a process of 'orderly urbanization', and this in turn would expand domestic demand from low-income black households for consumer goods and/or housing and social infrastructure. The proponents of this strategy argued that the production required to meet this increased demand for basic goods would be met largely by small, labour-intensive firms and would have a low import content. It would thus simultaneously reduce the demand for skilled labour and strengthen the balance of payments. However, it did not take much reflection to recognize that in the absence of a large – and improbable – policy of income redistribution, increases in domestic demand from the black population could only be a consequence of further growth, not a cause.

So the only remaining way in which South Africa could sustain its momentum would be to develop a new export-orientated strategy for manufacturing. If this could be accomplished it would both promote growth and also help to overcome the balance-of-payments constraint.

---

[22] Calculated from G. Marais, 'Structural changes in manufacturing industry 1916 to 1975', *SAJE*, 49, 1981, pp. 27 and 36–7.

[23] The ideas were originally proposed by Professor Jan Lombard of the South African Reserve Bank in J. Lombard et al., *Industrialisation and Growth*, Johannesburg: Mercabank, 1985.

From the late 1960s, numerous government commissions and committees proclaimed the necessity for such a change, and explored methods by which it might be achieved. In 1972, for example, the Reynders Commission endorsed the view that 'import replacement cannot be relied upon to maintain or regain its dominant position as the prime mover of a high rate of economic development'. Nor could South Africa continue to increase its foreign indebtedness:

The only alternative, if the country wished to avoid falling into the trap of stagflation, was to improve its export performance drastically, that is to say, in future exports would have to play a more important role as a generator of growth in the South African economy.

It is imperative to realise that the continuance of South Africa's economic development is likely in future to depend increasingly on its ability to produce large volumes and new forms of exports to augment the export performance of agriculture and mining. In this regard the fundamental long-term choice facing the country seems clear: A lower rate of economic growth or more intensive efforts to increase exports, thereby maintaining and if possible increasing growth.[24]

However, as one critic observed:

The Reynders Commission reported in 1972 in favour of export promotion while maintaining largely unchanged the distortions (such as infant-industry tariff protection, import control policies towards industrial location, agricultural price supports, transport pricing, labour deployment, and the development of human resources) which raise the real cost of domestic production and the relative cost of exportable goods, at a time when a number of countries have recognized the futility of export promotion without a thorough-going review of economic policies.[25]

Moreover, there could hardly have been a worse time than the early 1970s in which to initiate a switch to such a policy. The reasons for the intensification of the balance-of-payments problems in the 1970s and 1980s, the associated limitations on the growth of output, and the consequent rise in unemployment provide the main themes for the two final chapters.

A revolution finally comes to commercial agriculture

During the years following the end of the Second World War, South African taxpayers finally began to see some reward for the vast sums they had pumped into the commercial farming sector over the previous four decades. Although output increased quite rapidly in the 1950s and early

---

[24] Commission of Inquiry into the Export Trade (Reynders), *Report*, vol. 1, ch. 1, para. 23 and Ch. 15, para. 12.
[25] A. E. Ratcliffe, 'Export policy in perspective', *SAJE*, 43, 1975, p. 76.

1960s, this was almost entirely based on a comparable increase in the outlays on capital goods and other non-farm inputs, and there was virtually no improvement in farming efficiency. However, from the mid-1960s the sector made significant advances in its use of resources, particularly in horticultural and arable farming, and good progress continued during the 1970s. There was a steady decline in the number of farming units in the commercial sector, with a consequent increase in average farm size by over 40 per cent (from around 1,900 acres in 1948 to almost 2,700 in 1974). This generally meant that farmers had more to spend on capital equipment and on purchases of intermediate inputs such as artificial fertilizers, feedingstuffs, dips, and sprays, and was a contributory factor in the achievement of higher output and efficiency.

Subsistence farming in the reserves, and black labour-tenants on white-owned land, showed no such improvement; on the contrary, there was significant further deterioration. Resettlement policies conducted in pursuit of apartheid in the 1960s and 1970s forced millions of black people off farms and out of towns, making the reserves even more overcrowded and under-resourced. The disparity between white and black agriculture widened, and adverse factors discussed earlier in Chapters 3 and 6 remained as insuperable obstacles to change. The system of communal tenure had lost its original flexibility, and tribal – effectively government – officials maintained an inegalitarian and rigid distribution of land, grazing rights, and livestock. The majority of households in the reserves were only part-time farmers, predominantly women or elderly persons, and did not have sufficient land, infrastructure, or other services to produce even their subsistence needs, so that these areas were forced to import food from the commercial sector. Income from agricultural production provided only a small and diminishing part of household income; poverty-stricken rural communities were increasingly dependent on remittances from migrant workers, pensions, and other income transfers.

In the quarter of a century preceding 1948, the index of the physical quantities of goods produced by white farmers had increased at an average rate of about 2.1 per cent per annum. In the following period, from 1948 to 1980, the rate of increase of this index almost doubled to 3.9 per cent per annum. Over the same three decades, the average rate of growth of real gross value added in agriculture was somewhat slower, only 3.0 per cent per annum. The distinction between these two series, broadly speaking, is as follows. The former, shown in column (1) of Table 8.7, measures the output of farm goods produced each year, valued at constant prices. The latter, shown in column (2), measures the difference between the output of farm goods produced, and the input of non-farm goods purchased from other sectors, with both outputs and inputs

Table 8.7. *Farm output, prices, labour, and fixed capital, 1948–80*

	(1) Index of volume of agricultural production (1948=100)[a]	(2) Index of value added at constant prices (1948=100)[bc]	(3) Number of regular farm employees (000s)[d]	(4) Fixed capital stock at constant prices (1948=100)[c]
1948	100	100	(685)	100
1954	131	132	812	142
1960	186	148	756	164
1965	186	154	834	180
1974	263	209	713	234
1980	344	258	669	268

[a] Centred three-year averages of seasonal years (e.g. 1948 = average of 1946/7 to 1948/9).
[b] Centred three-year averages.
[c] Including forestry and fishing.
[d] Regular employees on commercial farms excluding both domestic servants and seasonal and casual labour. 1948 is a rough estimate based on a figure of 845,000 for 1947 including domestic servants, of whom there were 161,000 in 1954 when the first separate count was made.

Source: (1) and (2) *South African statistics, 2002*, pp. 9.3 and 19.1.2; (3) *Union Statistics*, G-3, *SA Statistics, 1970*, H-46 and 1995, p. 7.20; (4) South African Reserve Bank, *Quarterly Bulletin*.

again valued at constant prices. This second series, value added at constant prices, provides a more comprehensive basis for an assessment of the overall performance of the sector, and its slower growth is a pointer to the rapid increase in non-farm inputs that was one of the principal factors responsible for the post-war acceleration.

At the beginning of the post-war period the demand for farm labour was still increasing, and the number of full-time employees (all but 2 per cent of whom were black) rose to a peak of 873,000 in 1962. Thereafter the trend was downward, and by 1980 the regular labour force had fallen below its initial level in 1947 (see column (3) of the table). The number of seasonal and casual workers employed on farms fell even more steeply. To begin with, employers looked to well-tried measures of coercion, legislative controls, and discrimination to ensure that they could obtain all the labour they needed, and saw no need to break with tradition by paying higher wages. However, it was evident by the 1960s that this policy was not working, and when urban employers began to raise wages and improve working conditions for black workers in manufacturing, the effects were felt even in isolated rural areas. Farmers were forced to recognize the need for better remuneration and, after a long period of stability, real farm wages in the Transvaal and Orange Free State more than doubled between the mid-1960s and mid-1970s.

There was considerable short-term variation in output as a result of changing weather conditions, and the period of three decades covered by the table includes an initial phase of rapid growth in the physical volume of output from 1948 to 1960 at an average rate of 5.3 per cent per annum, a short period of stagnation at the beginning of the 1960s, and then a renewed spurt at 4.2 per cent per annum from the mid-1960s to the end of the 1970s. The combination of rising output and a regular labour force that was growing only very slowly or declining meant that there was a substantial increase in output for each worker over the period as a whole. The growth in labour productivity was especially rapid in this final phase, at about 5.7 per cent per annum.

The largest contribution to the improved output performance came from increased production of cereals, but significant advances were also made on wine farms in the western Cape, on Natal sugar plantations, and on fruit farms in the eastern Transvaal. There was a striking rise in the area of maize under cultivation: from about 3,000,000 acres after the war to over 5,500,000 by the early 1970s. Output was further boosted by an impressive increase of over 90 per cent in average maize yields on white farms: from 690 kg a hectare in the five years ending in 1949/50 to 1,310 kg a hectare in the five years to 1970/1. The sources for this markedly improved performance included a substantial increase in the area of irrigated land; the use of high-yield and drought-resistant hybrid maize seeds developed in South Africa; intensive application of chemical fertilizers and of sprays for weed and pest control; more efficient planting and harvesting; and better management of the soil. There was more recognition of the need to avoid monoculture; and the Soil Conservation Act (1946) and subsequent legislation provided a framework for the promotion of good farming practices, with assistance for conservation and reclamation of land. Public funds were also used to promote research and to diffuse better farming methods.

Output of wool, meat, and dairy products showed much less progress, and adverse environmental conditions continued to be exacerbated by poor management of the animals. The stock of cattle was broadly static over the period, and although sheep flocks rose in the early 1950s they declined when the price of wool came down from the high levels reached during the Korean War boom, so that there was no net change over the whole period. The result of this divergent experience was a marked increase in the contribution of arable and horticultural farming to the total value of production (at current prices), from 53 per cent at the beginning of the post-war period to 64 per cent at the end of the 1970s.

One crucial element behind both the rise in labour productivity and the increased outlays on non-farm inputs was the rapid increase in use of capital assets (see column (4) of Table 8.7) and the spread of mechanization. In 1947 there were only 20,000 tractors, equivalent to less than one for every six farming units. By 1960 the number had jumped to 121,000, with an average of at least one per farm, and the corresponding figure for 1975 was 173,000, equivalent to more than 2.2 tractors per farm. This was a marked rise in the capital intensity of production, even allowing for the larger size of farms. There was also a substantial increase in the use of combine harvesters and other machinery. Work such as weeding, planting, reaping, threshing, and gleaning that was previously done almost completely by hand or with the use of animal-drawn implements could be done by machinery with fewer workers and in a shorter time. Mechanization was also introduced for fertilizing and for delivery of the crops. The latter originally involved extremely labour-intensive and time-consuming tasks filling, weighing, and sewing 200lb bags of grain, loading them individually onto a trailer, transporting the trailer to a depot, and off-loading and stacking each bag. From the early 1960s this was progressively replaced by bulk handling and storage, in which grain was transferred directly from threshing machines or combine harvesters into bulk trailers, which were then driven to the depots where the grain was easily emptied into large silos. However, all these machines could not be 'fed' with produce grown on the farm – they required fuel, spares, repairs, and maintenance that had to be purchased from other sectors.

Farmers were encouraged to invest heavily in machinery and equipment by a combination of policy measures involving easy access to capital at low rates of interest, and favourable tax provisions allowing 100 per cent of the capital cost to be written off against tax in the year of purchase. An additional contributory factor in the 1970s and early 1980s was the overvaluation of the rand, which lowered the cost of imported capital goods. Despite the low wages paid to black farm workers, these factors made it profitable for farmers to substitute capital for labour.

Figure 8.1 illustrates the growth of output (in real terms), of total factor inputs, and of the relationship between them, or total factor productivity.[26] The factor inputs include land, labour (including the full-time equivalent number of casual and seasonal workers), capital (including

---

[26] The data are taken from World Bank, *South African agriculture*, Discussion Paper No. 6, World Bank, 1994, p. 123, and are based on research by C. Thirtle et al., *Explaining total factor productivity in South African commercial agriculture, 1947–91*, Discussion Paper Series G no. 7, University of Reading, 1993. It must be noted that the technical basis of their indices of output and inputs differs from those of the indices in Table 8.7, and they also use different definitions of labour and capital.

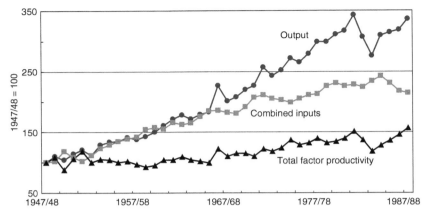

Figure 8.1. Farm output, inputs, and total factor productivity, 1947/48–1987/88

Source: World Bank, *South African agriculture*, Discussion Paper 6, Washington, DC: World Bank, 1994, p. 123.

machinery and equipment, improvements to land and buildings, and animals), and various types of intermediate inputs. The series for total factor productivity thus measures the changes in farm output per unit of all inputs. As the chart shows, there was an initial period – from the end of the Second World War until the mid-1960s – when total farm output and total inputs grew at roughly the same pace, so that all the extra output came from the use of additional inputs; there was no improvement in efficiency. After that, the growth of output was more rapid than the increase in inputs, and total factor productivity increased at a satisfactory rate of about 2 per cent per annum until the end of the 1970s. However, this overall productivity performance masks significant differences between the three farming sectors. The rate of growth of total factor productivity was consistently most rapid in the export-oriented and inherently labour-intensive horticultural sector (producing wine, fresh fruit, and vegetables), and slowest in the livestock sector producing largely for the domestic market.

Although the overall performance was thus much better, the standard of South African farming was still poor by international standards. It remained essential for the government to divert substantial funds to commercial agriculture, and it was calculated that state aid to white farmers accounted for about a fifth of their net farm income in the late 1960s.[27]

---

[27] Commission of Inquiry into Agriculture (Marais/Du Plessis), *Third (Final) Report*, 1972, para. 5.12.

The major form of support consisted of payments to marketing boards to help stabilize prices at times of excess supply, and only a small fraction (about 13 per cent) of farm produce was sold on the free market. The general policy of favouring producers at the expense of consumers introduced in the 1930s (see Chapter 6) remained firmly in place, and the pursuit of self-sufficiency kept out foreign competition regardless of the adverse effects on efficiency. Farmers were also assisted in many other ways, including drought and flood relief, cheap loans, rebates on fuel, subsidies for fertilizers, reduced railway rates on farm products, and payments for pest and weed control, irrigation, and soil conservation. As with manufacturing, the low efficiency of the largely illiterate labour force was a powerful factor restraining progress. To give just one illustration, it was estimated in 1971 that maintenance costs of farm equipment were 18 cents per hour, compared with 5 cents in the United Kingdom. The size of this differential was eloquent proof that the low nominal wages paid to black farm workers could in no way compensate for the inferior education and training that their white employers still insisted on.

9   Hitting the barriers: from triumph to disaster

Following the development of the diamond fields of Kimberley in the early 1870s, the South African economy achieved a hundred years of successful economic growth. Previous chapters have charted the process by which a relatively backward country, almost wholly dependent on a largely self-sufficient agricultural sector, was transformed into a dynamic, modern, capital-intensive economy. From the 1920s to the 1970s an expanding industrial sector was supported by a combination of high profits and abundant foreign exchange derived from unlimited international demand for gold. There was then a dramatic structural break and the economy switched from apparently triumphant progress to distressing decline.

The present chapter first establishes the main features of this turning point. This is followed by an analysis of the reasons for the severe downturn in gold mining, and of the problems experienced in the attempt to promote the expansion of exports of manufactures. The chapter ends with a review of the effects of the rise and fall in fixed capital formation.[1] The further consequences of these developments for the balance of payments and the labour market, and the eventual retreat from apartheid, are examined in the final chapter. Unfortunately, it is impossible to analyse these developments in a complex economy without using certain economic concepts and terms, and readers who find that at some point this chapter becomes too technical and difficult are encouraged to omit the remaining sections and go straight to Chapter 10.

From growth and stability to stagnation and inflation

Columns (1) and (2) of Table 9.1 reveal the many striking contrasts between a phase of growth and stability from 1948 to 1973, and one of

---

[1] This is the technical term for capital expenditure on fixed assets such as buildings and machinery.

Table 9.1. *Indicators of a structural break in economic performance c. 1973*

	(1) 1948–73	(2) 1973–94	(3) 1973–81	(4) 1981–94
Annual percentage growth rate				
Real GDP per head	2.2	−0.4	1.2	−1.3
Real output				
GDP	4.8	1.8	3.5	0.8
Manufacturing	7.3	1.9	5.2	−0.1
Gold mining	3.5	−1.8	−3.3	−0.9
Employment				
Agriculture	0.0	−1.4	−2.3	−0.8
Mining and quarrying	1.7	−0.9	0.7	−1.9
Manufacturing	4.2	0.9	3.0	−0.4
Real output per worker[a]	2.9	1.0	2.1	0.3
Real output per unit of capital[a]	−0.4	−2.2	−2.8	1.9
Real fixed capital formation	5.3	0.2	4.3	−2.3
Unemployment[b]	6.6	8.7	3.0	12.7
Exports at constant prices				
Merchandise	6.6	4.3	4.3	4.4
Total including gold[c]	4.7	1.6	0.3	2.4
Consumer prices	3.6	13.8	12.7	14.5
Exchange rate				
US dollar:rand	0.1	−7.5	−2.3	−11.9
Percentage of GDP (average for period)				
Current account	−2.5	1.1	−0.7	1.3

[a] In manufacturing.
[b] Dates are 1950, 1970, 1980, and 1995.
[c] Includes non-factor services.

Source: Employment and consumer prices: *South African statistics, 2002*; unemployment: see Annexe 3; volume of merchandise exports: 1948–60 from International Monetary Fund, *Yearbook of International Financial Statistics*, and all other series from South African Reserve Bank, *Quarterly Bulletin*.

stagnation and inflation from 1973 to 1994.[2] On every one of the indicators shown in the table there was a marked deterioration in performance, and on most of them there was a further worsening within that final phase, seen in columns (3) and (4). There was an actual decline in real output per head, and a marked slowdown in the rate of growth of output,

[2] The focus in this context is on these medium-term phases, not on short-run cyclical fluctuations within each phase. The three end points are roughly comparable in the sense that each is a cyclical peak.

employment, labour productivity, and exports. Other signs of crisis included a change from rapid growth to stagnation in real gross fixed capital formation, diminishing output per unit of capital, rising unemployment, rapid inflation, a steep depreciation in the exchange rate, and a persistent balance-of-payments problem.

Three main economic explanations are suggested for the deterioration. First, the position of the gold mines was transformed by far-reaching changes for the worse in both domestic supply and foreign demand. Costs of production rose rapidly as the richer seams were exhausted, and gold lost its special position as the ultimate reserve asset for the international monetary system. The crisis was not immediately apparent. On the contrary, while the price of gold was rising during the 1970s it seemed to many that the Republic was entering a new era of growth and prosperity. But when the price plunged downwards after 1980 the illusion was shattered. The engine which had once driven the whole economy forward so vigorously had clearly stalled.

Second, there was a succession of adverse external economic and political changes. From the 1970s, world output and trade ceased to grow at the exceptionally rapid pace enjoyed during the previous 'golden age'; a worldwide surge in the price of oil and other commodities increased inflationary pressures in South Africa; and rising demand for gold and other natural resources drove up the exchange rate, making it more difficult for manufacturers to export. Some of these trends were reversed in the 1980s, but international hostility to apartheid became substantially stronger, and there was an abrupt loss of confidence in the prospects for financial and political stability, leading to a massive outflow of capital.

The final, and most deep-seated cause, was the persistent underlying weakness identified in earlier chapters (and examined further below) that was responsible for low levels of efficiency and high costs of production in the industrial sector. The more the economy became dependent on industry for further growth, the greater the harmful impact of this low competitive capability. These three sets of economic factors interacted with, and added to, seething political discontent and militant activity by black people in mines and factories, townships and schools, farms and villages.

This failure of the economy was clearly one of the decisive forces that persuaded the new State President, F. W. de Klerk, to make the dramatic change in policy announced in 1990, leading to public negotiations with the African National Congress (ANC) and other parties, and culminating in democratic elections in 1994. A full analysis of this conclusive – and, to many observers, surprisingly sudden – collapse of white supremacy would need to assess the relative contribution of several major factors. Within South Africa, these included the growing success of the struggle waged by the ANC and its allies, forcing the authorities to resort to ever more violent and repressive measures; the failure of the 'homelands' policy to provide a genuine alternative to the unstoppable urbanization of the African population; changes in the character of the National Party and in the interests of its supporters; and the corrosive effects of white prosperity on their willingness to make economic sacrifices in the pursuit of white supremacy. Among the international forces were the replacement of white minority rule in neighbouring countries by black governments sympathetic to the ANC; the removal of the threat from international communism following the disintegration of the Soviet empire and the end of the cold war; and the mounting strength of the global campaign against apartheid.

Such an evaluation of all these domestic and international forces is beyond the scope of this survey of the economic history of South Africa, and the aim of this and the following chapter is to examine the reasons for the critical deterioration in economic performance, not to assert that it was uniquely important. The first theme to be considered is the turning point in the fortunes of the gold mines.

The decline of gold mining despite yet another windfall

By the late 1960s mining companies were beginning to feel the pressure of a familiar problem, one they remembered keenly from previous difficult episodes. As in the years before the First World War, in the 1920s, and in the 1940s, their costs of production were spiralling upwards, while the price of gold remained fixed and beyond their control. Many mines survived only with assistance from the government; others depended on the related profits from producing uranium or concentrated production on higher grades of ore which could be mined more cheaply. Once again the companies were hoping to be rescued by yet another windfall. From 1971 their wish was granted, when the United States took the first step towards the abolition of the fixed price for gold of $35 per fine ounce that had prevailed since 1934.[3]

---

[3] The United States achieved a devaluation of the dollar by increasing the price of gold to $38.0 per fine ounce in December 1971, and there was a further increase for the same reason to $42.2 in February 1973. The Bretton Woods system of fixed exchange rates was replaced by floating rates for all the leading currencies, and after prolonged discussion it was formally agreed in 1976 to abolish the official price of gold and to demonetize gold internationally (as it had previously been nationally). Since then, gold has no longer served as either a standard of value or a medium of exchange.

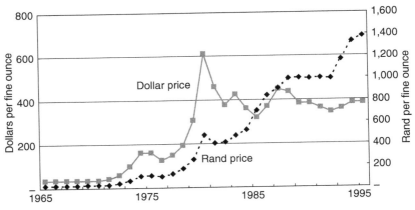

Figure 9.1. Price of gold in US dollars and in rand per fine ounce, 1965–95

From then on, the dollar price of gold, shown in Figure 9.1, was determined by market forces and rose rapidly in a decade of raging worldwide inflation. This was partly a response to the general dislocation of international financial markets following the demise of the Bretton Woods system, and partly because inflationary surges encouraged many people and institutions to hold gold, either as a hedge against rising prices, or simply in anticipation that the upward trend in the gold price would continue. By 1978 it had reached almost $200, and in January 1980 it soared to an over-exuberant peak of $850. The fever then subsided, and over the 15 years from 1982 the dollar price fluctuated in a narrow range around an average of $380 per fine ounce – at least ten times higher in nominal terms than it had been under the fixed price regime. Moreover, the sharp depreciation of the rand against the dollar after 1980 – from R0.78 to R2.23 by 1985 and R3.63 by 1995 – meant that the rand price of gold increased even more steeply than the dollar price (see Figure 9.1).[4] Initially the increase in price easily outpaced rising working costs, but while the price stabilized, costs continued to increase, and the profitability of mining operations fell sharply in the 1980s.

Mining companies reacted swiftly to the early rise in prices by shifting extraction to lower grades of ore that had not been profitable to exploit at lower prices, and by mining deeper and less accessible reefs. Until 1977, as the price of gold raced higher, they held the tonnage of ore treated roughly constant, and were able to improve profitability even while the

[4] For further discussion of movements in the exchange rate see p. 214 below.

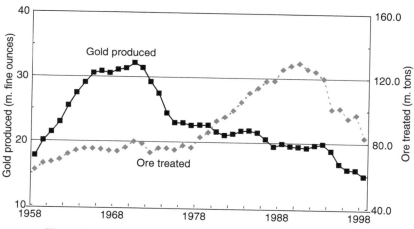

Figure 9.2. Gold produced and ore treated, 1958–98

average grade of ore was falling sharply. The result of these two trends was, however, a precipitous fall in the quantity of gold produced, from a peak of over 32,000,000 fine ounces in 1970 to 22,500,000 in 1977, and this decline had a strong negative impact on the overall rate of growth of real GDP.[5] The very different movements in the series for the amount of ore processed and the amount of gold produced are shown in Figure 9.2 and also in columns (1) and (2) of Table 9.2, with the average grade of ore in column (3).

In the next phase, from 1977 until 1990, the two series again moved in different directions, but this time the tonnage of ore milled was steadily increased, while the output of gold drifted gently downwards. The quantity of ore milled eventually reached a peak of 129,000,000 tons, 62 per cent above the level in 1970, but its gold content fell continuously, and by 1990 was only 3 dwts per ton. From the beginning of the 1990s the output of gold resumed its downward course, and by 2000 it had fallen to 13,800,000 tons, a reduction of almost 30 per cent over the final decade of the twentieth century. The inevitable consequence of this development and of the fall in price was a commensurate decline in the value of exports of gold, so that its contribution to total exports plunged from a peak of 45 per cent in 1979–84 to less than 24 per cent in the mid-1990s (as shown

---

[5] It is the quantity of gold produced that is used to measure the contribution of gold mining to overall GDP. Ore treated may be a better measure of the actual volume of work done by mines, but gold produced is more closely related to the income received and thus to value added by the industry.

Table 9.2. *South African gold mines: ore milled, output, price, and sales,*
1970–2000

	(1) Ore milled (million tons[a])	(2) Output of gold (million fine ounces)	(3) Average grade (dwts per ton[b])	(4) Price received (rand per fine ounce)	(5) Value of gold sales (R million)
1970	80.0	32.2	8.0	26	831
1977	76.7	22.5	5.9	125	2,815
1980	93.3	21.6	4.6	480	10,375
1985	113.8	21.6	3.8	702	15,140
1990	129.4	19.4	3.0	992	19,239
1995	101.5	16.8	3.3	1,382	23,219
2000	80.9	13.8	3.4	1,926	26,507

[a] Metric tons of 2,004.6 lb.
[b] 20 dwts (pennyweights)=1 fine ounce.

Source: Chamber of Mines, *96th Annual Report*, 1985, p. 58, continued from website
www.bullion.org.za, *South African mining industry, Statistical tables 2000*, pp. 15–16.

in column (1) of Table 9.5 below). By the late 1990s it had fallen below
18 per cent. Since this steep downward trend in output and exports could be
anticipated by the end of the 1980s, its damaging effects on domestic
and foreign confidence in the economy were felt well before the final
descent a decade later. Production and exports of other minerals – notably
diamonds, coal, copper, iron ore, and, in the 1990s, platinum –
were increasing, but they could not compensate for the decline of the
gold mines.

The increase in the price of gold was also associated with a revolutionary change in labour policy, though one that was largely forced on the
mining houses. They were increasingly worried about the extent of their
dependence on foreign labour from countries to the north that were
growing more hostile to South Africa, and considered it essential to
increase recruitment from within the country, in part from urban areas.
Given the extent to which wages in mining had fallen behind those offered
to African workers by industry, a very substantial increase was necessary
to make the mines more competitive. In addition, African workers were
gradually being allocated to skilled and semi-skilled work previously
undertaken by whites (see Chapter 6), and there was increasing recognition of the need to boost their productivity by greater attention to training
and the provision of incentives. Finally, there was mounting moral and
political pressure for higher wages, especially from abroad.

A leap of 36 per cent in the cash pay of African mine-workers in 1973 was followed by even greater advances, of 61 per cent and 68 per cent, in the two following years. After allowing for higher consumer prices, the average real wage of African mine-workers increased by 165 per cent in three years, though this was from a very low base. They made further but less spectacular advances in the remainder of the 1970s and through the 1980s, and since there were no corresponding increases for white miners, the ratio of white to black wages narrowed from over 15:1 in 1970 to 8:1 in 1975 and 5:1 in 1985.

The mining houses also used their increased profits to finance research and technological innovation, and to invest in the further mechanization required to contain the costs of mining lower grades of ore and of working at ever greater depths. A number of major advances were made in the 1980s, including general diffusion of hand-held hydraulic drills able to bore twice as many holes per shift as the pneumatic drills they replaced, and improvements in the equipment and techniques used to support the working face. Whereas the main thrust of technological advances made in earlier decades was the substitution of machinery for unskilled manual labour, what the mines were now seeking to achieve was increased productivity in the operation of machinery. There were also substantial investments in underground refrigeration and air-conditioning, as well as in new forms of underground transport.

Changes in government policy (discussed more fully in Chapter 10) finally eliminated all legal forms of job reservation and opened the way for the recognition of African trade unions. From 1981 agreement was reached enabling young people of all races to enter apprenticeships in a variety of artisan crafts on the mines; and in 1987 the Mines and Works Amendment Act was passed after protracted negotiations with the white unions, though the formal step necessary for its implementation was delayed for a further year. Removal of the 1926 regulation from the statute book finally cleared the way for Africans to obtain certificates of competency in blasting and other activities which had for so long been the exclusive preserve of white workers. The limit of 3 per cent that Verwoerd had previously imposed on the proportion of housing that could be allocated to miners' families was abandoned by the government, but the mining companies did not take advantage of this to build appreciably more family housing. They did, however, make some effort to stabilize their workforce by encouraging repeated re-engagement and, although the basic reliance on migrant labour remained, those recruited were predominantly men who were re-employed on successive contracts throughout their working lives.

The National Union of Mineworkers (NUM), under the astute leadership of Cyril Ramaphosa, was recruiting strongly and by 1986, two years after it was officially recognized, had a paid-up membership of 135,000. The union had a number of successes, but its bargaining position in major confrontations was gravely weakened by the conditions of general excess supply that existed in the labour market by the 1980s (see Chapter 10). In August 1987 a major strike, involving some 40 per cent of the workforce and lasting for three weeks, was defeated without any significant concession to the NUM's demands for a further large increase in pay, and was followed by large-scale dismissals.

The government also claimed a substantial share in the increased profits of the gold mines, and a large part of the ensuing additional tax revenue was devoted to improvements to the transport infrastructure, notably the development of new ports and associated railway lines at Saldanha Bay on the west coast and Richards Bay on the east coast. The former was designed particularly to serve new iron ore mines, and the latter was linked to the Natal coalfields. The national road system was also greatly extended and improved during the 1970s.

The final aspect to be considered is the outcome of these changes in terms of the mining companies' costs and profits. During the 1970s the impact of the unprecedented movements in the price of gold was very profitable for the mining houses, even after the payment of increased wages to black mine-workers. The combination of a higher dollar price and depreciation of the South African currency meant that the rise in the rand price for gold far outweighed the fall in quantity produced, so that the total value received from gold sales in rand was more than twelve times higher in 1980 than in 1970 (see columns (4) and (5) of Table 9.2). As can be seen in Table 9.3, working revenues per ton of ore milled raced ahead of working costs during this decade, even though there was little progress in labour productivity. As a result, working profits jumped from almost R4.00 per ton of ore milled in 1970 to R85.00 in 1980, and this very satisfactory level was broadly maintained until 1986. The benefits of the new labour arrangements and increased mechanization were seen in the improvement in productivity in the 1980s, when the mines were able to increase the tonnage of ore treated by almost 40 per cent with no growth in their total labour force (see column (4) of Table 9.3).

From the mid-1980s, however, conditions deteriorated, as the industry was crushed between a broadly stable dollar price for gold and sharply rising costs of production. On the demand side, the gold price was unable to break out of the range at which it had traded since the early 1980s. There was a substantial increase in the world supply of gold as new mines were developed abroad in response to the rise in price after 1971. But gold had lost its unique role in the world monetary system; and sales by the IMF, the US Treasury, and other central banks put downward pressure

Table 9.3. *South African gold mines: working revenue, costs, profits, and labour productivity, 1970–2000*

	(1) Working revenue	(2) Working costs (rand per ton of ore milled[a])	(3) Working profit	(4) Ore milled per worker (tons[a])
1970	11.2	7.3	3.9	193
1977	40.0	23.9	16.1	184
1980	120.6	35.5	85.0	199
1986	157.9	80.2	77.7	221
1990	163.5	130.3	33.2	273
1993	206.5	153.3	53.2	307
2000	284.2	219.5	64.7	410

[a] Metric tons of 2,004.6 lb.

Source: Chamber of Mines, *96th Annual Report*, 1985, p. 87, continued from website *www.bullion.org.za*, South African mining industry, *Statistical tables 2000*, pp. 19–20.

on the market price. Once inflation was brought under control, speculative demand to hold gold as an asset-hedge diminished. Other types of demand – for example, for jewellery, industrial use, and private hoarding of gold as a store of value – were not strong enough to counteract these forces.

With demand for gold and its dollar price thus constrained, gold mining needed to maintain its costs of production roughly constant, but it was not able to do this. On the contrary, South African producer prices continued to increase through the 1980s at an average rate of 12 per cent per annum, with consequent pressure on general expenses, including labour. Specific conditions on the mines added further to this economy-wide escalation of costs. Average grades of ore declined, better seams in the new mines developed after 1948 were worked out, and it became increasingly expensive to extract ore from the remaining gold-bearing seams as shafts deepened and the distance of the face from the shafts lengthened.

Even with the assistance of a further steep depreciation of the rand against the dollar, the value of sales could not keep pace with the rise in costs. From 1987 the favourable trend in the relationship between working costs and working revenue that the mines had enjoyed since 1970 was reversed. The ratio of costs to revenue climbed from 50 per cent in the mid-1980s to a crippling 80 per cent in 1990 (see columns (1) and (2) of Table 9.3). The resulting movements in working profit per ton milled are shown in column (3). The profit series reached a peak in the first half of the 1980s and then dropped sharply from R78.00 per ton to R33.00 a decade later. By 1987 one in five mines were producing at a cost that exceeded the current gold price. From that date the mining houses reacted to their rapidly deteriorating position by introducing massive programmes of rationalization. The number employed on the gold mines was cut from a peak of over 530,000 in 1986 to fewer than 200,000 at the end of the century. This sufficed to raise productivity and there was some improvement in profitability in the 1990s, but not to levels required to revive the industry.

On this occasion there was to be no external relief for gold mining; the history of 1932 or 1949 was not repeated. There were no new reefs waiting to be discovered by the geologists and prospectors; there was no prospect of a sustained and significant increase in the price of gold. The output of gold and its share in total exports fell steeply, old mines were closed, and the labour force was drastically reduced. The engine that had driven the South African economy forward so powerfully for 100 years was no longer functioning; indeed, as shown by the negative growth rates for the sector in Table 9.1, gold mining was now actually retarding the rest of the economy. The end of the 'wasting asset' so often predicted had finally become a reality.

The expansion of coal and platinum

The diversification of the mining industry noted earlier (see Chapter 8) continued, with the expansion of coal production as the dominant feature of the period after 1970. Prior to this, large deposits of easily accessible, cheap coal had supplied gold mining, electricity generation, and local industry, but exports were negligible because of high transport costs and the low quality of much of the coal. However, during the 1960s Anglo American engineers developed new washing techniques which removed sufficient of the high ash content to create good coking coal suitable for the iron and steel industries. In addition, large quantities of steam coal suitable for power stations and other industrial uses could be produced as a by-product of this low-ash coal. In the following decade, foreign demand for coal increased greatly as a result of the escalation of oil prices, and the oil crisis also encouraged the development of SASOL's oil-from-coal programme in South Africa.

Substantial new markets were found in Europe and Japan, both for coking coal and for steam coal for electricity generation, and production more than trebled from 55 million tons in 1970 to 175 million in 1985, while exports soared over the same period from just over 1 million tons to almost 47 million. The average value per ton of coal sold abroad raced to

R67.00 in 1985, so that the value of coal exports increased rapidly and became a significant source of foreign currency. Labour productivity was greatly increased by adopting more mechanized methods of extraction and introducing capital-intensive open-cast operations. By the mid-1980s over a third of the total output was produced by such mines. Massive new investments were also undertaken to improve the transport infrastructure and reduce the costs of moving and handling coal. A special electrified railway line was built, starting from the coalfields at Witbank in the eastern Transvaal, passing through those in Natal, and ending at Richards Bay on the east coast, where a new bulk coal terminal was constructed, capable of handling the huge carriers used in the international coal trade. Although the imposition of sanctions from the mid-1980s eliminated sales to Denmark, France, and the United States, alternative markets were found in South Korea, Taiwan, and certain Mediterranean countries, so that production and exports remained on a plateau at about the 1985 levels.

The other notable development in the mining industry was the emergence of the platinum group of metals (platinum, palladium, and rhodium). Production increased by 60 per cent between 1980 and 1994, while the price soared almost fivefold. The value of sales, almost all exported, thus increased to almost 12 per cent of total sales by the mining industry. In the late 1990s the price continued to rise rapidly, and by the end of the century the platinum group had displaced gold as South Africa's principal mineral. Increased demand was driven by several factors, including the growing popularity of platinum jewellery and use of the metal as a catalyst in new vehicle exhaust systems that were made compulsory in both the United States and European countries as a means of reducing pollution.

Manufacturing's failure to achieve export-led growth

The remarkable progress of manufacturing that started in the 1930s, continued during the Second World War, and accelerated after the war, was described in Chapters 6 and 8. In the early post-war period, from 1948 to 1973, both external and internal conditions were conducive to growth, so that expansion was particularly rapid. There was an almost threefold rise in employment, and the average rate of growth of real output was more than 7 per cent per annum over these 25 years. However, it was also noted that the peak growth rate of almost 10 per cent per annum was reached in the first half of the 1960s, and that growth was decelerating in the remainder of the period, though rates remained high (see Table 8.6).

Table 9.4. *Indices and growth rates of output, employment, fixed capital, and productivity in manufacturing, 1974–94*

	(1) Value added at constant prices	(2) Employment	(3) Labour productivity	(4) Fixed capital at constant prices	(5) Capital/labour ratio	(6) Capital/output ratio
Indices, 1974 = 100						
1974	100	100	100	100	100	100
1978	110	104	106	127	122	115
1981	141	120	118	172	144	122
1987	138	118	118	184	156	133
1994	139	113	123	216	191	156
Annual percentage growth rate						
1974–8	2.5	1.0	1.5	6.2	5.1	3.6
1978–81	8.5	4.8	3.6	10.6	5.6	1.9
1981–7	−0.4	−0.3	−0.1	1.1	1.4	1.5
1987–94	0.1	−0.6	0.6	2.3	2.9	2.3
1974–94	1.6	0.6	1.0	3.9	3.3	2.2

Sources: (1) and (2) *South African statistics, 2002*, Tables 19.1.2 and 7.1.1; (3) = (1) ÷ (2); (4) South African Reserve Bank, *Quarterly Bulletin*, June 1999; (5) = (4) ÷ (2); (6) = (4) ÷ (1).

The early 1970s marked the high point of South Africa's post-war economic performance. At some point between 1972 and 1975 – the precise date varies according to the series – there was a structural break and a shift to much lower rates of growth of output, employment, and productivity. The average annual rate of growth of real manufacturing output plunged from 7 per cent in 1948–74 to a miserable 1.6 per cent over the two following decades (see column (1) of Table 9.4). Even that slow pace owed much to a short-lived boom from 1978 to 1981 as the government took advantage of the exceptional surge in the gold price to boost the economy by a variety of expansionary measures, including large tax cuts and substantial increases in public expenditure in the budgets of 1979 and 1980.

After that spurt the sector suffered thirteen years of stagnation, ending with a level of real output marginally lower in 1994 than in 1981. In these circumstances there was no need to recruit additional workers, and the trend in employment was also downward from the early 1980s (see column (2) of the table). During this period there were, however, strong incentives for employers to substitute capital for labour (the reasons for this are discussed below), and capital per worker roughly doubled over the period, but with little benefit in terms of higher output per worker, as shown in columns (3) and (5). Furthermore, the growth of the stock of fixed capital also outpaced the growth of real output, so that there was a large rise in the capital/output ratio shown in column (6), in part because of the allocation of substantial resources to sectors such as metals and chemicals with above-average capital requirements for each unit of output. The inverse of this upward trend in the capital/output ratio indicates a considerable decline in the productivity of capital.

It was frequently stated that the balance of payments was the immediate constraint on the growth of manufacturing and of the economy more generally. Every attempt to accelerate the rate of growth of output led to a surge in imports and a weakening of the balance of payments. This could be accommodated if there was a sufficient inflow of long-term capital, but if that was not available the alternatives were either to resort to short-term borrowing to finance the deficit or to impose restrictive measures such as tighter import quotas and higher interest rates designed to make the economy grow more slowly. The former was inherently dangerous, and was not a sustainable long-term policy. The latter merely highlighted the nature of the low-growth equilibrium in which the economy was trapped. However, it is important to recognize that this binding balance-of-payments constraint should not be seen in isolation. It was not some exogenous force imposed on South Africa, but was itself part of the more general problem of low productivity and high costs which afflicted the economy and, in particular, the manufacturing sector.

If manufacturing was to take over as the engine of growth, it was thus essential that there should be a marked improvement in its export perform- ance in order to relieve the balance-of-payments constraint on growth. Ever since the inception of the policy of promoting industry in the 1920s, the sector had relied heavily on gold mining to cover the foreign exchange costs of the processed materials and capital goods it required from abroad. With the gold mines facing decline, the authorities believed that the time had come when manufacturing would have to pay its own way.[6] However, the good fortune which had attended South African development for so long appeared to have run its course, and the early 1970s was not a propitious time to attempt the conversion of manufacturing to export-led growth.

There were two crucial adverse factors, both of them outside South Africa's control: from 1973 the rate of growth of world output and trade dropped to a significantly slower pace as the long post-war boom enjoyed by the world economy reached its end (see Chapter 1), and there was a steep appreciation in South Africa's real effective exchange rate from 1970 to 1983.[7] The first severely restricted the growth of markets for South African exports; the second made them less competitive in those markets. The consequence was that manufacturing proved unable even to sustain its own standard of export performance during these years.

The appreciation of the rand was driven by the influence on South Africa of the worldwide upswing in general commodity prices. A fourfold increase in the price of oil at the end of 1973 as a consequence of the activities of the OPEC member states, was one powerful reason for the jump to much higher rates of increase in prices. There was a further 'oil shock' in 1979–80 after the revolution in Iran, and by early 1981 the dollar price of crude oil was more than ten times higher than it had been in 1973. On top of this, at the beginning of the 1970s food prices were driven sharply higher by crop failures in the United States and other countries, and at the same time a synchronized business cycle upswing in the major industrial countries caused prices of non-food industrial raw materials to accelerate. Total non-fuel commodity prices more than doubled between

---

[6] See the earlier discussion of this policy shift in Chapter 8.

[7] Exchange rates are normally quoted in terms of a single currency, but for an overall perspective it is helpful to have a measure of the rate of exchange against all a country's major trading partners. This is referred to as the nominal effective exchange rate. It is calculated by combining movements in each of the other currencies (dollar, sterling, yen, etc.) with weights based on their shares in trade with South Africa. The real effective exchange rate adjusts this measure for differences in movements in relative prices. If, for example, the nominal rate depreciated by 5 per cent, but South African prices rose by 10 per cent relative to those elsewhere, the real rate would appreciate by 4.5 per cent ($0.95 \times 1.10 = 1.045$), indicating a worsening in the country's competitive position.

1970 and 1974, paused at roughly that level until 1978, and then jumped again by a further one-third to a peak in 1980.

These large movements had powerful but mixed effects on the Republic. The rise in the price of imports during the 1970s far exceeded the rise in the price of non-gold exports. The terms of trade (excluding gold) thus worsened sharply over the decade and continued to fall until 1983, at which point there had been a deterioration of some 43 per cent in the ratio of export prices to import prices. However, this was more than offset by the steep increase in the price of gold, so that the overall terms of trade moved substantially in favour of South Africa in the 1970s and were then broadly stable in the 1980s and 1990s. The net effect was thus that the purchasing power of the country's residents was increased in the sense that a given amount of imports could be bought in the 1970s for fewer exports, and this advantage was retained in subsequent decades.

There was a huge increase in demand for mining exports such as metallic ores and minerals, while coal and uranium were in great demand as substitutes for oil (see column (4) of Table 9.5). A few manufactured products that were closely related to natural resources – notably iron and steel and non-ferrous metals – also experienced buoyant international demand (see column (3) of Table 9.6). As a relatively small country South Africa was essentially a price taker for these commodities; it could sell all it could produce at the prevailing prices and thus enjoyed a rapid increase in the value of these exports.

However, the 1970s commodity price boom also brought with it two significant adverse effects. Acceleration of inflation across the world triggered a huge increase in South Africa's import prices, and this added to domestic inflationary tendencies that were already very strong because of the higher wages conceded in mining, industry, and other sectors without compensating improvements in labour productivity.[8] As a result, the rate of increase of prices raced well ahead of rates in the country's main trading partners, and the disparity widened sharply in the 1980s and early 1990s, when South Africa was unable to emulate other developed countries in bringing inflation under control. After the initial external shock, the principal reasons for the persistence of rapid inflation in the Republic through the 1980s were largely domestic, with government policy playing a major role. The exchange rate was allowed to depreciate sharply after 1983 in the hope that this would stimulate exports, even though this raised the cost of imported materials and supplies, and thus spread higher prices through the economy. In addition, political pressures, sanctions, and the

---

[8] For reasons for this increase in wages see p. 206 above and pp. 230–2 in Chapter 10.

Table 9.5. *Composition of total and merchandise exports, 1967–96*

			Percentage of merchandise exports			
	Percentage of total exports		(3) Agriculture, forestry, and fishing	(4) Other mining and quarrying	(5) Manufactures	(6) _a_ Total
	(1) Gold	(2) Merchandise				
1967–9	34.6	65.4	20.0	20.8	58.2	100.0
1970–2	36.7	63.3	17.1	19.3	62.7	100.0
1973–5	43.9	56.1	17.8	19.0	62.5	100.0
1976–8	35.9	64.1	13.1	26.4	59.9	100.0
1979–81	45.2	54.8	11.4	32.7	55.5	100.0
1982–4	45.0	55.0	9.6	36.0	54.0	100.0
1985–7	40.9	59.1	6.6	33.7	59.3	100.0
1988–90	34.0	66.0	6.2	35.1	56.5	100.0
1991–3	29.0	71.0	5.1	36.5	55.9	100.0
1994–6	23.7	76.3	6.3	28.1	64.0	100.0

_a_ Including items not classified.

Source: South African statistics, various issues (adjusted to eliminate various inconsistencies in the published classification of manufactured goods) and Department of Trade and Industry website *http://www.thedti.gov.za/econdb.*

attempt to alleviate rising socioeconomic tensions induced the authorities to maintain more expansionary fiscal and monetary policies than the pursuit of inflation control alone would have dictated. Current government expenditure as a percentage of GDP raced from 15 per cent in the 1960s to over 23 per cent in 1980–4 and by 1990–4 exceeded 30 per cent. The rate of inflation was, nevertheless, relatively moderate by comparison with many developing economies, and the fiscal deficit was always covered by issuing debt, not by printing money.

The second adverse effect of the commodity price boom was that the surge in exports of gold and other natural resources sustained the nominal exchange rate at a broadly stable level from 1978 to 1983, despite the increase in relative prices, so that the real exchange rate appreciated by over 36 per cent in these five years. This was South Africa's version of the 'Dutch disease' from which the Netherlands (and Britain) also suffered.[9]

[9] This was the name given to the harm done to manufacturing and other sectors when a country's effective exchange rate appreciated steeply because of a large increase in the value of major natural resource exports (such as gold for South Africa, North Sea oil and gas for the Netherlands and Britain).

Table 9.6. *Composition of exports of manufactures, 1967–93*

	(1) Traditional industries[a]	(2) Paper, paper products, and chemicals[b]	(3) Iron and steel and non-ferrous metal basic industries	(4) Metal products, machinery, and vehicles[c]	(5) Jewellery and other industries[d]	(6) Total manufacturing
			(per cent)			
1967–9	28.0	19.1	33.4	12.4	7.2	100.0
1970–2	28.9	17.2	32.0	14.1	7.8	100.0
1973–5	31.9	14.0	34.5	11.2	8.4	100.0
1976–8	26.6	14.8	41.3	10.1	7.1	100.0
1979–81	22.5	13.7	48.7	9.1	6.0	100.0
1982–4	20.3	15.1	52.0	8.6	4.0	100.0
1985–7	17.8	15.6	53.2	8.5	4.8	100.0
1988–90	20.0	22.0	41.1	11.7	5.2	100.0
1991–3	21.2	26.5	32.6	17.8	1.9	100.0

[a] Food, drink, and tobacco; textiles, leather, and clothing; wood and furniture; glass, pottery, and other non-metallic minerals.

[b] Including products of petroleum and coal.

[c] Metal products: electrical and non-electrical machinery; motor vehicles; other transport equipment.

[d] Jewellery, professional and scientific equipment, and other manufacturing industries.

Source: South African statistics, various issues (adjusted to eliminate various inconsistencies in the published classification of manufactured goods) and Department of Trade and Industry website *http://www.thedti.gov.za/econdb.*

This reduction in competitiveness was very damaging for exports of manufactures that were not directly linked to natural resources. There could be no possibility of export-led industrialization while the gold and commodity price boom was sustained and the real exchange rate was appreciating.

Given the expansion of exports of minerals and metals, the failure to achieve the desired switch to export-orientated industrialization in the 1970s might not seem to matter. But the commodity price boom could not last; it was only a temporary phenomenon created by an unusual combination of circumstances. As soon as it abated, the South African economy would again find itself in difficulty and would need to expand its exports of a wider range of manufactures if it was to break out of its low-growth trajectory. After a severe contraction in the volume of manufacturing exports in the early 1980s, sales abroad did indeed recover, and expanded quite rapidly, once the upward trend in the exchange rate was reversed. This happened as soon as gold and commodity prices started to fall, and between 1983 and 1986 the nominal effective exchange rate lost more than half its value, while the real rate improved by a third. The recovery in many developed countries in the 1980s also improved the prospects for South African exports.

The authorities took advantage of the improvement in exports to resume the programme of dismantling import licences and quotas begun in the early 1970s. The change in policy had initially been instituted under pressure to meet the country's obligations as a member of the IMF and a signatory to international trade agreements, but it was also regarded as desirable as part of the move towards a more export-orientated system of trade. The abolition of quantitative restrictions could not be sustained without some compensating increase in customs tariffs, but the net outcome was a degree of progress between 1972 and 1976 towards the liberalization of trade. The process then stalled as the appreciation of the rand described above started to make conditions difficult for exporters. It was revived in 1983 when this trend was reversed and the rand started to depreciate, so that the authorities were optimistic about the prospects for exports and the balance of payments. Over the next two years, the proportion of the value of imports subject to quantitative restrictions was slashed from 77 to 23 per cent, and by 1991 it had fallen to 10 per cent. This was again only partly offset by higher tariffs, so that the overall effect was a significant reduction in the long-standing policy of protection.

Manufacturers were given a further incentive to expand their exports by the depressed condition of the home market and rising excess capacity. A substantial part of the increase in sales abroad was thus a replacement for domestic sales – undertaken to utilize spare capacity – not an addition to total output. Such exports did not call forth new capacity or promote growth. While some progress was made, the attainment of the desired goal of export-led growth remained elusive, and there were significant problems in the formulation and execution of an appropriate trade strategy. The issues involved were complex and contentious, and it proved difficult to attain a consensus or to follow a consistent and coherent policy. The increasing threat of sanctions (see below) further weakened enthusiasm for a switch, and ensured that projects such as SASOL I and II and Mossgas – designed to maintain strategic self-sufficiency in energy and other resources – remained priorities regardless of their true economic cost. Proposals to lower costs for exporters by reducing protection on industrial materials and capital goods roused opposition from powerful vested interests among employers and white trade unions engaged in local production of these goods. Instead, general incentives for exporters were introduced to offset the costs of protection, but they were prohibitively expensive and were criticized for tending to subsidize firms that would have exported anyway.

An alternative strategy was suggested to overcome this by means of targeted intervention designed to select particular industries for their export potential, and to improve their competitive capability by means of special incentives. However, the enhanced role this would have created for state bureaucrats was strongly rejected both by business and by other government departments. A more general criticism of many of the schemes proposed is that the trade strategy was seen in isolation, with too little attention given to the need to overcome fundamental supply-side weaknesses. Export-led growth could not be achieved without increased productivity, sustained technical progress, and new investment in physical and human capital.

Opponents of further state involvement in relation to exports found plenty of ammunition in the government's record in relation to the preceding twenty-five-year programme of import licensing (see Chapter 8). The system essentially required the authorities to decide how scarce foreign exchange should be allocated, rather than allowing the market to do so through the price mechanism. A few South African economists were willing to argue that state agencies had superior knowledge, could take a longer view, and moved more swiftly and flexibly than the market. But the general opinion was that the net effects of government intervention tended to be negative rather than positive. Selective intervention was not, in general, judicious and fine-tuned; bureaucratic administrators were more likely to introduce distortions and waste than to correct market failures.

This judgement was powerfully reinforced by mounting international evidence of the dismal record of experience in India and many parts of Latin America that had relied primarily on import substitution, contrasted with the success of outward-looking economies such as South Korea, Taiwan, Hong Kong, and Singapore. There was undoubtedly a significant degree of state intervention in the latter group, as there had earlier been in Japan, but always within a context in which private enterprise and market forces were dominant, so that prevailing prices (including exchange rates) provided a broadly reliable reflection of real resource costs. Critics of import substitution argued that industries that developed behind the shelter of protective tariffs and import controls were deprived of the crucial stimulus to increase efficiency that foreign competition provided. The most inefficient absorbed resources that might have been better deployed in other activities. The size of the domestic market was limited by high costs of production and the unequal distribution of income. More rapid growth of exports was obstructed because an industrial structure engendered by import substitution did not promote those industries in which the country had a true comparative advantage.

For all these reasons there was, therefore, a signal failure to attain a new growth path driven forward by rapid expansion of non-gold exports. The average rate of growth in the volume of merchandise exports was an impressive 7.3 per cent per annum from 1948 to 1972, but it then dropped abruptly to 1.7 per cent in 1972–84, including a terrible phase of sharply falling exports from 1981 to 1983 when the adverse effects of the appreciation of the real effective exchange rate were most damaging. The competitive position of exporters improved with the subsequent depreciation of the real exchange rate, and the growth rate of the volume of merchandise exports recovered to 6.1 per cent per annum after 1984.

This was a satisfactory performance, but well below what would have been required to launch the economy into a new orbit propelled by exports of manufactured goods. It was also significant that manufacturers of 'modern' products such as machinery and vehicles failed to increase their share of exports of manufactured goods (see column (4) of Table 9.6). Furthermore, the corresponding estimate for the volume of gold exported declined from 3.9 per cent per annum in 1948–72 to –2.1 per cent in 1972–84 and continued to decline at that rate from 1984 to 1994. The average rate of growth of the total volume of exports thus declined drastically from 5.2 per cent per annum in 1948–72 to –0.2 per cent in 1972–84 and then recovered, but only to 3.1 per cent from 1984 to 1994.

From the early 1980s the economy was thus trapped in a vicious circle. A generally low standard of efficiency and poor labour productivity kept costs of production high and retarded the rate of growth of exports. The resulting pressures on the balance of payments forced the authorities to restrict imports, both directly through quotas and controls, and indirectly through tight fiscal and monetary policy. These policies discouraged investment by dampening business confidence and limiting the supply of essential capital and intermediate goods from abroad. From the mid-1980s sanctions cut off the flow of funds from New York, London, and other financial centres. Slow growth and low investment then reinforced the basic weakness of the economy and prevented any escape from low levels of productivity.

The decline in fixed investment

The initial rise and subsequent decline in investment in fixed assets (gross domestic fixed capital formation) at current prices is charted in Figure 9.3 for the period 1954–94. The series is expressed as a percentage of gross domestic product to eliminate the effects of steeply rising prices. In addition to the overall investment ratio, the graph shows the corresponding percentages for the private and public sectors. The latter covers capital expenditure by both public corporations (such as ISCOR) and state-owned business enterprises (for example, those responsible for transport and communications) as well as by general government for school buildings, hospitals, and other fixed assets for public services. The overall investment ratio began to rise from 1963, as the economy recovered from the post-Sharpeville crisis, and swept upwards in three successive booms to peak in 1976 at almost 30 per cent. The movement was then reversed and the ratio started to fall, at first slowly and then, after 1981, more rapidly. By 1993 it had plunged below 15 per cent.

The critical factor in both the upswing from 1963 and the downward movement from 1976 was the behaviour of public-sector investment and, in particular, of the major corporations such as SASOL, ISCOR, and ESCOM. The share of government and public enterprises in total investment increased from 45 per cent in 1963 to 53 per cent in 1976, and then declined rapidly to 27 per cent in 1994.[10] At its peak the public-sector investment ratio was almost 16 per cent of GDP; by 1994 it had been cut to 4 per cent. Capital formation by private business enterprises was much less volatile, rising from 1963 by only 5 percentage points to peak in 1982 at over 15 per cent of GDP, and then falling back by 1993 to its previous level.

The peak years of fixed capital formation took the investment ratio to levels that were high – though not exceptional by international standards – and the dominant component of this increase was capital expenditure by the public

---

[10] The decline is slightly overstated because of the partial privatization of SASOL in 1987 and of ISCOR in 1989.

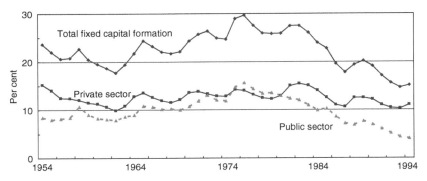

Figure 9.3. Fixed capital formation as per cent of gross domestic product, 1954–94

Source: South African Reserve Bank, *Quarterly Bulletin.*

sector. This was undertaken partly to promote self-sufficiency in oil and other requirements which were possible targets for external sanctions and embargoes, and partly to provide improvements to the economic and social infrastructure utilized by white households and by business enterprises. The former led to massive investment in the development of the synthetic fuels programme for the manufacture of oil from coal, and in the production of armaments; the latter led to the expansion of capacity for the provision of electricity, gas, and water, and of roads, railways, airlines, ports, and tele-phone services.

In both public and private manufacturing enterprises the attempt to overcome the scarcity of *skilled* workers by substituting capital for labour was encouraged by the rise in real wages of black workers in response to labour shortages from the 1960s (see Chapter 10 below), by the growing organization and militancy of the black workforce, and by state policies, notably influx controls, that artificially increased the cost of labour by restricting the numbers available for work in the urban areas. The reduction in the cost of capital also stimulated the adoption of more capital-intensive methods of production. This was partly the result of specific government policies, including generous tax concessions on machinery and equipment that favoured the most capital-intensive sectors (such as metals and chem-icals), and partly the effect of unplanned trends, notably the negative real interest rates that resulted from the failure of nominal rates to keep pace with the rapid increase in prices; and, in the period up to 1983, an over-valued exchange rate that favoured imports of capital equipment.

The public sector was also primarily responsible for the steep down-ward trend in the investment ratio after 1976. The imposition of financial sanctions after 1985 was an important cause of this sharp decline, since the public enterprises were cut off from their main source of funds and were forced to borrow in the domestic market at much higher rates of interest. Further investment in the public sector was also discouraged by the presence of substantial excess capacity created during the preceding expansion. Other factors that contributed to the decline in both public and private investment included worsening political and security conditions and a general loss of business confidence after 1985, the depreciation of the exchange rate, which increased the cost of imported capital equipment, and pressure on the government to divert tax revenues to current expenditures (such as increased pensions) accompanied by higher taxes and the phasing out of special allowances for investment.

During the 1960s and 1970s the growth of the economy was stimulated by the boost to aggregate demand given by the large programme of public and private investment, but this process was reversed in the two following decades as the downward trend in investment strengthened recessionary forces in the economy. Furthermore, public investment involved a large-scale allocation of resources to sectors with high capital/output ratios, but the additions to the capital stock that resulted from this were not matched by a commensurate increase in output. The decline in the productivity of capital (rise in the capital/output ratio) in the manufacturing sector – in which ISCOR, SASOL and other public corporations were prominent – and the unimpressive performance of total factor productivity was noted earlier with respect to the years 1948–73 and 1973–94.[11] There were broadly similar trends in several other sectors, and in the economy as a whole, so that the economy-wide productivity of capital was consistently falling from 1965 to 1994 (at an average rate of about –1.5 per cent per annum), and overall rates of growth of total factor productivity were very low. The poor productivity performance of the capital installed in both the public and private sectors thus contributed significantly to the low rates of growth of real output in the post-1973 phase.

The downward trend in output and exports of gold, the inability of manufacturing to achieve a more rapid expansion of exports, and the fall in the proportion of gross domestic product devoted to investment in fixed assets all contributed to the switch from progress to decline. The most important manifestations of the resulting crisis were seen in the balance of payments and in the labour market, and these developments are explored in the following chapter.

[11] See pp. 185 and 197, and Tables 8.5 and 9.4.

10 Confronting the contradictions: the final crisis and the retreat from apartheid

The problems of the mining and manufacturing sectors outlined in the previous chapter converged to create acute crises at two points at which the South African economy was most vulnerable. The development of these problems provides the main topic for this final chapter. A chronic balance-of-payments crisis compelled the authorities to restrain economic growth, while falling investment and a stagnant economy drove unemployment to intolerable levels. These were the critical symptoms of a more fundamental, chronic disease which fatally weakened the economy and helped to force the retreat from apartheid. The chapter ends with a brief discussion of the abiding fallacy of the benefits of 'cheap' labour, and of the principal reasons why the apartheid regime was ultimately unable to sustain a successful economy.

Sanctions, capital flows, and the balance-of-payments crises

The country's problems with respect to investment and the balance of payments were made more difficult to overcome by the growing momentum of anti-apartheid campaigns for sanctions, trade boycotts, and an end to investment in South Africa just as the temporary gains from the commodity price boom of the 1970s were coming to an end.

The earliest calls for sanctions were made in the 1960s, including a resolution of the General Assembly of the United Nations, but the movement had little effect until the mid-1980s. In 1985 and 1986 the European Community, the Commonwealth, the US Congress (which overrode President Ronald Reagan's veto to pass this legislation), the United Kingdom, and other individual governments voted to ban trade with South Africa in a wide range of products. Restrictions or bans were also placed on government and bank loans to South Africa and on private investment.[1]

---

[1] See further p. 228 below.

In addition to formal sanctions, more general political hostility, especially in Africa, also made it more difficult for exporters trying to build new markets. Nevertheless, the record suggests that, in the main, formal and informal *trade* sanctions had only very minor effects. Prohibitions on sales to South Africa were either not imposed or could be evaded, restrictions on exports had relatively little impact, with the notable exception of the widespread ban on purchases of South African iron and steel. However, *financial* sanctions were appreciably more damaging, and the virtual cessation of capital inflows described below was a source of really serious difficulty.

The problems that emerged in the 1980s were not initially anticipated. On the contrary, the remarkable surge in the gold price and the huge improvement in the balance of payments engendered a mood of great optimism. The prevailing attitude was well illustrated by Gerhard de Kock, governor-elect of the South African Reserve Bank, in his 1980 presidential address to the Economic Society of South Africa. He noted the substantial increases in the price of oil and gold, a structural increase in world demand for many other South African mineral exports, and the breakdown of the Bretton Woods system of fixed exchange rates, and judged that South Africa had come out well from these large changes: 'Because of the economy's increased fundamental strength, the long-term secular trend of economic activity will probably be strongly upwards'. There would inevitably continue to be cyclical fluctuations, but the higher gold price and stronger demand for other exports would loosen the balance-of-payments constraint, so that 'the South African economy can now afford stronger upswings and higher growth rates before deficits on the current account become large enough to bring about either a significant downward float of the rand or a marked decline in gold and other foreign reserves'.[2]

The impact on the balance of payments of the rise in price of gold and other commodities and of the resulting boom in exports of these natural resources in the 1970s can be seen in columns (1) to (3) of Table 10.1. Exports of goods other than gold rose from 13.5 per cent of GDP in 1964–73 to 17.9 per cent in 1977–80, and exports of gold from 7.9 per cent to 12.4 per cent. There was thus an increase in the ratio of total exports of goods and services to GDP of 9 percentage points. The authorities initially took advantage of the rise in exports to relax some of the quantitative restrictions on imports, while allowing the deficit on the current account to worsen from 3 per cent of GDP in 1964–73 to

---

[2] G. de Kock, 'The new South African business cycle and its implications for monetary policy', *SAJE*, 48, 1980, pp. 351–2.

Table 10.1. *Current account of balance of payments, 1946–94*

	(1) Merchandise exports	(2) Net gold exports	(3) Total exports of goods and services[a]	(4) Total imports of goods and services	(5) Net income paid abroad[b]	(6) Balance on current account[c]
	(percentage of GDP at current market prices)					
1946–58	17.3	9.7	30.5	31.2	5.1	−5.8
1959–63	16.6	10.4	30.3	23.3	4.1	2.9
1964–73	13.5	7.9	24.7	24.3	3.4	−3.0
1974–6	15.1	9.0	27.8	29.2	4.0	−5.4
1977–80	17.9	12.4	33.7	26.1	4.2	3.4
1981–4	12.7	10.7	26.3	25.1	4.2	−3.0
1985–8	16.0	10.5	29.3	21.8	4.2	3.3
1989–94	14.4	5.7	22.8	18.7	2.9	1.2

[a] Including net exports of services such as shipping and tourism.
[b] Net payments abroad of interest, dividends, and other income less net receipts of current transfers from abroad.
[c] (6) = (3) − (4) − (5)

Source: South African Reserve Bank, *Supplement to the Quarterly Bulletin*, June 2001, Table 1.

5.4 per cent in the mid-1970s (columns (4) and (6) of the table). However, when the rand started to appreciate in the late 1970s it quickly became necessary to use most of the further improvement in the export ratio to shift the current account from deficit into surplus, and the authorities were also compelled to act to reduce the import ratio from a level of more than 29 per cent during the mid-1970s.

From the mid-1970s, the relationship between the current and capital accounts that had prevailed in earlier decades changed markedly for the worse. In thirty-one years from 1946 to 1976 (inclusive), the only period in which there was not a continuous net *inflow* of capital was 1959–63, in the immediate aftermath of the shooting of protestors at Sharpeville. In the next eighteen years, from 1977 to 1994, the only period in which there was not a continuous *outflow* was 1981–4 (see column (2) of Table 10.2). South Africa could no longer compensate for current-account deficits by attracting either private or official capital from overseas. The first major crisis of this new period started in the winter of 1976, when the heroic student uprising in Soweto shattered the relative calm previously preserved by decades of ruthless suppression of political activity. Peaceful demonstrations against many features of Bantu education, most notably the imposition of Afrikaans as the medium of instruction for certain subjects, spread to

Table 10.2. *Balance of payments, current and capital accounts, 1946–94*

	(1) Balance on current account	(2) Investment and other capital flows[a]	(3) Net change in reserves [b]
	(percentage of GDP at current market prices)		
1946–58	−5.8	4.8	−1.0
1959–63	2.9	−1.5	1.4
1964–73	−3.0	3.0	0.0
1974–6	−5.4	3.2	−2.2
1977–80	3.4	−2.6	0.8
1981–4	−3.0	2.5	−0.5
1985–8	3.3	−3.4	−0.1
1989–94	1.2	−1.1	0.1

[a] Including unrecorded transactions; + = net receipts, − = net payments.
[b] Gold and foreign currency; + = net increase, − = net decrease.

Source: South African Reserve Bank, *Supplement to the Quarterly Bulletin,* June 2001, Table 1.

other parts of the country and were suppressed with great brutality and many deaths. From 1977 to 1980 there was a net outflow of capital, the first stage in a process which would culminate in the devastating debt crisis of 1985.

The primary reason for the intense balance-of-payments crisis that hit South Africa in the early 1980s was the sharp fall in the amount of foreign currency earned by exporters. Measured in current dollars, total exports plummeted from $26,000 million in 1980 to $16,000 million in 1985. The main damage was done by two factors. One was a fall in the dollar price of gold by approximately half, while the quantity of gold available for sale abroad remained broadly stable. The other was a depreciation of the rand against all major currencies by almost half. An increase in the volume of merchandise exports made possible by the depreciation of the currency was far too small to offset this massive movement in the exchange rate. In one sense, the depreciation of the currency was simply a desirable correction of an excessive previous appreciation, but the authorities had failed to take advantage of the preceding surge in the value of exports of gold and other natural resources to build up the country's net reserves of gold and foreign exchange, and there was almost nothing 'in the bank' with which to meet the developing crisis.

The position of the government was made more difficult by economic developments in the rest of the world during the same period. The rise in oil prices created massive current-account surpluses for the oil-exporting countries, but because many of them were not immediately able to spend commensurate amounts on domestic development, there were vast sums available for investment elsewhere. Much of this flowed towards developing countries. Unfortunately, the United States and many other developed countries were simultaneously raising interest rates in order to curb the inflationary surge of the 1970s. As this policy succeeded and prices started to fall, real interest rates (i.e. nominal interest rates corrected for the rate of increase of prices) reached very high levels. When the eventual fall in commodity prices caused a deterioration in their terms of trade, as export prices fell relative to those paid for imports, several developing countries suffered major foreign debt crises, including Mexico, Argentina, Chile, and Morocco. Failures in these financial markets initially made foreign bankers more eager to lend to South Africa, and in the early 1980s many lenders took a very optimistic view of the prospects for the price of gold and for the continued prosperity of the economy.

The immediate result of this impression that the Republic was a good credit risk – at a time when there were still large surpluses to be recycled from the oil producers – was a massive increase in the movement of capital to the country. However, the overwhelming bulk of the funds that flowed in during the early 1980s involved no long-term commitment to South Africa. The data on foreign liabilities assembled in Table 10.3 show an abrupt fall in the share of foreign direct and portfolio investment between 1980 and 1985, while the share of other types of investment jumped from 35 per cent to 62 per cent (see columns (2) to (4) of the table). This third category consisted predominantly of short-term loans and deposits, and the share of all short-term liabilities, shown in column (5), soared from 18 per cent in 1980 to 40 per cent in 1985. As soon as it became clear that the optimism induced by the surge in the price of gold was misplaced, these high levels of short-term borrowing placed South Africa in an extremely vulnerable position. Foreign lenders started to withdraw their funds, and there was also a high level of capital flight by domestic holders of assets as they too were infected by the loss of confidence.

This precarious situation was then made even more unstable as the growing international campaign against apartheid led to bans and restrictions on most forms of investment in South Africa. From this point, even financial and commercial interests still privately sympathetic to the regime decided that it was no longer advisable to show public support for apartheid. This political prudence was reinforced by rising pessimism about South Africa's economic prospects, with gold mining in decline, the recession dragging on, escalating political unrest, and repeated

Table 10.3. *Total and composition of gross foreign liabilities of South Africa,*
1960–94

	(1) Total foreign liabilities (R billions)	(2) Direct investment[a] (per cent)	(3) Percentage share of portfolio investment[b]	(4) Other investment[c] (per cent)	(5) Short-term loans and deposits as percentage of total[d]
1960	3.2	53.2	26.2	20.6	15.6
1970	7.9	53.0	28.7	18.3	16.9
1975	16.7	44.4	18.3	37.3	21.7
1980	26.6	46.1	19.0	34.9	17.6
1985	90.9	25.1	13.1	61.8	39.9
1990	90.1	26.2	24.0	49.8	17.4
1995	228.4	24.0	37.5	38.6	21.2

[a] Investment where foreign residents are potentially capable of exercising significant influence over a South African company or other organization, as defined, for example, by the ownership of at least ten of the voting rights.
[b] International equity and debt securities not classified as direct investment, where investors are primarily motivated by arms-length considerations such as income and capital appreciation.
[c] Loans and deposits not specified elsewhere.
[d] Liabilities payable on demand or within an original fixed period of twelve months or less.

Source: South African Reserve Bank, *Supplement to the Quarterly Bulletin*, June 2001, Table 9.

declarations of a 'state of emergency'. The crucial moment came in August 1985 when Chase Manhattan Bank of New York announced that it would not make any further loans, and called for the repayment of all outstanding loans and deposits as they fell due. Its lead was followed by a number of other banks in the United States and Europe. The authorities were forced to make a humiliating declaration that all debt repayment would be suspended for four months (subsequently extended to the end of March 1986). They also reintroduced the 'financial rand', which effectively ensured that any foreign investor withdrawing funds from South Africa would pay a heavy penalty. The debt standstill was followed by a period of complex international negotiations leading to an agreement on a schedule of repayments.

The debt crisis followed immediately after an infamous address on 15 August 1985 by the State President, P. W. Botha, that has come to be known as the 'Rubicon' speech. Botha allowed his Foreign Minister and other representatives to let it be thought abroad that he would announce significant new reforms, but the final content was brutally intransigent and contained no noteworthy initiatives. From then on the prospect of early reform faded, and financial pressures on South Africa became increasingly damaging. By June 1987, 120 US companies, including General Motors and IBM, had sold their investments in local subsidiaries and associated companies and withdrawn from direct operations in the country. The major withdrawal by a European company was the sale by Barclays Bank of its interest in its South African subsidiary, following a sustained political campaign in Britain, and the threat that many more would follow the lead of anti-apartheid protestors who transferred their accounts to other banks. The Republic's access to foreign credit, capital, and new technology was severely curtailed.

The only option left to the government to cope with the new conditions and to meet the terms of the agreement on debt repayments was to sacrifice growth and adopt drastic measures to maintain a surplus on current account. South Africa was thus forced into the inappropriate position for a developing country of being a net *exporter* of capital (see column (2) of Table 10.2). The authorities restricted imports directly by imposing import surcharges, and indirectly by raising interest rates in order to reduce aggregate demand; they also attempted to boost exports by allowing the commercial rand to depreciate very sharply. As shown in column (4) of Table 10.1, the ratio of imports to GDP was brought down from 26 per cent in 1977–80 to 19 per cent in 1989–94. Though unavoidable, this contraction was extremely damaging, because some 70 to 80 per cent of imports consisted of intermediate and capital goods. Reductions in supplies of essential intermediate goods (such as chemicals, plastics, and copper) retarded current growth, while shortages of foreign capital goods held back investment in new capacity required for future growth.

Changes in the labour market

As with the economy generally, the early 1970s also marked a critical turning point in the labour market. In the initial post-war years, during the phase of rapid economic growth, expansion of modern industry and related services was increasingly retarded by a lack of skilled and semi-skilled workers, while mines and farms faced their customary dilemma of how to recruit and retain sufficient unskilled labour at the low wages they were willing to offer. Employers initially delayed their response to these labour shortages, but then raised the real wages of black workers sharply just when the situation was changing and the supply of labour was starting to outstrip demand.[3]

---

[3] See also Chapter 8, p. 191.

The first move was made by manufacturing, and in the early 1960s there was a series of increases for both skilled and unskilled black workers, resulting in an overall rise in average real earnings by almost a quarter; as noted in Chapter 9, mining followed in the early 1970s with much larger increases. The growing pressure of demand for labour was felt even in some rural areas, so that commercial farmers were also compelled to raise cash wages significantly. The data are very imperfect, but suggest that real farm wages for regular farm employees more than doubled between the mid-1960s and mid-1970s in the Transvaal and Orange Free State, and also rose, though more slowly, in the western Cape.

After this initial spurt, increases in the manufacturing sector levelled off, but black workers had sensed that the labour market was turning and their bargaining position was improving, especially for those with some skill and experience. A new mood of confidence reinforced old grievances and demands, and a long period of industrial quiescence was finally broken by a remarkable wave of strikes. The movement started spontaneously in Durban at the end of 1972 and continued through 1973 and into 1974, spreading to the Witwatersrand and other key industrial centres, and to a wide variety of industries in both the private and public sectors. Despite the illegality of the strikes, the official response was very restrained; the police did not become directly involved, the leaders were not arrested, and management entered into negotiations. The strikers did not achieve their full demands, but succeeded in obtaining a marked improvement in their pay and working conditions, with increases in nominal wages sufficiently in excess of the rise in the cost of living to provide a significant improvement in their real wages.

Domestic pressure for improvements in pay and conditions were reinforced by external developments. In the United Kingdom, a subcommittee of the House of Commons issued a report in 1974, recommending a code of practice with regard to wages and working conditions to be observed by South African subsidiaries of British companies. This was followed in 1977 by the Sullivan Code in the United States, and by a European code, and in the same year local employers' organizations drew up their own codes. Like the others, these effectively required the elimination of racial discrimination in the workplace, and active promotion of the interests of black employees. The large differentials between white and black workers were increasingly difficult to justify and gave an impetus to advances in wages for the black workforce.

By 1976 average real earnings for African workers in manufacturing were almost 40 per cent higher than in 1970. White workers did not get comparable increases in this period, so the gap between white and black wages narrowed slightly but remained high. White wages in private manufacturing were 5.5 times African wages in 1960, and the multiple declined to 4.8 in 1975 and 3.8 a decade later. By South African standards this was a marked improvement; by international standards it was still evidence of unconscionable discrimination. However, the rate of increase in wages from the early 1960s to the mid-1970s far exceeded the improvement in output per worker, and was thus responsible for a substantial rise in labour costs per unit of output. The average real wage of black workers in manufacturing generally continued to rise after 1975, but most of the gains in the later period came from upward occupational mobility and increasing levels of skill. In most industries, increases in nominal wages for specified occupations failed to keep pace with the rapid increases in consumer prices, and the consequent fall in real wages for such workers was greatest for the unskilled.

The old policy of job reservation was formally retained, but surreptitious erosion was permitted to cope with the unsatisfied demand for skilled workers that was increasingly apparent from the mid-1960s. In 1965 only one in ten of the non-farm skilled workforce was black; by 1990 the proportion had risen to four in ten. There was a net increase in the total number of artisans and apprentices over this period of 115,000, and of these 59,000 were African, 47,000 were coloured or Asian, and only 9,000 were white.[4] There was also some limited progress by black workers into positions as foremen and other supervisory occupations. However, this advance into skilled work was generally restricted to certain of the smaller industries in which organized resistance by white workers was relatively limited. Progress in the important metals, engineering, motor vehicle, and electrical industries was much more modest. The industrial colour bar was thus effectively allowed to 'float' upwards in certain industries, with white workers moving higher up the occupational hierarchy into managerial, professional, and supervisory posts, while black workers took the semi-skilled and skilled jobs they vacated. The number of white employees in managerial and professional posts rose from 170,000 to 341,000, while those in supervisory employment increased from 34,000 to 128,000.

The position in the tertiary sectors was rather different, with a much greater degree of racial integration within higher-level occupations, though not normally within individual establishments or institutions. Within the semi-professional category, a significant expansion in the number of African and other black workers was heavily concentrated in

---

[4] Statistics on occupations in this and the following paragraph are based on the detailed classification of Manpower Survey data by Crankshaw, *Race, class and the changing division of labour*, pp. 141–51.

schoolteaching and nursing; there were relatively few black technicians, lecturers, or bookkeepers. By contrast, black employment increased in most of the routine white collar occupations including clerks of various descriptions, shop and counter assistants, cashiers, bus and train conductors, and postal sorters and deliverers. Black advancement in both these semi-professional and white-collar occupations was closely associated with services for the black population, and was acceptable to the government on this basis. Furthermore, unlike much of secondary industry and mining, there was little resistance from white trade unions to the movement of black workers into these occupations. The number of black workers in these two broad occupational categories thus increased from 221,000 (28 per cent of the total) in 1965 to 937,000 (53 per cent of the total) in 1990.

One consequence of these occupational changes, as well as of other forces in the labour market to be analysed below, was a very striking divergence in the movements of male and female participation rates and an increase in the relative importance of female labour.[5] The participation rate is a measure of the proportion of the population – for any specific population, gender, and age group, for example, African females aged 20–24 – who are economically active, that is, either in employment or unemployed. For all males, the participation rate dropped steeply from 97 in 1960 to 65 per cent in 1996, whereas for females it rose continuously over the same period from 30 to 49 per cent. As a result of these very different movements the proportion of females in the labour force climbed from just over one in five in 1960 to almost one in two at the end of the century. The change between 1960 and 1996 is set out for females for each population group in the upper panel of Table 10.4, and for males in the lower panel. The movements in the rates for the population as a whole for males and females in each age group are represented in Figure 10.1, and the change for males and females in each population group are shown in Figure 10.2 for combined age groups from twenty to sixty-four.

There was a fall in participation rates for both males and females in the two extremes of the working age groups – the youngest, aged fifteen to nineteen, and the oldest, aged sixty-five and over. The former was evident in all population groups, but was particularly large for African and coloured males. It was a result partly of longer involvement in school and college education, which may itself have reflected the greatly increased difficulty in finding employment in the final decades of the

---

[5] The derivation of the estimates underlying the remainder of this section is described in Annexe 3.

Table 10.4. *Change in labour force participation rates between 1960 and 1996 by age group, gender, and population group*

	(1) African	(2) Coloured	(3) Asian	(4) White	(5) Total
	(percentage points)				
Females					
15–19	−11.5	−35.1	18.8	−10.4	−13.0
20–24	20.1	22.7	51.5	25.1	19.5
25–34	31.9	29.9	43.4	36.1	31.9
35–44	32.6	20.9	34.0	32.9	30.8
45–64	16.6	5.4	13.9	18.2	15.2
65+	−4.7	−1.2	1.0	5.0	−1.3
All ages	19.3	11.3	31.6	24.2	19.3
20–64	26.3	20.5	33.3	27.1	25.8
Males					
15–19	−48.1	−52.0	−23.1	−11.1	−40.7
20–24	−33.1	−22.1	−13.2	−20.9	−30.6
25–34	−28.2	−17.0	−12.2	−15.2	−25.9
35–44	−29.5	−16.9	−10.6	−12.8	−25.9
45–64	−34.6	−21.9	−13.6	−18.3	−29.6
65+	−49.9	−23.6	−18.9	−25.1	−39.3
All ages	−37.2	−25.2	−11.4	−16.1	−32.8
20–64	−31.0	−18.8	−12.5	−16.4	−27.7

century (see below), and partly of the diminished scale of the workforce on commercial farms, a sector which had traditionally employed large numbers of young people. For older workers, the fall in the participation rate reflected a marked increase in retirement, and was heavily influenced by the improved state pensions available to Africans from the 1980s. The number of African beneficiaries (males aged sixty-five and over, females aged sixty and over) increased from 200,000 in 1979/80 to 1,300,000 in 1993/4 and their average pension rose from under R 300 to over R 4,400 per annum.

Even more significant changes occurred in the central age groups that were largely unaffected by the effects of either education or retirement. The rise in the female participation rate is evident in all age groups from twenty to sixty-four (see Figure 10.1), and in all population groups (see Figure 10.2). By 1996 the average rate for this age range as a whole was highest for coloured and white females, at 60 and 57 per cent respectively,

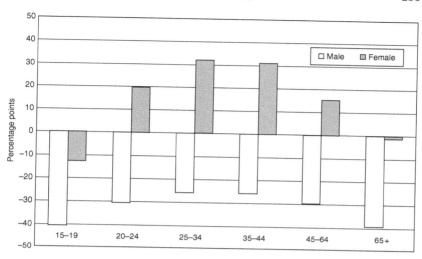

Figure 10.1. Change in male and female participation rates by age group, 1960–96

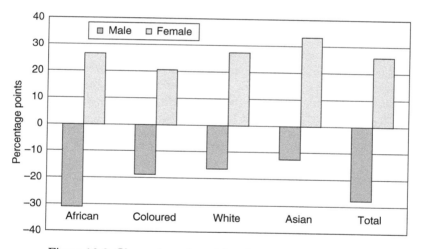

Figure 10.2. Change in male and female participation rates aged 20–64 by population group, 1960–96

and was 53 per cent for African females, but was appreciably lower for Asian females, at 43 per cent. The increasing propensity for women to participate in the labour force can be explained partly by the changing structure of the economy (shown in Figure 10.3 and in more detail in

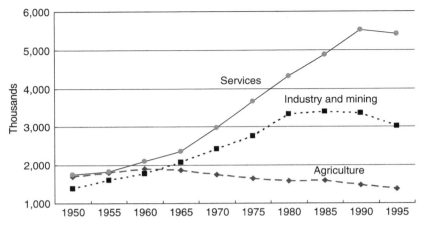

Figure 10.3. Employment classified by economic sector, 1950–95

Table A3.2 in Annexe 3). There was a substantial rise in the scope and scale of the service sectors, creating more employment opportunities for women. Growing numbers were required as nurses, schoolteachers, secretaries, typists, receptionists, and clerical workers, and some of the occupations traditionally filled by men, such as bank clerks, cashiers, and shop assistants, were increasingly taken over by women. In addition, there were significant social changes which made it more acceptable for women to remain in employment after marriage and childbearing. The economic pressure for greater female participation may also be in part a response to the decline in male participation.

The contrasting decline in male participation is again evident in all population groups and all ages (see the lower panel of Table 10.4 and Figure 10.1). In 1960 the overall participation rate for males aged twenty to sixty-four was between 96 and 99 per cent for all population groups; by 1996 it had fallen by 17 percentage points for white males, by 19 points for coloured males and by a remarkable 31 points for Africans (see Figure 10.2). The most rapid decline occurred in the 1980s. A large part of this change must reflect the decline in the availability of work in traditional male sectors, notably commercial agriculture, mining, manufacturing, and construction. It is also likely that the exceptionally large decline in labour force participation for African males in this age range was in part the result of a rise in the number who might be described as 'ultra discouraged workers'. This refers to men who saw no prospect of getting a job and ceased even to think of themselves as wanting to work, so that they had effectively withdrawn from the labour force. They would thus be classified in the census as not economically active rather than as active but unemployed. The current estimates of unemployment published in South Africa include under the heading of 'expanded unemployment' those who want to work even if they have not taken steps to look for work (see Annexe 3, p. 270 for further details), but this would not cover these 'ultra discouraged workers'. We will return to this issue below.

The widespread rise in black wages noted above was one of several factors that contributed to a devastating rise in unemployment in the last part of the twentieth century. For three centuries since settlers arrived in South Africa, the dominant theme in all economic discourse had been a shortage of manpower. There was incessant coercion of black people to supply the labour required by white-owned farms, mines, and factories. But by the 1970s this position was beginning to change radically. From this time onwards, the central problem was no longer the inability of employers to find workers, it was the inability of workers – especially those who were unskilled – to find jobs.

The precise extent and timing of movements in unemployment are difficult to measure accurately, both because of inherent ambiguities in the concept in an economy where subsistence and informal sectors offer considerable scope for disguised unemployment or under-employment, and because of severe deficiencies in the available data, not only for employment or unemployment, but even for such basic measures as the total population. An attempt to compile a consistent series from census and other data for every five years from 1950 to 1995 is described in Annexe 3, and the results are shown in Figure 10.4. For reasons discussed in the annexe, the estimates are at best a rough approximation, but are probably sufficient to indicate the broad trends in the three series shown in the diagram: the population aged fifteen to sixty-four, the number in employment, and the number unemployed.

The two major features immediately evident are the slow growth and eventual decline in employment, and the sharp rise in unemployment. Comparison with other evidence (for example, household and labour force surveys) suggests that the census of population does not cover all employed, but the jobs omitted are mainly those of people working only a few hours per week, so that their omission does not seriously distort the position.

The estimates of unemployment in Figure 10.4 are consistent with the measure of 'expanded unemployment' which does not take into account the 'ultra discouraged' men aged twenty to sixty-four mentioned above. Such 'ultra discouraged' men – and also a smaller number of women – would represent what one government statistical report referred to as 'very expanded' unemployment. This was measured by adding to

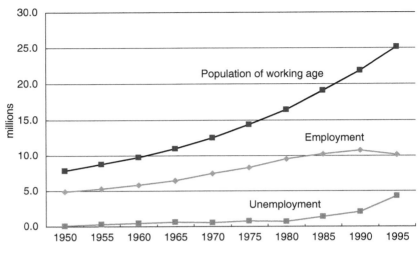

Figure 10.4. Employment and unemployment, 1950–95

the expanded unemployed all those who were returned in household surveys as not economically active, but did not fall into any of the standard categories that normally make up the bulk of those who are not active (such as full-time homemakers, full-time students, pensioners, or disabled persons), and who were not recorded as 'unwilling to accept a suitable job if it were offered within a week'. If the estimates of the 'expanded' and 'very expanded' rates of unemployment given in that report are applied to the census data for 1996 it can be calculated that there were approximately 1,400,000 of such 'ultra discouraged' potential workers in 1996.[6] This is clearly a very uncertain and subjective estimate, but it is essential to make some allowance for people in this category in order to indicate the full dimensions of the unemployment problem in South Africa.

Whatever the precise level of unemployment, it was clearly a human tragedy on a staggering scale. The estimated number of employed and unemployed in 1960, the changes between 1960 and 1996, and the resulting levels in 1996 are shown in Table 10.5. In the 1960s, shown in column (2), the economically active population available for work increased by 1,690,000, and only 75,000 of these failed to find jobs.

---

[6] Calculated from Statistics South Africa, *Unemployment and employment in South Africa*, 1998 pp. 64–5 and 71, and *October household survey 1996*, adjusted to include miners, Tables 2.1.1, 2.2.1 and 5.1.

Table 10.5. *Employment and unemployment, 1960–96*

	(1) Level in 1960	Changes in			(5) Level in 1996
		(2) 1960–70	(3) 1970–80	(4) 1980–96	
		million			
Employed	5.84	1.62	2.07	0.32	9.85
Unemployed	0.46	0.07	0.18	4.17	4.88
'Ultra discouraged workers'[a]	0.00	0.00	0.00	1.40	1.40
Total economically active[b]	6.30	1.69	2.25	5.89	16.13

[a] See Annexe 3 for discussion of this concept.
[b] Including 'ultra discouraged workers'.

In the following decade, shown in column (3), there was an increase in the total economically active population of 2,250,000, and all but 180,000 of these obtained employment. The position deteriorated dramatically in the subsequent period, from 1980 to 1996, when the potential labour force available for work according to the census data increased by almost 4,500,000, and almost all of these (4,170,000) became unemployed (see column (4) of the table).

If the estimated 1,400,000 'ultra discouraged workers' are taken into account, the estimate of additional unemployment in 1980–96 rises to an appalling 5,570,000. There was an increase in employment in commerce and in social, communal, and personal services of over 1,000,000 during these years, but roughly half of this was offset by the loss of jobs in agriculture, mining, and manufacturing (see Figure 10.3 above). The overall result of these changes was that by 1996, shown in column (5), only three out of five potential workers were actually employed, and two out of five – or almost 6,300,000 – were either formally unemployed or had become so discouraged about the prospect of ever finding work that they had effectively withdrawn from the labour market. The overwhelming majority of these were Africans, and it was clearly this group which was most severely afflicted by the failure of the economic system to provide jobs.

Why were around 6,300,000 people unable to find work in 1996? There was some pressure from the supply side as a result of a rise in the proportion of the total population aged fifteen to sixty-four (see Annexe 3). After falling slightly until 1970, the proportion of the population in the working-age range then rose from 55 per cent to almost

61 per cent. This effectively added some 1,400,000 persons to the potentially economically active population in 1996. But far more fundamental problems occurred on the demand side. There were two crucial developments. The first was the dismal trend in economic performance already examined, with the average annual growth rate for real GDP shrivelling to less than 1 per cent after 1981.

The second was the tendency to replace labour by capital, as a result of which the slow growth that was achieved generated fewer jobs. In agriculture there was extensive mechanization, including a large increase in the number of tractors and the introduction of combine harvesters, while government pressure on farmers to reduce the number of Africans living on white-owned land was also an important additional factor. There was also mechanization in mining, where a new wage structure was linked to significant improvements in the use of African labour. From the mid-1980s the contraction of gold mining (described in Chapter 9) significantly reduced demand for mine-workers, and stabilization policies meant that a much smaller number of migrant workers were rotating through the mines. This was an important reason for the rise of open unemployment in rural areas from which mine labour was traditionally recruited. In manufacturing, firms responded to a number of factors noted in the discussion of fixed investment in Chapter 9, including the rise in real wages, the growing militancy and organization of the labour force, and government policies that made labour more expensive and capital cheaper.[7]

The retreat from apartheid

With the emergence of serious economic difficulties from the early 1970s, the economic cost of apartheid ideology and practice became ever more onerous, and the government started to retreat gradually from many of its positions. Even while growth was slowing, skill shortages remained a severe problem. There were growing demands for change from many sections of industry and commerce, and even of commercial agriculture, from black organizations, and from abroad. But piecemeal reform was

[7] In addition to these two developments (corresponding in economists' terms to an inward shift in the labour demand curve) it is likely that there was also a movement along the demand curve. This means that some workers may have been priced out of the formal labour market by the extent to which black wages increased. Even if other conditions – such as the amount or type of capital equipment – remained constant, employers may have responded by hiring less labour, either because they found that it was no longer profitable to produce at the higher labour cost, or because they were able to exact greater effort from a smaller number of better-paid workers.

difficult; in Lipton's phrase: 'the system hung together'.[8] Erosion of the colour bar to provide more skilled workers required improvements in education and training, recognition of trade unions, and the right to bargain about wages and conditions. It also needed stabilization of the urban labour force, leading to demands for secure and permanent status in the towns. That in turn made it impossible to evade consideration of the issues of African citizenship and political rights.

To assist the government in initiating reforms, two major commissions were established in 1977, the first, under Wiehahn, to look into all aspects of labour relations, including trade union rights; the second, under Riekert, to consider other aspects of the use of labour. Both reported in 1979 and their work led to a series of fundamental reforms. The Wiehahn Commission recommended that Africans should in future be included in the definition of 'employee' under the Industrial Conciliation Act, and should have full trade union rights. The government at first attempted to restrict such union rights to Africans with permanent urban residence (under Section 10 of the Urban Areas Act) and to prohibit racially mixed unions, but this stance was gradually modified, and by 1984 all restrictions had been dropped. The reform was quickly followed by a substantial increase in the number, membership, and militancy of African unions, though difficult economic conditions and rising unemployment meant that their activity had only a marginal effect on the outcome of wage negotiations.

The commission also noted that as a result of the

ever-increasing process previous of industrialization ... the already thinly stretched resources of skilled manpower in the country were placed under severe strain. There were simply not enough skilled workers to fill all the vacancies during this period of intensive economic activity, with the result that increasing numbers of unskilled and semi-skilled workers, particularly Blacks [i.e. Africans] had to be trained and utilized to perform higher-level skilled jobs.[9]

Against this background, the commission concluded that the existence of statutory job reservation was 'immensely injurious to sound race relations'; that it imposed restrictions 'on the very category of workers ... whose better training and utilisation are a *sine qua non* for the future economic growth and stability of the Republic', and that it could 'only be seen as an impractical and inadequate measure' that was 'no longer tenable'.[10] Its recommendation that work reservation should be neither maintained nor modified but abolished was accepted by the government,

---

[8] Lipton, *Capitalism and apartheid*, p. 181.
[9] Commission of Inquiry into Labour Legislation (Wiehahn), *Report*, 1979, Part 1, para 1.2.
[10] Ibid., para. 3.129.

and implemented in industry by 1984 and in mining by 1988. A further proposal to allow Africans to enter apprenticeships made less headway, largely because of opposition from white trade unions.

The other commission had a more difficult task and made less impact. Its chairman and sole member was Dr P. J. Riekert, economic adviser to the Prime Minister. He exposed the lamentable effects of the multiplicity of state interventions in the labour market with admirable clarity:

The commission was particularly struck by the extensive, complicated, and in many respects, fragmented and overlapping measures, i.e. statutes, regulations, administrative rules and practices having a bearing on manpower matters in South Africa, which not only lent a strong institutional character to the labour market but also gave rise to all kinds of market failures, for example, discrimination, labour shortages or surpluses, the rise of sub-markets, wage levels that were not related to productivity, imperfect mobility – vertical and horizontal – defective knowledge of the labour market, the sub-optimal allocation of labour, the limitation of economic growth and development in certain regions and sectors, dissatisfaction and frustration among workers and employers at some measures and the consequent disturbance of relations between population groups.[11]

Riekert was anxious to eliminate these market failures and frictions, and thus to contribute to the more effective development and utilization of labour in all sectors of the economy, but considered that this could be done only 'within the framework of certain political parameters which were taken as given'. In particular,

Control over the rate of urbanization is, in the light of circumstances in South Africa, an absolutely essential social security measure. Even though, as some witnesses contend, the abolition of such control would lead to faster economic growth, the price to be paid for it in terms of direct and indirect social costs would be too high.[12]

He attempted to reconcile these divergent aims by improving conditions for African 'insiders', those with Section 10 rights who were permanently settled in urban areas, while still preserving – and indeed strengthening – the broad framework of apartheid and of controls on movement and residence for rural 'outsiders'. 'Insiders' should have greater freedom of movement, the right to change jobs and housing within larger areas than single municipalities, and better training. There should be improvements in housing with more promotion of home-ownership, and their families should be allowed to live with them. Various discriminatory provisions should be removed, for example, the 'discriminatory, archaic and highly

---

[11] Commission of Inquiry into Legislation affecting the Utilization of Manpower (Riekert), *Report*, 1979, para. 6.4.

[12] Ibid., para. 4.204.

irritating' general curfew on Africans prescribed by a 1945 Act. The business and property rights of African traders should be recognized, and there should be more opportunities for African entrepreneurs. 'Outsiders', by contrast, should be prevented from moving to urban areas by strict control over both employment and accommodation of 'unauthorized' persons.

The Commission's main ideas were accepted by the government, but the proposed benefits for 'insiders' were not implemented fully, largely because of opposition from within the mammoth bureaucracy that was both ideologically committed to apartheid controls and also dependent on them for its own employment. Furthermore, the fact that the 'insiders' were expected to bear the costs of the urban development encouraged by Riekert aroused hostility in urban areas, and residents focused their anger on the newly responsible black councillors. There was, however, a marked fall in the number of prosecutions under the 'pass laws' during the 1970s, and finally, under mounting pressure, the whole system of influx control was abolished in 1986.

Industry's other major demand was for a huge improvement in African education and training, and here too the government accepted the need for significant reform. Verwoerd's policy of limiting expenditure on African education to the amount raised from the African population in direct taxes was discarded, and expenditure rose very rapidly through the 1970s. This permitted a large increase in the number of pupils enrolled and some reduction in the enormous disparity between expenditure per pupil for white and African children. Restrictions on the provision of higher education in white areas (see Chapter 7) were withdrawn and many high schools were built. In 1983 the government accepted the principle of 'equal opportunities for education, including equal standards for every inhabitant, irrespective of race, colour or creed'. However, the amount spent in that year on each white pupil was still seven times higher than the amount spent on each African pupil. There was some increase in the proportion of African pupils passing at the higher grades, but the numbers remained woefully low by comparison with those for white children. It was clear that raising the quality of education of black children to a satisfactory standard still required very much higher expenditure to provide more school buildings, better teachers, and adequate supplies of books and other equipment, as well as more fundamental reforms to improve the nutrition, health, and motivation of the pupils.

From the early 1980s the government also initiated far-reaching policy reforms and structural adjustments in the commercial farming sector. These were driven by a variety of factors, including the general deterioration in the economy described above; greater awareness of the adverse effects of the prevailing policies on farm efficiency and on the economy as a whole; diminishing political power of white farmers; and a combination of new spending priorities and tighter budget constraints which made it difficult to sustain the high costs of the existing structure of subsidies and support for agriculture, including the burden of exporting surplus grains at a loss.

The main thrust of the reforms involved the progressive introduction of market forces in place of the system of administered prices and marketing regulations that had operated since the 1930s. Among the steps towards liberalization were a decline in the real prices received by producers for major products such as maize and wheat; the lifting of price controls on milk, bread, maize meal, and other staple foods; extensive deregulation of control under the Marketing Act and the dissolution from 1993 of a number of smaller control boards; and a reduction in protective measures and tariffs. The level of financial support for the farm sector was reduced by various measures, including the introduction of market-related interest rates on loans to farmers and less generous tax subsidies for capital expenditure. The reforms made capital more expensive relative to labour and reduced the support for spending on non-farm inputs, but the World Bank assessment in 1994 was that 'despite the efforts at reform, the legacy of past policies is such that the sector remains highly capital intensive and has not been able to fulfil its potential in terms of employment creation'.[13] There was, however, acceleration in the rate of growth of total factor productivity, from about 2 per cent per annum in the period 1965–81 to almost 3 per cent per annum from 1981 to 1991.[14]

The fallacy of 'cheap' labour

By 1986 many of apartheid's major economic institutions and policies had been dismantled. Black people continued to be denied access to decision-making over all aspects of economic life, white children continued to benefit from massive discrimination in the provision of public education, and the inequitable distribution of land imposed by the Acts of 1913 and 1936 was not changed.[15] In most other respects, however, the retreat from the economic dogmas of previous decades was largely complete, and there was also a significant relaxation of social apartheid.

---

[13] World Bank, *South African agriculture*, p. 20.
[14] Ibid., pp. 123–4; for more detail about this measure of productivity and performance in the earlier post-war period see Chapter 8.
[15] The Land Acts of 1913 and 1936, and related legislation regulating land rights on a racial basis, were finally removed from the statute book in 1991.

But the reforms had minimal impact: stagnation persisted, the economy remained in the grip of the balance-of-payments constraint, businesses lacked confidence in the future and became more reluctant to undertake new investments. Under these conditions real incomes continued to fall and unemployment rose remorselessly.

At the root of the problem was South Africa's poor standard of labour productivity relative to that elsewhere. There are considerable difficulties in making reliable comparative measurements, but the broad picture is reasonably clear. Figure 10.5 draws on the results of a major international research programme to show unmistakably how output per worker in South African manufacturing in 1994 fell well below that in many other countries.[16] At the end of the apartheid period, labour productivity in South Africa was only between 20 and 50 per cent of the level in a representative sample of developed nations, and between 50 and 75 per cent of the level in developing countries such as South Korea, Brazil, Taiwan, Mexico, and Morocco. South Africa's level of output per worker in manufacturing was superior to that of only four of the twenty countries in the chart (Egypt, Poland, India, and Indonesia).

In the context of international competitiveness in export markets, lower standards of productivity would not matter if they were matched by correspondingly lower wages. What matters, in other words, is not the level of wages alone, but the relationship between wages and productivity, more precisely, the average wage for each worker divided by the average output of each worker. This relationship is known as the 'unit labour cost' and is generally regarded as the best single indicator of international competitiveness. If unit labour costs are roughly the same in two countries at any given exchange rate, then neither has any competitive advantage in competing for exports, even if wages are much lower in one of the countries.

The evidence suggests that this is broadly the position in comparisons between South Africa and developed countries. According to the results of a recent study, South Africa's unit labour costs in manufacturing in 1990–94 were only 9 per cent lower than those for a sample of developed countries including the United States, the United Kingdom, France, Italy, and Spain. However, when the same comparison was made with a

---

[16] For South Africa relative to the United States see M. van Dijk, 'South African manufacturing performance in international perspective, 1970–99', *SAJE*, 71, 2003, p. 131. Estimates for all other countries relative to the United States were taken from the Groningen Centre's ICOP Industrial Database, Table 4, available at their website http://www.eco.rug.nl/medewerk/ark/ark.htm. These bilateral comparisons with the United States were then used to estimate the level in South Africa relative to that in each of the other countries.

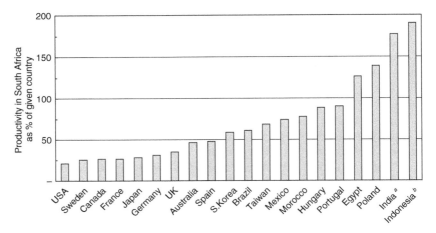

Figure 10.5. International comparison of labour productivity in manufacturing in 1994

Each bar shows the level of labour productivity in South African manufacturing relative to the level in the given country; for example it is only 21 per cent of the level in the USA, but 190 per cent of the level in Indonesia.

[a] Establishments with 20 or more employees or with 10–20 employees

sample of eleven developing countries, including South Korea, Hong Kong, Singapore, India, Mexico, Chile, and Turkey, South Africa's unit labour costs were found to be on average 59 per cent higher.[17] While South Africa was in many respects a low-wage country, wages in these developing countries were even lower and/or their output per worker was higher.

It is these newly industrializing countries which are major exporters of manufactured goods in competition with South Africa in the markets of the rich nations, and the Republic's higher unit labour costs thus constitute a serious problem. Costs of inputs which can be traded internationally, such as capital and raw materials, tend to be approximately the same in different countries, so it is the cost of those inputs which cannot be traded – of which labour is the most important – that are crucial in determining a country's success both in export markets and in attracting foreign direct investment. Given the scale of South Africa's competitive

[17] S. Golub and L. Edwards, 'South African international cost competitiveness and exports: a sectoral analysis', *Trade and Industry Monitor*, 25, 2003, p. 3.

disadvantage, its hope of achieving export-led growth based on the manufacturing sector was doomed to fail.

One final question remains for discussion. Why did an initial confidence in a beneficial relationship between apartheid and economic performance prove so wrong? During the early post-war decades the view that apartheid was fully consistent with a successful capitalist economy and rising prosperity was held by the government and by most of the white electorate. Many radicals and Marxists went even further, and contended that apartheid was *necessary* for capitalism, the two were not only not inconsistent, they were mutually reinforcing. The conflict between their views and that of an earlier generation of liberal economists and historians was summarized in a review of the two schools as follows: "'liberal' political economists argued that apartheid laws and institutions retarded and distorted economic growth. In contrast, scholars in the emerging "revisionist" school argued that, far from undermining capitalist economic growth, apartheid policies delivered the cheap labour necessary for the survival and expansion of South African capitalism.'[18] The opinions of the electorate might be attributed simply to prejudice and inertia. White supremacy, racial discrimination, and growing prosperity had coexisted comfortably in South Africa for 300 years, and it was not unreasonable for voters to believe that this would continue indefinitely. But where did both the policy makers of the National Party government and the revisionist theorists go wrong?

Perhaps, like the voters, they extrapolated too readily from the past to the future, and the view that apartheid was fully compatible with successful economic growth would have been strengthened by the good performance from 1948 to 1974. Both groups clearly failed to recognize the extent to which the needs of manufacturing diverged from those of mining and farming, and ignored the difficulty of achieving high productivity in industry on the basis of a migrant labour force.[19] The government's justification for this was its preoccupation with white supremacy, as Prime Minister Strijdom made explicit:

Is there any man who uses his brain who can tell me that he thinks it is possible for White South Africa to continue to exist if we allow Natives to enter by the million and to outnumber the Whites by millions and millions? . . . We must let industrial development continue in such a way that it will not endanger the existence of the White race in South Africa. Unless we do that we would be committing suicide.

---

[18] Crankshaw, *Race, class and the changing division of labour*, p. 2. See also the authors quoted in Chapter 7, pp. 162–3.
[19] These differences were outlined in Chapter 6, pp. 128–9.

Therefore the matter must be controlled. For that reason we say that the Native labour which comes to a particular area must be migrant labour, as the mines had.[20]

It is also likely that both government and radicals failed to appreciate fully the potential for growth based on a more skilled and more productive black labour force, with improvements in productivity generating higher real wages as well as higher profits. The apartheid ideologues probably failed to recognize this because of endemic racial prejudice, the Marxists because of their flawed economic analysis. One of the latter's fundamental errors was clearly expressed in a seminal paper by Harold Wolpe:

The point is that reforms which would have resulted in higher real wages and improved economic conditions for Africans could only be introduced *without a corresponding fall in the rate of profit* provided they were bought at the cost of the White working class – that is to say, either through a drop in the wages of White workers, or the employment of Africans, at lower rates of pay, in occupations monopolized, until then, by White workers.[21]

This is an unequivocal expression of the view that 'cheap' African labour was essential to the preservation of the rate of profit, formulated in the context of a zero-sum game in which higher productivity is allowed to play no part. In this framework the task of apartheid was to hold down African wages as the basis for the survival of capitalism. Exponents of the cheap labour power thesis remained convinced that it 'was a major breakthrough' in understanding the relationship between apartheid and capitalism. As late as 1987 it was claimed that 'The argument that the capitalist system in South Africa was dependent for its survival and expansion on low wages, and a repressed African labour force tied to the Bantustans, has not been debunked in over a decade of debate. On the contrary, it has given rise to a generation of radical scholarship which ... deepened our historical knowledge and theoretical understanding.'[22]

But modern economic growth in a developed industrial economy does not depend on crude exploitation of wage labour with low pay and long hours. It is achieved by means of technical progress, better human capital, and advances in productivity. What was true for mining in 1870 was not

---

[20] *House of Assembly Debates*, 18 April 1955, cols 4021–2. See also the statement by Verwoerd quoted in Chapter 7, p. 159.

[21] Wolpe, 'Capitalism and cheap labour power', p. 309 (emphasis added). For a very similar denial of the possibility of changing the character of the African labour force to meet the interests of manufacturing, see M. Legassick, 'Gold, agriculture, and secondary industry in South Africa, 1885–1970: from periphery to sub-metropole as a forced labour system', in R. Palmer and N. Parsons (eds.), *The roots of rural poverty*, Berkeley: University of California Press, 1977, p. 191.

[22] D. Hindson, *Pass controls and the urban African proletariat*, Johannesburg: Ravan Press, 1987, p. 7.

true for manufacturing a century later. The constant emphasis by radicals on super- and ultra-exploitation of migrant labourers highlighted the very real suffering imposed on black workers, but ignored its adverse consequences for the economy. So too, until it was too late, did supporters of apartheid. Even those who saw some scope for productivity improvements continued to attach too much significance to the alleged advantages of 'cheap' labour; for example, the many manufacturers who continued to rely on it.

Low levels of skill, inadequate nutrition, poor health, bad housing, social instability and insecurity, weak motivation, denial of industrial and political rights, the disruptive effects of migrant labour, bureaucratic interference in the allocation of workers – all ensured that 'cheap' black labour was not really cheap. On the contrary, some 80 per cent of South Africa's labour force was compelled by apartheid to live and work under conditions that were profoundly prejudicial to vitally necessary improvements in productivity. Legal, social, and customary barriers to occupational mobility restricted the supply of black skilled and semi-skilled workers, while the low quality of education and training depressed the standards attained by the minority of blacks who were able to move up the occupational ladder. The cost of 'cheap' black labour was also inflated by a system which imposed white supervisors on black workers. The subservience which the *'baas'* expected from his 'boys', and the racial friction and antipathy which were almost always present in such relationships, meant that the supervisory system raised rather than lowered the impediments to higher efficiency.

A further crucial consequence of 'cheap' labour was that growth was inhibited because the domestic market was tightly constrained by the low incomes of the black population, at the same time as their low productivity prevented South Africa from competing effectively in export markets. Individual capitalists might have benefited from low wages; capitalists as a whole suffered from lack of markets and the absence of economies of scale.

Even when the various dimensions of the problem were clearly identified by an authoritative government commission, as in the following forceful and comprehensive statement in 1972, the malign legacy of discrimination, and of inferior and insufficient education and training, could not be corrected by a white minority government in the limited time available.

Shortages of skilled labour, some categories of higher semi-skilled labour, technicians, and professional and management labour exist and are expected to increase in future years ... At the same time, the Republic has a large reservoir of Coloured, Asian and above all of Bantu labour who, because of lack of training (formal and technical) and because they are prevented by statutory and traditional barriers, by the attitude of some trade unions and/or by management practices, are unable to make the contribution to economic growth of which they are capable. There exist, therefore, restrictions of all kinds on the optimum use of the total labour force of the country. This situation makes for decreased overall labour productivity and increased wages in some labour categories, resulting in higher costs which weaken the competitive ability in the domestic and foreign markets; it also has a restricting effect on the purchasing power of the total labour force, thereby limiting the size of the local market which, in turn, is reflected in higher unit costs and decreased competitiveness. Thus a major inhibiting factor is the underutilization of the human resources of the Republic which not only limits growth but causes cost-increasing and inflationary pressures and also creates a climate adverse to gearing productive capacity to exports.[23]

Even the productivity of white workers was adversely affected by the system. As long as their jobs were artificially shielded from competition from black workers, there was little incentive for them to improve their performance; discriminatory legislation 'tended to generate easy-going ways, born of the assumption that the skilled, supervisory, administrative and technical occupations would forever remain the preserve of the white man'.[24] In addition, implementation and enforcement of apartheid represented a massive waste of resources. An economy suffering from shortages of high-level manpower diverted the work of thousands of well-educated men and women to the bureaucracies established to operate influx controls and all the other administrative measures that were imposed on black people in the name of apartheid, and of thousands more to the police force and other agencies that were required to suppress resistance to government policies. There was yet further misallocation of resources in largely fruitless attempts to encourage decentralization of industry to homelands, and in 'show' capitals with parliaments and other ostentatious public buildings constructed for these 'independent' Bantustans.[25]

All these dysfunctional elements of the relationship between apartheid and economic growth thus heavily outweighed those elements which were beneficial for at least some individual capitalists who still relied primarily on unskilled, low-wage, African labour. The reforms introduced by the National Party governments in the 1970s and 1980s were unable to save the situation. Many decades of deliberately diminishing

---

[23] Commission of Enquiry into the Export Trade (Reynders), *Report*, 1972, Vol. 1, ch. 9, para. 41.
[24] W. F. J. Steenkamp, 'Labour problems and policies of half a century', *SAJE*, 51, 1983, p. 75.
[25] It was estimated by S. R. Lewis, *The economics of apartheid*, New York: Council for Foreign Relations Press, 1990, p. 145, that the dividend from the elimination of the costs of the apartheid system would add as much as $2,000 million to the country's GDP.

the quality of the work done by the majority of the labour force – by relying on migrant labour, providing inferior education, denying access to training, preventing the acquisition of skills, paying poverty wages, doing too little to combat the resulting disease and malnutrition – finally exacted their inevitable penalty. Most other countries strive to raise the quality of their human resources; only South Africa made it an express purpose of official policy to lower standards and frustrate the aspirations of those who wished to improve their contribution to the economy.[26] As long as gold could be mined at a good profit, the economy could carry this heavy burden. Once the gold had gone, the huge costs of irrational discrimination could no longer be sustained.

With the transition to non-racial democracy in 1994, it became the task of an ANC-led government to attempt to resolve the economic contradictions that apartheid had created. To achieve this requires massive economic and social changes, great programmes of investment and structural change. It is necessary to create the vital human capital needed at every level, from rudimentary literacy to the highest ranks of science and technology; to overcome enormous deficiencies in all forms of social infrastructure, including housing, schools, health, and transport; to return land to the black population and restore ravaged rural areas; to expand black ownership of mining, industry, commerce, and finance; and to diminish enormous inequalities in income and wealth. The new regime has made a promising start, but South Africa's past will exert a powerful influence on its present and future for a long time to come, and these huge tasks will not be swiftly or easily accomplished.

---

[26] The only parallel is perhaps those societies which deny economic and social rights to women, but economic performance in such countries is also very poor.

Annexe 1: the people of South Africa

The black population before 1900

There is no basis for an accurate estimate of the size of the African population for any date before the beginning of the twentieth century. A recent study by Etherington brought together various estimates made in the nineteenth century for different regions, and suggested as 'only the roughest of guesses' a total population of less than one million by the eighteenth century for the entire region bounded by the Kalahari, the Limpopo, and the Indian Ocean.[1] A rough check on this estimate can be made by starting from the more comprehensive evidence available for the twentieth century.

When the first nationwide census was taken in 1904, the African population was stated to be 3,490,000. The addition of the population of the three British protectorates of Basutoland, Bechuanaland, and Swaziland would raise the total to a little over 4,000,000.[2] A range of estimates for the African population of the entire region at earlier dates can be derived by backward extrapolation from this level at higher or lower rates of increase. One possible assumption is that the population increased at broadly the same rate as in the first half of the twentieth century, about 2.0 per cent per annum.[3] This implies that a number of critical determinants of birth and death rates, including high infant mortality, excess mortality during periodic harvest failures or drought- and disease-related cattle deaths, and relatively long birth intervals associated with abstention during the period of suckling were common to both

---

[1] N. Etherington, *The great treks: the transformation of southern Africa, 1815–1854*, Harlow: Longman, 2001, p. 25.

[2] *Year Book*, No. 14, 1931–2, pp. 816–7, 995, 1007, and 1029. It is likely that there was a degree of under-enumeration at this first attempt to count the entire African population.

[3] According to the official census data the rate of growth of the African population of the Union was 1.9 per cent per annum between 1904 and 1951: Statistics South Africa, *Statistics, 2002*, p. 1.3. This may be an over-estimate if the degree of under-enumeration was greater at the earlier date.

periods, and also that any beneficial effects of modern medical intervention and public health measures such as smallpox inoculation were offset by deteriorating living conditions, especially in the increasingly crowded rural areas. Growth at this relatively high rate would give a lower bound for the population at the end of the eighteenth century of about 500,000, well below Etherington's estimate. The corresponding estimate for the mid-nineteenth century would fall a little short of 1,500,000.

To derive an upper bound for the population we need to consider various factors that would have caused a lower rate of population growth during the nineteenth century. Foremost among factors that might be thought to have lowered the growth rate were the numerous wars fought by Africans, both among themselves, notably during the *mfecane* in the 1820s and 1830s, and against the settlers and the imperial government.[4] However, according to de Kiewiet:

> The death rate in purely Native wars was never high, and there is even much reason to suppose that the devastation of the Zulu, Matabele and Mantati 'hordes' was very greatly exaggerated. Even in their wars with the Europeans, although occasional commandos and military expeditions resulted in bloody encounters, it was notorious that the Natives lost few lives. Sir Harry Smith's 'drive' on the Eastern Frontier in 1851 and the long agony of the Basuto wars were more cattle-raids than genuine warfare.[5]

Other relevant factors that should be considered include the severe droughts that occurred between the years 1817 and 1831, and are believed by some to have been a primary cause of the upheavals during that period, and out-migration of the Ndebele and Ndwandwe across the Limpopo into Southern Rhodesia and Portuguese East Africa in the aftermath of the *mfecane*. There was also widespread starvation and disaster following the Xhosa's horrendous cattle-killing catastrophe in 1856–57, though single events such as this would be of limited significance in the context of a century of growth.[6]

With regard to birth rates, the dominant features were early marriage and the great importance attached to having many children, 'especially in the strongly patrilineal and competitive societies of cattle-keepers'. The relatively long intervals between births were generally associated with the widespread custom of abstention from intercourse during suckling, as

---

[4] For the *mfecane* see Chapter 2, p. 37.
[5] Walker (ed.), *Cambridge history*, p. 838; see also J. Iliffe, *Africans, the history of a continent*, Cambridge: Cambridge University Press, 1995, p. 117.
[6] W. M. Macmillan, *Bantu, Boer and Briton: the making of the South African native problem*, London: Faber & Gwyer, 1929, p. 294, quotes an estimate by Theal for the number of Xhosa deaths of not fewer than 25,000 and 'possibly double that number', but comments: 'The likelihood is, as usual, that contemporary estimates would be exaggerated'.

well as the practice of breast-feeding for 'three hoeing seasons' or even longer. Paradoxically, the effect (and perhaps the purpose) of this extended suckling and birth spacing was not to limit population but rather to enhance the survival of infants, and possibly also to protect the health of mothers by reducing the frequency of childbirth.[7]

Taking all these factors together with the generally favourable environment and virtual absence of tropical diseases, it seems reasonable to assume a minimum rate for the long-run growth of the African population in southern Africa during the nineteenth century of 0.5 per cent per annum. This is approximately the rate at which the population of England increased between the mid-sixteenth and late eighteenth centuries, and has been suggested as the intrinsic rate elsewhere in Africa.[8] Backward extrapolation from 1904 on this basis would put the population in 1850 at about 3,000,000 and in 1800 at almost 2,500,000.

On the basis of this exercise, a level of between 500,000 and 2,500,000 for the entire African population south of the Limpopo seems to be the extreme range of possibilities for the beginning of the nineteenth century, with 1,500,000 to 3,000,000 as the corresponding range for the middle of the century. A central point estimate of 1,500,000 in 1800 (corresponding to a growth rate over the whole century of just under 1 per cent per annum) might thus serve as a suitable order of magnitude, though with due recognition of the essential uncertainties. For a corresponding estimate for mid-century it would be appropriate to make some allowance for the probability that the rate of increase was actually lower in the first half of the century – because of droughts, wars, and out-migration in the time of the *mfecane* – than in the second, and to replace the average of the upper and lower bounds by a best estimate of about 2,000,000 in 1850.[9]

Early estimates for the other groups comprising the black population are also very uncertain. It is estimated that the total Khoisan population south of the Orange River was of the order of 200,000 when the Dutch landed in the mid-seventeenth century, but their numbers were drastically reduced by the smallpox epidemics of 1713, 1735, and 1767, and by murderous attacks on them by white settlers.[10] Raiding parties were

---

[7] Walker (ed.), *Cambridge history*, pp. 838–40; M. Hunter, *Reaction to conquest*, Cape Town: David Philip, 1979, p. 158; Iliffe, *Africans*, pp. 68–9, 114–15; and V. van der Vliet, 'Growing up in traditional society', in W. D. Hammond-Tooke (ed.), *The Bantu-speaking peoples of Southern Africa*, 2nd edn, London: Routledge, 1974, p. 219.

[8] P. Manning, *Slavery and African life: occidental, oriental, and African slave trades*, Cambridge: Cambridge University Press, 1990, pp. 82–5.

[9] These two point estimates are broadly consistent with those of 1,500,000 in 1800 and 1,850,000 in 1850 given by C. McEvedy and R. Jones, *Atlas of world population history*, London: Allen Lane, 1978, pp. 258–61.

[10] Wilson and Thompson, *Oxford history*, vol.1, p. 68.

especially violent in their treatment of the San hunters. The toll taken by disease and slaughter was so high that the San effectively lost their separate identity by the end of the eighteenth century, though brutal onslaughts on the small number of survivors in Namaqualand, on the northern frontier of the Colony, continued into the middle of the following century. Those few who remained in the Cape were absorbed into the larger coloured population, and small numbers sought refuge in the arid land and deserts across the Orange River.

Fewer than 18,000 Khoisan (described as 'Hottentots') were enumerated in 1806, when the first count was made after the British had taken over the Cape, but this excludes those in Namaqualand. A contemporary estimate for 1820 put their number at 28,000.[11] At the census of 1865, taken after the incorporation of this territory, the number was over 80,000. In 1891 it was given as 50,000, but presumably by that date it was becoming increasingly difficult to distinguish between the original Khoisan and the general coloured population.

The first slaves were brought to the Cape by the VOC in 1658. Thereafter they were imported in roughly equal numbers from four sources: the east coast of Africa, the island of Madagascar to the east of the continent, India, and Malaya, Java, and other islands in the Indian Ocean. This continued until the abolition of the slave trade by the United Kingdom in 1808. The total slave population of the Cape was just over 1,800 in 1700, including slaves purchased by the Dutch East India Company for its own purposes, and those of the company's officials, as well as slaves owned by free burghers. The number climbed steadily to 6,700 in 1750 and 26,300 in 1800, and had reached 36,300 at emancipation in 1834.[12] Their descendants and those of the Khoisan form part of the larger coloured population that was subsequently enumerated in official censuses. In the Cape census of 1875 they numbered 196,000, and in the census of 1891, 312,000. Both these totals include those classified as Hottentots, but exclude the small coloured population living outside the Colony. By 1904 the total coloured population of South Africa was some 445,000, of whom about 89 per cent were resident in the Cape.[13]

[11] W. M. Macmillan, *The Cape colour question, a historical survey*, London: Faber & Gwyer, 1927, p. 141.
[12] R. C.-H. Shell, *Children of bondage: a social history of the slave society at the Cape of Good Hope, 1652–1838*, Hanover, NH: Wesleyan University Press, 1994, pp. 445–8.
[13] *Official Year Book*, 14, 1931–2, pp. 816–7.

The white population before 1900

The authorities thought it more important, and found it easier, to count the white population, and there are several official and other censuses from which it is possible to track their expansion. However, it was not until 1904 that a count was taken on the same date across the entire country, and there are large margins of error around some of the estimates, changes in classifications of the population, shifting geographical boundaries, and omission of some areas prior to their incorporation into the Cape Colony.

When the first count was made in 1658, the Dutch population of the Dutch East India Company settlement numbered only 166, and subsequent growth was very slow. At the beginning of the eighteenth century there were about 1,300 Europeans at the Cape. This had increased to 1,544 when a survey was taken in 1731, and thereafter to about 10,000 by 1778, and to 22,000 at the end of the century.[14] Table A1.1 brings together what are judged to be the best of the available estimates for the two British colonies and the two Boer republics to show the subsequent rise over the course of the nineteenth century. The final column of the table incorporates a number of adjustments and additions in an attempt to provide a consistent and comprehensive total for 'South Africa'. This indicates growth to about 160,000 in 1855, and then more rapidly, with the aid of increased immigration, to over 1,100,000 in 1904.

The population in the twentieth century

The growth of the total population during the twentieth century was measured by official censuses at various dates, but there were significant problems of undercounting and of changing geographical boundaries when the nominally independent homelands were excluded during the apartheid era. Annual estimates of the mid-year population were given in various official publications, but were not always revised in the light of later census data, and there does not appear to be a continuous series published on a consistent basis. Table A1.2 attempts to provide such a series for the total population for all years from 1904 to 1996, and the racial composition of the totals is shown at decadal intervals in Table A1.3.

---

[14] Walker (ed.), *Cambridge history*, pp. 155 and 164 and N. Worden et al., *Cape Town: the making of a city*, Cape Town: David Philip, 1998, pp. 26 and 50.

Table A1.1. *European population of South Africa, 1798–1904*

	(1) Cape	(2) Natal	(3) Orange Free State	(4) Transvaal	(5) 'South Africa'
			(thousands)		
1798	21.7	–	–	–	21.7
1806	26.6	–	–	–	26.6
1815	37.3	–	–	–	37.3
1825	50.6	–	–	–	50.6
1832	66.0	–	–	–	66.0
1845	81.6	–	–	–	94.0[h]
1855	<u>112.0</u>	8.5[a]	15.0[d]	25.0[d]	161.0[i]
1865	181.6	17.0[b]	21.0[e]	33.0[e]	252.0[i]
1875	236.8	18.6[c]	<u>27.0</u>[f]	40.0	342.0[ij]
1880	..	<u>25.3</u>	61.0	<u>50.0</u>	–
1891	377.0	46.8	77.7[g]	119.1[g]	<u>632.0</u>[i]
1904	579.7	97.1	142.7	297.3	1,116.8

Notes: Only figures below the rule in each column are based on official censuses.
[a] 1856.
[b] 1866.
[c] 1874.
[d] 1854.
[e] Rough estimate, obtained by interpolation.
[f] 1873.
[g] 1890.
[h] Including an estimated 12,000 trekkers who left the Cape between 1835 and 1843.
[i] Including components adjusted where necessary by interpolation to obtain estimates for the given year.
[j] Including a rough addition of 12,000 to cover the population of the diamond fields in Griqualand West, which was not annexed by the Cape Colony until 1880, and of East Griqualand, the Transkei, and other territories in the eastern Cape annexed between 1879 and 1894.

Sources: Official Year Book, 14, 1931–2, pp. 816–17 for all official census data. Other estimates from Schumann, *Structural changes*, pp. 38–9, except for the Cape in 1798, taken from Walker (ed.), *Cambridge history*, p. 164; the Cape in 1832 and Natal in 1856 are from M. H. de Kock, *Selected subjects in the economic history of South Africa*, Cape Town: Juta, 1924, pp. 135 and 142; and Natal in 1880 is from *Statistical Yearbook for the Colony of Natal, 1899*, quoted in D. Hobart Houghton and J. Dagut (eds.), *Source material on the South African economy, 1860–1970*, Cape Town: Oxford University Press, 1972, 1, p. 294. The estimate of the number of trekkers is given by Walker (ed.), *Cambridge history*, p. 328, and the white population of the territories annexed by the Cape Colony after 1875 by D. M. Goodfellow, *A modern economic history of South Africa*, London: Routledge, 1931, p. 16.

Table A1.2. *Mid-year de facto total population of South Africa, 1904–96 (millions)*

Year	Pop.	Year	Pop.	Year	Pop.
1904	5.192	1935	9.855	1966	20.440
1905	5.299	1936	10.077	1967	20.997
1906	5.409	1937	10.304	1968	21.569
1907	5.521	1938	10.532	1969	22.157
1908	5.635	1939	10.762	1970	22.740
1909	5.751	1940	10.991	1971	23.338
1910	5.877	1941	11.223	1972	23.936
1911	5.992	1942	11.452	1973	24.549
1912	6.103	1943	11.686	1974	25.179
1913	6.214	1944	11.920	1975	25.815
1914	6.325	1945	12.158	1976	26.468
1915	6.436	1946	12.399	1977	27.130
1916	6.547	1947	12.692	1978	27.809
1917	6.658	1948	13.003	1979	28.506
1918	6.769	1949	13.311	1980	29.252
1919	6.727	1950	13.596	1981	30.018
1920	6.838	1951	13.926	1982	30.829
1921	6.957	1952	14.265	1983	31.664
1922	7.150	1953	14.624	1984	32.523
1923	7.356	1954	14.992	1985	33.406
1924	7.559	1955	15.369	1986	34.230
1925	7.760	1956	15.755	1987	35.046
1926	7.964	1957	16.152	1988	35.873
1927	8.165	1958	16.558	1989	36.724
1928	8.370	1959	16.975	1990	37.597
1929	8.575	1960	17.417	1991	38.397
1930	8.782	1961	17.870	1992	39.173
1931	8.992	1962	18.357	1993	39.927
1932	9.208	1963	18.857	1994	40.655
1933	9.419	1964	19.371	1995	41.353
1934	9.636	1965	19.898	1996	42.021

Sources: Figures for 1904–10 are by interpolation starting from estimate based on census for 1904 adjusted to a mid-year basis. Those for 1911–45 are based on mid-year population given in *Union Statistics*, A-8, increased progressively from 1922 to allow for undercounting in censuses of 1936 and 1946 as estimated by J. L. Sadie, *A reconstruction and projection of demographic movements in the RSA and TBVC countries*, University of South Africa, Bureau of Market Research, Research Report No. 148, Pretoria, 1988, p. 4. Linked to mid-year series for 1946–49 in J. L. Sadie, *A projection of the South African population, 1991–2011*, University of South Africa, Bureau of Market Research, Research Report, No. 196, Pretoria, 1993, pp. 33–4 and for 1950–85 in United States Bureau of the Census, International data base, www.census.gov/cgi-bin/ipc/idbsprd. From 1986 this series was increased progressively to link to mid-year population given for 1991–96 in C. J. Van Aardt et al., *A projection of the South African population, 1996–2021*, University of South Africa, Bureau of Market Research, Research Report No. 270, Pretoria, 1999, p. 121.

Table A1.3. *Mid-year de facto population of South Africa by population group, 1904–2000*

	(1) Total (millions)	(2) African	(3) Coloured	(4) Asian	(5) White
		(percentage)			
1904	5.192	67.4	8.6	2.4	21.6
1910	5.877	67.3	8.8	2.6	21.4
1920	6.838	67.7	7.9	2.4	21.9
1930	8.782	68.9	8.0	2.3	20.8
1940	10.991	69.5	8.2	2.4	19.9
1950	13.596	69.5	8.6	2.7	19.2
1960	17.417	70.3	9.0	2.9	17.9
1970	22.740	70.7	9.4	2.9	17.0
1980	29.252	72.4	9.3	2.8	15.5
1990	37.191	75.5	8.6	2.6	13.3
2000	43.686	79.0	8.9	2.5	9.6

Sources: For 1904–40 estimates were derived directly from, or by interpolation between, official census data adjusted from 1936 for undercounting as for Table A1.2 and *Year Book*, No. 14, p. 813. For 1950–80 they are based on Sadie, 'Projection', pp. 33–4, for 1990 on Van Aardt et al., *Projection of the South African population*, p. 121, and for 2000 on census results for 2001 from Statistics South Africa website: www.statssa.gov.za.

Annexe 2: the land and the geographical environment

This annexe is provided primarily for readers who are not familiar with South Africa. Its purpose is to provide a very brief resumé of the main geographical and environmental features of the country, with particular reference to those that influenced its economic history with respect to the settlement and migration of people, the pattern of farming, and the development of mining. Nature could scarcely have been more generous in endowing South Africa with minerals, or more niggardly in providing water for the land. It was only the good fortune of the mines that enabled the country to overcome the misfortunes of the farms.

The land area and the geological legacy

Modern South Africa is in large part a political rather than a geographical construct. The area of the Union from its formation in 1910 was approximately 472,000 square miles (302,000,000 acres). This is big by European standards, almost as large as the territories of Great Britain, France, and Germany combined, but small by comparison with the 3,000,000 square miles of Australia and the even larger area of Canada. With a population in 1911 of almost 6,000,000, South Africa had an overall density of less than thirteen persons a square mile, but this covered a wide range: from large, sparsely settled regions in the western half of the country with fewer than one person to the square mile to the more settled areas to the east with densities of over seventy-five to the square mile.

The figure given for South Africa does not include the vast area (275,000 square miles) of the British protectorate of Bechuanaland, or the smaller territories of Basutoland and Swaziland, all of which played an important role in the political history of the region prior to 1910, and were effectively incorporated into the South African economy after Union. The political division between South Africa and Rhodesia was also politically determined in the late nineteenth century. In earlier periods African people had moved freely within the larger region, as did the British South Africa Company of Cecil Rhodes when it was exploring in the north and when it advanced into Mashonaland in the 1890s to overthrow Lobengula and claim the territory for Britain.

South Africa is bounded to the west by the Atlantic Ocean and to the south and east by the Indian Ocean, but there are few good natural harbours. At the time of the Union the two major ports were Cape Town and Durban, and substantial amounts of cargo also passed through Port Elizabeth and East London. The port of Delagoa Bay (Lourenço Marques), further north in Portuguese territory, also handled a large volume of South African traffic because of its proximity to the country's principal industrial centre in the Transvaal. To the north the country was bordered (from west to east) by South West Africa, Bechuanaland, Southern Rhodesia, and Portuguese East Africa, with the boundaries formed primarily by the Orange, Molopo, and Limpopo rivers (see Map 1). None of South Africa's rivers are navigable (though in earlier times many river beds were used as convenient roads and tracks for transport by ox-wagon in the long dry season), and there is not a single river mouth with sufficient depth for sea-going ships to enter.

One of the distinctive geological features of the entire sub-continent is a U-shaped escarpment which follows the outline of the coast from a point north of the Orange River in the west to the Limpopo valley in the east. The escarpment (sometimes Great Escarpment) forms the edge of a vast interior plateau which extends northwards across Africa to reach its highest levels in east Africa. In the Cape, a number of parallel mountain ranges lie between the sea and the escarpment, running north–south in the west and west–east in the south. Many of the valleys are deep, narrow gorges that impeded transport until the advent of dynamite, together with systematic organization and financial resources, facilitated the making of proper roads during the first half of the nineteenth century. There are also two arid plains in this region of the Cape; the Great Karroo, running west–east for about 300 miles between the mountains and the escarpment, and the Little Karroo south of this between the Langenberg and Swartberg mountains (see Map 2). Elsewhere the coastal plain is very narrow, and the escarpment rises upwards – progressively in some places, more steeply in others – to the large interior plateau. On the western side it is about 3,000 feet above sea level and runs northwards through the Kalahari Desert in a broad strip from the Orange River to the Zambesi. To the east, this plateau is known as the highveld, and in the Transvaal is about 6,000 feet above sea level, a factor which helped to moderate temperatures and promote settlement at latitudes where hot summers might otherwise have been unbearable. However, the bushveld region to the north and east of the highveld is subject to malaria and so is much less attractive to European settlers.

The feature of most significance for the economic development of the country was formed over millions of years in the long sequence of geological events that created precious metals and minerals. From the late nineteenth century all commercial attention was focused on the volcanic pipes containing diamonds and the extensive rock system in which gold was embedded, and from which it was later possible to extract uranium. The diamonds were located in the north-eastern Cape in the district of Kimberley, the conglomerates or reefs bearing gold and uranium in the Transvaal and Orange Free State. As discussed in Chapter 5, the character of the South African mining industry was essentially geologically determined. The main supplies of gold were lying at great depths and were finely distributed in very hard rock, so that the extraction and production of gold required the resources of giant corporations; there was no place for individual miners. In the late twentieth century, large deposits in the northern Transvaal of platinum (and its allied metals such as palladium) have become increasingly important, and there has been such an enormous expansion in world demand for this metal that by the end of the century the value of the country's sales of platinum exceeded those of gold.

Geology's rich legacy also gave South Africa good supplies of base metals and of non-metallic minerals. The mining of gold was greatly facilitated by the discovery close by of coal in thick, unbroken, horizontal seams, at relatively shallow depths, and there are further large deposits of coal (of even better quality) in Natal. The development of a domestic iron and steel industry in the inter-war period was based on the presence of large reserves of high-grade iron ore, and other base metals found in significant quantities include chromium, manganese, vanadium, titanium, antimony, and copper. The non-metallic minerals include fluorspar, phosphates, mica, and vermiculite. Asbestos is no longer regarded as an economic asset because of its role in causing mesothelioma and other diseases of the lung, but was until recently produced in substantial quantities. All these minerals are located in the north of the country, predominantly in the northern and north-eastern Transvaal or in the northern Cape.

Rainfall, soil, and vegetation

The extent and elevation of the interior plateau, the narrow coastal belt, and the coastal ocean currents combine to influence the atmospheric circulation and pattern of rainfall, which was the crucial climatic factor in the economic history of South Africa. Over most of the country the rain falls in summer. However, there is a small zone of Mediterranean winter rainfall in the southwest corner of the Cape, and a narrow belt to the east of this that receives rain all year, though it is only along the southern coast between the Breede River and East London that precipitation is high.

In general both the frequency and the regularity of the rainfall increases from west to east. Only about one-tenth of the territory of South Africa – in the south-western corner, along the southern coastal belt, and on the south-eastern side – receives at least 30 inches (750 mm) of rain per year, roughly the minimum amount required for successful arable farming. At the other extreme, about one-third of the country – including the desert of Namaqualand and the southern edge of the Kalahari, and the semi-desert of the Karroo and north-western Cape – has an annual rainfall of less than 10 inches (250 mm), and a further third receives less than 20 inches (500 mm). This coincides broadly with the region of extensive farming shown on Map 5 below. The problem is not simply that the amount of rain received over so much of the country is very inadequate, but that it is also highly irregular. The historical record indicates an average of one severe drought every six years, usually leading to significant losses of cattle and sheep as well as poor harvests. Even well-watered areas are subject to frequent droughts which can last for two or three years, and the variability is far greater in areas with poor rainfall. When rain does come, particularly in the summer rainfall zone, it is typically not a gentle shower but a torrential storm that runs off the hard, dry, treeless surface of the land, and often causes heavy damage to both soil and vegetation. Overstocking and poor management of the land have hastened the deterioration wrought by adverse natural conditions. The threat that the entire country might become one great desert (expressed by the Drought Investigation Commission of 1923) was clearly exaggerated, but soil erosion has been a massive problem, especially but not only in areas farmed by Africans. The soil is generally thin and of poor quality, with vast areas of sandy and desert soil, and there are only a few exceptional places with rich alluvial soil of high fertility, such as the valleys in the zone of winter rainfall.

Climatic conditions combined with soil variations to determine the character of the vegetation. The four principal types of cover are the numerous varieties of evergreen shrubs (fynbos) in the south-western Cape, karroo shrub in the semi-desert and desert areas of the Cape, grasslands in the highveld of the Transvaal and Orange Free State, and the bushveld (or savannah) which lies in a semi-circle around the highveld grasslands and consists of a mixture of sparse trees and grasses suitable for stock farming. Less than 0.5 per cent of the surface area is covered by true forests with timber of commercial value. These are confined to the region of all-year rainfall on the southern coast or to the seaward slopes and deep ravines of the escarpment in the eastern Transvaal and Natal.

The karroo vegetation has been described as having 'a superficial resemblance to a European heath in a very dry and poor condition'.[1] It is composed of small shrubs and succulents but, despite the unfavourable impression it gives, has the dual advantage that it is better adapted to withstand prolonged droughts than the grassland, and that it provides nutritious grazing for sheep and goats, enabling the region to be used for stock-farming on an extensive basis. For cattle farmers the crucial aspect of the grasslands is whether they are 'sweet' or 'sour'. The sweet grass is succulent and nourishing, and can be consumed by cattle throughout the year, even during the dry season. The sourveld (also referred to as zuurveld) is found in many parts of the country and is unpalatable to stock in the winter, although it provides good grazing in the early months of growth during summer rainfall.

Seasonal variation in the rainfall played a significant part in determining the early patterns of settlement and movement by the Khoisan in the Cape and by the African peoples as they moved south along the eastern seaboard (see Chapter 1). It also explains the types of farming and the crops grown by the indigenous population in different regions. Following the settlement by Europeans in the mid-seventeenth century, the east–west direction of the Cape mountain ranges between the sea and the escarpment was responsible for the direction of their movement away from the original settlement around Cape Town towards the interior. When they finally crossed the mountains and settled in the Karroo, they remained relatively isolated and found it very difficult to bring their products to market in Cape Town in any form except as live animals. These transported themselves, but lost much weight on the journey. The difficulties created by the escarpment also discouraged and delayed the ascent of settlers to the high plateau. In the nineteenth and twentieth centuries the pattern of rainfall, supplemented by other environmental factors such as temperature, frost, soil, and vegetation, was the fundamental determinant of the characteristic types of agriculture outlined below.

Diseases and pests

It was not only drought against which farmers had to contend. As the Director of the Transvaal Department of Agriculture noted when he surveyed the position in 1908,

---

[1] Walker (ed.), *Cambridge history*, p. 13. It should be noted that the karroo veld covers a much larger area than the specific regions designated as the Great and Little Karroo.

In many respects our farmers are in a worse plight now than they have ever been, for owing to a lack of care in dealing with contagious diseases of animals and plants, new diseases have been allowed to enter this colony, and diseases native to certain parts of it permitted to spread, until a collection of pests has been accumulated that for variety and virulence could scarcely be equalled, and certainly not surpassed, by any country in the world.[2]

Some of the diseases were endemic in South Africa, others flared up in periodic epidemics. Each animal had its own special scourge: rinderpest and east coast fever for cattle, the parasitic scab for sheep and goats, and horse sickness – carried by insects flying at night – for horses, mules, and donkeys. Other cattle diseases included redwater, anthrax, bovine tuberculosis, and lung sickness (pleuro-pneumonia). Sheep flocks were also vulnerable to jackals and other predators. Arable farmers periodically lost their crops of maize and wheat to rust, smut, and other fungous diseases, to insect pests such as the maize stalk-borer, and to unimaginably vast swarms of locusts. Their vines fell victim to phylloxera. There was little advance in methods of control before the twentieth century, and, until the formation of the Union, divisions and differences between the four independent colonies aggravated problems by making it easy for plagues and pests to cross artificial boundaries. Many of South Africa's fiercely independent white farmers regarded any form of government directive as unacceptable interference with their personal freedom. Black farmers tended to distrust all government policies and especially those that sought to dictate how they should treat their stock. The lack of any form of natural barrier also made the country particularly vulnerable to the advance of diseases and pests from tropical Africa.

Perhaps the worst such invasion from the north was rinderpest, a highly infectious febrile disease, which entered South Africa in the 1890s, probably from the Sudan, and rapidly wiped out millions of cattle. Eventually a serum was discovered with which herds could be inoculated, and the disease was first arrested and then eradicated. Cattle were also subject to periodic epidemics of east coast fever, a parasitic disease carried by ticks that was as deadly as rinderpest though not as contagious. The first outbreak was recorded in Natal at the beginning of the twentieth century, and was believed to have taken hold when animals lacking a natural immunity to the fever were imported from Australia. It then spread to other parts of the country and the mortality among infected animals at each subsequent outbreak was commonly 90 per cent. The initial response was to restrict cattle movements and slaughter all infected cattle, but the technique of

---

[2] F. B. Smith, *Some observations upon the probable effect of the closer union of South Africa upon agriculture*, Pretoria: Government Printer, 1908, p. 4.

using dipping to destroy the ticks was borrowed from Australia and proved effective both against east coast fever and against redwater, one of the endemic cattle diseases. It was, however, a long and costly process to develop the infrastructure necessary for dipping all cattle and to ensure the compliance of all farmers, both white and black. There were numerous anti-dipping campaigns among African cattle owners in the reserves, and they were particularly hostile to the dipping fees that they were obliged to pay and to restrictions on the sale and movement of their stock.

The principal problem for owners of sheep (and also goats) was scab, a contagious disease of the skin with a purely parasitic origin. It had been a problem for hundreds of years, and was mentioned in the late seventeenth century by one of the governors of the Dutch settlement at the Cape as the cause of heavy losses of sheep owned by the VOC. The irritation and itching which are the symptoms of the disease cause much suffering to the animals, there is heavy mortality, and the value of the wool and skins is greatly reduced. Unlike Australia, the country was slow to tackle the problem, and it was not until the very end of the nineteenth century that the Cape Colony introduced an Act making it compulsory for every owner of sheep and goats to have a dipping tank and to dip the entire stock during the summer months. The Act also established an efficient system of inspectors to ensure that the dipping was done thoroughly. This framework of inspection, compulsion, and simultaneous dipping was later extended to the whole country under an Act passed by the Union government in 1911.

Agricultural regions

South Africa is predominantly a pastoral country and less than 15 per cent of its area is suitable for cultivation. Intensive agriculture is possible in only three small parts of the country, two on the coast and one inland. These are shown on Map 5 by vertical hatching. The first comprises the coastal areas of the south-western Cape and the southern and eastern Cape coastlands, and the main farming activities in this region include fruit, vines, wheat and other cereals, sheep, ostriches, dairying, and timber. The second, on the Natal coast, is predominantly devoted to the cultivation of sugar, but also produces subtropical fruits and timber. In the third area of intensive farming, located in the northern Orange Free State and southern Transvaal, maize is the principal crop, and this is supplemented by cattle, sheep, and dairying. The maximum production of maize is concentrated in an inverted triangle with its apex at Ladybrand in the south, and sides running north-west to Lichtenburg and north-east to Ermelo. This central area of intensive farming is surrounded by more

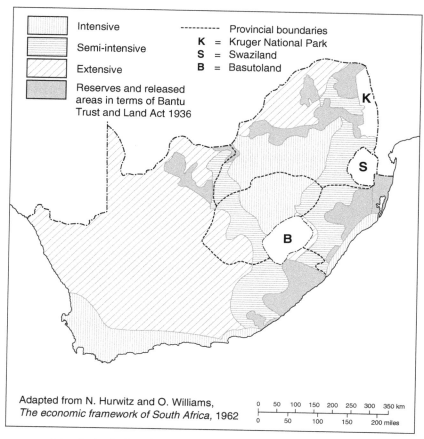

Intensive

Semi-intensive

Extensive

Reserves and released areas in terms of Bantu Trust and Land Act 1936

---------- Provincial boundaries
K = Kruger National Park
S = Swaziland
B = Basutoland

Adapted from N. Hurwitz and O. Williams,
The economic framework of South Africa, 1962

Map 5. Agricultural regions of South Africa, *c.*1960

marginal land devoted to semi-intensive farming (marked on Map 5 by horizontal hatching). To the west and east this intermediate zone is used for maize, sheep, cattle, dairying, citrus fruit, and timber, and in the north-east for timber, vegetables, citrus fruit, and subtropical fruits.

The remaining area of European-owned land covers a very large part of the country, and is suitable only for extensive farming. The standard South African farm of 6,000 acres was sufficient for sheep farming on the eastern karroo veld, but further west at least 10,000 acres were required, and farms of more than 20,000 acres were not exceptional. Large flocks of sheep and goats were carried on the vast area of karroo vegetation in the Cape, and on the foothills of the Drakensberg in Natal, and large herds of cattle on vast ranches in the northern Cape and northern Transvaal. Substantial parts of the eastern Transvaal and Natal were also set aside for game reserves, most notably the Kruger National Park on the eastern frontier with Portuguese East Africa.

Finally, there are the areas of African subsistence farming (coloured grey on the map) in the reserves (later homelands) and on land that was released for future acquisition under the Bantu Trust and Land Act, 1936, though much of this was not actually purchased. For reasons discussed in Chapters 3 and 6, these areas have suffered throughout the twentieth century from lack of resources, overstocking, and erosion, and produce extremely low yields.

Annexe 3: the labour force and unemployment

For much of the apartheid period the government omitted to compile data on the number of Africans without work, and when a regular survey was finally initiated an unduly narrow definition of unemployment was adopted. As it became apparent during the 1970s and 1980s that the number out of work was rising, the issue became the subject of heated debate. There were disputes over both theoretical aspects of the nature and possibility of voluntary unemployment in a market economy, and over the validity of various attempts at empirical measurement. Such measures were typically either indirect estimates that were necessarily highly sensitive to their underlying assumptions and definitions or depended on one-off surveys, often with quite small samples. Both provided useful information, but neither is of much help to historians trying to trace the emergence and changing scale of unemployment over time. For the purpose of the present study an attempt was made to do this by using the one other available source, information on employment and unemployment collected at periodic censuses of the population.[1]

The quality of the data available is very poor, and the results are, at best, rough orders of magnitude.[2] The original census enumerations suffered from changing levels of undercounting of the black population, from inconsistencies in the definition of employment, and from exclusion of the

---

[1] Two of the most influential of the earlier empirical studies that also made some use of census data were J. B. Knight, 'Labour allocation and unemployment in South Africa', *Oxford Bulletin of Economic Studies*, 40, 1978, and C. Simkins, 'Measuring and predicting unemployment in South Africa, 1960–77', in C. Simkins and D. Clarke (eds.), *Structural unemployment in Southern Africa*, University of Natal, 1978. The present exercise differs appreciably from these studies in both aims and methods; in particular, it does not attempt to estimate under-employment. It also has the benefit of data for a much larger number of years with which to evaluate trends in employment and unemployment.

[2] C. Meth, *Sorry, wrong number, a critical examination of African labour force estimates, 1970–87*, University of Natal, 1988, was a devastating onslaught on the official data, but his most trenchant comments were directed at the Current Population Survey, which is not used at all in this exercise, and at the problems created by the removal of the home-lands from the 1980 census, an issue on which there is now much more information.

notionally independent states of the Transkei, Bophuthatswana, Venda, and Ciskei (the TBVC states) from the censuses of 1980, 1985, and 1991. The present estimates attempt to adjust for all these factors to obtain a consistent set of benchmarks for selected census years, but inevitably the adjustments are highly approximate, and in some cases can only be informed guesses.

The resulting uncertainty is especially large in relation to estimates of employment and unemployment. These are not precise concepts, and there is ample scope for ambiguity in an economy with a large informal sector and with large numbers of people living in the subsistence sector. The straightforward category of full-time employment shades into successive states of part-time employment, irregular, and casual employment, and varying degrees of under-employment or disguised unemployment. The rest periods taken by migrant workers between stints on the mines add a further complication. There is certainly no single statistic that can claim to be an accurate measure of the level of 'employment' or 'unemployment' at any particular time. All that the present estimates hope to achieve is to provide a guide to the evolution of the broad dimensions of unemployment over the last half of the twentieth century.

The first stage in the compilation of these estimates was the derivation of benchmarks for census years. In the second stage the resulting information was extended to every fifth year from 1950 to 1995 by various forms of interpolation. The broad outlines of these procedures are described below. The main purpose of the exercise was to compile consistent estimates for the total population and four of its components: the population of working age (all those aged from fifteen to sixty-four inclusive), the number who were economically active (all those who were either in work or unemployed), and the division of the latter series between employment and unemployment.

The South African statistical agency currently publishes two estimates of unemployment. One, referred to as 'official', defines the unemployed as those people who (i) did not work during the seven previous days, (ii) want to work and are available to start work within a week, and (iii) have taken active steps to look for work or to start some form of self-employment in the four previous weeks. The second, referred to as 'expanded unemployment', omits the third requirement. The results derived from the census are closest to the expanded definition, since the census did not apply a 'looking-for-work' test. Derivation of these series also yielded internally consistent data for two other series: the dependent population (aged under fifteen or over sixty-four), and those of working age who were not economically active, for example full-time students, housewives, or disabled people who were unable to work. A further by-product was a classification of the employed population by economic sector.

The census benchmarks

The benchmark estimates were derived from six successive post-war censuses of population, taken between 1951 and 1996.[3] A small number of persons aged sixty-five and over were returned at the censuses as economically active, and are included in the present estimates. All children below the age of fifteen are excluded automatically from the definition of economically active, though no doubt some were employed in various ways.

The basic procedure used to derive estimates for five of the census years (1951, 1960, 1970, 1980, and 1996) required three sets of data, all subdivided by age, gender, and population group. These were (i) the enumerated total population, (ii) the enumerated economically active population, and (iii) the corrected total population after adjustment for undercounting, and – in 1980 – for the exclusion of the TBVC states.[4] The corrected economically active population was then calculated by assuming that the activity rates (the number of economically active persons as a percentage of the total population) were the same for the corrected as for the enumerated population in each separate age, gender, and population group. An example may help to clarify the procedure: in the initial census enumeration for 1960 the total number of African males aged fifteen to nineteen was given as 523,000, and the number economically active as 404,000, an activity rate of 77.3 per cent. After adjustment for under-enumeration the number of African males in this age group was raised to 604,000, and it was assumed that 77.3 per cent of the additional 81,000 were also economically active, bringing the total number to 467,000.

---

[3] A census was also taken in 1985, but an initial attempt to make the necessary adjustments for undercounting and omission of the TBVC states for the present exercise was judged unsatisfactory on various criteria, and the results were discarded. The results of the census in 2001 have been released recently, but the Census Sub-Committee of the South African Statistics Council has reported that preliminary investigations reveal a number of 'mutually compensating distortions in the composition of the population by gender, age and population group', and has given a 'special warning about labour market statistics'. It was decided, therefore, that data for 2001 should not be included in the tables given in this annexe.

[4] Data on the total enumerated population classified by age, gender, and population group were extracted from each of the relevant census reports. The sources for the corresponding corrected de facto population were Van Aardt et al., *Projection of the South African population*, p. 2 for 1996, and Sadie, *Reconstruction*, pp. 60–1, 68–70, 76–8, and 88–9 for earlier census years. The classification of the economically active population by age, gender, and population group was extracted from the census reports for 1960 and 1970; for other years the age distribution was not given and was reconstructed as described in the text.

For 1960 and 1970 full information was found for all three of the necessary data sets. For 1951 the required classification of the economically active population by age was not published, and it was assumed that the activity rates for each age, gender, and population group were the same as in 1960, subject to an overall adjustment to maintain consistency with the 1951 activity rate for the total of each population group. For 1970 it was also necessary to reduce the figures reported by the census for employment in agriculture. The numbers were greatly inflated by comparison with all other census years because abnormally large numbers of females in the subsistence sector were treated by the census enumerators as economically active. Male employment was also overstated because enumerators classified as employed in agriculture a substantial number of males living in rural areas who described themselves as unemployed.[5] The excess number of females was transferred to the economically inactive category, and the excess males were classified as unemployed.

For 1980, the shortcomings of the census data were bypassed by extrapolating 1970 activity rates (adjusted for changes to the numbers in agriculture noted above) by means of the change in activity rates between 1970 and 1980 in each age group estimated by Sadie for each population group and gender.[6] For 1996, the necessary age distribution of the enumerated economically active population classified by population group and gender was reconstructed by applying the activity rates projected by Sadie for 1995 and scaling the resulting estimates to agree with the census totals.[7] The corrected participation rates were then applied to the revised population data to obtain the required corrected estimates of the economically active population classified by age, gender, and population group. The remaining census year for which estimates were required was 1991. The estimates for this year were taken directly from census data for the Republic of South Africa, corrected for

[5] For the females see G. Maasdorp, 'Unemployment in South Africa and its implications', in L. Schlemmer and E. Webster (eds.), Change, reform and economic growth in South Africa, Johannesburg: Ravan Press, 1978, p. 145; for the males see N. Bromberger, 'South African unemployment: a survey of research', in C. Simkins and C. Desmond, South African unemployment: a black picture, Pietermaritzburg: University of Natal, 1978, p. 12.

[6] J. L. Sadie, The South African labour force, 1960–2005, University of South Africa, Bureau of Market Research, Research Report, No. 178, Pretoria, 1991, pp. 44, 55, 62, 69, 102, 105, 109, and 115.

[7] The projected 1995 participation rates for females were given in Sadie, South African labour force, pp. 102, 105, 109, and 115. Those for males were not published but can be reconstructed from his corresponding estimates of the male labour force, ibid., pp. 164–8 and of the male population in Sadie, Reconstruction, pp. 61, 70, 78, and 89.

undercounting, with an addition for the TBVC states compiled by the Development Bank of Southern Africa (DBSA).[8]

The corrected economically active totals for each gender and population group in each census year were then obtained as the sum of the corresponding age groups, and the corrected aggregate economically active population in each year as the sum of the eight gender and population groups. This in turn yields for each census year a set of correction factors given by the ratios of the corrected to the enumerated estimates of the economically active population for each gender and population group. The variation in these correction factors was large enough to justify the work involved in making all the component estimates; for 1980, for example, they ranged from an addition of 2.4 per cent for white males to one of 29 per cent for African females. These correction factors were then applied to the corresponding census counts of the numbers employed and unemployed in each gender and population group, and to the corresponding classification of the employed by economic sector. The resulting benchmark estimates for the principal population and labour force series are set out in Table A3.1, and the classification by economic sector is given below in Table A3.2.

Labour market ratios

The data in the upper panel of Table A3.1 can be used to calculate various ratios. The *dependency rate* (the proportion of the total population aged under fifteen or over sixty-four) rose from 42 per cent in 1951 to almost 45 per cent in 1970, and then dropped sharply to 39 per cent in 1996. The proportion aged sixty-five and over was actually rising at the end of the century, but there was a fall in the proportion of non-working dependents aged under fifteen of some 6 percentage points between 1970 and 1996. This reflects a substantial reduction in fertility that occurred as a result of increased urbanization of the population and various socio-economic developments associated with that.

---

[8] The principal sources for the Republic of South Africa were *Statistics 2002*, pp. 1.6 and 7.5, and the United States Bureau of the Census, International data base: www.census.gov/cgi-bin/ipc/idbsprd, Table 069. The estimate of the economically active population including the TBVC states was taken from Development Bank of Southern Africa (DBSA), *South Africa's nine provinces*, DBSA, 1994, p. 105, and the division of the population between those of working age and those under fifteen or over sixty-four was based on data for 1989 in Development Bank of Southern Africa, *South Africa, an inter-regional profile*, DBSA, 1991, p. 38. The number employed in the TBVC area was allocated by economic sector in proportion to DBSA estimates for 1985; *South Africa, an inter-regional profile*, p. 47.

Table A3.1. *Population and labour force, benchmark estimates, 1951–96*

	(1) 1951	(2) 1960	(3) 1970	(4) 1980	(5) 1991	(6) 1996
	(thousands)					
A. Total population	13,864	17,482	22,666	29,111	37,945	42,273
B. Less under 15 and over 64	5,830	7,738	10,185	12,683	15,668	16,396
C. Population of working age	8,034	9,744	12,481	16,428	22,278	25,877
D. Total employed	4,936	5,847	7,462	9,532	10,613	9,847
E. Total unemployed	196	457	532	713	2,331	4,882
F. Economically active population	5,133	6,304	7,994	10,245	12,944	14,730
G. Not economically active	2,901	3,440	4,487	6,183	9,334	11,147
Percentage rates						
Dependency rate (B/A)	42.1	44.3	44.9	43.6	41.3	38.8
Activity rate (F/A)	37.1	36.1	35.3	35.2	34.1	34.8
Participation rate (F/C)	64.0	64.7	64.0	62.4	58.1	56.9
Males	98.4	96.8	88.1	83.8	69.9	64.8
Females	25.5	30.0	38.7	40.8	47.1	49.3
Absorption rate (D/C)	61.5	60.0	59.8	58.0	47.6	38.1
Unemployment rate (E/F)	3.9	7.3	6.7	7.0	18.0	33.1

The *activity rate* measures the ratio of the number economically active to the total population. It can be interpreted as the outcome of the combined movements in the proportion of the population of working age (=100 – the dependency rate) and in the *participation rate* (the proportion of the population of working age that are economically active). The fall in the activity rate from 37 per cent in 1951 to 35 per cent in 1996 was thus primarily explained by a fall in the participation rate, offset by a slight rise in the proportion of the population of working age as a consequence of the fall in the dependency rate mentioned earlier.

The fall in the overall participation rate from 64 per cent in 1951 to 57 per cent in 1996 conceals two remarkably divergent trends in the component male and female labour force participation rates which are discussed in Chapter 10. The *absorption rate* (the proportion of the population of working age in employment) shows a dramatic and persistent decline from 62 per cent in 1951 to 38 per cent in 1996, and mirrors the large rise in the *unemployment rate* (the proportion of the economically

Table A3.2. *Classification of employed labour force by economic sector, 1950–1995*

	(1) 1950	(2) 1955	(3) 1960	(4) 1965	(5) 1970	(6) 1975	(7) 1980	(8) 1985	(9) 1990	(10) 1995
					(thousand)					
Number										
Agriculture, forestry, and fishing	1,699	1,799	1,902	1,872	1,750	1,647	1,585	1,598	1,482	1,378
Mining and quarrying	584	615	668	717	751	852	966	977	925	751
Manufacturing	530	659	740	886	1,098	1,249	1,690	1,651	1,667	1,538
Electricity, gas, and water	26	38	33	39	50	70	93	122	114	114
Construction	244	296	334	424	518	581	583	651	658	600
Commerce	285	342	485	550	754	999	1170	1285	1472	1,404
Transport and communication	220	248	259	321	364	431	482	507	537	532
Financial and business services	55	82	126	157	199	255	307	462	606	657
Other services[a]	1,191	1,158	1,227	1,332	1,654	1,983	2,377	2,630	2,910	2,813
Not classified	33	50	74	156	324	251	279	306	336	277
Total in employment	4,867	5,287	5,847	6,454	7,462	8,318	9,532	10,189	10,707	10,065
Percentage										
Agriculture, forestry, and fishing	34.9	34.0	32.5	29.0	23.4	19.8	16.6	15.7	13.8	13.7
Mining and quarrying	12.0	11.6	11.4	11.1	10.1	10.2	10.1	9.6	8.6	7.5
Manufacturing	10.9	12.5	12.7	13.7	14.7	15.0	17.7	16.2	15.6	15.3
Electricity, gas, and water	0.5	0.7	0.6	0.6	0.7	0.8	1.0	1.2	1.1	1.1
Construction	5.0	5.6	5.7	6.6	6.9	7.0	6.1	6.4	6.1	6.0
Commerce	5.9	6.5	8.3	8.5	10.1	12.0	12.3	12.6	13.8	13.9
Transport and communication	4.5	4.7	4.4	5.0	4.9	5.2	5.1	5.0	5.0	5.3
Financial and business services	1.1	1.6	2.1	2.4	2.7	3.1	3.2	4.5	5.7	6.5
Other services[a]	24.5	21.9	21.0	20.6	22.2	23.9	24.9	25.8	27.2	28.0
Not classified	0.7	0.9	1.3	2.4	4.3	3.0	2.9	3.0	3.1	2.7
Total in employment	100.0	100.0	100.0	100.0	100.0	100.0	100.0	100.0	100.0	100.0

[a] Community, social, and personal services, and domestic service.

active population unemployed) over the same period from 4 per cent to 33 per cent, and to almost 39 per cent if an allowance is made for an additional 1,400,000 'ultra discouraged' potential workers. The reasons for these two trends are also discussed in Chapter 10.

Interpolation and classification by economic sector

To complete the exercise, some additional estimates were made for non-census years for the purpose of Figure 10.3 (p. 236). For the total population, interpolation was based on the annual mid-year estimates in Table A1.2. The inter-censal population of working age was then obtained by applying interpolated estimates of the ratio to the total population; and the corresponding economically active population was obtained by applying interpolated estimates of the participation rate to the population of working age.

In order to maximize the information used in estimating employment, the census benchmarks were disaggregated into nine economic sectors, and a residual group of those not classified. An exceptionally large number of persons were not classified by economic sector in the 1996 census, and it was clear from comparison with earlier years – and with labour force surveys – that levels in subsistence agriculture were substantially understated, and that there were smaller understatements of mining and manufacturing. Rough transfers from the unclassified category were made to correct for this. Inter-censal employment was then derived by interpolating between these benchmarks on the basis of annual employment series for these sectors.[9] Linear logarithmic interpolation was used where no such information was available, and for the unclassified group.

The results of the initial interpolation were modified in a few cases where it was judged that a correction was needed to obtain a more consistent relationship between the level of employment and the phase of the business cycle in a given inter-censal year; for example, 1950 was a year close to the peak of the upswing, while 1955 was close to the trough of the downswing. The resulting series are set out in the upper panel of Table A3.2, with the corresponding percentage composition in the lower panel. The main categories are also shown in Figure 10.4 (p. 238). The final series, for unemployment, was then obtained as the difference between the number economically active and the number in employment.

---

[9] The main sources were *Statistics 2002*, p. 7.2, South African Reserve Bank, website: http://www.resbank.co.za, series 7000L–7009L, and information on the numbers employed in commercial agriculture given in issues of *SA Statistics* and in agricultural censuses.

Guide to further reading

The aim of this guide is both to indicate the principal sources used in writing the present text and to suggest further reading for those who wish to obtain additional analysis and information on particular topics. The abbreviations used for journals are listed on p. 288.

General economic history

C. W. de Kiewiet, *A history of South Africa, social and economic* (1941) was a brilliant contribution to the economic history of South Africa, and is still a delight to read for its intellectual insights, broad humanity, clarity, and sparkling style. Nothing comparable has appeared since then. The main later works are S. Jones and A. Müller, *The South African economy, 1910–1990* (1992), and the volume edited by F. L. Coleman, *Economic history of South Africa* (1983), in which two chapters by P. L. Wickins, on 'Land and labour' and 'Agriculture', are particularly good. Stuart Jones has also edited two special issues of the *South African Journal of Economic History*, one in 1994 on the 1980s and the other in 1999 on the 1970s, and has recently published a further collection of articles, *The decline of the South African economy* (2002), covering the whole period since 1970. The three volumes of commentary and extracts from documents by D. Hobart Houghton and J. Dagut (eds.), *Source material on the South African economy, 1860–1970*, vol. 1, *1860–1899*, vol. 2, *1899–1919*, and vol. 3, *1920–1970*, (1972) are an invaluable resource.

The studies by D. Hobart Houghton, *The South African economy* (4th edn, 1976), R. Horwitz, *The political economy of South Africa* (1967), and J. Nattrass, *The South African economy, its growth and change* (2nd edn, 1988), were primarily intended as introductions to the contemporary working of the South African economy, but all adopt a historical perspective and offer much of interest to economic historians. So too does the collection of papers by radical economists edited by S. Gelb, *South Africa's economic crisis* (1991). The extended review of the economic position in the early 1990s undertaken for the World Bank by P. Fallon and L. A. Pereira de Silva, *South Africa: economic performance and policies*, Discussion Paper 7, World Bank (1994), is illuminating on many aspects of the recent past.

Two collections edited by B. Guest and J. M. Sellers, *Enterprise and exploitation in a Victorian colony* (1985) and *Receded tides of Empire* (1994) cover various aspects of the economic and social history of Natal and Zululand; and there are essays on the social and economic history of the western Cape in W. G. James and M. Simons (eds.), *The angry divide* (1989). Finally, there are three historiographical reviews that readers of this book are likely to find helpful: J. Lonsdale, 'From colony to industrial state', *Social Dynamics*, 9, 1983; W. M. Freund, 'Economic history in South Africa: an introductory overview', *SAHJ*, 34, 1996; and J. Iliffe, 'The South African economy 1652–1997', *Economic History Review*, 52, 1999.

There are also a number of older works which are worth consulting for interesting ideas and for detailed information often omitted in later studies. These include two books by M. H. de Kock, *Selected subjects in the economic history of South Africa* (1924) and *The economic development of South Africa* (1936); W. M. Macmillan, *Complex South Africa* (1930); D. M. Goodfellow, *A modern economic history of South Africa* (1931); L. C. A. Knowles, *The economic development of the British overseas empire*, vol. 3, *The Union of South Africa* (1936); C. G. W. Schumann, *Structural changes and business cycles in South Africa, 1806–1936* (1938); and the chapters on South Africa in S. H. Frankel, *Capital investment in Africa* (1938), and K. Hancock, *Survey of British Commonwealth affairs*, vol. 2, *Problems of economic policy 1918–1939, Part 2* (1942).

General political history

It is seldom possible to understand South Africa's economic history without reference to its changing political history. The most comprehensive and up-to-date of many general surveys is R. Davenport and C. Saunders, *South Africa, a modern history* (5th edn, 2000). For more concise accounts see R. Ross, *A concise history of South Africa* (1999), or W. Beinart, *Twentieth-century South Africa* (2nd edn, 2001). The nature and origins of apartheid policies can be studied in S. Dubow, *Racial segregation and the origins of apartheid in South Africa, 1919–1936* (1989); D. Posel, *The making of apartheid, 1948–1961* (1991); P. Bonner, P. Delius, and D. Posel (eds.), *Apartheid's genesis, 1935–1962* (1993); and W. Beinart and S. Dubow (eds.), *Segregation and apartheid in twentieth-century South Africa* (1995). H. Giliomee, *The Afrikaners: biography of a people* (2003), is a superb synthesis of the changing activities and attitudes of the group who came to occupy such a dominant position in the history of the country, and were then forced to surrender it.

From the 1970s South Africa's problems and prospects stimulated numerous lively debates and conferences that resulted in a succession of thought-provoking collections with articles on overlapping aspects of economics and politics. They include L. Schlemmer and E. Webster (eds.), *Change, reform and economic growth in South Africa* (1978); H. Giliomee and L. Schlemmer (eds.), *Up against the fences: poverty, passes and privilege in South Africa* (1985); J. Butler, R. H. Elphick, and D. Welsh (eds.), *Democratic liberalism in South Africa* (1987); N. Nattrass and E. Ardington (eds.), *The political economy of South Africa* (1990); R. Schrire (ed.), *Critical choices for South Africa: an agenda for the 1990s* (1990) and *Wealth or poverty?: critical choices for South Africa* (1992); and M. Lipton and C. Simkins (eds.), *State and market in post apartheid South Africa* (1993).

There is also a disciplinary overlap at many points with economic and historical geography, evident in books such as A. J. Christopher, *Southern Africa* (1976), and A. Lester, *From colonization to democracy: a new historical geography of South Africa* (1998).

The early inhabitants of South Africa

For information on the life of the indigenous population historians are largely dependent on the work of anthropologists and archaeologists. The available evidence for the continent as a whole is superbly surveyed in J. Iliffe, *Africans, the history of a continent* (1995), and for southern Africa by S. Marks in her chapter in J. D. Fage and R. Oliver (eds.), *The Cambridge history of Africa*, vol. 4, *c. 1600 to 1790* (1975). The leading archaeological account is M. Hall, *The changing past: farmers, kings and traders in Southern Africa, 200–1860* (1987). Studies by anthropologists include W. D. Hammond-Tooke (ed.), *The Bantu-speaking peoples of South Africa* (2nd edn, 1974); M. Hunter, *Reaction to conquest* (1979); and the three chapters by the same author, now M. Wilson, on 'The hunters and herders', 'The Nguni people', and 'The Sotho, Venda, and Tsonga' in M. Wilson and L. Thompson (eds.), *The Oxford history of South Africa* (vol. 1, 1969). L. Thompson (ed.), *African societies in southern Africa* (1969) is a wide-ranging collection of articles by anthropologists and historians.

The main sources for the history of the Khoisan and coloured population are W. M. Macmillan, *The Cape colour question* (1927); J. S. Marais, *The Cape coloured people, 1652–1937* (1962); R. Elphick, *Kraal and castle: Khoikhoi and the founding of white South Africa* (1985); and many high-quality papers in R. Elphick and H. Giliomee (eds.), *The shaping of South African society, 1652–1840* (2nd edn, 1989). N. Worden, *Slavery in Dutch South Africa* (1985) is a fine survey; and R. C.-H. Shell, *Children of bondage* (1994) is a rich and innovative study that provides new analysis and information on many aspects of this institution. The subsequent impact of slavery is explored in N. Worden and C. C. Crais (eds.), *Breaking the chains: slavery and its legacy in the nineteenth-century Cape Colony* (1994); and E. E. Eldredge and F. Morton (eds.), *Slavery in South Africa* (1994). P. Scully, *Liberating the family? Gender and British slave emancipation in the rural western Cape, 1823–1853* (1997) provides a fresh perspective on the emancipation.

The early economic history of the Cape and of the interaction between its indigenous population and the European settlers was the subject of a seminal article by H. M. Robertson, '150 years of economic contact between black and white', *SAJE*, 2, 1934 and 3, 1935. S. D. Neumark, *Economic influences on the South African frontier, 1652–1836* (1957), was a pioneering monograph on the extent of the commercial relationships of the first white farmers. There are new data series in P. van Duin and R. Ross, *The economy of the Cape Colony in the eighteenth century* (1987); and relevant aspects of the economic development of the colony are examined in R. Ross, *Beyond the pale* (1993); T. J. Keegan, *Colonial South Africa and the origins of the racial order* (1996); chapters in Elphick and Giliomee, *The shaping of South African society* (1989); and in Part I of James and Simons, *The angry divide* (1989). D. Denoon, *Settler capitalism, the dynamics of dependent development in the southern hemisphere* (1983) is unusual and interesting for its comparative perspective.

Conquest and dispossession

The full history of the process of conquest and dispossession was only very partially revealed in standard early histories of South Africa such as E. Walker (ed.), *Cambridge history of the British Empire*, vol. 8, *South Africa* (2nd edn, 1963). However, the subject was subsequently transformed by a several studies that were based on a much wider range of sources and gave much more attention to the views and acts of the African people. The primary themes are political rather than economic, but there is much of interest for the economic historian. Among the major contributions to this body of work are J. Guy, *The destruction of the Zulu kingdom* (1979); P. Delius, *The land belongs to us: the Pedi polity, the Boers and the British in the nineteenth-century Transvaal* (1983); P. Bonner, *Kings, commoners and concessionaires: the evolution and dissolution of the nineteenth-century Swazi state* (1983); K. Shillington, *The colonialization of the southern Tswana 1870–1900* (1985); C. C. Crais, *The making of the colonial order: white supremacy and black resistance in the eastern Cape, 1770–1865* (1992); and C. Murray, *Black mountain: land, class and power in the eastern Orange Free State, 1880s–1980s* (1992). Many of these authors are also represented in the important collection of papers edited by S. Marks and A. Atmore, *Economy and society in pre-industrial South Africa* (1980). The sharp debate about the nature and causes of the upheavals in African societies in the early nineteenth century can be reviewed in C. A. Hamilton (ed.), *The mfecane aftermath* (1995). P. L. Wickins, 'The Natives Land Act of 1913: a cautionary essay on simple explanations of complex change', *SAJE*, 49, 1981, gives a fresh assessment of this momentous act.

Agriculture

Much of the material on individual sectors of the economy is contained in the general studies already listed and there are relatively few specialist works. The early work by W. M. Macmillan, *The agrarian problem* (1919), still repays reading. The leading research on the economic development of an independent African peasantry in the second half of the nineteenth century is presented in C. Bundy, *The rise and fall of the South African peasantry* (2nd edn, 1988). This second edition also includes the author's reply to critics of the first edition (of 1979), notably J. Lewis, 'The rise and fall of the South African peasantry', *JSAS*, 11, 1984. Wilson and Thompson, *Oxford history* (vol. 2, 1971) has a very good chapter by M. Wilson on the growth of peasant communities, followed by a lucid and comprehensive survey of the general history of farming by F. Wilson. S. Marks and R. Rathbone (eds.), *Industrialization and social change in South Africa* (1982), has a number of excellent papers on developments in farming and mining after 1870. For an analysis of the way in which the 'poor white' problem was eventually solved see I. Abedian and B. Standish, 'Poor whites and the role of the state', *SAJE*, 53, 1985.

The best introduction to the crucial, interrelated issues of dispossession of Africans, creation of a labour force for white farmers, and conditions in the African reserves, is W. Beinart, P. Delius, and S. Trapido (eds.), *Putting a plough to the ground: accumulation and dispossession in rural South Africa, 1850–1930* (1986). Other significant contributions include J. B. Knight and G. Lenta, 'Has capitalism underdeveloped the labour reserves of South Africa?', *OBES*, 42, 1980; C. Simkins, 'Agricultural production in the African reserves of South Africa, 1918–1969', *JSAS*, 7, 1981; M. Lacey, *Working for Boroko: the origins of a coercive labour system in South Africa* (1981); S. Greenberg, *Race and state in capitalist development* (1980); W. Beinart, *The political economy of Pondoland, 1860–1930* (1982); and T. J. Keegan, *Rural transformations in industrializing South Africa* (1986). Later research is reported in L. Switzer, *Power and resistance in an African society, the Ciskei Xhosa and the making of South Africa* (1993); J. Lambert, *Betrayed trust: Africans and the state in colonial Natal* (1995); and A. H. Jeeves and J. Crush (eds.), *White farms, black labour: the state and agrarian change in Southern Africa, 1910–1950* (1997). W. Beinart and C. Bundy, *Hidden struggles in rural South Africa* (1987), reveals many of the acts of resistance to official policy offered in the eastern Cape in the period 1890 to 1930; and the brief life of the Industrial and Commercial Workers' Union as an influential mass movement in rural South Africa is well chronicled in H. Bradford, *A taste of freedom* (1987).

A sense of the theoretical controversies that were prominent in the 1970s and 1980s in the historiography of agrarian development can be gained from M. Morris, 'The development of capitalism in South African agriculture', *Economy and Society*, 3, 1976; M. J. Murray, 'The origins of agrarian capitalism in South Africa: a critique of the "social history" perspective', *JSAS*, 15, 1989; and T. J. Keegan, 'The origins of agrarian capitalism in South Africa: a reply', *JSAS*, 15, 1989. The marketing arrangements introduced in the 1930s were strongly criticized at the time by C. S. Richards, 'Subsidies, quotas, tariffs and the excess cost of agriculture in South Africa', *SAJE*, 3, 1935. Their origins are explained in retrospect by one of the key participants in S. J. J. de Swardt, 'Agricultural marketing problems in the nineteen thirties', *SAJE*, 51, 1983; and their operation in the post-war period is scrutinized in World Bank, *South African agriculture*, Discussion Paper 6 (1994). This also contains a very thorough analysis of other recent developments in commercial farming and of the position in the reserves. Many aspects of contemporary farm labour are discussed in F. Wilson, A. Kooy, and D. Hendrie (eds.), *Farm labour in South Africa* (1977); and the impact of mechanization is carefully examined in M. de Klerk, 'Seasons that will never return', *JSAS*, 11, 1984.

Mining and migrant labour

The outstanding work on the history of gold mining is F. Wilson, *Labour in the South African gold mines, 1911–1969* (1972). F. A. Johnstone, *Class, race and gold* (1976), had an enormous impact on interpretations of the relationship between mining capital and the state, and on the origins of the colour bar, though E. N. Katz, 'Revisiting the origins of the industrial colour bar in the Witwatersrand gold mining industry, 1891–1899', *JSAS*, 25, 1999, adds some important qualifications. Two very different views of the role of the Anglo American Corporation are given in T. Gregory, *Ernest Oppenheimer and the economic development of southern Africa* (1962), and D. Innes, *Anglo American and the rise of modern South Africa* (1984); both are essential reading. D. Yudelman, *The emergence of modern South Africa* (1984), presents a carefully argued case for revision of earlier views on the relationship between the state and the mining industry.

The history of the diamond mines can be studied in the volumes by Gregory and Innes, and in C. Newberry, *The diamond ring: business, politics and precious stones in South Africa, 1867–1947* (1989); R. V. Turrell, *Capital and labour on the Kimberley diamond fields* (1987); W. H. Worger, *South Africa's city of diamonds: mine workers and monopoly capitalism in Kimberley, 1867–1895* (1987); and C. Newberry 'South Africa and the international diamond trade', *SAJEH*, 10, 1995, and 11, 1996.

For the system of migrant labour that was central to the operation of the mines see Wilson, *Labour in the South African gold mines;* and also A. Jeeves, *Migrant labour in South Africa's mining economy: the struggle for the gold mine's labour supply, 1890–1920* (1985); W. G. James, *Our precious metal, African labour in South Africa's gold industry, 1970–1990* (1992); and P. Harries, *Work, culture and identity: migrant labourers in Mozambique and South Africa, c. 1860–1910* (1994). E. Katz, 'Silicosis on the South African gold mines', in F. Wilson and G. Westcott (eds.), *Economics of health in South Africa* (1980), is excellent on the incidence of disease and on the disparity in compensation payments to white and black miners, and R. M. Packard, *White plague, black labor: tuberculosis and the political economy of health and disease in South Africa* (1989) is a very thorough study of another major disease associated with mining.

Industry and trade

Specialized histories of industrial development and of particular industries are largely confined to journal articles in the *South African Journal of Economics* and the *South African Journal of Economic History*. On the overall growth of manufacturing see G. Marais, 'Structural changes in manufacturing industry 1916 to 1975', *SAJE*, 49, 1981; S. P. Viljoen, 'The industrial achievement of South Africa', *SAJE*, 51, 1983; and C. L. McCarthy, 'Structural development of South African manufacturing industry – a policy perspective', *SAJE*, 56, 1988. The best starting point for a history of the key policy of industrial protection is D. J. J. Botha, 'On tariff policy: the formative years', *SAJE*, 41, 1973. Other sources include A. J. Norval, *A quarter of a century of industrial progress in South Africa* (1962); D. E. Kaplan, 'The politics of industrial protection in South Africa, 1910–1939', *JSAS*, 3, 1976; A. B. Lumby, 'Tariffs and gold in South Africa, 1886–1939', *SAJE*, 44, 1976; and S. Archer, 'Industrial protection and employment creation in South Africa during the inter-war years', *SAJEH*, 4, 1989. The forces behind the expanding economic activity of the Afrikaners in finance and industry from the 1930s is investigated from a Marxist perspective in D. O'Meara, *Volkskapitalisme* (1983); and the development of the early parastatals ESCOM and ISCOR is the central focus of N. L. Clark, *Manufacturing apartheid: state corporations in South Africa* (1994).

There are good discussions of various aspects of industrial and trade policy in the post-1948 period in J. A. Lombard (ed.), *Economic policy in South Africa* (1973); D. Lachman, 'Import restrictions and exchange rates', *SAJE*, 42, 1974; and two articles by A. E. Ratcliffe, 'Export policy in perspective', *SAJE*, 43, 1975 and 'Industrial development policy: changes during the 1970s', *SAJE*, 47, 1979. A. Black, 'The role of the state in promoting industrialization', and T. Bell, 'Should South Africa further liberalise its foreign trade?', in M. Lipton and C. Simkins (eds.), *State and market* (1993), are both valuable discussions of key issues.

Further thoughtful and thorough analysis of factors influencing South Africa's overseas trade and its relationship to the growth of manufacturing in recent decades are provided by T. Bell in his chapters in J. Michie and V. Padayachee (eds.), *The political economy of South Africa's transition* (1997); (with N. Madula) in S. Jones (ed.), *The decline of the South African economy* (2002); and (with G. Farrell and R. Cassim) in J. M. Fanelli and R. Medhora (eds.), *Finance and competitiveness in developing countries* (2002). The effect of sanctions is examined in R. T. Bell, 'The impact of sanctions on South Africa', *Journal of Contemporary African Studies*, 12, 1993; and by C. Jenkins, 'Adjusting to economic sanctions in South Africa', in O. Morrissey and F. Stewart (eds.), *Economic and political reform in developing countries* (1995).

The issue of decentralization and regional policy attracted considerable attention in the light of government policies to restrict the black population of the urban areas. Articles on this subject include R. T. Bell, 'Some aspects of industrial decentralization in South Africa', *SAJE*, 41, 1973; C. L. McCarthy, 'Industrial decentralization – reflections on new initiatives', *SAJE*, 50, 1982; F. Pretorius et al., 'History of industrial decentralization (Part II): historical development and the impact of policy', *Development Southern Africa*, 3, 1986; and R. Tomlinson and M. Addleson, 'Trends in industrial decentralization: an examination of Bell's hypothesis', *SAJE*, 54, 1986. These technical discussions should be read together with L. Platzky and C. Walker, *The surplus people, forced removals in South Africa* (1985).

Labour, the colour bar, unemployment, wages, and poverty

The most authoritative account of labour policy from the mid-nineteenth to the mid-twentieth century is S. van der Horst, *Native labour in South Africa* (1942). It can be supplemented by her chapter, 'Employment', in S. van der Horst (ed.), *Race discrimination in South Africa* (1981), and her contribution, 'Labour policy in South Africa (1948–76)', in M. L. Truu (ed.), *Public policy and the South African economy* (1976). See also W. F. J. Steenkamp, 'Labour problems and policies of half a century', *SAJE*, 51, 1983. The archives of the Department of Native Affairs and other government departments are used to good effect by D. Duncan, *The mills of god: the state and African labour in South Africa, 1918–1948* (1995). K. E. Atkins, *The moon is dead! Give us our money!* (1993) is an illuminating investigation of the cultural origins of the work ethic of Africans in Natal in the second half of the nineteenth century. O. Crankshaw, *Race, class and the changing division of labour under apartheid* (1997), clarifies and explains many aspects of the changing occupational structure of industry and services in the period 1960–90.

J. Lewis, *Industrialization and trade union organization in South Africa, 1924–55* (1984), is excellent on the nature of the mechanization of manufacturing and its impact on white trade union attitudes. Other studies of trade union and political activity include J. and R. Simons, *Class and colour in South Africa, 1850–1950* (1969), written by two of South Africa's leading Marxists; E. Webster, *Cast in a racial mould* (1985); B. Hirson, *Yours for the union* (1989); B. Freund, *Insiders and outsiders: the Indian working class of Durban, 1910–1990* (1995); and P. Alexander, *Workers, war and the origins of apartheid* (2000).

The emergence of significant levels of unemployment provoked many controversial articles exploring both theoretical concepts and attempts to measure it in the absence of reliable official data. The key issues as seen at the end of the 1970s were summarized in N. Bromberger, 'South African unemployment: a survey of research', in C. Simkins and C. Desmond (eds.), *South African unemployment: a black picture* (1978); and in G. Maasdorp, 'Unemployment in South Africa and its implications', in L. Schlemmer and E. Webster (eds.), *Change, reform and economic growth in South Africa* (1978).

Substantial later contributions were made by two economists, J. B. Knight and C. Simkins. For Knight's work see 'Labour allocation and unemployment in South Africa', *OBES*, 40, 1978, and 'The nature of unemployment in South Africa', *SAJE*, 50, 1982. For Simkins see 'Measuring and predicting unemployment in South Africa, 1960–77', in C. Simkins and D. Clarke (eds.), *Structural unemployment in Southern Africa* (1978), and *Structural unemployment revisited* (1982). Their views were challenged by J. Gerson, 'The question of structural unemployment in South Africa', *SAJE*, 49, 1981, and the subject was also reviewed by R. T. Bell, 'Issues in South African unemployment', *SAJE*, 53, 1985.

Trends in wages in the post-war period are examined in J. Nattrass, 'The narrowing of wage differentials in South Africa', *SAJE*, 44, 1976; J. B. Knight and M. D. McGrath, 'An analysis of racial wage discrimination in South Africa', *OBES*, 39, 1977; and in three papers by J. F. Hofmeyer, 'African wage movements in the 1980s', *SAJE*, 61, 1983; 'The rise in African wages, 1975–1985', *SAJE*, 62, 1994; and 'Black wages: the postwar experience', in N. Nattrass and E. Ardington (eds.), *The political economy of South Africa* (1990). The most comprehensive amongst numerous accounts of poverty is F. Wilson and M. Ramphele, *Uprooting poverty* (1989). H. Bhorat et al., *Fighting poverty* (2001), offer a more analytical investigation of contemporary labour markets and inequality in South Africa; and J. Seekings and N. Nattrass, *From race to class* (2005) is a splendid exploration of many facets of inequality, unemployment, and the social structure.

Finance and transport

These topics are not fully covered in the present text, but the chapters on 'Transport' and 'Money and banking' by V. E. Solomon in F. L. Coleman (ed.), *Economic history of South Africa* (1983), survey the ground well. The history of banking, currency, and finance can be studied in more detail in E. H. D. Arndt, *Banking and currency development in South Africa, 1652–1927* (1928); G. de Kock, *A history of the South African Reserve Bank* (1954); and S. Jones, *The great imperial banks in South Africa: a study of the business of Standard Bank and Barclays Bank, 1861–1961* (1996). Good surveys of monetary and fiscal policy and of public finance are provided by D. G. Franzsen, 'Monetary policy in South Africa 1932–1982', *SAJE*, 51, 1983; G. W. G. Browne, 'Fifty years of public finance', *SAJE*, 51, 1983; T. Moll, 'Macroeconomic policy in turbulent times', in M. Lipton and C. Simkins (eds.), *State and market* (1993); and P. D. F. Strydom, 'Macroeconomic policy, 1970–2000' in S. Jones (ed.), *The decline of the South African economy* (2002).

The liberal–radical controversy

For basic expositions of the 'liberal' view, see W. H. Hutt, *The economics of the colour bar* (1964), R. Horwitz, *Political economy* (1967), and M. Lipton, *Capitalism and apartheid* (1985). The primary statements of the position variously described as Marxist, radical, or revisionist were made by F. Johnstone, 'White prosperity and white supremacy in South Africa today', *African Affairs*, 69, 1970; S. Trapido, 'South Africa in a comparative study of industrialization', *Journal of Development Studies*, 7, 1971; H. Wolpe, 'Capitalism and cheap labour power', *Economy and Society*, 1, 1972; and by M. Legassick in several articles including 'Legislation, ideology and economy', *JSAS*, 1, 1974; 'South Africa: forced labour, industrialization and racial differentiation', in R. Harris (ed.), *The political economy of Africa* (1975); and 'Gold, agriculture, and secondary industry in South Africa, 1885–1970: from periphery to sub-metropole as a forced labour system', in R. Palmer and N. Parsons (eds.), *The roots of rural poverty* (1977).

Some of the wider theoretical implications of the debate were vigorously contested in B. S. Kantor and H. F. Kenny, 'The poverty of Neo-marxism', *JSAS*, 3, 1976, and the response by H. Wolpe, 'A comment on the poverty of Neo-marxism', *JSAS*, 4, 1977. For overviews of the debate and later interventions see H. M. Wright, *The burden of the present, liberal–radical controversy over Southern African history* (1977); D. B. Posel, 'Rethinking the "race–class debate" in South African historiography', *Social Dynamics*, 9, 1983; N. Nattrass, 'Controversies about capitalism and apartheid, an economic perspective', *JSAS*, 17, 1991; and T. Moll, 'Did the apartheid economy fail?', *JSAS*, 17, 1991.

Neglected voices

It is probably inevitable that black workers will appear as passive and anonymous figures in a concise economic history written from a macro-economic perspective. For a proper sense of their individuality and personality, as well as of their private pain and suffering, it is necessary to read those writers who have made effective use of oral history and/or made leading contributions to social history. Notable examples of the former include T. Matsetela, 'The life story of Nkgono-Pooe', in Marks and Rathbone (eds.), *Industrialization and social change*; T. J. Keegan, *Facing the storm, portraits of black lives in rural South Africa* (1988); T. D. Moodie with V. Ndatshe, *Going for gold: men, migrants and migration* (1994); and C. van Onselen, *The seed is mine: the life of Kas Maine* (1996).

Vivid contributions to South African social history which give valuable insights into economic life include B. Bozzoli (ed.), *Labour, townships and protest* (1979); C. van Onselen, *Studies in the social and economic history of the Witwatersrand*, vol. 1, *New Babylon*, vol. 2, *New Nineveh* (1982); and N. Penn, *Rogues, rebels, and runaways: eighteenth-century Cape characters* (1999). The important role of women emerges more fully than usual in B. Bozzoli, *Women of Phokeng* (1991); C. Walker (ed.), *Women and gender in Southern Africa to 1945* (1990); I. Berger, *Threads of solidarity, women in South African industry, 1900–1980* (1992); and A. K. Mager, *Gender and the making of a South African Bantustan* (1999).

Black South Africans were seldom able to express publicly their ideas and opinions for themselves, but they can be glimpsed in works such as S. Plaatje, *Native life in South Africa* (1916), D. D. T. Jabavu, *The black problem* (1920), A. 'Luthuli, *Let my people go* (1963), and S. Biko, *I write what I like* (1978). See also political documents and addresses by leaders of the ANC and other black organizations reproduced in the five volumes of T. Karis and G. M. Carter (eds.), *From protest to challenge, a documentary history of African politics in South Africa, 1882–1990* (1973–1997). Accounts of the experiences, struggles, and achievements of individual Africans can be read in a handful of autobiographies, including B. Modisane, *Blame me on history* (1963), N. Mokgatle, *The autobiography of an unknown South African* (1971), Z. K. Matthews, *Freedom for my people* (1981), M. Resha, *My life in the struggle* (1991), and M. Ramphele, *Across boundaries* (1996).

References

The following list covers all sources cited in the text. Works cited only in the preceding 'Guide to further reading' are not included. The abbreviations used here and in the guide are:

JSAS	*Journal of Southern African Studies*
OBES	*Oxford Bulletin of Economics and Statistics*
SAHJ	*South African Historical Journal*
SAJE	*South African Journal of Economics*
SAJEH	*South African Journal of Economic History*

Books and articles on South Africa

Agar-Hamilton, J. A. I., *The native policy of the voortrekkers, 1836–1858*, Cape Town: M. Miller, 1928.

Bhorat, Haroon, et al. (eds.), *Fighting poverty: labour markets and inequality in South Africa*, Cape Town: University of Cape Town Press, 2001.

Biesheuvel, S., 'Black industrial labour in South Africa', *SAJE*, 42, 1974, 292–311.

Bleloch, William Edwin, *The new South Africa, its value and development*, London: Heinemann, 1901.

Bromberger, Norman, 'South African unemployment: a survey of research', in Charles Simkins and Cosmas Desmond (eds.), *South African unemployment: a black picture*, Pietermaritzburg: University of Natal, Development Studies Research Group, 1978, 3–25.

Chamber of Mines of South Africa, *96th Annual Report*, Johannesburg: Chamber of Mines, 1985.

Crankshaw, Owen, *Race, class and the changing division of labour under apartheid*, London: Routledge, 1997.

de Kiewiet, C. W., *A history of South Africa, social and economic*, London: Oxford University Press, 1941.

de Kock, Gerhard, 'The new South African business cycle and its implications for monetary policy', *SAJE*, 48, 1980, 349–58.

de Kock, M. H., *Selected subjects in the economic history of South Africa*, Cape Town: Juta, 1924.

Delius, Peter, *The land belongs to us: the Pedi polity, the Boers and the British in the nineteenth-century Transvaal*, Johannesburg: Ravan Press, 1983.

Development Bank of Southern Africa, *South Africa, an inter-regional profile*, Midrand: Development Bank of Southern Africa, 1991.

Development Bank of Southern Africa, *South Africa's nine provinces*, Midrand: Development Bank of Southern Africa, 1994.

du Plessis, J. C., 'Investment and the balance of payments of South Africa', *SAJE*, 35, 1965, 311–40.

Etherington, Norman, *The great treks: the transformation of southern Africa, 1815–1854*, Harlow: Longman, 2001.

Frankel, S. Herbert, *Capital investment in Africa, its course and effects*, London: Oxford University Press, 1938.

  Investment and the return to equity capital in the South African gold mining industry, Oxford: Blackwell, 1967.

Franzen, D. G., and J. J. D. Willers, 'Capital accumulation and economic growth in South Africa', in R. Goldsmith and C. Saunders (eds.), *The measurement of wealth*, Income and Wealth series VIII, London: Bowes & Bowes, 1959, 293–322.

Germond, Robert Charles (ed.), *Chronicles of Basutoland*, Morija: Morija Sesuto Book Depot, 1967.

Gilbert, Donald Wood, 'The economic effects of the gold discoveries upon South Africa', *Quarterly Journal of Economics*, 47, 1933, 553–97.

Golub, Stephen, and Lawrence Edwards, 'South African international cost competitiveness and exports: a sectoral analysis', *Trade and Industry Monitor*, 25, 2003, 2–5.

Goodfellow, D. M., *A modern economic history of South Africa*, London: Routledge, 1931.

Gregory, Theodore, *Ernest Oppenheimer and the economic development of southern Africa*, Cape Town: Oxford University Press, 1962.

Hamilton, Caroline (ed.), *Mfecane aftermath, reconstructive debates in southern African history*, Johannesburg: Witwatersrand University Press, 1995.

Hellmann, Ellen (ed.), *Handbook on race relations in South Africa*, Cape Town: Oxford University Press, 1949.

Hindson, Doug, *Pass controls and the urban African proletariat*, Johannesburg: Ravan Press, 1987.

Hobart Houghton, D., *The South African economy*, 4th edn, Cape Town: Oxford University Press, 1976.

Hobart Houghton, D. and Jenny Dagut (eds.), *Source material on the South African economy, 1860–1970*, 3 vols., Cape Town: Oxford University Press, 1972.

Hunter, Monica, *Reaction to conquest*, Cape Town: David Philip, 1979.

Hurwitz, Nathan, and Owen Williams, *The economic framework of South Africa*, Pietermaritzburg: Shuter & Shuter, 1962.

Innes, Duncan, *Anglo American and the rise of modern South Africa*, Johannesburg: Ravan Press, 1984.

Johnstone, Frederick A., *Class, race and gold*, London: Routlege & Kegan Paul, 1976.

  'White prosperity and white supremacy in South Africa today', *African Affairs*, 69, 1970, 124–40.

Julius, A. B., and A. B. Lumby, 'Phases I, II and III of the local content programme in the South African motor car manufacturing industry, 1961–1976', *SAJEH*, 13, 1998, 17–35.

Karis, Thomas, and Gwendolen M. Carter (ed.), *From protest to challenge, a documentary history of African politics in South Africa*, vol.1, *Protest and hope, 1882–1934*, Stanford, CA: Hoover Institution Press, 1972.

Keegan, Timothy J., *Rural transformations in industrializing South Africa: the Southern Highveld to 1914*, Broamfontein: Ravan Press, 1986.

Leary, P. M., and J. E. S. Lewis, 'Some observations on the state of nutrition of infants and toddlers in Sekhukhuniland', *South African Medical Journal*, 39, 1965, 1156–8.

Legassick, Martin, 'Legislation, ideology and economy in post-1948 South Africa', *JSAS*, 1, 1974, 5–35.

'Gold, agriculture, and secondary industry in South Africa, 1885–1970: from periphery to sub-metropole as a forced labour system', in Robin Palmer and Neil Parsons (eds.), *The roots of rural poverty*, Berkeley: University of California Press, 1977, 175–200.

Lehfeldt, R. A., *The national resources of South Africa*, Johannesburg: University of the Witwatersrand Press, 1922.

Lewis, Stephen R., *The economics of apartheid*, New York: Council of Foreign Relations Press, 1990.

Lipton, Merle, *Capitalism and apartheid: South Africa, 1910–1986*, London: Gower/Temple Smith, 1985.

Lomard J., et al., *Industrialisation and Growth*, Johannesburg: Mercabank, 1985.

Maasdorp, Gavin, 'Unemployment in South Africa and its implications', in Lawrence Schlemmer and Eddie Webster (eds.), *Change, reform and economic growth in South Africa*, Johannesburg: Ravan Press, 1978, 139–48.

Macmillan, W. M., *The Cape colour question, a historical survey*, London: Faber & Gwyer, 1927.

Bantu, Boer and Briton: the making of the South African native problem, London: Faber & Gwyer, 1929.

Marais, G., 'Structural changes in manufacturing industry 1916 to 1975', *SAJE*, 49, 1981, 26–45.

Marais, J. S., *The Cape Coloured people, 1652–1937*, Johannesburg: Witwatersrand University Press, 1962.

Matsetela, Ted, 'The life story of Nkgono-Pooe', in S. Marks and R. Rathbone (eds.), *Industrialisation and social change in South Africa*, Harlow: Longman, 1982, 212–37.

Mokgatle, Naboth, *The autobiography of an unknown South African*, London: Hurst & Co., 1971.

Moll, Terence, 'Did the apartheid economy fail?', *JSAS*, 17, 1991, 271–91.

Nattrass, Jill, *The South African economy, its growth and change*, 2nd edn, Cape Town: Oxford University Press, 1988.

Nattrass, Nicoli, 'Economic power and profits in postwar manufacturing', in Nicoli Nattrass and Elisabeth Ardington (eds.), *The political economy of South Africa*, Cape Town: Oxford University Press, 1990, 107–28.

Noble, John, *Descriptive handbook of the Cape Colony*, Cape Town: Juta, 1875.

Norval, A. J., *A quarter of a century of industrial progress in South Africa*, Cape Town: Juta, 1962.

O'Meara, Dan, *Volkskapitalisme: class, capital and ideology in the development of Afrikaner nationalism, 1934–1948*, Johannesburg: Ravan Press, 1983.

Plaatje, Sol T., *Native life in South Africa*, London: P. S. King & Son, 1916.

Platzky, Laurine, and Cherryl Walker, *The surplus people – forced removals in South Africa*, Johannesburg: Ravan Press, 1985.

Ratcliffe, Anne, E., 'Export policy in perspective', *SAJE*, 43, 1975, 74–91.

Richards, C. S., *The iron and steel industry in South Africa with special reference to ISCOR*, Johannesburg: Witwatersrand University Press, 1940.

'Subsidies, quotas, tariffs and the excess cost of agriculture in South Africa', *SAJE*, 3, 1935, 365–403.

Sadie, J. L., *A reconstruction and projection of demographic movements in the RSA and TBVC countries*, Research Report 148, University of South Africa, Bureau of Market Research, Pretoria, 1988.

A projection of the South African population, 1991–2011, Research Report 196, University of South Africa, Bureau of Market Research, Pretoria, 1993.

The South African labour force, 1960–2005, Research Report 178, University of South Africa, Bureau of Market Research, Pretoria, 1991.

Sansom, Basil, 'Traditional economic systems' in W. D. Hammond-Tooke (ed.), *The Bantu-speaking peoples of Southern Africa*, 2nd edn, London: Routledge, 1974, 135–76.

Schumann, C. G. W., *Structural changes and business cycles in South Africa, 1806–1936*, London: P. S. King & Son, 1938.

Shell, Robert C.-H., *Children of bondage, a social history of the slave society at the Cape of Good Hope, 1652–1838*, Hanover, NH: Wesleyan University Press, 1994.

Smith, F. B., *Some observations upon the probable effect of the closer union of South Africa upon agriculture*, Pretoria: Government Printer, 1908.

Simkins, Charles, 'Agricultural production in the African reserves of South Africa, 1918–1969', *JSAS*, 7, 1981, 256–83.

South African Institute of Race Relations, *A survey of race relations in South Africa*, annual.

Steenkamp, W. F. J., 'Labour problems and policies of half a century', *SAJE*, 51, 1983, 58–87.

Thirtle, C., H. S. von Bach, and J. van Zyl, *Explaining total factor productivity in South African commercial agriculture, 1947–91*, Discussion Paper Series G no. 7, University of Reading, Department of Agricultural Economics and Management, 1993.

Trollope, A., *South Africa*, reprint of 1878 edn, ed. J. H. Davidson, Cape Town: A. A. Balkema, 1973.

van Aardt, C. J., and J. L. van Tonder with J. L. Sadie, *A projection of the South African population, 1996–2021*, Research Report 270, University of South Africa, Bureau of Market Research, Pretoria, 1999.

van der Horst, Sheila, *Native labour in South Africa*, London: Oxford University Press, 1942.

van der Vliet, Virginia, 'Growing up in traditional society', in W. D. Hammond-Tooke (ed.), *The Bantu-speaking peoples of Southern Africa*, 2nd edn, London: Routledge, 1974, 211–45.

van Dijk, Michiel, 'South African manufacturing performance in international perspective, 1970–99', *SAJE*, 71, 2003, 119–42.

van Riebeeck, Jan, *Journal of Jan van Riebeeck*, ed. H. B. Thom, 3 vols., Cape Town: A. A. Balkema for the Van Riebeeck Society, 1952–8.

Van Riebeeck Society, *The reports of Chavonnes and his council and of Van Imhoff, on the Cape*, Cape Town: Van Riebeeck Society, vol. 1, 1918.

van Wyk, H. de J., *Personal disposable income in South Africa by population group, income group and district, 2000*, Research Report 279, University of South Africa, Bureau of Market Research, Pretoria, 2000.

Verwoerd, Hendrik Frensch, *Verwoerd speaks, speeches 1948–1966*, ed. A. N. Pelzer, Johannesburg: APB Publishers, 1966.

Viljoen, S. P., 'The industrial achievement of South Africa', *SAJE*, 51, 1983, 29–57.

Walker, Eric A., *Historical atlas of South Africa*, Oxford: Oxford University Press, 1922.

Walker, Eric A. (ed.), *Cambridge history of the British Empire*, vol. 8, *South Africa*, 2nd edn, Cambridge: Cambridge University Press, 1963.

Wilson, Francis, *Labour in the South African gold mines, 1911–1969*, Cambridge: Cambridge University Press, 1972.

Wilson, Monica, and Leonard Thompson (ed.), *The Oxford history of South Africa*, vols. 1 and 2, Oxford: Oxford University Press, 1969, 1971.

Witwatersrand Chamber of Mines, Industrial Commission of Enquiry, *Evidence and Report*, Johannesburg: Witwatersrand Chamber of Mines, 1897.

Wolpe, Harold, 'Capitalism and cheap labour power in South Africa: from segregation to apartheid,' in Harold Wolpe (ed.), *The articulation of modes of production*, London: Routledge, 1980, 289–320.

Wolseley, Garnet, *The South African journal of Sir Garnet Wolseley*, ed. Adrian Preston, *1879–1880*, Cape Town: A. A. Balkema, 1973.

Worden, Nigel, Elizabeth van Heyningen, and Vivian Bickford-Smith, *Cape Town, the making of a city*, Cape Town: David Philip, 1998.

World Bank, *South African agriculture*, Discussion Paper 6, Washington, DC: World Bank, 1994.

Other books and articles

Acemoglu, Daron, Simon Johnson, and James A. Robinson, 'The colonial origins of comparative development', *American Economic Review*, 91, 2001, 1369–401.

Baldwin, Robert E., 'Patterns of development in newly settled regions', *Manchester School of Economic and Social Studies*, 24, 1956, 161–79.

Brown, Henry Phelps, *The inequality of pay*, Oxford: Oxford University Press, 1977.

Davis, Ralph, *The industrial revolution and British overseas trade*, Leicester: Leicester University Press, 1979.

Domar, E., 'The causes of slavery or serfdom: a hypothesis', *Journal of Economic History*, 30, 1970, 18–32.

Eatwell, John, Murray Milgate, and Peter Newman (eds.), *The new Palgrave, a dictionary of economics*, London: Macmillan, 1987.

Iliffe, John, *Africans, The history of a continent*, Cambridge: Cambridge University Press, 1995.

International Monetary Fund, *Yearbook of International Financial Statistics*, annual.

Keynes, John Maynard, *Collected works*, Vol. 9 *Essays in persuasion*, London: Macmillan, 1972.

Lewis, W. Arthur, *Growth and fluctuations, 1870–1913*, London: George Allen & Unwin, 1978.

McEvedy, Colin, and Richard Jones, *Atlas of world population history*, London: Allen Lane, 1978.

Maddison, Angus, *The world economy: a millennial perspective*, Paris: OECD, Development Centre Studies, 2001.

Manning, Patrick, *Slavery and African life: occidental, oriental, and African slave trades*, Cambridge: Cambridge University Press, 1990.

Nieboer, H. J., *Slavery as an industrial system: ethnological researches*, The Hague: M. Nijhoff, 1900.

Rockoff, H., 'Some evidence on the real price of gold, its costs of production, and commodity prices', in M. D. Bordo and A. J. Schwartz (eds.), *A retrospective on the classical gold standard 1821–1931*, Chicago: Chicago University Press, 1984.

Routh, Guy, *Occupation and pay in Great Britain, 1906–70*, 2nd edn, London: Macmillan, 1980.

World Bank, *World development indicators, 2003*, Washington, DC: World Bank, 2003.

Official publications

South Africa

Statistical abstracts, year books, and other official publications

Board of Trade and Industries, Report No. 282, *Investigation into manufacturing industries in the Union of South Africa, 1945*.

Bureau of Census and Statistics, *Census of industrial establishments, 1948/49 to 1949/50*.

Bureau of Census and Statistics, *Union Statistics for Fifty Years, 1910–1960*, 1960.

Department of Agriculture and Forestry, *Report of the reconstruction committee*, 1944–45.

Department of Labour, *Report for the year ended 31 December 1955*, 1956–7.

Department of Statistics, then Central Statistical Service, then Statistics South Africa, *South African Statistics*, biennial from 1970 to 1995, annual from 2001.

Republic of South Africa, *House of Assembly, Debates*.

Republic of South Africa, *Senate, Debates*.

South African Reserve Bank, *Quarterly Bulletin.*
Statistics South Africa, *October household survey, 1996,* 1999.
Statistics South Africa, *Unemployment and employment in South Africa,* 1998.
Union Office of Census and Statistics, *Official Year Book,* annual from 1917.

Reports of commissions

T.G. (Transvaal Government) 2 – 1908, Transvaal Mining Industry Commission, 1907–08, *Evidence and Report.*

T.G. 13 – 1908, Transvaal Indigency Commission, 1906–8, *Report.*

U.G. (Union of South Africa) 10 – 1912, Trade and Industries Commission (Cullinan), *Report.*

T.P. (Province of Transvaal) 1 – 1922, Transvaal Local Government Commission (Stallard), *Report.*

U.G. 36 – 1925, Mining Regulations Commission (Pittman), *Report.*

U.G. 14 – 1926, Economic and Wage Commission (Clay), *Report.*

U.G. 22 – 1932, Native Economic Commission (Holloway), *Report.*

U.G. 5 – 1936, Customs Tariff Commission (Holloway), *Report.*

U.G. 40 – 1941, The Industrial and Agricultural Requirement Commission (van Eck), *Third Interim Report.*

U.G. 21 – 1944, Witwatersrand Mine Natives' Wages Commission (Lansdown), *Report.*

U.G. 32 – 1946, Social and Economic Planning Council, *Report No. 9, Native reserves and their place in the economy of the Union of South Africa.*

U.G. 28 – 1948, Native Laws Commission of Enquiry (Fagan), *Report.*

U.G. 61 – 1955, Commission for the Socio-Economic Development of the Bantu areas within the Union of South Africa (Tomlinson), *Report.*

U.G. 36 – 1958, Commission of Inquiry into Policy relating to the Protection of Industries (Viljoen), *Report.*

R.P. (Republic of South Africa) 19 – 1972, Commission of Inquiry into Agriculture (Marais/Du Plessis), *Third (Final) Report.*

R.P. 69 – 1972, Commission of Inquiry into the Export Trade of the Republic of South Africa (Reynders), vols. 1 and 2, *Reports.*

R.P. 32 – 1979, Commission of Inquiry into Legislation Affecting the Utilization of Manpower (Riekert), *Report.*

R.P. 47 – 1979, Commission of Inquiry into Labour Legislation (Wiehahn), *Report.*

United Kingdom Command Papers

Correspondence relating to the Natives Land Act, 1913, Cd. 7508, pp 1914, LIX.
Further correspondence respecting the affairs of South Africa, C. 2000, pp 1878, LV, No. 12.

Index

African Explosives and Chemical Industries Ltd (AE & CI) 174, 175
African National Congress (ANC) 149, 202, 251
African population
  definition 19
  diet 19
  dispossession of 33, 34, 35, 43
  economic development 20
  economic independence 43
  farmers 47, 60–2, 63, 135–8, 265
  income 9
  miners 62–7, 63, 77, 78, 81, 85, 88, 93, 109, 167, 169, 206
  occupations in industry 127
  relationship with Khoisan 13
  resettlement 151, 194
  settlement patterns 264
  size 1, 152, 156 , 252, 254
  standard of living 19, 142
  trade with Europeans 20
  way of life 16–21
Afrikaanse Handelsinstituut (Afrikaans Commercial Institute) 180
Afrikaner population 82, 118
  and capitalism 176, 180
  commandos 80, 84, 87
  contribution to economy 177
  definition 19
  farmers 84, 87
  intellectuals 153
  miners 79
  nationalism 83, 85, 179
  see also Boer population
agriculture 266
  arable farming 25, 138, 196
  commercial 48, 49, 73, 109, 135, 138, 139, 142, 193–9, 243
  communal tenure 43, 73, 156, 194
  contribution to GDP 107, 115, 144
  dependence on 2, 200
  employment in 107

expenditure on 71
farm prices 7, 140, 141
food prices 73
government assistance 108, 113, 141 , 199, 244
horticulture 196, 198
labour tenancy 44, 53, 61, 62, 136
livestock 198
loan farms 25, 31
mechanization 140, 197, 240
output 70, 136, 138, 140, 142, 196, 197
pastoral farming 17, 31, 91, 138
quit-rent farms 40
rent tenancy 60, 62
sharecropping 45, 61, 62, 136, 137
subsistence farming 49, 194, 268
techniques 19, 139
total factor productivity 197
training 199
wage labour 62, 136
wages 62, 196, 199, 231
yields 139, 196
Albany 27
Albu, George 63, 97
Anglo American Corporation 82, 104, 167, 171, 174, 175, 176, 177, 179, 189, 210
apartheid
  campaigns against 149, 203, 224, 228
  economic cost 240
  and economic growth 146, 162, 163, 247–251
  international hostility to 202
  policies 143, 149, 151, 153, 154, 158, 161, 164, 180, 194, 242, 244
  retreat from 224, 240
Apprenticeship Act (1922) 77, 157
apprenticeships 77, 191, 207, 242
Argentina, industrialization of 119
armaments, manufacture of 184, 222
ARMSCOR 184
Ashley, Cecil 36

Asian population
 definition 20
 restrictions on 74, 88
Association of Mines 63
Australia
 comparisons with 132
 industrialization of 119
 as model of export economy 91

backwardness, opportunities of 173
balance of payments 108, 131, 148, 180,
 182, 188, 192, 202, 213, 221, 223,
 224–30, 245
Bank of England 79
Bantu population, definition of 19
Bantu Education Act (1953) 158
Bantu Trust and Land Act (1936) 44, 45,
 244, 268
Bantustans 250 see also homelands
Barclays Bank 177, 178, 230
Barnato, Barney 97
Basuto people 31, 37
Basutoland 34, 44, 83, 86, 252, 260 see also
 Lesotho
Beaumont Commission 43
Bechuanaland 44, 83, 86, 252, 260 see also
 Botswana
Bethelsdorp 51
black population, definition of 20
Bloemfontein Convention (1854) 31
Board of Trade and Industries 117, 119, 173
Boart and Hard Metals 176
Boer population 19, 31, 34
 commandos 37
 conflict with Pedi 40, 41
 farmers 83, 85–9
 relationship with British 30
 see also Afrikaner population
Botha, Louis 79, 80, 82, 149
Botha, P. W. 150, 229
Botswana (formerly Bechuanaland) 14, 17
Bretton Woods system 8, 22, 204, 225
British Kaffraria 28
British protectorates 44, 65, 252 see also
 Lesotho; Botswana; Swaziland
British South Africa Company 260
Burgers, Rev. Thomas 41
Bushmen see San population

Caledon, Lord 52, 57
Calvinia 25
Canada
 comparisons with 132
 industrialization of 119
 as model of export economy 91

Cape Town 24, 47, 98, 113, 261, 264
 District six see District six, Cape Town
capital
 accumulation 48
 capital/output ratio 185, 186, 213, 223
 expenditure 163, 221
 fixed capital formation 200, 202, 221
 flows 5, 91, 189, 202, 213, 226
 foreign 93, 109, 148
 human 92, 93, 219, 248, 251
 investment 90
 lack of 48, 72, 114, 137
 private 148, 156
 substitution of for labour 91, 185, 197,
  213, 222, 240
Carnarvon, Lord 41
Carnegie Commission 85, 87
Casalis, J. E. 34
Cato Manor, Durban 150
cattle
 diseases 17, 84, 86, 264
 role in African societies 18, 20, 72
Central Selling Organisation 172
cereal production 196
Ceres 55
Cetshwayo 37
Chamber of Mines 45, 64, 75, 79, 80, 81,
 82, 88, 117
Chase Manhattan Bank 229
chemical industry 171
children
 child labour 53, 271
 inboekelinge 53
Chinese population
 restrictions on 75
 settlers 54, 75
church schools 158
Ciskei 70, 72 see also homelands; reserves
climate 24, 97 see also geography
coal
 demand for 210, 215
 discovery of 103, 262
 exports 210
 production 210
colonialism 5
colour bar 74, 75, 84, 87, 118, 152, 157, 241
coloured population 255
 definition 14, 19
 occupations 49, 127
 resettlement 150
 restrictions on 74, 88, 150
 size 255
commodity prices 96, 214, 215, 216,
 218, 228
Consolidated Gold Fields 104

consumer goods 187, 188, 189
  demand for 192
copper 172
cost of living 81, 109, 133
crop failure 24
Cullinan Commission 117
currency 20
  'blocked rand' 189
  depreciation 208, 227
  devaluation 95, 96, 123, 165
  'financial rand' 229
  use of sterling 27
Customs Tariff Act (1914) 117
Customs Tariff Act (1925) 119, 124

De Beers Consolidated Mines 99, 171
de Kiewiet, C. W. 106, 253
de Klerk, F. W. 150, 202
de Kock, Gerhard 225
Delagoa Bay 20, 38, 261
Delius, Peter 36
depression
  Great Depression (1929–33) 5, 7, 85, 87,
    94, 99, 121, 123, 140
  post-war 80
Development Bank of South Africa
    (DBSA) 273
diamonds
  demand for 122, 171
  discovery of 3, 41, 99, 262
  economic role of 49, 106
  output 99, 171
  price 99
  see also mining sector
Discount Bank 27
disease 70, 164 see also health
District Six, Cape Town 150
Dithakong, Battle of 37
Domar, E. 33, 46
drought 24, 140, 253
Drought Investigation Commission 263
Durban (formerly Port Natal) 31, 113, 156,
    231, 261
'Dutch disease' 216
Dutch East India Company (VOC) 22
  departure of 30
  monopoly of trade 23, 24
  objectives of 1, 22, 34
  restrictions imposed by 113
  use of slaves 51, 255

East London 261
East Rand 103
economic growth 3, 48, 98, 162, 164, 200,
    224, 242, 248, 250

export-led 90–3, 211–20, 247
economic performance
  international comparisons 3, 5, 144
  macroeconomic performance 149
education 77, 93, 98, 129, 130, 158, 160,
    164, 188, 192, 241, 243, 244, 249
  Bantu 159, 160, 226
  expenditure 164, 243
  higher 108, 243
  post-primary 77, 159, 233
  primary 159, 160
  teacher training 158, 160
Electricity Supply Commission (ESCOM)
    120, 221
engineering industry 123, 127, 171
entrepreneurship 97, 156, 172
Etherington, Norman 252, 253
European population
  establishment of institutions 97–9
  job reservation for 75, 119, 158
  settlers 1, 97, 98
  size 2, 23, 256
exchange controls 189
exchange rate 202, 214, 215, 216, 220,
    222, 223
  fixed 94
  rand against dollar 22
  rand against sterling 20
export economy, types of 90–3
exports 190, 249
  international comparisons 3, 29

Factories Act 83, 86
Fagan, H. 152, 156
Fagan Commission 153
Federale Mynbou (Fedmyn) 179
Federated Chamber of Industries 190
Federation of Afrikaans Cultural
    Associations 178
financial sector 176
  banking 100, 108
  infrastructure 177
  institutions 177
  private banks 27
First World War, stimulus to industry
    of 115
fiscal policy 8, 216, 221
Ford 181
Fort Willshire 59
FOSKOR see Phosphate Development
    Corporation
France
  Huguenots 19, 23
  settlers from 19
franchise 2, 43, 76, 93, 98, 150, 151

Frankel, S. Herbert 83, 85, 106, 111, 141
Franschhoek 23
free trade 117, 180
freedom of movement 57, 58, 154, 242
fruit production 196

Genadendal 51
General Agreement on Tariffs and Trade
    (GATT) 180
General Mining and Finance Corporation
    104, 179
General Motors 181, 230
Germany
    acquisition of South West Africa 83, 86
    industrialization of 119
    settlers from 19, 28
geography 260–8
geology 261–2
globalization 4
gold
    contribution to GDP 107
    demand for 200, 202
    discovery of 3, 41, 262
    economic role of 49, 90, 93, 106, 203–10
    exports 100, 107, 108, 205, 210, 220,
        223, 225
    gold standard 5, 79, 95, 122, 166
    output 104, 105, 166, 169, 205, 210, 223
    price 67, 79, 93–7, 103, 104, 165, 169,
        202, 203, 208, 225, 227
    production 100, 144, 146, 165
    as 'wasting asset' 118, 210
    see also mining sector
government
    government borrowing 148, 213
    representative government 98, 149
Graaff Reinet 25, 51
Grahamstown 113, 114
grazing rights 15, 136, 194
Great Trek 30, 31
    British reaction 31
Grey, Sir George 54
Griqualand East 58
gross domestic product (GDP)
    as indicator of economic progress 3, 146
    international comparisons 9, 143, 146
Group Areas Act (1950) 150, 151

Hartebeespoort Dam 140
health 243, 249, 254
    expenditure 164
    public 253
    see also disease
Hertzog, J. B. M. 83, 85, 118, 120, 149, 152
Highveld Steel and Vanadium 176

Holland, settlers from 1, 13, 19, 23, 34, 256
    see also Dutch East India Company
Holloway Commission 55
homelands 70, 151, 155, 250, 256
    policy 203
    see also reserves
Hottentots see Khoikhoi population
Houghton, D. Hobart 106, 173
housing 164, 167, 192, 207, 242, 249
human rights 35, 128

IBM 230
immigration 100, 256
    international comparisons 3
Imperial Chemical Industries (ICI) 175
Imperial Economic Conference (1932) 132
imports 188
    controls 189, 221
    licensing 180, 189, 218, 219
    quotas 218, 221
    substitution 119, 135, 173, 189, 192, 220
inboekelinge see children
income
    differentials 75, 83, 86, 110, 135, 231
    inequality 9, 11, 220, 251
    per capita 5, 9, 70, 145
Indian population
    occupations 127
    resettlement 150
    settlers 20, 54
indigenous population 1, 16, 19
Industrial Conciliation Act (1924) 84, 87
Industrial Conciliation Act (1956) 150,
    157, 241
Industrial Development Corporation (IDC)
    124, 179, 183
industrial relations 81, 130, 167, 241 see also
    strikes; trade unions
industrial sector 48, 135, 172, 188, 200
    colour bar in 77, 88, 232
    contribution to GDP 128, 144, 146, 173
    costs 130
    development of 123
    employment in 49, 124
    factory production 126, 127
    international comparisons 132
    investment in 120, 125, 174
    mechanization 132, 158
    output 121–125, 129, 174
    productivity 124, 132
    relationship with mining 109, 135
    secondary industry 118, 119, 121, 125,
        127, 128, 135
    training 152, 191
    wages 48, 132, 191

industrialization 111, 120, 151, 180,
     218, 241
inflation 95, 115, 148, 201, 209, 215
interest rates 213, 222, 228, 230
International Monetary Fund (IMF) 189,
     208, 218
Iron and Steel Industrial Corporation
     (ISCOR) 120, 121, 124, 183, 221, 223
iron and steel 120, 125, 225, 262
  demand for 215
  iron ore 262
  steel production 121

Johannesburg 47, 79, 100, 108, 154, 171
Johannesburg Consolidated Investment
     Company 104
Johannesburg stock exchange 177
Johnstone, Frederick A. 162
Joint Stock Companies Limited Liabilities
     Act (1861) 98

Keynes, J. M. 95
Khoikhoi population 19, 24, 52, 57
  dispossession of 22, 37
  herders 13, 16
  relationship with Europeans 15
  as a source of labour 51, 53
  trade with VOC 23
  way of life 14–16
Khoisan population 264
  definition 19
  size 1, 254, 255
  as a source of labour 24
  see also Khoikhoi population; San
     population
Kimberley 47, 100, 108, 114, 171, 200
Klerksdorp 166

labour
  bureaux 154, 163
  'cheap' 163, 183, 224, 248, 249
  'civilized' 84, 86, 118, 119, 122, 134
  competition for 49
  control of 34
  costs 155, 183
  dop system 53
  flow 5
  indentured 54
  job reservation 118, 157, 158, 207, 232,
     241
  migrant 64, 66, 129, 152, 153, 161, 167,
     207, 248, 249
  occupational mobility 130, 232, 249
  productivity 103, 124, 168, 170, 184,
     196, 197, 202, 220, 245

ratios 79, 80, 81, 167
  shortages 127, 158, 188, 222, 230
  supply 59, 70, 172, 230
  surplus 48
  unit labour cost 245
Labour Party 82, 83, 85, 117
land
  distribution 194, 244
  ownership 2, 34
  rights 43
Land Act (1913) see Natives Land Act
Land Act (1936) see Bantu Trust and Land
     Act
Land and Agricultural Bank 141
Lanyon, Sir Owen 56
legal system
  lack of 40
  reforms 98
Legassick, Martin 163
Lehfeldt, R. A. 107
Lesotho (formerly Basutoland) 17
Lipton, Merle 241
literacy 20, 159, 251
Lithuania, settlers from 97
locations see reserves
Lombard Bank 27
London Missionary Society 52
Low Grade Mines Commission 78
Lydenburg 31, 53

Maddison, Angus 3
maize 19, 49, 139, 196
Malan, D. F. 149
Malawi (formerly Nyasaland) 65
malnutrition 71, 164
Mandela, Nelson 149
manufacturing sector 131, 182, 188,
     190, 211
  contribution to GDP 115
  costs 213, 232
  dependence on gold 131
  development of 107, 108, 109, 113,
     118, 123
  domestic market 128
  economic role of 173
  exports 218, 220, 223
  government assistance 113
  labour force 118
  labour requirements 129
  output 116, 132, 185, 192, 213
  private 184
  total factor productivity 223
  wages 133, 135, 195, 222, 231
Marketing Act (1937) 142, 244
marketing control schemes 142

marriage 236
  age at 253
  customs 18
  mixed marriages 150
Mashonaland 261
Masters and Servants Act (1856) 57
masters and servants acts 56, 64
Masters and Servants Ordinance (1841) 57
men, employment of 49, 114, 233, 236, 272
metal-working industry 127, 188
mfecane 37, 253
Mine Workers' Union 79, 85, 88
mineral resources 2, 35, 172, 206, 262
Mines and Works Act (1911) 75, 77, 84, 87
Mines and Works Amendment Act (1926)
  88, 111
Mines and Works Amendment Act (1987)
  207
Mining Regulations Commission 85, 87
mining sector
  colour bar in 74, 77, 78, 88, 130, 169
  compounds 63, 64, 128, 151, 167
  contribution to GDP 115, 144, 146
  costs 45, 77, 80, 81, 96, 105, 202,
    203, 208
  discrimination in 67, 74, 88, 98
  employment in 107, 210
  investment in 99, 168
  labour policy 206
  labour requirements 129, 240
  occupations in 63
  productivity 81, 208
  profits 104, 105, 111
  recruitment 45, 62, 64, 66
  as source of government revenue 100,
    108, 118
  techniques 101–3, 167, 168, 207
  training 129, 168, 206
  wages 45, 46, 63, 67, 81, 109, 111, 133,
    170, 206, 208, 231
missionaries 59
  mission schools 158
  missionary institutions 51
Mokgatle, Naboth 57
monetary policy 8, 177, 216, 221
Moshoeshoe 37
motor vehicle industry 158, 181, 182
Mozambique (formerly Portuguese East
  Africa) 65
Mswati 38

Namaqualand 255
Namibia (formerly South West Africa) 14
Nasionale Pers (National Press) 178
Natal 30, 54, 55

coalfields 211
National Finance Corporation 177
National Party 82, 117, 118, 143, 150, 153,
  154, 161, 180, 203, 247, 250
  election of 58, 149, 178
National Union of Mineworkers (NUM) 207
Native Building Workers Act (1951) 157
Native Labour Regulation Act (1911) 64, 78
Native Labour (Settlement of Disputes) Act
  (1953) 157
Native National Congress 44
Native Recruiting Corporation 66
Natives (Abolition of Passes and
  Coordination of Documents) Act
  (1952) 154
Natives Land Act (1913) 43, 44, 45,
  61, 244
Natives (Urban Areas) Act (1923) 58
Netherlands East India Company *see* Dutch
  East India Company
New Zealand
  comparisons with 132
  as model of export economy 91, 92
Nguni people 16, 17, 19

Ohrigstad 38
oil
  price 8, 202, 210, 214, 225, 227
  self-sufficiency in 222
Oppenheimer, Ernest 82, 97, 167, 171
Oppenheimer, Harry 167
Orange Free State goldfield 165, 166
Ordinance 50 (1828) 52, 57
Organization of Petroleum Exporting
  Countries (OPEC) 8, 214
output
  international comparisons 245
  trends 184–8

Paarl 23
Pact government 81, 82, 117, 124
  policies 83, 85–9, 119, 120, 135
Paris Evangelical Missionary Society 34
pass laws 64, 128, 152
  convictions under 155, 243
  introduction of 56, 58
  protests against 148
Pedi people 16, 36
  dispossession of 36, 37–42
pensions 9, 83, 86, 223, 234
petrochemical industry 183
Phalaborwa 172
Philip, Dr John 52
Phosphate Development Corporation
  (FOSKOR) 183

Plaatje, Sol T. 45
Plant, Sir Arnold 68
platinum
    demand for 211, 262
    price 211
    production 211
political rights 130, 153, 241, 249 *see also*
    franchise
Pondoland 58
population data 70, 237, 256, 273
    birth rates 84, 86, 252, 253
    child mortality 71, 252
    death rates 66, 252
    population density 260
    population growth 252
Population Registration Act (1950) 150
Port Elizabeth 25, 261
Port Natal 31 *see also* Durban
Potchefstroom 31
Potgieter, Andries Hendrik 38, 40
poverty 64, 72, 82, 84, 86, 87, 118, 128,
    138, 141, 145, 192
Pretoria 121
prison labour 54
private sector, discrimination in 84, 86
property rights 98, 243
protective measures 114, 180, 188,
    219, 244
    government policies 119, 120, 124, 218
    opposition to 117
    tariffs 107, 109, 116, 119, 130, 142
public sector 222
    discrimination in 84, 86

race
    interracial contact 20, 150
    racial discrimination 72, 74, 85, 87, 99,
        128, 132, 137, 195, 231, 249
    racial integration 232
    racial prejudice 135, 136, 248
railways 108
    investment in 91
    state ownership of 120
    see also transport
rainfall 2, 17, 24, 138, 262–3, 264 *see also*
    geography
Ramaphosa, Cyril 207
Rand Mines 104
Rand Native Labour Association 66
Rembrandt Corporation 179
Reservation of Separate Amenities Act
    (1953) 150
reserves 43, 44, 55, 66, 136, 139, 151, 155,
    156, 160, 194, 268
    deterioration of 70–3

lack of government support for 71
Reynders Commission 193
Rhodes, Cecil 97, 99, 260
Rhodesia 260
Richards, C. S. 141
Richards Bay 211
Riekert, P. J. 242, 243
Riekert Commission 160, 241
roads 24, 208, 261 *see also* transport
Roosevelt, F. D. 93, 95
'Rubicon' speech 229
Rupert, Anton 179
Russia, industrialization of 112, 119

Sadie, J. L. 272
San population 13, 19
    extermination of 74
    treatment of 255
    way of life 13–14
sanctions 148, 211, 215, 219, 221,
    222, 224
Sanlam 178, 179, 189
Sansom, Basil 17
Sauer Report 153
Scaw Metals 176
Schoemansdal 31
scientific advances 20
Second World War 95, 152, 170
    stimulus to industry 123
segregation 149, 150, 152, 153
Sekhukhune 41, 42
Sekhukhuniland 71
Sekwati 37, 38, 40, 41
separate development 143, 155, 157
service sector
    growth 147, 236
    output 147
Sharpeville 148, 155, 179, 189, 226
silicosis 66
slavery 19, 33, 51, 255
    abolition 52
    introduction 51
    treatment of slaves 74
smallpox 14, 254
Smithsonian agreement 22
Smuts, J. C. 80, 82, 117, 124, 149, 152
Social and Economic Planning Council 152
Soil Conservation Act (1946) 196
Sotho people 16, 19, 34
South African Coal, Oil and Gas Corporation
    (SASOL) 183, 210, 221, 223
South African Party 81, 82
South African Pulp and Paper Industries
    Ltd (SAPPI) 181
South African Reserve Bank 177, 225

South African War (1899–1902) 84, 87
South West Africa 83, 85 see also Namibia
Soweto 226
squatters' laws 62
stagflation 9, 146, 193
stagnation 161, 200, 213, 245
Stallard Commission 151, 153
Standard Bank of South Africa 177, 178
steel see iron and steel
Stellenbosch 23
Strijdom, J. G. 149, 151, 247
strikes 157, 231
  general 80
  in mining 64, 79, 80, 208
sugar industry 54, 196
Sullivan Code 231
Surplus People Project 151
Swazi people 16
  conflict with Pedi 37, 40, 41
Swaziland 44, 252, 260
Swellendam 25, 57

Table Bay 22, 23
taxes 64, 128, 159, 223
  on gold mines 108
  hut tax 55, 56
  labour tax 54
  poll tax 55, 56
  as source of government revenue 164
  tax cuts 213
  tax concessions 222
Thema, Selope 76
Tomlinson, F. R. 155, 156
Tomlinson Commission 156
trade
  foreign 5, 224
  international comparisons 3
  liberalization 218
  promotion 59
trade unions 130, 150, 157, 158, 241, 250
  black 157, 207, 241
  white 79, 123, 168, 191, 207, 219,
    233, 242
Transkei 43, 70, 72 see also reserves
transport 100, 108
  as aid to trade 49
  as barrier to trade 20
  infrastructure 91, 208, 211
Transvaal goldfields 98, 99, 165
Transvaal Indigency Commission 83, 85, 88
Transvaal Legislative Council 75
trekboers 25, 29, 32 see also Great Trek
Trollope, Anthony 50, 69
Tswana people 16
Tulbagh 25, 51

unemployment 80, 141, 148, 202, 224,
    237–40, 241, 245, 269–70, 274, 276
  'disguised' 48, 237
Union Corporation 104, 179, 181
Union Defence Force 79
Union Government 116, 266
United Kingdom
  annexation of Basutoland 83, 86
  anti-apartheid protests 230
  concern for equality 76
  control of the Cape 2, 27, 35, 41, 97
  devaluation of sterling 95
  financial links with 177
  and gold standard 94
  industrial co-operation with 176
  industrialization of 111
  influence on working conditions 231
  objectives 34, 35
  opposition to indentured labour 54
  settlers from 19, 28, 31, 34, 82
United Nations 184, 224
United States of America
  abolition of fixed price for gold 203
  financial policy 94
  industrial co-operation with 176
  industrialization of 111, 119
  influence on working conditions 231
  as model of export economy 91
  United States Treasury 208
uranium
  demand for 170, 215
  output 171
  production 203, 262
Urban Areas Act (1923) 152
Urban Areas Act (1952) 153, 241
urbanization 100, 130, 143, 152, 153, 203,
    242, 273

Vaal-Haarts irrigation scheme 140
vagrancy laws 52, 58
vanadium 176
Van Eck Commission 131, 135, 138, 165
van Imhoff, Baron 50
van Riebeeck, Jan 1, 13, 15, 24
Vereeniging 121
Verwoerd, H. F. 149, 156, 159, 161, 167,
    207, 243
Viljoen Commission 154
VOC see Dutch East India Company
Volkskas (People's Treasury) 178, 179
Vorster, B. J. 149
voting rights see franchise

Wage Board 127, 157
Wages Act (1925) 84, 87

water rights 2, 43
Welkom 166
white population
  definition 19
  farmers 34, 47, 51, 59, 73, 113, 114, 136,
    138, 244, 265
  income 9
  miners 77, 78, 80, 82
  objection to manual labour 50, 85, 88
  objectives 44
  'poor whites' 45, 82, 83–5, 86,
    118, 124
  size 2, 23, 156, 191, 256
Wiehahn Commission 241
wine
  export 28
  production 28, 196
Witbank coalfields 211
Witwatersrand goldfield 54, 100, 114, 166
Witwatersrand Native Labour Association 66
Witzieshoek 56
Wolpe, Harold 163, 248
Wolseley, Sir Garnet 42
women

employment of 49, 114, 118, 233,
  235, 272
introduction of passes for 154
role of in agriculture 18
wool
  export 28, 49
  output 196
  price 196
  production 28
Workmen's Compensation Acts 83, 85
World Bank 244
world economy 4, 7, 9, 143, 146, 202, 214
world trade 5, 9, 202, 214
  effect of tariffs on 5
world wars, effect on economy of 5, 7

Xhosa people 16, 25, 27, 32, 253
  dispossession of 37
  farmers 22
  relationship with Europeans 28

Zululand 70 *see also* reserves
Zulu people 16, 31, 42
  conflict with Pedi 37

Lightning Source UK Ltd.
Milton Keynes UK
UKHW040921121218
333861UK00001B/123/P